*Judgement and*
*Choice*

# Judgement and Choice

Second Edition

## The Psychology of Decision

**Robin M. Hogarth**

*University of Chicago*
*Graduate School of Business*
*Center for Decision Research*

*A Wiley—Interscience Publication*

**JOHN WILEY & SONS**
Chichester · New York · Brisbane · Toronto

Copyright © 1980, 1987, by John Wiley & Sons, Ltd.
2nd Edition

Reprinted June 1988

**Library of Congress Cataloging-in-Publication Data:**

Hogarth, Robin M.
    Judgement and choice.

    'A Wiley–Interscience publication.'
    Includes bibliographical references and index.
    1. Decision-making. 2. Judgment. 3. Choice
(Psychology) I. Title.
BF448.H64 1987      153.8'3      86–32481

ISBN 0–471–91479–7

**British Library Cataloguing in Publication Data:**

Hogarth, Robin M.
    Judgement and choice : the psychology
of decision.—2nd ed.
    1. Decision-making
    I. Title
    153.8'3      BF441

    ISBN 0 471 91479 7

Typeset by Photo·Graphics, Honiton, Devon
Printed and bound in Great Britain
by Anchor Brendon Ltd, Tiptree, Essex

*To*
*Hilly and the CDR*

# Contents

# Preface

Although it sounds trite, decision making is one of the most important recurrent human activities. Nonetheless, three observations about decision making strike me as paradoxical: (1) people are generally unaware of *how* they make decisions and often *why* they prefer one alternative to others; (2) they show little concern for the quality of their own decision-making processes (although the failures of others are often indicated with haste); and (3) the scientific study of decision making has not in my view attracted the attention it merits.

One argument could resolve these paradoxes, namely: people are effective decision makers. However, although it is true that people have been observed to be effective at making some kinds of decisions, the available empirical evidence also indicates important deficiencies across a range of problems with both trivial and important consequences.

A major goal of this book is to help people make better decisions. The orientation, however, is quite different from the standard texts on decision-making methodology, statistical decision theory, and related subjects. I write as a psychologist who recognizes that almost all decisions are based on the anticipations people make about the immediate and/or distant future. Anticipations, or predictive judgements as I call them, lead to choices, i.e. decisions. I further recognize that the basis of predictive judgements is largely intuitive; however, I believe, and indeed show in the book that intuition can both be studied and educated. Although formal decision-making methods are also discussed, the emphasis is on the unstructured, natural way people make judgements and exercise choice. Since this accounts for almost all real decision-making activity, the emphasis is more than justified.

This book is written for an audience that consists of neither professional psychologists nor decision theorists. It is written for decision makers, people who manipulate their specialist knowledge in making choices, be it in industry, commerce, government service, medicine or indeed any other professional activity. Consequently, the book is written at a non-technical level. Notes placed at the end of each chapter do however provide references to the specialized literature and a detailed bibliography, or guide to further reading, is contained in an appendix. Many of the examples chosen for illustration actually concern business applications; however, this should not diminish the appeal or usefulness of the book for other classes of decision makers. The choice simply reflects the kind of decision makers to whom I have been most exposed.

## PLAN OF THE BOOK

The book consists of ten chapters and five appendices. It is organized as follows. Chapter 1 discusses the nature of human judgement emphasizing limitations on human ability to process information. In Chapter 2 an important implication of these limitations is explored, viz the necessity to treat the environment as probabilistic. Experiments describing difficulties in thinking probabilistically are discussed and means suggested to overcome these shortcomings. Chapter 3 continues this theme but generalizes to situations where people have to combine multiple sources of information for prediction. Chapter 3 stresses the point that whereas good judgement typically requires viewing the world within a probabilistic framework, much intuitive judgement is causal in nature. Often, however, there is conflict between the implications of causal and probabilistic thinking.

Chapters 4 and 5 discuss choice. Whereas uncertainties about either features of alternatives or events that could affect outcomes are not emphasized in Chapter 4, decision making under uncertainty is the focus of Chapter 5. This includes both situations where the decision maker has good estimates of the relevant uncertainties and those where such knowledge is vague. The two chapters present principles of rational choice that have been developed in economics and statistics and discuss how these differ from the more intuitive strategies, or psychological mechanisms, people use in their actual choice behaviour.

Two important issues in decision making concern how people learn the relations they use in making predictions and the role of memory. These topics are discussed in Chapters 6 and 7, respectively.

Chapter 8 recognizes that the quality of judgement and choice are crucially dependent upon imagination and creativity. For example, I argue that without imagination, free choice is impossible. A conceptual model of creative processes is outlined and related to an overview of creativity techniques.

In Chapter 9, decision aids and methods of structuring problems are presented and discussed within the framework of *decision analysis* with its emphasis on the two key questions of rational choice: (1) assessing the consequences of alternative actions (i.e. utilities); and (2) estimating the probabilities of future events. Whereas I acknowledge that decision analysis is no panacea, I do believe it to be superior to other methodological approaches that have been suggested for making decisions. Choosing a method of analysing decisions is itself a decision. One should therefore choose the best even if it falls short of perfection.

Chapter 10 integrates the various findings discussed in the book and provides a conceptual overview of human judgement. It also contains discussions of what is or is not a 'good decision' (which is not evident prior to knowing the outcomes of actions) and some speculation concerning the origins of judgemental deficiencies noted in the preceding chapters.

There are five appendices. Appendix A outlines the rules of probability theory and is designed to help readers understand some of the issues raised in Chapters 2 and 3. Appendices B, C, and D all have a specific decision aiding orientation and, in this sense, can be seen as complementary to Chapter 9. Appendix B is a tutorial on probability assessment. This was originally written in 1973 and has been widely used by many different groups of people interested in learning how to assess probabilities. Following a procedure recently proposed by Mark McCord and Richard de Neufville, Appendix C shows how to assess a utility function under uncertainty over a single attribute, e.g. money. Appendix D outlines a method advocated by Ward Edwards for assessing the utility of outcomes that can be characterized on several attributes. Finally, Appendix E provides a guide to further reading in the form of a bibliography organized by topics.

In addition to updating topics, readers familiar with the first edition will notice several changes. These include: (1) a reorganization and expansion of Chapters 2 and 3 to make more explicit the relation between probabilistic and causal thinking; (2) greater coverage of choice processes in terms of both models of choice under certainty (Chapter 4) and risky decision making (Chapter 5); and (3) a new Appendix (C). Risky decision making received but brief attention in the first edition and I have made a conscious effort to correct this imbalance at the cost of increasing the length of the book by a chapter. My views on some of the issues discussed in the first edition have also evolved with time (hopefully in an appropriate manner) and such changes are reflected in almost all chapters. On the other hand, having received many favourable comments on the style of the first edition (level of discussion, use of examples, and so on) I have tried to preserve this aspect in the new version.

## ACKNOWLEDGEMENTS

First, and foremost, this book owes a great debt to those researchers whose early efforts laid the groundwork of what has become an exciting, active field of research, a field that one could probably now describe as 'established'. My list contains seven names. However, I will keep the list secret for fear of offending the very worthy reputations of several who are not on that special list.

The manuscript of the first edition benefited from conversations, critical comments and the encouragement of several colleagues, notably Carlo Brumat, Hillel J. Einhorn, Spyros Makridakis, Dennis Lindley, and Paul Slovic. In addition, the students in my elective course at INSEAD in 1979, and particularly Derek Nutt, gave much useful detailed feedback. The original manuscript was written before the wide-scale adoption of word processing

xii

equipment and several people were involved in converting my various hand-written and corrected drafts into text form. For doing this, I was extremely fortunate in being able to rely on the expert skills of Marie-José Rouault at London Business School, Lindsey Hill at INSEAD, and Charlesetta Wren at the University of Chicago. I thank them all.

I have also had many advantages in preparing the second edition. These have included: daily contacts and conversations with my colleagues at the Center for Decision Research at the University of Chicago. It would be hard to imagine a more stimulating group; Charlesetta Wren, who has handled, in exemplary fashion, a mass of details involving word processing, the preparation of figures, requests for permissions, and so on; my students in various courses at the University of Chicago who both directly and indirectly questioned my thinking and have contributed greatly to the way in which much material in the book is now organized and presented. Permission to reproduce material that has appeared in print elsewhere was granted by several publishers and specific acknowledgements are made in the appropriate places in the text.

Most of my research during the last five years has been supported by contracts from the Office of Naval Research obtained jointly with Hillel J. Einhorn. Without such support, this second edition would have been quite different. My own research efforts have naturally fuelled how I think about many of the topics discussed.

At an emotional level, my wife Hélène, and our three children have supported me in ways that are hard to evaluate. My indebtedness to them is probably far greater than I can realize.

Finally, at both an emotional and intellectual level, I owe a tremendous debt to my friend, colleague, and former teacher, Hillel J. Einhorn. I have profited enormously from being able to work closely with him over many years—and through times that have been both good and bad. As I stated, at the end of the preface of the first edition: 'His intellect, humanity, and infectious enthusiasm have both encouraged and sustained my work in this field'. Once again, I have little hesitation in dedicating this book to him and the Center for Decision Research that he brought into existence.

*Chicago, USA*
*August 1986*

Robin M. Hogarth

*Postscript added in proof*

Hillel J. Einhorn died at the age of 45 on January 8, 1987, leaving a great void amongst those working in decision research. He also left a considerable intellectual legacy, part of which is reflected in the influence he had on the contents of this book.

# CHAPTER 1

# The nature of human judgement

Judgement and choice are pervasive activities. For example, as you read this text you will probably make judgements concerning the quality of the book and its interest to you. Right now, you may also be anticipating how long it will take you to read this chapter, or indeed the whole book. These examples illustrate two kinds of judgement that are common to almost all choice situations.

First, people make value judgements by which they express preferences: for example, concerning the quality and interest of this book, for more as opposed to less money, for one job over another, for the relative beauty of works of art, for one kind of vacation compared to another, and so on. Second, people make predictions that reflect what they expect to happen: for example, how long you will need to read this chapter, how someone might react to what you say or do, whether a colleague will be successful in a new job, the extent to which the sales of your company will exceed a given figure next year, or whether a football team will win a particular game.

In short, judgement is an inevitable aspect of living. However, for the most part judgements are made intuitively—that is, without apparent reasoning and almost instinctively. And indeed, for much that affects us, intuitive choices are adequate. Either the outcomes of judgement are relatively unimportant, for instance your choice of which sweater to wear on a particular day, or they involve skills acquired under conditions that have allowed you to test their adequacy, as in driving a car.

However, the increasing interdependency and complexity of modern life mean that judgement now has to be exercised on matters with more important consequences than was ever the case in the past. Moreover, the frequency with which people are called upon to make important judgements in unfamiliar circumstances is growing.

Consider, for example, advances made only this century. The development of modern transportation systems, e.g. air travel, large urban transit systems and motorways, imply that many judgements have to be made daily which affect the safety of millions. Consider, for instance, the judgements made by air traffic controllers. The growth of large corporations implies that the decisions of a few persons can affect the livelihoods of many more people than would have been the case several years ago. For example, the decision

1

by a few managers in a large corporation to locate a new plant in one location rather than another can affect the lives of thousands of workers and their dependents as well as local economies.

The debate over nuclear power is another striking example. People make judgements about its relative advantages, and disadvantages, and public officials have to make decisions involving both enormous sums of money and risks that no one has ever experienced. In the realm of economics, recent history indicates a striking lack of agreement concerning which policies can most effectively deal with inflation and unemployment, and indeed the causes of these social ills. However, decisions have to be made on economic issues and such decisions are based on judgement. Development of modern means of warfare has also increased the need for good judgement, since the consequences of mistakes in this area are too horrible even to contemplate.

It could be argued that tools now exist to help decision makers take more reasoned choices and that this offsets the increased risks and stakes that have accompanied technological advances. It is true that many tools exist.[1] However, it is not true that such decision aids are equal to their task. First, one cannot eliminate the need for judgement. Even with the most sophisticated computer system someone has to make decisions concerning design, choice of variables, mode of use, and so on. Second, most tools lack the flexibility necessary to capture the essence of many important problems. Third, decision making takes place in situations involving people and judgements have to be made about those situations and the people in them, whether in the boardroom, parliament, or on the shop floor. Formal decision aids frequently cannot handle these important contextual considerations.

Despite the increasing complexity of modern technology and life, it might also be claimed that our organizations have adapted to facilitate decision processes. However, this is patently not true. The writings of both Peyrefitte in France and Crossman in the UK are quite explicit concerning the fact that cabinet members have neither the time nor information necessary to make reasoned judgements on the wide range of issues with which they are confronted.[2] Ministers must either delegate decisions to civil servants (which implies making judgements about their competence), or decide by themselves on an intuitive basis. The same could be said of chief executives. For example, there is evidence that managers are sometimes incapable of understanding the situations in which they have to make crucial judgements concerning the survival of their organizations.[3]

Whereas most people reading this book will probably never be called upon to make decisions of the magnitude described above, it is true that the technological, economic, and social environment in which they must now operate has also changed considerably in recent decades. Today even the humblest of us must make choices affecting others, and frequently under time pressure.

However, what is common to both the more humble and eminent persons in our society is the increasing necessity to handle and process information for judgemental purposes. Indeed, it has been said that we are now living a second industrial revolution, but instead of steam, the new revolution is being propelled by *information*. And, as in the first revolution, relative success will be determined by the ability to handle the propelling force. In the not so distant past human survival and progress depended upon physical skills, e.g. for hunting, fighting, fishing, and so on. There can be little doubt that the need today is for conceptual skills, that is the ability to process information and make judgements.[4]

Despite the above, it is a curious fact that whereas most professionally trained persons (for example, engineers, lawyers, physicians, managers), have both followed courses and received on-the-job training concerning the subject matter of their expertise, almost none has given serious thought, or received instruction concerning conceptual skills and, in particular, the intuitive processes they use to manipulate their substantive knowledge.

Intuition, flair, and judgement are, it seems, sacrosanct. Indeed, the questioning of a person's judgement can be likened to an attack on his or her moral and professional character. Furthermore, whereas most people recognize that nonsense fed into a computer will result in nonsensical output (i.e. 'garbage in—garbage out'), few question the notion that good information given to a human brain will result in anything but good judgement.

The issue to be faced is whether the intuitive processes that have apparently served the human race well until now are adequate for the future. Recent research suggests that they are not and, what is more disturbing, that people are unaware of this situation.

The purpose of this book is to bring the psychological study of judgement and choice to the attention of a wider, non-specialist audience. As indicated above, two forms of judgement are considered, evaluations and predictions. Evaluations, or as we shall say evaluative judgements, reflect individual preferences. Thus, it cannot be categorically said that they are 'wrong' in any case although a series of such judgements could be inconsistent. Similarly, it cannot be said that a person's opinions in the form of predictive judgements are wrong at the moment they are expressed. On the other hand, reality can subsequently show that the predictions were inaccurate.

The theme of this book is that since choice reflects both evaluative and predictive judgements, the quality of choice depends upon the extent to which (1) evaluative judgements really translate true preferences, and (2) predictive judgements are accurate. Moreover, we shall be particularly concerned with exploring the bases of intuitive judgement.

The book has three underpinnings: (1) the findings and theories of judgemental psychology; (2) probability theory or, as it has been more aptly named, the 'logic of uncertainty'; and (3) principles of decision theory that prescribe how evaluative and predictive judgements should be combined to determine choice.

## THE BASES OF JUDGEMENT

Intuitive judgements are based on information that has been processed and transformed by the human mind. Thus, it is appropriate to consider the characteristics of the human mind as an information-processing system. Unfortunately, neither the techniques of neurology nor psychology have reached the stage where one can observe what happens to information as it passes through the human mind. However, recent decades have seen considerable interest and advances within cognitive psychology, an area which encompasses the study of perception, problem solving, judgemental processes, thinking, memory, concept formation and human information processing in general.

These studies have produced at least two firm conclusions: first, compared to the complexity of many tasks, people have limited information-processing capacity; second, they are adaptive. Therefore, the nature of the judgemental task with which a person is faced determines to a large extent the strategies that can be used for dealing with the task (these notions will be explained below). Consequently, to understand judgement it is necessary to have clear notions of human possibilities and limitations as well as of the structure of judgemental tasks.[5]

### Limited information-processing capacity

There are four major consequences of limited human information-processing capacity. These concern: (1) perception of information; (2) the nature of processing; (3) processing capacity; and (4) memory.

(1) Perception of information is not comprehensive but *selective*. For example, it has been estimated that only about 1/70th of what is present in the visual field can be perceived at one time. Thus since we are literally bombarded with information we have to select; however, to select it is necessary to know what to select. *Anticipations* therefore play a large part in what we actually do see. Physical as well as motivational reasons account for why 'people only see what they want to see'. Indeed, the fact that we are confronted by more information than we can deal with at any given time, leads to an apparent paradox in the way that we cope with this predicament. Specifically, although faced with too much information relative to our processing capacity, we add even more information to external stimuli in order to make sense of the latter. We shall explore this issue further in Chapter 7.

(2) Since people cannot simultaneously integrate a great deal of information, processing is mainly done in a *sequential manner*. This can, of course, be misleading in the sense that the actual sequence in which information is processed may bias a person's judgement. However, it should be realized that our normal way of acquiring information is across time and that the sequence of events observed is important in making anticipations leading to

actions. For example, the simple act of walking several yards along a busy street involves a constant series of minor adjustments to some initial anticipations. That is, when walking we constantly adjust our path to avoid bumping into objects or people we may not have seen when starting. We acquire information across time (e.g. where people are relative to us on our path), and we are constantly making minor adjustments on the basis of this information.

It should be emphasized that this kind of judgemental 'strategy' will be quite successful in many circumstances.[6] Consider, for example, short-term anticipations of sales returns, stock-market prices, or the weather. When anticipations of the immediate future are based on the latest information observed they are often quite accurate. If the weather is fine today, for instance, it will probably be fine tomorrow (weather comes in spells). In addition, whereas stock-market prices oscillate at random from day to day, it is also true that if the price of a particular stock is high today, it will usually still be high tomorrow. In a relatively stable environment, predictions based on the most recent observations of a series will be fairly accurate. Indeed, this is almost guaranteed by the sheer inertia of human and natural activity.

However, when the environment is unstable, such judgemental strategies are deficient. Consider, for example, what happens when a sudden change in events causes larger changes between successive observations than are normally expected. People are unable to adjust their predictions to a different level of 'stability' and confusion reigns. A striking example was the economic chaos engendered by the Arab oil embargo of 1973.

(3) People do not possess intuitive 'calculators' that allow them to make what one might call 'optimal' calculations. Rather, they use fairly simple procedures, rules or 'tricks' (sometimes called 'heuristics') in order to reduce mental effort. For example, if you were asked to predict how well someone would do in a particular job, it is unlikely that you would make a detailed mental investigation and calculation of the predictive ability of the person's characteristics (e.g. by combining information such as the track records of people of equivalent age, schooling, and past performance). Instead, you would probably use a simpler procedure, for example by considering how similar the person was to people who had already succeeded in the kind of job envisaged.[7]

Heuristic strategies are also common in choice. For example, imagine that you are in a supermarket deciding which can of peas to buy. You are conscious of the need to consider price and quality in your choice and do so by adopting the following decision rule: if the price difference between brands is less than or equal to 5 cents, choose the higher quality product; otherwise, choose the cheaper brand.[8] Whereas one could quibble about the amount of the 5 cents limit, this heuristic rule is easy to apply. Moreover, to most people it seems sensible in that the two important attributes of price and quality are explicitly considered. Indeed, many people openly acknowledge using rules of this type when shopping. However, consider the implications of the rule if you were faced with the following alternatives:

| Brand | Price | Quality |
|-------|-------|---------|
| X | 60 cents | High |
| Y | 55 cents | Medium |
| Z | 50 cents | Low |

Specifically, consider what would happen if you were to choose between pairs of the alternative brands. In a comparison between $X$ and $Y$, you would prefer $X$; between $Y$ and $Z$, you would choose $Y$; however, a comparison between $X$ and $Z$ leads to the choice of $Z$. In other words, the apparently sensible heuristic that considers both price and quality implies an inconsistent ordering of your preferences over the three brands of peas. (That is $X$ is preferred to $Y$; $Y$ is preferred to $Z$; but $Z$ is preferred to $X$.)

This example illustrates three important issues in the use of choice rules. First, despite the fact that the rule seems sensible, *a priori*, it can lead to undesirable consequences in the form of contradictory choices. Second, in adopting what seem to be reasonable heuristics, we often lack insight into how such rules interact with characteristics of the choice task (in this case the characteristics of the particular alternatives). Moreover, unless the inherent contradictions in such rules are brought to our attention, not only may we never be aware of them, we might persist in using them to our disadvantage. And third, the example raises the issue of what the desirable properties of heuristic choice rules should be. These issues are explored further in Chapters 4 and 5.

(4) People have limited memory capacity. Although there is considerable uncertainty as to how memory processes actually work, current theories support the view that memory works by a process of associations that reconstructs past events.[9] Thus, unlike a computer, which can access information intact in its original form (i.e. as input), human memory works by an active process of reconstruction. Therefore, depending upon which association is used, memory can change. A nice example concerns two scientists who were trying to remember the dates of a conference that they both remembered as having being announced to last 4 to 5 days. One scientist maintained that the dates were from March 30 to April 3, the other from April 30 to May 3. The first scientist was sure because he specifically remembered March 30 in the circular announcing the conference. The other was equally sure since he specifically recalled the date of May 3. They consulted the circular letter to settle the dispute. The letter, to their mutual surprise, gave the dates as March 30 to May 3. This was obviously a mistake but it illustrates the point that memory is formed by reconstructing fragments of information. In this case, disagreement arose because the scientists reconstructed from different bits of information.[10]

Reconstruction can, however, be of considerable use as demonstrated in an experiment by de Groot.[11] He asked both master and ordinary chess players to memorize chess positions on a board. There were two experimental conditions. In one, the pieces were placed on the board at random; in the other, the positions were taken from actual chess games. Both master and ordinary players had similar, poor powers of recall for the random placements. However, the masters outperformed the others in reconstructing positions from actual chess games. It appears that reconstruction is important in memory, not only from the viewpoint of recreating situations for 'recall', but also in processing information as patterns rather than as distinct units. In the experiment described, the masters were apparently able to recognize patterns from real games as units and to reconstruct them, subject to the exceptions relevant to particular situations. In the random situation, they were unable to do this. The role of memory in judgement is discussed further in Chapter 7.

## The meaning of information

From the above, one might conclude that people, whom I have depicted as selective, sequential, limited-capacity information processors, can be likened to ineffective computers. However, the computer analogy is inappropriate. People have emotions, they can reverse thought chains in ways that computers cannot and have powers of imagination and creativity that would be extraordinarily difficult to program into computers.[12] Furthermore, people attach *meaning* to information and such meaning is often the clue to understanding how human thought processes work. To illustrate, consider how difficult it would be to endow a computer with general human knowledge. People have available to them vast numbers of possible connections betwen items of information that allow them to interpret and give meaning to the various messages they receive. For a computer to act like a human, it would be necessary to specify all these connections together with some appreciation of the circumstances in which particular interpretations are appropriate. At present, this seems like an impossible task. An illuminating example is provided by a computer program developed at a leading research university and designed to interpret newspaper headlines. This was made operational by programming the computer to restate headlines that were read into it. One headline was 'World shaken; Pope shot'. The program interpreted this as 'Earthquake in Italy; one dead'.

Contrary to computers, for humans the selection of specific items of information and anticipations concerning them are based on the meaning given to that information in particular environments. Through experience, people acquire an understanding of the world they live in and they use that understanding to select information, to interpret it, and to anticipate events.

I shall argue throughout the book, that to understand a person's judgements, it is necessary to understand how that person conceptualizes the world and the meaning he or she gives to information.[13] Consider an economic example. Imagine you believe that the rate of inflation is inversely related to the level of unemployment. Furthermore, you have been told that there has recently been a substantial drop in inflation. If asked to make a forecast of economic trends, you would probably anticipate an increase in unemployment. However, consider someone who does not believe there is a relation between the rates of inflation and unemployment. On receiving the same information as yourself, this person will not make the same inference. You give different meanings to the same information since it is interpreted within different conceptualizations, or models of the world.

Despite the emphasis on meaning *per se*, it should still be recognized that the meaning people give to information, and its interpretation, is effected within the constraints of the human information-processing system described above.

## The context of judgement

Before reading this section, attempt to answer the following questions:

(1) What will be the revenue (in dollars, pounds or francs as appropriate) of your organization (viz., company, school, institution) in the next calendar year?
(2) How tall is the Queen of England?

Now think about the process by which you generated your responses. It is unlikely that you could have answered the questions other than by making some comparisons with known points of reference. For example, consider the revenue of your organization. You probably started to answer this question by thinking of points of reference such as the level of this year's revenue, trends in your sector of the economy, general economic conditions, and so on. In other words, your judgement was made on the basis of points of reference you believe to be related to the target to be predicted (i.e. next year's revenue) or, in the terminology to be used in this book, cues. It was not made in any absolute sense. Similarly your judgement of Queen Elizabeth's height was probably made by reference to your memory of her size relative to other people (e.g., the 'average' male or female with whom you have seen her pictured).

Most judgements are the result of a number of comparisons with such points of reference or cues. This process was conceptualized by the psychologist Brunswik in his so-called 'lens model' illustrated in Figure 1.1.[14] In that conceptualization Brunswik and his followers have been concerned with understanding the interrelations between two systems. One system is the 'real' network of relations between cues in the environment and the event to be predicted; the second is the network of relations between cues in the individual's mind and his or her predictions. For example, consider your prediction of next year's revenue of your organization. The first system is the economic environment in which the organization operates (including

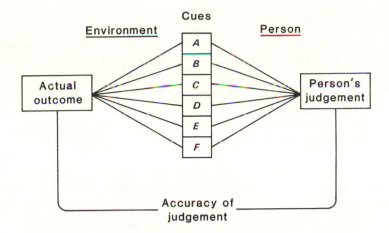

Figure 1.1 Brunswik's lens model. The model is to be understood as follows: The person makes judgements about an uncertain event (e.g. next year's revenue) on the basis of 'cues', *A*, *B*, *C*, ..., *F* (e.g., this year's revenue, competitive reactions, etc.). The relations between the person's judgement and the cues are represented by the lines between the 'person' box and the cues; the relations between the cues and the uncertain event are shown on the environmental side of the lens model. Accuracy of judgement depends on the extent to which the relations on both sides of the lens are the same

the actions taken by your organization, competitors, etc.). This system can be said to generate (i.e. produce) the outcomes you are trying to predict, that is revenue. The second system represents your mind. It indicates the relations you perceive or imagine between cues in the environment, e.g. anticipated trends and competitive reactions, and your prediction of revenue. In other words, the first system is the environment; the second is the model or representation of the environment in your mind that you use for prediction. Accuracy of prediction therefore depends on the extent to which your model matches the environment, i.e. in terms of cues, relations between cues, and between cues and the target event, as well as the relative importance of the cues.

It must be emphasized that Brunswik's conceptualization is only a model. Thus, it cannot claim to describe actual thought or environmental processes accurately although it can be said to represent them. The importance of Brunswik's lens model is to stress:

(1)  Judgement results from a series of operations on information that is related to other items of information or events;
(2)  such interrelations in the human mind have an analogue in nature;
(3)  judgement will be accurate to the extent that the individual's picture

of reality and judgemental rules match those of reality;

(4) Brunswik also stressed that judgement takes place in a probabilistic environment. That is, the relations between cues in the environment and the target outcome can not be represented by strict functional rules. Rather the rules are probabilistic—which roughly means that they are not exact in 100% of cases. This notion is explored further in Chapter 2; and

(5) judgemental accuracy is a function of both individual characteristics and the structure of the task environment.

In this book, examination is made of the kinds of rules people have been found to use in particular task environments. This will lead to an evaluation of these rules and suggest where one should seek remedial action.

## SUMMARY

Judgement and choice are essential and pervasive activities. Two kinds of judgement are involved in choice: evaluations and predictions, i.e. judgements of preference and belief. It was argued that intuitive judgemental processes are no longer adequate to deal with the modern world and that it is incumbent upon decision makers to examine their judgemental processes.

However, such an examination entails an understanding of judgemental processes. The nature of the human mind as a selective, sequential information-processing system with limited processing and memory capacity was described. Nonetheless, the apparent analogy with the computer is inappropriate. People give meaning to information and it is necessary to understand that meaning within a person's limited information-processing system.

It was further emphasized—through the conceptual device of Brunswik's lens model—that accuracy of judgement depends upon the extent to which the mind mirrors the environment it attempts to predict. Human judgemental ability is a function of both the person and the task.

## NOTES AND REFERENCES

1. Developments in decision theory and particularly multi-attribute utility theory are good examples of progress made in recent years—see R. L. Keeney (1982). Decision analysis: An overview. *Operations Research*, **30**, 803–838. These approaches will be discussed in Chapter 9.
2. See A. Peyrefitte (1976). *Le Mal Français*, Paris: Plon; and R. H. Crossman (1975). *The Diaries of a Cabinet Minister*, Vol. 1 London: Hamilton and Cape. The plethora of books about the Watergate crisis are also most revealing in this respect.
3. An illuminating example of this is contained in R. I. Hall (1976). A system pathology of an organization: The rise and fall of the Old Saturday Evening Post. *Administrative Science Quarterly*, **21**, 185–211.
4. See also R. F. Sinsheimer (1971). The brain of Pooh: An essay on the limits of mind, *American Scientist*, **59**, 20–28.

5. Supporting evidence for this paragraph as well as parts of the following section can be found in H. A. Simon and A. Newell (1971). Human problem solving: The state of the theory in 1970, *American Psychologist*, **26**, 145–159; and P. Slovic and S. Lichtenstein (1971). Comparison of Bayesian and regression approaches to the study of information processing in judgment, *Organizational Behavior and Human Performance*, **6**, 649–744, as well as in the references contained in these two works. For some implications of these issues for decision making in business and economics, see H. A. Simon (1979). Rational decision making in business organizations. *American Economic Review*, **69**, 493–513.
6. This issue is treated in greater detail in R. M. Hogarth (1981). Beyond discrete biases: Functional and dysfunctional aspects of judgmental heuristics, *Psychological Bulletin,* **90**, 197-217.
7. More evidence on this point will be presented in Chapter 3.
8. This example is taken from H. J. Einhorn (1980). Overconfidence in judgment. In R. A. Shweder (ed.), *New Directions for Methodology of Social and Behavioral Science: Fallible Judgment in Behavioral Research* (No. 4). See also A. Tversky (1969). Intransitivity of preferences. *Psychological Review, 76*, 31–48.
9. For an overview of research on memory, see R. L. Klatzky (1980). *Human Memory: Structures and Processes* (2nd edn), San Francisco: W. H. Freeman. The classic work on memory by reconstruction is F. C. Bartlett (1932). *Remembering*, Cambridge, England: Cambridge University Press.
10. B. Fischhoff, P. Slovic, and S. Lichtenstein (1977). Knowing with certainty: the appropriateness of extreme confidence, *Journal of Experimental Psychology: Human Perception and Performance,* **3**, 552–564.
11. A. D. de Groot (1965). *Het denken van den schaker (Thought and Choice in Chess)*, The Hague: Mouton.
12. U. Neisser (1963). The imitation of man by machine, *Science*, **139**, 193–197.
13. The role of meaning in judgement has, incidentally, been largely ignored in judgement research, although there are signs that this situation is changing. For example, researchers are now investigating the 'cognitive maps' that people use to interpret the world. An illustrative example of an actual decision making situation is provided by R. M. Hogarth, C. Michaud, and J.-L. Mery (1980). Decision behavior in urban development: A methodological approach and substantive considerations, *Acta Psychologica*, **45**, 95–117. See also Reference 3 above.
14. A useful description of Brunswik's model and research related to it are provided in Slovic and Lichtenstein, Reference 5. Brunswik's own writings are far from easy to digest. However, his views of psychology have been summarized by L. Postman and E. C. Tolman (1959). Brunswik's probabilistic functionalism. In S. Koch (ed.), *Psychology: A Study of a Science*, Vol. 1. New York: McGraw-Hill.

# CHAPTER 2

# Randomness and the probabilistic environment

A few years ago, a man won a huge prize in Spain's national lottery. Curious journalists inevitably asked him how he did it. The winner replied that he had deliberately sought and selected a ticket that ended with the numbers 4 and 8. As he explained, 'I dreamed of the number 7 for seven straight nights. And 7 times 7 is 48.'[1]

This story illustrates a key issue in judgement: namely, the problem of determining whether outcomes of action are due to skill or luck. Whereas most would argue that the lottery winner was lucky rather than skilful, this distinction is not so clear in other circumstances. The reason is simple: outcomes of actions result from combinations of factors that either are or are not within one's control; that is, factors that are due to skill or luck. However, it is often difficult to separate the effects of skill and luck in order to assess their relative contributions. In this and the next chapter, we shall explore issues concerning how people assess uncertainty, or the luck factor, in predictive judgement. Moreover, since prediction is often based on one's causal understanding of how the world works, we shall also explore conflicts between our attempts at causal comprehension, on the one hand, and our need to assess the luck factor, on the other.

A statement was made in the preceding chapter that we live in a probabilistic environment. In fact, this is not true. A more accurate statement is that the world is perceived by us as being probabilistic since we are unable to see and comprehend the myriad factors that cause events to occur. Moreover, as indicated above, we may even experience difficulty in accurately assessing the probabilistic elements of our environment.

To illustrate, consider first a case where we can judge the luck factor; specifically the familiar exercise of tossing a fair coin. What does it mean to say that the coin has 1 chance in 2 of coming down 'heads' and 1 chance in 2 of coming down 'tails?' The meaning is simply that we are uncertain whether it will be heads or tails on any particular throw. Furthermore, the chances of 1 in 2 reflect that uncertainty. Note that this statement does not mean that there are no causes for the coin to fall on one side or the other on a particular throw. Indeed, there must be causes. The statement simply implies that we are unaware of the relative forces of the various causes and so are prepared to assess chances of 1 in 2. The probabilistic statement expresses our degree of knowledge and is not a property of the coin *per se* (although the statement can be made in light of the coin's properties, e.g. it is not bent).

However, this admission of uncertainty lying within ourselves, rather than being a property of events in the environment, is something people have much difficulty in accepting. Indeed, there is considerable evidence to suggest that even in the 'rational' world of business, managers tend to deny the presence of uncertainty and, when they do accept it, to think of it as some kind of physical property of the environment rather than attributing it to themselves.[2] However, from a logical viewpoint, it is absurd to make a statement of the kind that one situation or venture is more uncertain than another; it is simply you who are more uncertain about one of the situations. Nonetheless, this is not the way society teaches us to think about uncertainty and our use of language obscures this basic point. A prominent investigator has put it this way:

> The usual tests and language habits of our culture tend to promote confusion between uncertainty and belief. They encourage both the vice of acting and speaking as though we were certain when we are only fairly sure and that of acting as though the opinions we do have were worthless when they are not very strong.[3]

Why should you accept that uncertainty lies within you rather than in the environment? After all, suppressing our uncertainties is both more comfortable and a considerable simplification. The reasons are important. First, explicit recognition of uncertainty can save you from deluding yourself.* Second, although there is often an emotional block in accepting uncertainty, in that one feels a loss of control over the environment, accepting uncertainty may paradoxically help you gain greater control over your environment. Indeed, Langer has demonstrated a phenomenon that she terms the 'illusion of control'.[4] This refers to a systematic tendency to assess the subjective probability of success in certain kinds of tasks as higher than objective circumstances would warrant. In particular, Langer argues that this is most likely to occur when factors associated with situations governed by skill (such as competition, choice, personal involvement), are introduced into situations governed by chance. For example, in one study Langer investigated the effects of permitting people to choose their own ticket numbers in a lottery as opposed to having tickets allocated by the organizer. That is, a situation where people could exercise some 'control' (by choosing specific tickets) was contrasted with one where lack of control was highlighted. Subsequently, and prior to the outcome of the lottery, it was determined that those who

---

* Whereas you may wish to delude others, I submit that deluding oneself is counter-productive.

chose their own tickets valued them about four times more than those to whom tickets had been allocated. The behaviour of the Spanish lottery winner referred to above is not unique. Indeed, it is significant that many state lotteries have adopted a marketing tactic of allowing players to choose their own 'lucky' numbers thereby implicitly capitalizing on the illusion of control.

In a further experiment, Langer and Roth showed that in predicting the outcomes of several tosses of a coin, people will readily believe that they can predict 'better than chance' if informed that their initial predictions in a series are generally accurate.[5] Since these experimental results were obtained in a laboratory situation, using a well-defined random device and with highly educated college students as subjects, one can easily imagine how such illusory powers of prediction can be created in more realistic environments where the role of luck is less apparent. In the economic domain, for instance, 'success' in stock-market predictions is a good example as witnessed by the plethora of pundits' newsletters that are willingly consumed by the investing public. Langer also argues that merely thinking about an uncertain event can induce illusions of control—possibly because one narrows one's focus of attention and thus becomes less capable of imagining alternative outcomes. For example, in one experiment Langer showed that the longer people had to think about the outcome of a lottery, the more confident they became in their chances of winning.[4] To the extent that these findings generalize, they have important implications for activities involving planning in many walks of life. In business, for instance, it is relatively easy to engender feelings of control through planning; however, extensive planning could well lead to misplaced confidence.

In this chapter, these and related issues will be explored by discussing concepts from the discipline developed to deal with uncertainty: probability theory. In particular, four key concepts from probability theory are examined. These are randomness, statistical independence, sampling variability, and regression. Experimental evidence is reviewed indicating deficiencies in people's untutored appreciation of these basic concepts. Subsequently, the kinds of judgemental errors resulting from such misunderstandings are discussed, as are possible ways of overcoming such deficiencies.

Finally, I do not underestimate the emotional difficulty of accepting uncertainty, both because of the uncomfortable feelings it engenders and the manner in which this tends to promote delays in action. However, there can be little doubt that people who accept uncertainty, and yet are not paralysed in action, will be more successful in the long run.[6]

## RANDOMNESS AND STATISTICAL INDEPENDENCE

In any predictive context, the amounts of unexplainable irregularity or randomness in the phenomenon limit the ability to predict. For example, we accept that the outcomes (heads or tails) of tosses of a fair coin are random in that it is impossible to predict heads or tails accurately on each of a long series of tosses. That is, although *on average* we may expect to see about as many heads as tails, the exact sequence of heads and tails is irregular and thus unpredictable. Similarly, we can think of the event 'next year's sales' as being random in the sense that although we may 'know' bounds within which next year's sales will lie, the actual level of sales within those bounds is uncertain. However, whereas people can accept these ideas at an intellectual level, most have great difficulty in dealing with randomness in the real world.[7] People want to treat the world as though it were more predictable than it is.

An important statistical concept related to randomness is the notion of statistical independence. Two events, for example the outcomes of successive throws of a die, or turns of a roulette wheel, are said to be statistically independent if knowledge of the outcome of one provides no information concerning the outcome of the second, or vice versa.

However, independent, random events are not limited to games of chance such as coin tossing or roulette. Many real-life processes have these characteristics and we all have considerable experience in dealing with them. For example, extensive evidence exists that daily changes in stock-market prices (i.e. up or down compared to the previous day's price) are of this nature.[8] Similarly, the output of many industrial processes can be considered to vary randomly around some average value. Consider, for example, a machine that is set to produce bolts of a certain width. Not all bolts will be precisely the required width; rather there will be small, irregular variations around this standard. However, as long as the bolts are within certain tolerance limits, this is acceptable. Indeed, almost all time series (i.e. events generated across time such as sales figures, export statistics, etc.) have a random component due to the fact that what occurs on any given occasion is the result of many different factors that are impossible to enumerate. For example, in considering the monthly sales of a company, one may be able to attribute certain rises and falls to specific factors such as a time trend or seasonal effects: however, a myriad of other factors also 'cause' monthly sales and thus induce irregularities or randomness.

Despite extensive experience with independent, random observations, people are extraordinarily inept at recognizing and dealing with the concept. Consider the following evidence.

One well-known phenomenon is the so-called *gambler's fallacy*. This refers to the behaviour of many people who, despite knowledge that they are dealing with gambling devices with fixed and known properties (e.g. roulette wheels), behave as though those properties—for example, the chance of observing a Red on the next throw—change. In particular, after a long sequence of, say, observing Reds in roulette, there is an almost compulsive belief that Black will become more likely. (Witness, for example, sports commentators who, on discussing a player performing below average, are prone to state that the player is now 'due' to perform well.)

| Series A | Series B |
|---|---|
| H | H |
| T | H |
| T | T |
| H | H |
| T | H |
| T | T |
| H | H |
| H | T |
| T | T |
| T | H |
| T | T |
| T | H |
| T | T |
| T | H |
| T | T |
| H | T |
| T | T |
| H | H |
| T | H |
| T | H |

Figure 2.1   Two series of coin tosses: one imaginary, and one real

Some investigators have sought the explanation to these types of phenomena by considering development across the life cycle. For example, a study by Cohen and Hansel aimed to discover how children aged 6 to 15+ acquire the concept of statistical independence.[9] The experimental task required the children to guess which of two outcomes would occur in a sequence of outcomes generated at random (i.e. similar to a coin-tossing experiment). Results indicated that the younger children frequently made their choices in order to balance the outcomes of the series (in other words, similar to making sure in a coin-tossing experiment that there are as many heads as tails). Indeed, according to Cohen and Hansel, the concept of independence does not even seem to start to form until children reach the age of 12+ to 15+. The behaviour of the children in these experiments exhibited aspects of the gambler's fallacy described above.

As previously mentioned, adults also have difficulty with the concept of independence and particularly with respect to random sequences. To illustrate this point, see whether you are able to generate a random sequence yourself. For example, imagine a series of 20 tosses of a fair coin and write down, in sequence, the outcomes of each of the 20 tosses.

Now compare your results with those of Figure 2.1. There I have reproduced two series of 20 tosses, series A and series B. One of these series, like yours, was generated intuitively; the other resulted from an actual coin-tossing experiment. Which series resembles most the one you generated?

Which series was artificially generated, and which was the result of the actual coin-tossing experiment?

How can you judge? Most people use two criteria. First, since the coin is presumed fair one should observe roughly as many heads as tails. Based on experience of giving this task to people, I can tell you that it is highly unlikely that either your series or that of the person whose series is reproduced in Figure 2.1 would have anything other than 9, 10 or 11 heads.[10] However, a quick calculation based on probability theory tells us there is only about a 50% chance of actually observing 9, 10 or 11 heads in a real sequence of 20 tosses of a fair coin. That is, in 20 tosses there can be anything from 0 to 20 heads and the probability of observing outcomes across the whole range of possibilities is greater than most people imagine. Instead, people tend to judge likelihood by how close outcomes are to what they believe the ideal should look like.[11] In this case, the ideal is 10 heads in 20 throws.

Second, it is unlikely that one would observe, say, 10 heads followed by 10 tails, or at the other extreme, to see heads and tails alternate in sequence, viz. H, T, H, T, H, .... The observed pattern should be somewhere between these two extremes. Statisticians have devised a method for assessing whether such intermediate patterns correspond to random sequences. The idea is the following: define a sequence of the same outcomes, e.g. heads, as a *run*, and count the number of runs in the series. For example, in Series A (the outcome of the real experiment), there are 10 runs; in Series B, there are 13 runs. In 20 tosses of a fair coin one should expect to see approximately 11 runs, and reasonable limits of variation would be between 7 and 15 runs.[12] The main characteristic of the number and type of runs observed in artificially generated human series is that, compared to random sequences, individual runs tend to be too short (i.e. there are too many runs). Wagenaar has explicitly investigated the ability of adults to detect random from non-random sequences. He summarizes his experiments by stating that

> Subjects are unable to produce a randomized sequence of two, three or more alternatives even if they are explicitly instructed and motivated to do so. Generally S's show a tendency towards too few repetitions and too many alternations.[13]

Wagenaar also investigated people's ability to detect the amount of randomness in sequences of data.[13] Subjects observed sequences of black and white dots under varying conditions of dependence between successive observations of the same colour. That is, unlike fair coin-tossing experiments, the observation of outcomes affected the chance of succeeding outcomes. For example, to continue the analogy with a coin-tossing experiment, if heads were observed, heads would not be equally likely as tails on the subsequent throw. Heads could be more or less likely depending on how the scheme was arranged to depend on the observation of heads. In Wagenaar's experiments, the schemes tested varied the chances that successive observations would be of the same colour from 1 in 5 to 4 in 5. It turned out that schemes where the chances were set at 2 in 5 were judged by the subjects to be 'the most random'.

These experiments illustrate two points. First, people have a tendency to expect what they observe, i.e. sequences of data, to be *representative* of the process generating them: for example, in 20 tosses of a fair coin one expects to see 10 heads, or the tendency of the children in the Cohen and Hansel experiments to balance the series. Second, people have little appreciation of the concept of randomness. In particular, they underestimate the extent to which deviations from what they expect to see in random processes are quite normal.[14]

## Variability and sampling variability

An important point related to the preceding discussion is that prediction is difficult because we rarely have all the necessary information. For example, imagine that you are observing a production line and that the items produced can be classified as acceptable or defective. You see, say, 100 items which include 5 defectives. Is this reasonable? How many defectives should you expect to see?

In this example, as in most judgemental activity, you are involved in a process of sampling; that is, observation of partial information on the basis of which you need to make an inference or judgement about the whole—in the example above the proportion of defectives produced by a particular machine. As should be apparent from the discussion of human information-processing capacity in Chapter 1, sampling is a fundamental activity. Almost all that we learn is by way of samples and most of our actions are based on sample information. For example, as a reader you have already sampled part of this book. You are probably trying to anticipate whether it will be worth the effort to finish it. However, as illustrated above, samples are rarely wholly representative, and this is particularly true of small samples. Most of what we can observe exhibits variation and, as will be illustrated below, an understanding of variation is important in judgement.

## Two basic principles

There are two basic principles for estimating variability when observing outcomes that are random and independent:

(1) *The amount of variability is positively related to the degree of randomness exhibited by the phenomenon.* For example, tosses of a fair coin exhibit more irregularity than tosses of a bent coin where the chances of observing heads are fixed at, say, 4 in 5. Observations made from measuring instruments (e.g. psychological tests, thermometers, cardiographs, seismic recorders, or reports concerning, *inter alia*, stock levels, trade statistics, etc.), usually reflect two sources of variation: variation in the underlying traits or

dimensions being measured, and variation due to lack of reliability of the instruments. Other factors being equal, the more reliable an instrument, the less the variability one will observe in actual measurements.

(2) *Averages\* of observations show less variation than the observations that have been averaged. Furthermore, variation is reduced as the number of observations included in the average increases.* As an example, consider a factory producing cars and concentrate on the number of cars produced per day. Across a year, the average number of cars produced per day will show less variation on a weekly basis than the actual numbers produced per day. Similarly, the average per month will show less variation than the average per week, and the average per quarter less than the average per month.† Another way of looking at this principle is to realize that if you want to estimate the average daily production of the factory, a weekly average is liable to be more accurate than a day picked at random, the average for a month more accurate than the average for a week, and so on. In other words, you can be more confident in your average, the more days you used to estimate it.

The above two principles seem quite straightforward and one would expect people to apply them in a relative if not absolute sense. The ability of people to do just this was tested in an ingenious series of experiments by Kahneman and Tversky.[11] Subjects in these experiments were faced with problems of the following kind:

(1)    There are two programs in a high school. Boys are a majority (65%) in program *A*, and a minority (45%) in program *B*. There is an equal number of classes in each of the two programs. You enter a class at random, and observe that 55% of the students are boys. What is your best guess—does the class belong to program *A* or to program *B*?[11]

(2)    A certain town is served by two hospitals. In the larger hospital about 45 babies are born each day, and in the smaller hospital about 15 babies are born each day. As you know, about 50% of all babies are boys. The exact percentage of baby boys, however, varies from day to day. Sometimes it may be higher than 50%, sometimes lower. For a period of 1 year, each hospital recorded the days on which more (less) than 60% of the babies born were boys. Which hospital do you think recorded more such days? The larger hospital? The smaller hospital? About the same (i.e. within 5% of each other)?[11]

(3)    A medical survey is being held to study some factors pertaining to coronary diseases. Two teams are collecting data. One checks three men a day, and the other checks one man a day. These men are chosen randomly from the population. Each man's height is measured during the checkup. The average height of adult males is 5 ft 10 in, and there

---

\* By average is meant 'arithmetic mean'.
† For the sake of this illustration, assume that there are no seasonal effects.

are as many men whose height is above average as there are men whose height is below average.

The team checking three men a day ranks them with respect to their height, and counts the days on which the height of the middle man is more (less) than 5 ft 11 in. The other team merely counts the days on which the man they checked was taller (shorter) than 5 ft 11 in. Which team do you think counted more such days?

The team checking 3? The team checking 1? About the same (i.e. within 5% of each other)?[11] (Reproduced by permission of Academic Press Inc.)

To answer these three questions correctly requires an understanding of the two principles enumerated above. The first problem concerns the first principle. That is, sampling from a population where 65% are boys (program A) produces less variation than when sampling from a population where 45% are boys (program B). Thus although the majority of students in the class sampled (55%) were boys—and thus the class seemed more representative of program A—it is in fact slightly more probable that the class sampled came from program B. Incidentally, if you answered 'program A,' you too are 'representative'; 67 of Kahneman and Tversky's 89 subjects also gave that answer.

Second, consider the hospital problem. This problem tests your appreciation of the second principle. That is, the larger the size of sample you observe, the more confidence you can have that a statistic (e.g. the mean or a proportion) is close to the true value.* With small samples you should expect high variability in such estimates, in larger samples less variability. Indeed this principle has been given the name of 'the law of large numbers' and does seem quite intuitive. More information should lead to greater confidence. However, this principle was not evident to Kahneman and Tversky's subjects. Only 10 out of 50 subjects realized that in the smaller hospital there would probably be a larger number of days where over 60% of babies born were boys; furthermore, only 9 out of 45 realized that in the larger hospital, there would be less than 60% male births on more days than in the smaller hospital.

If you understood the hospital problem, then you should also appreciate the third problem. Taking the mid-value of three heights will reduce observed variability relative to recording a single height. Consequently you would observe more heights over 5 ft 11 in by the team checking 1 person, and more mid-values less than 5 ft 11 in by the team checking 3 persons. Once again, a majority of Kahneman and Tversky's subjects failed to answer these questions correctly.

The subjects whose responses are indicated had not been formally trained

---

* Incidentally, note that in this problem the true proportion (50%) is the same in both populations (i.e. hospitals). Thus, lack of differences in the proportions is not a factor.

in statistical reasoning. Consequently, it is legitimate to ask whether 'experts' would fall prey to the same kinds of questions. Tversky and Kahneman developed analogous problems which they presented to trained scientists and which concerned the interpretation and design of experiments.[15] They found that these statistically sophisticated scientists made the same kinds of judgemental errors as the naive subjects in the other experiments. In particular, they overestimated the extent to which they should have confidence in data. Tversky and Kahneman dubbed this failing 'the law of small numbers', i.e.

> The law of large numbers guarantees that very large samples will indeed be highly representative of the population from which they are drawn. If, in addition, a self-corrective tendency is at work, then small samples should also be highly representative and similar to one another. People's intuitions about random sampling appear to satisfy the law of small numbers, which asserts that the law of large numbers applies to small numbers as well.[15]

One must be careful, however, not to overgeneralize from these examples. There are circumstances under which people do recognize the implications of concepts such as the law of large numbers in naturally occurring circumstances. For example, most of us would place more faith in the results of a survey based on 1000 as opposed to 10 respondents. On the other hand, we are often called upon to make probabilistic inferences when it is not so easy to understand the type of problem confronting us. And in these circumstances, the statistically appropriate response is not evident to our intuition. Nisbett and his colleagues have suggested that the two types of situation can be distinguished by the extent to which people have a good causal understanding of the phenomenon of concern such that they can clearly distinguish the relative roles of causal influences and chance factors in affecting outcomes.[16] Thus, experts should be less prone to statistical errors than novices when reasoning in their own domains. On the other hand, even experts can make responses similar to novices when problems are complex. Nisbett and his colleagues also show that training in statistical reasoning can help people recognize how the luck factor should affect inference and thus increase the chances that they will make appropriate responses.

To summarize the essence of this chapter so far, I have argued that people often exhibit little appreciation for the concepts of randomness, statistical independence, and sampling variability. However, given that they have extensive real-world experience of these phenomena, it is legitimate to ask why. Two reasons are advanced here. First, it is difficult for people to perceive accurately the extent to which the luck factor affects observable phenomena. The world, both social and physical, is complicated and establishing 'what causes what' is often problematic. In particular, whereas receiving appropriate feedback from the environment is essential for learning, many judgemental tasks are structured in a way that systematically distorts the feedback available to us. This topic is explicitly developed in the next section as well as in different parts of this book. Second, given limited information-processing capacity, people have a great need to structure and interpret their environment. Findings from the psychology of perception show that what we are able to perceive is often structured by so-called 'Gestalt' forces. Such forces, however, are not restricted to perception. Other branches of psychology have shown, for example, how people seek to find patterns in music as well as in rather banal letter-series completion tasks. Indeed, it has been said,

> Patterns, temporal as well as spatial, occur in many spheres of life besides music. People appear to have strong propensities, whether innate or learned, to discover patterns in temporal sequences presented by the environment, and to use these evidences of pattern for prediction. The ability and desire to discover temporal patterns undoubtedly has had great value for the survival of Man: in predicting the seasons for example, or the weather. The urge to find pattern extends even to phenomena where one may well doubt whether pattern exists (e.g. in the movements of the stock market).[17]

## RELIABILITY AND REGRESSION

When using information for predictive purposes, two important concepts are (1) the reliability of the source and (2) its predictive ability. It is important to distinguish these related concepts. Reliability refers to the extent to which an information source actually reports what has happened. For example, trade statistics are reliable to the extent that they are accurate. A person is reliable to the extent that he or she is truthful. Whereas reliability is an inherent characteristic of the information source, predictive ability can only be defined in relation to another event. For example, trade statistics have a given level of reliability but are differentially predictive of, say, stock-market prices or the level of unemployment.

The predictive ability of an information source therefore refers to the extent to which the information source can be used for predicting a particular event. Moreover, predictive ability can only be defined with respect to that event. However, whereas reliability and predictive ability are distinct concepts, they are related in the sense that a totally unreliable information source can have no predictive ability. Furthermore, reducing the reliability of an information source must reduce its predictive ability.

A common error in judgement is to overlook the fact that lack of reliability increases observed variability. Thus, failure to consider the reliability of data sources can lead to misinterpreting observed variations in data. In 1965, for example, a crime wave was proclaimed in New York City. The cause, however, subsequently turned out to be an improvement in record keeping.[18] In another example, lab technicians were blamed by their superiors for the inaccuracy of their work. However, it was later determined that the level of accuracy required of them was impossible to achieve given the inherent lack of reliability in their measuring instruments.[19]

Whereas it is well known that economic data lack perfect reliability, this fact is often overlooked, even by sophisticated economists. For example, in a book published in 1974, a noted French economist attempted to analyse the relation between the rate of inflation and the level of industrial investment in France since 1962. Basing his analysis on figures issued by INSEE, the official French government statistics body, he noted a positive relation between levels of investment and increases in the rate of inflation. This observation led him to develop the thesis that the rate of increase in inflation was caused by the demand stimulated by increased investment. Furthermore, to diminish the rate of inflation it would be necessary to reduce the level of industrial investment. However, when the empirical basis for these conclusions was examined more closely in the light of subsequent statistical investigations, it turned out that (a) industrial investment in France between 1962 and 1970 had been overestimated by amounts of up to 35%, and (b) inflation had been initially underestimated in the period under consideration. In other words, the intriguing thesis of a leading economist (and others) was based on a spurious empirical relation induced by errors of measurement.[20] The story therefore again illustrates how people frequently fail to consider the vagaries of irregular fluctuations when interpreting information. Awareness that economic statistics are inherently unreliable should, in this case, have been sufficient to forewarn the economists from attempting unwarranted, causal explanations.

To summarize, it is important to remember that unreliable data sources exhibit more variability than they would if they were reliable. Moreover, the assessment of a cue's predictive ability should be moderated by considerations of reliability. Incidentally, the importance of these two remarks can be emphasized by the results of a study that showed that the mere variability of a cue can enhance its perceived salience for prediction.[21]

What are the implications of failing to appreciate the nature of random fluctuations? As both the preceding and following examples show, the major consequence concerns the meaning we attach to what we observe. This can by itself engender self-delusion as well as other undesirable consequences.

## Managing by exception[22]

Imagine that you have the responsibility of a department where a number of people have periodic targets to meet (e.g. weekly sales targets, daily output or production rates). Since you are conscientious, you always check each person's performance against target at the end of each period. When doing so, you often find that at least one individual has performed well below target. Consequently, you speak to that person. Moreover, you find that the performance of the individual concerned typically improves in the next time period. What inference can you draw from observing this improvement? Most people tend to believe that their interventions (i.e. reprimanding

24

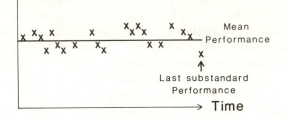

Figure 2.2    Performance plotted across time. (Reproduced by permission of CEDEP)

substandard performance) are justified by subsequent outcomes. However, consider the structure of the task more carefully.

A possible representation of the above situation is given in Figure 2.2. Here the target performance of one individual is represented by a straight line. The crosses represent actual performance achieved. As can be seen, and indeed as would be expected, performance does not match target exactly on every occasion. Rather, performance is sometimes more, sometimes less, than target, although on average target is being achieved. The actual performance of this individual can be described by irregular fluctuations around some average value, in this case the target. Now consider the last cross (i.e. performance level) of the series shown. This is some way below target performance and thus you would wish to speak to the individual after this occasion.

However, consider what would happen if you did not intervene. If the individual's performance can be represented by a series of irregular fluctuations around some average value, then it is highly probable that it will be closer to the average (i.e. improve) in the next time period. That is, irregular—or random—fluctuations in performance will always produce the occasional substandard performance. Moreover, it is highly likely that performance will improve on the next occasion *without intervention on your part.*

There is also another side to this situation. What is likely to happen after someone has produced an exceptionally high level of performance? On the next occasion, performance is likely to be closer to the mean level, that is decrease. Consequently, if you were to praise your outstanding performers, you would probably observe that your praise is followed by deterioration in their output. After extreme performance (high or low), it is highly likely that the next observation will be closer to the mean level.

The point being made here is that in many situations, observed outcomes (e.g production rates, sales statistics, athletic performance) vary irregularly around some average level. Thus the best prediction for a future observation is the average of the series. Consequently, an exceptionally good outcome is liable to be followed by a lower (i.e average) one, and an exceptionally bad outcome will probably be bettered. We all have our good and bad days and these are accentuated or offset by specific circumstances. From a judgemental viewpoint, the danger is over-reaction. For instance, in the example given above, the manager acts in an entirely 'reasonable' manner: he or she is busy and manages by 'exception', reprimanding bad performers (to keep them 'on their toes'). However, the feedback received from the environment is misleading: the manager is led to a false attribution concerning the efficiency of his or her interventions. Performance does not improve because the manager spoke to those who performed below standard. Performance would have improved anyway.

## Other examples

The experience of flight school instruction in Israel provides a further example.[23] Psychologists had advised instructors that each successful execution of a flight manoeuvre should be positively reinforced by the instructors (with praise). On the other hand, the instructors' experience with this approach was that praise for successful completion of complex manoeuvres was counter-productive. Praise was typically followed by less competent performance. What the instructors failed to realize, however, was that the difficulty of executing manoeuvres was such that variations in performance were inevitable. Thus, irregular fluctuations should have been expected. Instead, the instructors incorrectly attributed decrements in performance to the policy of praising previous good performance.

Kahneman and Tversky comment on this incident as follows:

> This true story illustrates a saddening aspect of the human condition. We normally reinforce others when their behavior is good and punish them when their behavior is bad . . . therefore, they are most likely to improve after being punished and most likely to deteriorate after being rewarded. Consequently, we are exposed to a lifetime schedule in which we are most often rewarded for punishing others, and punished for rewarding.[23] (Reproduced by permission of the American Psychological Association)

The above examples all indicate how individuals can and do make false attributions because they fail to understand the concept of random fluctuations. In a somewhat different vein, Campbell has discussed the problems of inferring causation in the evaluation of 'social experiments', for example assessing whether a reduction in traffic accidents follows from lowering speed limits or the introduction of breathalyser tests.[24] In such situations, which involve recording observations across time periods both before and after introduction of the social measure, the attribution of causation is difficult precisely because of the nature of random fluctuations. In elaborating on these issues, Campbell points out that an understanding of sampling fluctuations can also help 'trapped administrators whose political predicament requires a favorable outcome whether valid or not'. If such politicians want to be seen to have been successful, Campbell's advice concerns both when to start a social experiment and to whom the treatment should be given: '... the advice is pick the very worst year, and the very worst social unit. If there is inherent instability, there is nowhere to go but up, for the average case at least.'[24]

## The regression phenomenon

Several of the above examples are special cases of the so-called 'regression phenomenon', an understanding of which is critical to prediction in an uncertain environment. To illustrate this principle, consider that you are using a cue such as a test score to predict the future performance of a job candidate. Furthermore, imagine that extensive experience of the test exists and that the relation between score and job performance can be described by the graph illustrated in Figure 2.3.

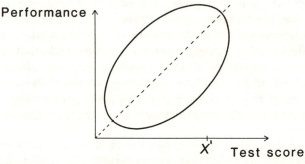

Figure 2.3  Relation between an imperfect test and performance

The ellipse in Figure 2.3 indicates the extent to which the test is predictive, the narrower the ellipse, the more predictive the test and vice versa. Thus, a test with perfect predictability is one where the relation between test scores and subsequent job performance is represented by a straight line (the dotted line in Figure 2.3). The so-called regression phenomenon simply reflects the inability of information sources with imperfect predictive ability to predict perfectly. This can be illustrated by comparing the predictions based on sources having, alternatively, imperfect and perfect predictive ability. Consider the test score $X'$ indicated on Figure 2.3 and ask yourself:

(1)  What performance level is someone with a score of $X'$ or higher on the imperfect test likely to achieve? and
(2)  If the test had perfect predictive ability, how would your answer differ?

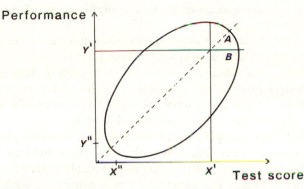

Figure 2.4  Illustration of the regression phenomenon. Note that a person scoring $X'$ or higher on the test has a greater probability of showing performance below $Y'$. (The area $B$ exceeds the area $A$.) By drawing analogous lines, the reader can confirm that someone scoring $X''$ or less stands a greater chance of performing above rather than below $Y''$

Figure 2.4 illustrates what would happen. For a test with perfect predictive ability performance corresponding to a test score of $X'$ is indicated by the point $Y'$. For each larger value of the test score, there will also be an associated, and unique value of performance. However, with an imperfect test, there is a range of possible levels of performance associated with test scores of $X'$ or more. This is represented by the area of the ellipse to the right of $X'$. Contrast the straight dotted line (for the perfect test) with the area just defined (for the imperfect test). Furthermore, note that the area of the ellipse to the right of $X'$ can be split into two parts at the level of performance $Y'$. One of these parts, $A$, denotes cases with test scores above $X'$ that are associated with performance above $Y'$; the other, $B$, denotes test scores above $X'$ but with performance below $Y'$. The key point to note, however, is that the area $B$ exceeds the area $A$. In other words, a person scoring $X'$ or more on the test has a greater probability of showing performance below rather than above $Y'$. In other words, there is regression toward the mean.

The reader will find it instructive to draw lines associated with $X''$ and $Y''$ at the bottom left of the ellipse. It should be noticed that for low test scores regression toward the mean still applies. There is a greater chance (with an imperfect test) that a person with a test score of $X''$ or less will perform at a level above rather than below $Y''$.

The implications of the regression phenomenon concern cases where prediction is based on sources with imperfect predictive ability. Here predictions should be less extreme than the information generated by the sources. The term 'regression phenomenon' simply means that, with imperfect information sources, predictions should be 'regressed' toward the mean, e.g. in this case toward average performance which, with a totally unreliable test, would be the best prediction.

This discussion of the regression phenomenon has been couched in terms of predictive ability of data sources and has made little reference to reliability *per se*. However, recall that lack of reliability of data sources reduces their predictive ability and therefore contributes to the regression phenomenon. Thus, failure to recognize that data are not perfectly reliable leads to predictions that are more extreme than they should be.

Evidence indicates that people are strongly influenced by predictive cues that exhibit extreme values. These are salient for them and lead to the belief that they should be accompanied by correspondingly extreme values of the variable being predicted. For example, it is a common mistake to believe that someone with superior performance on, say, an IQ test, will be as successful relative to his or her peers on related tests of academic achievement. However, since IQ tests are not perfectly reliable, this is rarely the case. In general, unreliable sources exhibit more extreme values than reliable sources. Thus, in these circumstances, a judgemental strategy that matches predictions to inputs such as test scores is particularly vulnerable to bias due to the presence of regression effects.[23]

**More on unreliable data sources**

The issue of reliability of data sources can enter judgemental problems in many subtle ways. For example, consider situations where you have to make a prediction based on a report which might itself be uncertain. An instance of this could be the following:[25] Imagine that you are a businessman facing a highly competitive marketing situation. In fact you are aware that the next move by you or your competitor could well be crucial in determining who establishes the larger market share. One of the possible weapons open to both of you is price reduction. However, given rates of profitability in the present market, this is not something you would be willing to do unless forced by competition. Nonetheless, you feel there is a fair chance (say evens) that your main competitor will reduce prices within the next week. You receive a message from one of your field sales force that your competitor has just booked large amounts of advertising space to go out in the next few days. What do you do?

First, note that there are several sources of uncertainty involved in this situation concerning: (1) whether your competitor will drop prices; (2) whether his booking of advertising space is related to a reduction in prices; and (3) whether your salesman's report is reliable (he may not, of course, be deliberately untruthful, merely misinformed). Note therefore that if these three sources of uncertainty are dichotomized, i.e. will or will not drop prices, advertising space is or is not related to the announcement of a price reduction, and the salesman's report is or is not reliable, then you should be considering the probabilities of six different scenarios as illustrated in the

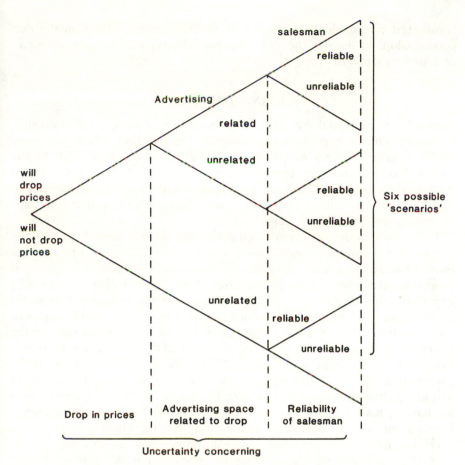

Figure 2.5   Combination of three sources of uncertainty

tree diagram of Figure 2.5. However, for most people situations such as these require the manipulation of far too much information and one is unlikely to handle it effectively without some mechanical means, be they merely pencil and paper. Experimental evidence indicates that in these kinds of situations people tend to eliminate some of the uncertainties and focus attention on what they consider to be the most likely combinations of outcomes.[26] This strategy, known as the 'best guess' strategy, is clearly a result of limited information-processing capacity. In many cases, one of the uncertainties suppressed concerns data source reliability.

To summarize, sources of information should be weighted in predictive activity relative to their ability to predict. However, people often fail to recognize the implications that lack of perfect reliability has for prediction. There are at least two reasons. First, people's experience of predictors is frequently insufficient for assessing their true predictive accuracy. This issue is explored in some depth in Chapter 6. Second, judgemental strategies that people adopt to simplify the task of prediction can lead to ignoring issues of source reliability.

## AVOIDING THE TRAPS

Above I have discussed the nature of randomness, statistical independence, variability, and the regression phenomenon. Furthermore, I have presented evidence indicating that people have difficulty in recognizing and dealing with phenomena that have these properties. In particular, since people are motivated to order and make sense of their world, they have tendencies to seek patterns where none exist and to make unjustified causal attributions. How does one avoid these traps?

There are two defences, one attitudinal, the other technical. *At the attitudinal level it is necessary to recognize that we live in a probabilistic environment.* However, the environment is not probabilistic because of its inherent properties; it is probabilistic because our representation of it is necessarily imperfect. *That is, the source of the uncertainty lies in us rather than in the environment.* One way to think about this is to note that random fluctuations are typically caused by a large number of factors. It is impossible for the human mind to identify and assess the effects of all these sources of variation. Consequently, the mind must accept the apparently random nature of the environment. At the attitudinal level, therefore, it is necessary to be humble and accept 'the probabilistic environment'. However, this is not easy since we have a natural tendency to anticipate and seek simple explanations. Perhaps one way to induce an appropriately humble attitude is to keep a 'track record' of occasions when you make causal attributions about people or events, and observe the number of times you were right or wrong. Another is to ask yourself systematically each time that you impose a causal explanation on a situation whether the 'random' hypothesis is not equally or even more likely. People have a strong need to feel that they control situations. However, by giving up 'illusory control' and concentrating on just the non-random aspects of a situation, you may in fact learn to exercise greater control over your environment.

At a technical level, one needs tools to be able to recognize when one is dealing with random observations (or more accurately 'apparently random' irregularities). Tools are in order since, as discussed above, when left to our own devices we are inept at recognizing randomness.

### Two simple tools

Two 'quick and dirty' tools are available when you are simply trying to determine whether observations are varying at random around some level of performance. Reconsider, for example, Figure 2.2. How would you know whether this series is produced at random, and what are reasonable limits

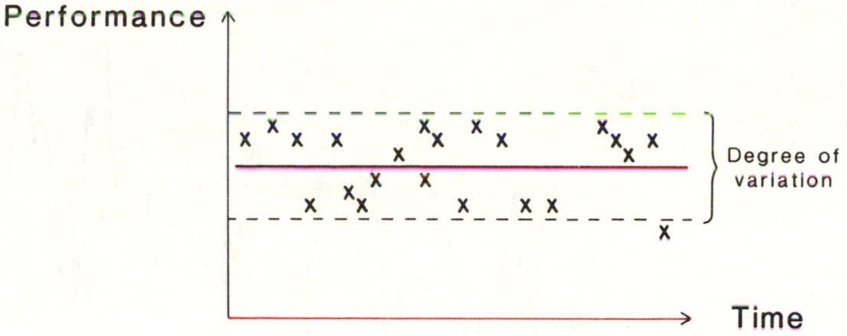

Performance ↑

Figure 2.6  Performance across time and degree of variation

of variation? The first necessity is to record the observations in sequence on a graph such as Figure 2.2 When this is done, calculate the arithmetic mean and draw a straight line through the data passing through the average you have calculated, as illustrated in Figure 2.2. Now assess limits of variation by drawing lines on either side of the average line which include most of the observed points and yet are parallel to the average line. Such lines are indicated by the dotted lines in Figure 2.6. The distance between the dotted lines will give you a fair idea of the amount of variation you can expect.

Figure 2.6 represents irregularities around a mean performance level. However, performance might be improving or deteriorating across time. In this case it is necessary to estimate such a trend by a straight line, and to follow the process indicated above.

The parallel line test will help you estimate the limits of variation; however, it will not show you whether the observations themselves are statistically independent of each other. An easy way to do this is to use the so-called 'unfolding test'.[12] Take a sheet of paper and cover all observations in Figure 2.6 except the first (in time). Now try to predict, given the first observation, where the second point will lie. Uncover, and observe the second point— but keeping the other points hidden from view. Now try to predict the third point; uncover, predict the fourth point—and so on. If you do have a series of independent observations you should find it impossible to predict where the points will lie. This unfolding test is both simple and effective (try it with the data in Figure 2.6 or better still with data from your own experience).

## Handling complex series

The two above aids can be used effectively without technical knowledge and are useful for simple series of the type illustrated here. In many situations, however, series are more complex. They can have trends coupled with seasonal and/or cyclical components. For example, consider Figure 2.7, which shows shipments of petrol to service stations in France. This series is clearly difficult to interpret: there are wide fluctuations, possible seasonal factors and some kind of upward trend across time. In such cases you should either

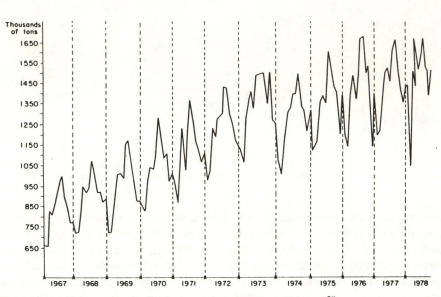

Figure 2.7   Shipments of petrol to service stations in France[28]

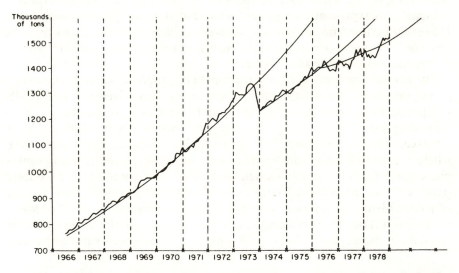

Figure 2.8   Shipments of petrol to service stations in France (after eliminating seasonality and randomness)[28]

consult someone with statistical expertise or attempt an analysis yourself using a time-series computer package.[27] In either case, however, you have to be aware of the questions to be posed. Is there really pattern in the data? Or are all irregular fluctuations within reasonable limits? For instance, Figure 2.8 presents the data of Figure 2.7 after elimination of seasonal and random components. (Incidentally, Figure 2.8 took less than two hours to produce with the aid of a computer package—including entering the raw data, checking for mistakes, adjusting months for comparability, drawing the figure, and so on.) The real underlying trends that were not apparent in Figure 2.7 are clear in Figure 2.8. The drop in 1973 corresponds to the Arab oil embargo; decreases in 1976 and afterwards coincide with large increases in the price of petrol.

## SUMMARY

This chapter has argued that our limited information-processing capacities oblige us to accept the environment as probabilistic. However, the source of the uncertainty lies within us rather than in the environment. Four important statistical concepts related to interpreting probabilistic phenomena were discussed—randomness, statistical independence, sampling variability, and regression—together with evidence of intuitive human misunderstanding of these concepts. It was emphasized that to accept randomness is counter-intuitive. People are motivated to seek explanations and thus try to impose patterns on what they observe. However, such patterns are often illusory.

Examples were given of how actions based on observing extreme values of outcomes often lead to false attributions of causality. Lack of reliability in data sources, for example economic statistics, induces inherent instability in observations which can lead to spurious causal explanations.

People need to adopt an attitude of mind that accepts the uncertain nature of the world. Some techniques for assessing the extent of random fluctuations in practical settings were briefly outlined.

## NOTES AND REFERENCES

1. S. Meisler (1977). Spain lottery—Not even a war stops it, *Los Angeles Times*, 30 December.
2. See, for example, D. H. Woods (1966). Improving estimates that involve uncertainty, *Harvard Business Review*, **44**, 91–98, as well as R. M. Cyert and J. G. March (1963). *A Behavioral Theory of the Firm*, Englewood Cliffs, NJ: Prentice-Hall (especially p. 20).
3. L. J. Savage (1971). Elicitation of personal probabilities and expectations, *Journal of the American Statistical Association*, **66**, 800.
4. E. J. Langer (1975). The illusion of control, *Journal of Personality and Social Psychology*, **32**, 311–328.
5. E. J. Langer and J. Roth (1975). Heads I win, tails it's chance: The illusion of control as a function of the sequence of outcomes in a purely chance task, *Journal of Personality and Social Psychology*, **32**, 951–955.
6. It is interesting to note that in asking the rhetorical question of why one should study philosophy, Bertrand Russell stated 'To teach how to live without certainty, and yet without being paralysed by hesitation, is perhaps the chief thing that philosophy, in our age, can still do for those who study it.' *History of Western Philosophy* (2nd edn), London: George Allen & Unwin, 1961, p. 14.
7. It should also be added that the meaning of randomness is not precisely defined

from a scientific viewpoint. See, for example, the illuminating discussion by L. L. Lopes (1982). Doing the impossible: A note on induction and the experience of randomness, *Journal of Experimental Psychology: Learning, Memory, and Cognition,* **8**, 626–636.

8. See for example, P. H. Cootner (ed.) (1964). *The Random Character of Stock Market Prices,* Cambridge, Mass: The MIT Press; and C. W. J. Granger and O. Morgenstern (1970). *Predictability of Stock Market Prices,* Lexington, Mass: D. C. Heath.

9. J. Cohen and C. E. M. Hansel (1955). The idea of independence, *British Journal of Psychology,* **46**, 178–190. See also J. Cohen (1972). *Psychological Probability: Or the Art of Doubt,* London: George Allen & Unwin.

10. See also the study by P. Bakan (1960). Response tendencies in attempts to generate random binary series, *American Journal of Psychology,* **73**, 127–131.

11. See D. Kahneman and A. Tversky (1972). Subjective probability: A judgment of representativeness, *Cognitive Psychology,* **3**, 430–454.

12. See for example H. V. Roberts (1974). *Conversational Statistics,* Cupertino, California: Hewlett Packard, Chapter 4.

13. W. A. Wagenaar (1970). Appreciation of conditional probabilities in binary sequences, *Acta Psychologica,* **34**, 348–356.

14. It is interesting to enquire *why* people have such difficulty with the concept of randomness. Recent evidence shows that, when given appropriate feedback (as opposed to being simply instructed to generate random sequences), people can exhibit variability in behaviour that appears random in nature. Thus the difficulty people experience in generating random sequences would not appear to be due to biological limitations *per se*, but rather to reflect perceptions of the environment. See A. Neuringer (1986). Can people behave 'randomly'?: The role of feedback, *Journal of Experimental Psychology: General,* **115**, 62–75.

15. A. Tversky and D. Kahneman (1971). The belief in the law of small numbers, *Psychological Bulletin,* **76**, 105–110.

16. R. E. Nisbett, D. H. Krantz, C. Jepson, and Z. Kunda (1983). The use of statistical heuristics in everyday reasoning, *Psychological Review,* **90**, 339–363.

17. H. A. Simon and R. K. Sumner (1968). Patterns in music. In Kleinmuntz, B. (ed.) *Formal Representation of Human Judgment,* New York: Wiley, p. 220.

18. A. Etzioni (1968). 'Shortcuts' to social change? *The Public Interest,* **12**, 40–51.

19. L. Zieve (1966). Misinterpretation and abuse of laboratory tests by clinicians, *Annals of New York Academy of Science,* **134**, 563–572.

20. Y. Renard (1976). Les incertitudes de la statistique et la baisse dite tendancielle de la rentabilité du capital. *Le Monde,* 17 February, p. 17. Incidentally, a classic study on the inherent unreliability of economic statistics is by O. Morgenstern (1965). *On the Accuracy of Economic Observations* (2nd edn), Princeton, New Jersey: Princeton University Press.

21. P. Slovic and S. Lichtenstein (1971). Comparison of Bayesian and regression approaches to the study of information processing in judgment, *Organizational Behavior and Human Performance,* **6**, 649–744, reference an unpublished study to this effect by C. N. Uhl and P. J. Hoffman.

22. Carlo Brumat suggested this particular scenario to me. See also R. M. Hogarth (1979). How valid is your judgment? *CEDEP Journal,* **3**, 47–56.

23. D. Kahneman and A. Tversky (1973). On the psychology of prediction, *Psychological Review,* **80**, 237–251.

24. D. T. Campbell (1969). Reforms as experiments, *American Psychologist,* **24**, 409–429.

25. This scenario, albeit in a different form, was suggested by Hillel J. Einhorn.

26. C. F. Gettys, C. W. Kelly III, and C. R. Peterson (1973). The best guess

hypothesis in multistage inference, *Organizational Behavior and Human Performance*, **10**, 364–373.
27. For example, S. Makridakis and S. C. Wheelwright (1978). *Interactive Forecasting: Univariate and Multivariate Methods* (2nd edn), San Francisco: Holden-Day.
28. The data and graphs presented in Figures 2.7 and 2.8 were kindly supplied by S. Makridakis and B. Majani who have authorized their presentation here.

# CHAPTER 3

# Combining information for prediction

Predictions and evaluations are usually based on a combination of different information sources. For example, an impression of a job candidate gained from an application form can be modified during an interview. A judgement concerning the probable level of next year's sales of a company depends on many factors, e.g. this year's sales, industry trends, marketing strategy, anticipated reactions by competitors, etc. An evaluation of a work of art, for example a play, can be made on several dimensions: structure, style, humour, pathos, and so on.

In the preceding chapter the necessity of considering the environment as probabilistic was discussed as well as notions related to probabilistic thinking. In most examples, however, single information sources were considered, for instance observations of a measure of an individual's performance across time. In this chapter, the problems of making predictions from several information sources are discussed.

Given limited information-processing capacity, it is difficult for humans to combine information from different sources. Consider what has to be done. Information from both the environment and the individual's memory needs to be selected. Meaning is given to the information and, indeed, such meaning may even guide the search process in the first place. The various sources of information selected then have to be weighted and combined to form a final judgement. Since people do not have the mental capacity to do these operations in the manner of a computer, they employ simplifying strategies. However, whereas these strategies reduce the cost of processing information, they sometimes induce errors that could be avoided by more systematic, but effortful procedures.

Statistical theory embodies several commonsense principles for combining information for prediction. These are also discussed in this chapter together with indications of the extent to which intuitive judgement can and does follow such principles. Specifically, the following issues are considered: (1) combining information sources that are or are not statistically independent; (2) conflicts between principles of statistical reasoning and people's natural tendency to think causally; and (3) the manner in which cognitive strategies interact with aspects of judgemental tasks such as the order in which information is presented, differential availability of information, and so on.

Finally, the chapter concludes with a discussion of mechanical aids for predictions based on several information sources.

## INDEPENDENT VERSUS DEPENDENT DATA SOURCES

In the discussion of sampling in Chapter 2, it was noted that confidence in judgement should be related to the amount of information sampled. However, this assumed that each item of information sampled was independent of the others. Consider, therefore, what should happen when information sources are not independent. At the limit, if when forming an opinion you observe the same information twice, you should clearly not treat it as two independent items of information. However, the more common situation is that of multiple sources of information with varying degrees of dependence on each other. For example, imagine that you are predicting a person's job potential on the basis of biographical details and an interview. Much of the information you receive will be redundant in the sense that knowledge of part of the information is related, albeit imperfectly, to other parts. For instance, assume that you are trying to assess the person's intelligence. This can be gauged from several sources: scholastic record, type of past employment, comments and answers made in the interview, etc. Whereas all these data sources are not identical, they are related, and in the prediction of intelligence, part of the information is redundant when you know the rest. For example, intelligence is often related (albeit imperfectly) to academic success. Although the redundancy principle may seem straightforward, evidence indicates that people have considerable difficulty in its application.

The employment interview provides a case in point. Research indicates that in a half-hour interview situation, the interviewer typically forms a hypothesis about the candidate (e.g., favourable or unfavourable) and then spends the rest of the interview seeking information consistent with the hypothesis.[1] Apart from the fact that this is not a good strategy for learning about the candidate (see Chapter 6), in most situations a lot of the information gleaned will be redundant in the sense described above. It is, of course, true that much of the information gained in this way will also be consistent (indeed, if it is redundant it is almost bound to be consistent). However, consistency of data sources that are not independent adds little to predictive validity.

When a person has a lot of information to process it is difficult to assess the degree of redundancy among different sources. Thus, well-documented cases with little inconsistency are often cues people use to infer how much confidence to place in judgement. An instructive example is a study by Oskamp where the judgements of clinical psychologists were studied as a function of the amount of information presented to them.[2] The psychologists were required to make predictions on the basis of case studies. In addition, they were asked to state their degree of confidence in their judgements when they had different amounts of information available to them. Results indicated that as the amount of information about cases increased, so did the psychologists' confidence in their judgements. However, there was no corresponding increase in predictive accuracy. In general, when predictions are based on several dependent data sources, the consistency of their implications is not an accurate indicator of the confidence to be placed in such predictions.

Strategies people use for making predictive judgements are influenced by consistency, and related concepts such as the degree of similarity between the features of an object and the class to which it is supposed to belong.[3] For example, a job candidate may be judged by the extent to which his or her characteristics match one's image of successful managers. Such 'stereotyping' was also noted in Chapter 2, when the problems of assessing random sequences of coin tosses were considered. The following exercise provides a further example.

Consider this description of Tom W. which was written by a psychologist when Tom was in his senior year in high school.

> Tom W. is of high intelligence, although lacking in true creativity. He has a need for order and clarity and for neat and tidy systems in which every detail finds its appropriate place. His writing is rather dull and mechanical, occasionally enlivened by somewhat corny puns and by flashes of imagination of the sci-fi type. He has a strong drive for competence. He seems to have little feel and little sympathy for other people and does not enjoy interacting with others. Self-centered, he nonetheless has a deep moral sense.[4]
> (Reproduced by permission of the American Psychological Association).

Now imagine, that you are told that Tom W. is currently a graduate student. Rank the following nine topics as to the likelihood that they are the area of Tom's graduate specialization:

> business administration
> computer science
> engineering
> humanities and education
> law
> library science
> medicine
> physical and life sciences
> social science and social work.

If you are like the subjects in an experiment by Kahneman and Tversky, then you would rank computer science and engineering as most likely, and humanities and education and social science and social work as least likely. Indeed, the consistency of the information in the personality sketch is compelling. However, as will be explained later in this chapter, such a judgement contradicts statistical reasoning.

The mental strategy of stereotyping by degree of similarity has been named 'representativeness' by Kahneman and Tversky.[3] They and others have shown that it plays a pervasive role in judgement. Unfortunately, it is valid only to the extent that data sources are not redundant or if it does not induce you to ignore other information (a point that will be explored in depth below).

The importance of consistency of data sources is emphasized when one considers how people make predictions on the basis of inconsistent cues. One strategy is to downplay or ignore the inconsistent information. This issue was specifically investigated in a study by Slovic concerning the assessment of intelligence on the basis of consistent and inconsistent profiles.[5] Slovic presented subjects with profiles of individuals based on nine cues—represented by scores on each of the nine dimensions. Previous work had indicated that two of the cues, high-school grade rating and English effectiveness, accounted for most of the differences in judgements. Consequently, these cues were manipulated to create a series of consistent and inconsistent profiles. Results indicated that judgements were dependent upon the two main cues when they were consistent; however, when the cues had contradictory implications, subjects relied on only one cue and excluded the other from consideration. Other investigators have reported similar results.[6]

The use of consistency, similarity, and representativeness seem to be reasonable strategies for making judgements. And indeed, in cases where information sources are not redundant and other relevant information is not ignored, the strategies can be effective. Problems occur in determining whether or not information sources are redundant and in handling apparently inconsistent information. For many judgemental tasks, such assessments exceed intuitive information- processing capacity and, as will be explored at the end of this chapter, are better handled by mechanical means.

## The illusion of validity

In discussing the regression phenomenon in Chapter 2, it was noted that judgemental strategies that involve matching the characteristics of cues to those of the criterion can lead to systematic errors. Specifically, extreme values of cues (e.g. test scores) are typically accompanied by less extreme values of the criterion (e.g. performance measures). Thus, a sensible judgemental strategy is to regress predictions based on extreme observations toward the mean of the variable predicted. However, people frequently make implicit use of extreme values of predictive cues, together with consistency of data sources, to justify confidence in their predictions. Thus, paradoxically, characteristics of information that inspire confidence are often inversely related to the predictive accuracy of that information. This has led to what Kahneman and Tversky have termed the 'illusion of validity':

... factors that enhance confidence, for example, consistency and extremity, are often negatively related with predictive accuracy. Thus people are prone to experience much confidence in highly fallible judgments, a phenomenon that may be termed the *illusion of validity*. Like other perceptual and judgmental errors, the illusion of validity often persists even when its illusory character is recognized. When interviewing a candidate, for example, many of us have experienced great confidence in our prediction of his future performance, despite our knowledge that interviews are notoriously fallible.[4]
(Reproduced by permission of the American Psychological Association)

Finally, at an anecdotal level, it is worth noting that the use of consistency of information as a cue to confidence in judgement seems to be well appreciated by 'con-men'. Successful con-men succeed in creating such consistent behaviour patterns that their victims never think of seeking other, independent evidence to check on them.

## STATISTICAL VERSUS CAUSAL REASONING[7]

As noted previously, intuitive predictions are largely based on one's causal understanding of the world. Moreover, given the complexity of the environment relative to the capabilities of the human mind, people are highly motivated to discover causal patterns for prediction. Indeed, as illustrated in Chapter 2, causal relations are often inferred where none exists. However, this does not mean that we have no intuitive appreciation for probabilistic concepts such as randomness. Rather, our difficulty lies in distinguishing between pattern and noise and our attributions of cause in specific circumstances are typically accompanied by feelings of uncertainty. Stated more concisely, much of our mental activity involves making judgements of *probable cause*.

The nature of causal reasoning, however, differs in important respects from the dictates of probability and statistical theory. First, unlike the nature of cause, probability and statistics are logical systems based on principles that allow one to state precisely the implications of certain assumptions. For example, given certain inputs, one can calculate the extent to which regression effects can be expected in specific situations. Second, certain aspects of probability theory are antithetical to causal reasoning. Indeed, probability theory is acausal. For example, causal reasoning is generally unidirectional in nature. That is, whereas one might state that $X$ (e.g. effort) precedes and causes $Y$ (e.g. fatigue), one would not simultaneously maintain that $Y$ causes $X$ (e.g. that fatigue causes effort). In statistical logic, on the other hand, the relation between $X$ and $Y$ can be described or discussed in either direction (i.e. $X$ to $Y$, or $Y$ to $X$). Moreover, neither $X$ nor $Y$ has any claim to, for example, temporal priority. Third, whereas statistical reasoning is entirely based on the logical structure of information, causal reasoning is responsive to both content and structure.

## Judging probable cause

The concept and definition of cause have long been the subject of scientific and philosophical debate. Nonetheless, people do have strong intuitions concerning the presence or absence of cause in particular circumstances. Moreover, these form the bases of judgements of probable cause. In a review of psychological work on causal reasoning, Einhorn and Hogarth argue that probable cause judgements are affected by four types of consideration. These are: (a) the causal field or context in which such judgements are made; (b) the use of various imperfect indicators of causal relations called 'cues-to-causality'. These include temporal order (causes precede effects), covariation, contiguity in time and space, and similarity of cause and effect; (c) judgemental strategies employed for combining the causal field with the cues-to-causality; and (d) the role of alternative explanations in discounting the strength of particular causal beliefs. To illustrate, consider the following example:

> Imagine that a watch face has been hit by a hammer and the glass breaks. How likely was the force of the hammer the cause of the breakage? Since no explicit context is given, an implicitly assumed neutral context is invoked in which the cues-to-causality point strongly to a causal relation; i.e. the force of the hammer precedes the breakage in time, there is high covariation between glass breaking (or not) with the force of solid objects, contiguity in time and space is high, and there is congruity (similarity) between the length and strength of cause and effect. Moreover, it is difficult to discount the causal link since there are few alternative explanations to consider. Now imagine that the same event occurred during a testing procedure in a watch factory. In this context, the cause of the breakage is more often judged to be a defect-in-the-glass.[7]

This example raises several issues that relate to how people make probabilistic judgements. First, note that whether information about a possible cause is deemed relevant depends on the context in which the information is considered. Thus, whereas the force of the hammer is deemed to be causally relevant in the first or neutral scenario, it is the defect in the glass that is relevant in the watch factory. More specifically, judgemental processes are attuned to differences and the relevance of potential causal candidates depends on whether these are perceived as differences in the context of the problem (the 'causal field'). Second, the strength of a causal hypothesis depends both on whether it is supported (or 'makes sense') in terms of the cues-to-causality and the presence or absence of alternative explanations. Thus, three critical aspects of causal reasoning involve: (a) the definition of the context or causal field against which relevant information is selected; (b) the extent to which the cues-to-causality imply a coherent scenario, and (c) the strength of alternative explanations. These considerations are now contrasted with the logic of probability theory.

42

## Base-rate and specific information

Consider the following problem:

> A cab was involved in a hit-and-run accident at night. Two cab companies, the Green and the Blue, operate in the city. You are given the following data:
> (1)   85% of the cabs in the city are Green and 15% are Blue.
> (2)   A witness identified the cab as a Blue cab. The court tested his ability to identify cabs under the appropriate visibility conditions. When presented with a sample of cabs (half of which were Blue and half of which were Green), the witness made correct identifications in 80% of the cases and erred in 20% of the cases.
>
> *Question*: What is the probability that the cab involved in the accident was Blue rather than Green?[8]

If you are like the typical subjects who have answered this question, you will assess the chances of the cab being Blue at about 80%. However, the statistical answer to this question is quite different; it is 41%. Moreover, for many people this answer is surprising in that it does not seem intuitively plausible. The source of the difficulty lies in the failure to realize that the question involves two kinds of information, one of which is typically ignored. First, there is what is called *a priori* or *base-rate* information. In this case, for example, it is known that 85% of the cabs in the city are Green. Second, there is information concerning the case at hand, namely the ability of the particular witness to distinguish Blue from Green cabs. The first kind of information is called the 'base-rate' in the sense that it provides the background to the judgemental situation; the second kind of information is referred to as *specific* or *case* data. Probability theory argues that one should modify base-rates by case data such that the ensuing judgement reflects both. (The technical details of how such calculations are done are contained in Appendix A.) People's intuitions, however, do not always correspond to the laws of probability in this instance. Indeed, considerable evidence has been documented of the failure to consider base-rate data.[9]

The above example indicates that readily available base-rate data may be ignored. However, frequently base-rate data are important for prediction even though they may be absent from the definition of a problem. A case in point is the example presented earlier in this chapter concerning Tom W. Recall that you were asked to estimate, on the basis of a personality sketch, the relative likelihoods of different areas of Tom W.'s graduate specialization. Most people respond to this question by suggesting computer science or engineering as most likely, and humanities and education and social sciences and social work as least likely. However, such judgements ignore the relative numbers of people, or base-rates, of students in the different areas of specialization. If these are taken into account, your answer should be quite different. An additional and interesting point here is that in a series of experiments using the Tom W. example, Kahneman and Tversky[4] found that: (1) even if people were aware of the inherent lack of reliability of such personality sketches, this did not affect their judgements (see also Chapter 2); and (2) their respondents were quite aware of the fact that different numbers of students were enrolled in the different areas of graduate specialization. However, this knowledge was not used when judgements were made.

There is often emotional resistance to the inclusion of base-rate data in problems like those involving the cabs. In particular, many feel that the base-rate data are not relevant to the question. However, before pursuing this issue, consider the following intuitive explanation for the rationale of probability theory. Probability theory makes the following kind of argument: Assume first that the only information you have is the base-rate data. That is, all you know is that 85% of the cabs are Green, and that 15% are Blue. If you were told that one cab had been involved in an accident, what are the chances that it was a Blue cab? Most people would say 15% (assuming, of course, that there is no reason to believe that drivers of Blue cabs are more or less reckless than drivers of Green cabs, etc.). Now assume that you are given additional informaton, which is not perfectly reliable, concerning the colour of the cab. Surely this information should modify your prior (or base-rate) estimation by a factor related to its inherent reliability. For instance, if specific or case information came from a totally unreliable source, it should be ignored; if it came from a 100% reliable source it should dominate the base-rate information. Intermediate levels of reliability will combine with the base-rate to form the normative judgement in accord with the rules of probability theory.[10]

Despite the above arguments, many people still do not consider the base-rate data as relevant. However, consider the following variation of this problem.

A cab was involved in a hit-and-run accident at night. Two cab companies, the Green and the Blue, operate in the city. You are given the following data:
(1)  Although the two companies are roughly equal in size, 85% of cab accidents in the city involve Green cabs, and 15% involve Blue cabs.
(2)  A witness identified the cab as a Blue cab. The court tested his ability to identify cabs under appropriate visibility conditions. When presented with a sample of cabs (half of which were Blue and half of which were Green) the witness made correct identifications in 80% of the cases and erred in 20% of the cases.

*Question*: What is the probability that the cab involved in the accident was Blue rather than Green?[8]

Note the distinction between the first and second versions of this problem. In the first, the base-rate data simply reflect the relative number of Blue and Green cabs in the city. In the second, however, the base-rate information appears as a distinct difference against the background of equal numbers of Blue and Green cabs. Thus, there is a change of context compared to the first version such that the base-rate information can now be given a causal interpretation. Indeed, whereas answers to the second question reflect greater variability than answers to the first, more people do make use of both the base-rate and specific data when answering the second. Here the average response is 55% compared to the statistical answer of 41% and the average response of 80% to the first version. In other words, whereas many do not consider the base-rate to be relevant in the first version of the problem, the change of context (or causal field) is such that the base-rate information is deemed relevant in the second. The above examples raise two interesting issues. First, under what general conditions do people attend or not attend to base-rates? Second, should people attend to base-rates?

There are many studies that demonstrate failure to attend to base-rates.[9] However, as just noted, people do attend to this information if it appears causally relevant to them. This can occur because the nature of the background or context highlights the information (as in the second cab problem), or because people possess substantive expertise in an area (based presumably on some underlying causal model) such that they 'know' base-rates are relevant. People also use base-rate information in the absence of specific or case data. For example, if as a manager you knew that, on average, 1 out of 5 salespersons succeeds in exceeding targeted sales, you would, in the absence of other information, predict a 1 in 5 success rate for any particular salesperson.

Should one always attend to base-rates? One difficulty in dealing with this issue is that it is not always clear what figure is the apppropriate base-rate. For example, in the cab problem, should the appropriate base-rate be the relative numbers of Green and Blue cabs (or differential accident rates) in the city, in the country, or in a specific neighborhood?[11] There is no easy answer to this question. However, whatever position one adopts with respect to the first version of the cab problem, there is little doubt that ignoring base-rates can, on occasion, lead to substantial judgemental errors, not least of which are certain forms of self-delusion. For example, imagine that you wish to determine how good your judgement is. This could be done in several contexts: for example, personnel decisions, stock purchases, decisions concerning sales outlets, medical prognosis if you are a physician, and so on. If you assess your judgemental ability simply on the basis of observed success rates this could be misleading. For instance, when checking your predictions, the relevant question to be asked is not how many predictions are successful, but how many would have been successful if you had no judgemental ability? In other words, your judgemental ability can only be assessed relative to a base-rate. For instance, if in a job selection situation 70% of candidates would have turned out to be successful whether or not you selected them, a success rate of, say, 80% may not be too impressive. Unfortunately, and as will be explored in Chapter 6, determining the base-rate is not easy in judgemental situations since the requisite information is not necessarily available. Thus, base-rate data are often ignored. However, it is necessary to keep the base-rate concept firmly in mind. Perhaps one way to remember it is to recall the comment attributed to the humorist Thurber. When asked what his spouse 'was like', he replied 'Compared to what?'

## Confusion of the inverse[12]

Imagine you are a physician who has just completed the examination of a female patient with a breast mass. Moreover, you believe that this is highly likely to be benign. That is, after thinking through the case carefully, you assess the probability that the patient's breast mass is malignant to be only 1%. Now imagine that you have ordered an X-ray test in the form of a mammogram and the result is positive, i.e. the test indicates that the patient's breast mass is malignant. You are aware that the test is not 100% reliable and thus consult the medical literature to assess its reliability. There you find statements of the form: 'The accuracy of mammography is approximately 90% ....''The accuracy of mammography in correctly diagnosing malignant lesions of the breast average 80 to 85 percent ....''The results showed 79.2 percent of 475 malignant lesions were correctly diagnosed and 90.4 percent of 1105 benign lesions were correctly diagnosed, for an overall accuracy of 87 percent.'[13]

If you were the physician, what would you now estimate the probability that the patient's breast mass is malignant (i.e. cancerous) given that you know that the test result was positive?

When this scenario and question were given to physicians, most (95 out of 100) gave an estimate of about 75%.[13] From a statistical viewpoint, there are two types of error in this response. First, most physicians ignored or gave little attention to the 1% base-rate (see above). Second, whereas the physicians used the information about test reliability to answer the question, they did this in a totally inappropriate manner. To see this, denote the event that the breast mass is malignant by the symbol $X$, and the positive outcome of the test result by $Y$. Observe that the question asked of the physicians was to estimate the probability of $X$ (malignancy) given $Y$ (the outcome of the test). In formal probabilistic notation, this is written $p(X|Y)$. Moreover, most of the physicians justified their answers to this question by referring to the test reliability data. However, it should be noted that these data do not provide estimates of $p(X|Y)$. Instead, these data provide information about $p(Y|X)$—that is, the probability of a positive test result ($Y$) given an underlying malignancy ($X$). As summarized by Eddy:

> When asked about this, the erring physicians usually report that they assumed that the probability of cancer given that the patient has a positive X-ray ... was approximately equal to the probability of a positive X-ray in a patient with cancer .... The latter probability is the one measured in clinical research programs and is very familiar, but it is the former that is needed for clinical decision making. It seems that many if not most physicians confuse the two.[13]

Dawes has referred to this error as 'confusion of the inverse' in that probabilities of the form $p(X|Y)$ are sometimes referred to as inverse probabilities.[12] However, what are the consequences of confusing $p(X|Y)$ and $p(Y|X)$ and why might such confusion occur? First, it should be noted that $p(X|Y)$ and $p(Y|X)$ are only equal when $p(X)$ is the same as $p(Y)$. In other words, from a mathematical viewpoint the confusion does not matter if the probability of a person having a malignancy is matched by the probability of the test giving a positive result. However, in this situation $p(Y)$ is typically much larger than $p(X)$. Thus, if physicians confuse $p(X|Y)$ and $p(Y|X)$ they will diagnose many more people as having malignant lesions than is in fact the case. Furthermore, if the treatment recommended for diagnosed malignancy is surgery, the practical implication is too many unnecessary surgeries.

To see why the confusion might exist, note that when thinking causally the order in which events occur is an important cue-to-causality. For example, if an event occurs and one wishes to infer its cause, a first reaction is to ask whether something unusual occurred prior to the event. Causes generally precede effects. When examining the structure of the problem given above, however, note that it has the following peculiarity. First, we know that the presence of a malignancy $(X)$ precedes the effect of a positive test result $(Y)$. However, in terms of the information obtained from the environment, we first learn of the test result $(Y)$ and it is this that is used to infer malignancy $(X)$. Thus, the test is used to predict a prior state (malignancy) that itself existed before the test and indeed is the cause of the outcome of

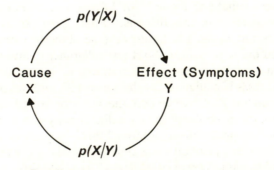

Figure 3.1   Loop-like structure for confusion of inverse probabilities. Copyright (1986) by American Psychological Association. (Reprinted by permission)

the test. This situation implies a loop-like structure, illustrated in Figure 3.1, that implies considerable ambiguity in the use of temporal order as a cue-to-causality. Einhorn and Hogarth comment:

Note that the causal probability, $p(Y|X)$, is not predictive in the usual sense; i.e. while having cancer predicts the test, this hardly seems relevant to the practical matter. On the other hand, the test (which is known first in time), is used to predict the disease that preceded it (since the disease causes the test result). Therefore, there are two temporal cues in problems of this type: causes precede effects, but, effects are seen first and used to predict their prior causes. Under such conditions, confusion of inverse probabilities is quite under-standable.[7]

## Plausible, and not so plausible scenarios

Recall the description of Tom W. given on page 38. Please read the description again and then consider the following questions: What is the probability that (a) Tom W. will select journalism as his college major (b) but quickly become unhappy with his choice and (c) switch to engineering?

Slovic, Fischhoff and Lichtenstein asked three groups of subjects to answer these questions.[14] The first group estimated the probability of (a) Tom's selection of journalism; the second was asked to assess the joint probability of (a) and (b) both occurring; and the third the joint probability of (a) and (b) and (c) all occurring. Mean estimates of the different groups were: .21 for (a); .39 for (a) and (b); and .42 for (a) and (b) and (c). In other words, as more detail was added to the events judged, they were assessed as more likely.

The answers given by the three groups contradict the logic of probability theory. To understand why, it helps to think of the structure of the problem in an abstract manner. Imagine two distinct events denoted $D$ and $E$. Moreover, assume that you have assessed the probability of $D$ occurring as, say, .50. Now imagine being asked to asess the probability that both $D$ and $E$ will occur. Moreover, assume that the probability of $E$ occurring is very high, say, .99, i.e. almost a certainty. However, even if the probability of $E$ were 1.0 (i.e. a certainty), it should be clear that the probability of $D$ and $E$ both occurring cannot exceed .50 since even if we are sure that $E$ will occur, there is still the uncertainty about $D$. In general, the logic of probability theory states that the joint probability of two events cannot exceed the smaller of the probabilities associated with the two events (see Appendix A). Moreover, this restriction holds whether or not the events are statistically independent.

Thus, returning to the Tom W. example, probability theory implies that the assessment of event (a) cannot be exceeded by that for the event defined by both (a) and (b), and this in turn cannot be exceeded by that for the event (a) and (b) and (c). However, the mean assessments provided by Slovic, Fischhoff and Lichtenstein's subjects reverse this rank ordering.

To consider why judgements might violate the logic of probability theory in this instance, it is important to consider the content and not just the structure of this scenario since people clearly respond to meaning and not just structure. Indeed, we infer structure through meaning. There are two important aspects of the example cited. First, parts (b) and (c) of the question make a coherent causal story in relation to part (a). That is, if one deems *a priori* that journalism is an unlikely choice for Tom, then it seems highly plausible that he would find it unsuitable and thus subsequently take up something more in line with his character. In many ways, the scenarios defined by the events [(a) *and* (b)] and [(a) *and* (b) *and* (c)] do seem more likely than (a) alone in that (a) just does not seem too likely by itself. Second, it is possible that in evaluating the two joint probabilities, people do not interpret their task as assessing joint probabilities but rather as assessing probabilities conditional on the event (a). Thus, for example, when asked to assess [(a) *and* (b)], people encode this event in a causal manner whereby they implicitly answer the question 'What is the probability that Tom will become quickly unhappy with his choice of journalism?' Note that in this question the event of having chosen journalism is considered as a certain event rather than a source of uncertainty to be evaluated. In other words, when evaluating complex events, people respond to the causal implications of the stimuli which can sometimes mask the logical structure of the problem.

People are sensitive to how problems are presented and react to implicit causal suggestions in the way these are worded. For example, noting that the English language conjunction 'and' often indicates temporal order when used in narrative, Einhorn and Hogarth illustrated the subtle effects of temporal order as a cue-to-causality, and the manner in which this can confuse probabilistic reasoning.[7] Two groups of MBA students (all of whom had taken courses in statistics) were told to let the symbol $S$ represent the event 'going into the supermarket' and $K$ stand for the event 'buying some coffee'. One group was then asked to consider the question 'What is the probability of going into the supermarket and buying some coffee?' and to state whether this should be represented in probabilistic notation by the expression $p(S \cap K)$, $P(K/S)$, $P(S/K)$ or 'none of the above'. Note that in this formulation, the order of the events $S$ and $K$ is such that the conjunction 'and' seems to imply causally that event $K$ followed event $S$. However, there is no logical reason why 'and' should have this implication and a statistician would respond to the question by selecting $p(S \cap K)$. Einhorn and Hogarth, however, reasoned that because of the temporal implication of 'and', the ordering of the events could induce confusion concerning the statistically appropriate interpretation. Thus, whereas the second group of students was given the same responses to choose from as the first, they received the probabilistic question in a different order, namely 'What is the probability of buying some coffee and going into the supermarket?' Once again, the statistical answer is $p(S \cap K)$. However, in this case 'and' has no temporal implication such that people should demonstrate less confusion in interpreting the statement in probabilistic terms. Responses supported these hypotheses: 75% of respondents chose $p(S \cap K)$ in the second group compared to 58% in the first. Moreover, whereas 38% of respondents in the first group selected $p(K|S)$ (which accords with the commonsense 'causal' order of the events), nobody in the second group chose this response. When interpreting probabilistic statements, it is difficult for people not to reason causally and thus easy to confuse statements of joint and conditional probabilities.

Tversky and Kahneman have argued that the force of causal reasoning is such that scenarios that include both a possible cause and an outcome could appear more probable than scenarios involving the outcome alone.[15] In one experiment, a group of professional forecasters was asked to assess (in 1982) the probability of 'a complete suspension of diplomatic relations between the USA and the Soviet Union, sometime in 1983'. A second group of subjects was also asked to evaluate this outcome but jointly with another causally coherent event, 'a Russian invasion of Poland, and a complete suspension of diplomatic relations between the USA and the Soviet Union, sometime in 1983'. The experimental results showed that these relatively sophisticated subjects evaluated the probability of the second scenario as greater than the first, thereby violating the logic of probability theory.

As the above example indicates, the causal coherence of a scenario is a cue that people use to assess the likelihood of its occurrence. Thus the outcomes of long, detailed, and coherent scenarios may often be judged as more likely than an assessment of the components of such scenarios would warrant. To the extent that scenarios, of both formal and informal natures, are used in forecasting and planning, this tendency points to people expressing inappropriately high levels of confidence when predicting the outcomes of these activities.[16]

## Updating and alternatives

An interesting, and classic example of a systematic discrepancy between intuitive and statistical reasoning is provided by the following experimental task that investigates how people update probabilistic opinion upon the receipt of new evidence. Imagine that an experimenter is standing in front of you and holding one of two bookbags.

> This bookbag contains 1000 poker chips. I started out with two such bags, one containing 700 red and 300 blue chips, the other containing 300 red and 700 blue. I flipped a fair coin to determine which one to use. Thus, if your opinions are like mine, your probability at the moment that this is the predominantly red bookbag is 0.5. Now, you sample, randomly, with replacement after each chip. In 12 samples, you get 8 reds and 4 blues. Now, on the basis of everything you know, what is the probability that this is the predominantly red bag?[17]

If your answer is like that of the typical subject, it would lie in the range of 0.7 to 0.8. In fact, the statistical answer is 0.97. That is, you should be 97% sure that the bag contains 700 red and 300 blue chips (as opposed to 300 red and 700 blue). The failure to revise the initial uncertainty of 0.5 to the

0.97 prescribed by statistical theory has been named 'conservatism'. That is, this type of experimental result has been interpreted as suggesting that people are conservative in that they do not extract as much meaning from sample evidence as they should. Arguments have been rife as to how or why people are conservative in the sense described here. However, the fact remains that they are. My preferred explanation is that strategies people use to update beliefs in everyday inference differ in two critical ways from the dictates of probability theory. Moreover, people use their everyday strategies even when confronted with artificial laboratory tasks such as that described here.

First, it should be noted that the statistical procedure used to evaluate sample evidence in problems such as the above explicitly evaluates the relative likelihoods of observing the evidence both under the hypothesis of interest and its complement. Thus, in the example given, this requires assessing and contrasting the sample evidence both that the bookbag is predominantly red and that it is predominantly blue. However, in everyday inference, problems are usually less explicitly structured than this task and people typically concentrate attention on a single hypothesis. That is, you may wish to evaluate how some evidence affects a hypothesis, but unless you also have some specific alternative hypothesis (or hypotheses) in mind, the evidence is only evaluated relative to the hypothesis of interest.[18] For example, imagine that you are uncertain whether a competitor in business is going to take a particular action, e.g. raise prices on a certain date. Now imagine that you receive information bearing on this issue. How are you going to evaluate this information? Most people would try to evaluate the information *vis-à-vis* the hypothesis that the competitor will increase prices. However, in probability theory, the evidence should also be evaluated relative to the complementary hypothesis, i.e. that the competitor will not raise prices. It is the ratio of these two assessments that is critical to the statistical evaluation of the impact of the evidence. However, most people have difficulty with evaluating evidence against an alternative hypothesis that has not been well specified. In particular, a complementary hypothesis such as 'the competitor will not raise prices' could mask a host of other possible actions of which you are not even aware, e.g. the competitor is preparing an advertising campaign, will raise prices next month, will launch a new product, and so on. Thus, how does one evaluate the evidence? In other words, when updating beliefs, humans do not typically make a simultaneous evaluation of the impact of evidence *vis-à-vis* all alternative hypotheses. Probability theory, on the other hand, prescribes that they should.

The second difference between statistical and human updating of beliefs can be illustrated by the following example. In Agatha Christie's *Murder on the Orient Expresss*, Inspector Poirot has, it seems, twelve possible suspects concerning the murder that has taken place on the train.[19] However, as we subsequently discover, all twelve did it! Now imagine what Poirot would have had to do if he had used statistical theory to assess the evidence. To start, he would have had to consider twelve alternative hypotheses for each of the individual suspects as well as all possible combinations of suspects considered in pairs, triples, foursomes, and so on up to and including the hypothesis of all twelve. Keeping track of all these hypotheses (there are 5019 in total), let alone evaluating the evidence in respect of each, would present a formidable task in information processing, even for the remarkable Poirot. This therefore suggests that in evaluating evidence, people construct, alter and replace hypotheses rather than update their degree of confidence in particular hypotheses. This is not to say that, for particular tasks, people do not use evidence to change the level of confidence held in particular hypotheses (e.g. one's confidence in a football team's chances of winning a game would doubtless decrease on learning that its two star players were injured). On the other hand, I maintain that much updating of opinion involves changing hypotheses rather than the probabilities attached to hypotheses. Moreover, this is an active and constructive cognitive process that depends heavily on causal reasoning.

How does evidence concerning alternative hypotheses affect judgements of probable cause? In general, people discount the strengths of belief accorded to particular hypotheses by the extent to which they can imagine alternative explanations. The difference between causal and probabilistic reasoning, however, is the following: whereas in both modes of thought the presence of strong alternatives will discount beliefs that are initially either strong or weak, the absence of alternatives can have different impacts in the two systems. Specifically, in probabilistic reasoning the absence of alternatives to a hypothesis implies strong belief in that hypothesis since the probabilities assigned to an hypothesis and its complement must always sum to one. In judgements of probable cause, however, this need not be the case. On the one hand, the strength of belief in one's hypothesis can be increased precisely because one cannot think of alternative explanations. Consider, for instance, the example of the hammer hitting the watch face in the neutral context (page 41). Here one has a good explanation (the force of the hammer) and this is strengthened by the inability to imagine alternatives. On the other hand, the fact that one cannot think of alternatives to a weak hypothesis (such as your explanation as to why the outer rings of Saturn are braided), does not necessarily imply strong belief in that hypothesis.

## TASK EFFECTS

A central theme of this book is that judgements are the result of interaction between the structure of tasks and the nature of the human information-processing system. Thus it may seem strange to have a section of this chapter specifically entitled 'task effects'. The purpose, however, is to present further examples of how task structures interact with information-processing strategies that people use for predictive judgement.

## Context

As noted above, the context within which judgements are made is important. This particularly affects intuitive estimates of variability, a concept which, as discussed in Chapter 2, is usually not well appreciated, although it is most important for understanding the nature of uncertainty.[20] An example will illustrate the point.

Consider the following two series of numbers:

| A: | 6, | 18, | 4, | 5, | 17 |
|----|----|-----|----|----|-----|
| B: | 1110, | 1122, | 1108, | 1109, | 1121 |

Which series exhibits the more variability?

Whereas most people answer Series A, the statistical measure of *variance*—which indicates the amount of irregular variations from the mean of a series of numbers—is the *same* for both series. Series B is simply Series A plus a constant of 1104. However, the absolute size of the series or objects provides the context against which intuitive judgements of variability are made and thereby influences this process. That is, relative variability is subjectively more salient than variability *per se*. The following intuitive explanation of this phenomenon has been offered:

> Think of the top of a forest. The tree tops seem to form a fairly smooth surface considering that the trees may be 60 or 70 feet tall. Now, look at your desk top. In all probability it is littered with many objects and if a cloth were thrown over it the surface would seem very bumpy and variable. The forest top is far more variable than the surface of your desk, but not relative to the sizes of the objects being considered.[21]

As has been argued in both this and the preceding chapter, when drawing inferences it is important to understand the nature and amount of variability. Thus, if perceptions of variability are distorted by contextual effects, the necessity of using mechanical methods to estimate variability, as illustrated in Chapter 2, is emphasized.

## Availability

The lens model diagram shown in Chapter 1 illustrated the point that predictive judgements are not made in a vacuum but by reference to other information sources or cues. These cues can either be seen physically at the time a judgement is made or imagined; that is, reference to 'imaginary' cues is made from memory. Thus, an important aspect of judgement is the extent to which cues are *available* to the individual.[22]

Tversky and Kahneman argue that the 'availability' of information is an important clue people use in making judgements of frequency or relative frequency. Specifically, if you can imagine or see several instances of one kind of event as opposed to another, you can be led to believe that the former is more frequent than the latter. For example, your estimate of the divorce rate in your country is probably heavily influenced by the number of divorced people you know. People often have the feeling that a traffic accident is more likely just after they have observed one than before. It has also been noted that the purchase of earthquake insurance increases after an earthquake but decreases subsequently as memory of it diminishes.[23]

To explore the operation of availability, experiments have tested people's intuitions of the relative frequency of diseases or causes of death. Results indicate that the relative frequencies of diseases or causes that are much publicized, such as homicide, cancer or tornadoes are overestimated, whereas the relative frequencies of less newsworthy others such as asthma, emphysema, and diabetes are underestimated.[24] The point being made here is that to the extent that our environment differentially emphasizes certain types of events, our judgement will be biased by the ease with which we recall instances of these events and thus in how we estimate their frequency.

A further example of availability bias is provided by geologists who were estimating the potential oil yields of some prospective sites. They did this by comparing the geological features of the sites with areas that had been exploited and where, as a consequence, the oil yields were known. The bias induced by this strategy was that no comparisons were made with other sites that had not been exploited but that had features similar to the prospective sites.[25]

Tversky and Kahneman argue that availability of instances is often a valid rule for prediction. That is, events which occur frequently, either by themselves or in the presence of others, will usually occur frequently in the future.[22] Thus relative availability of past instances is a useful clue to the likelihood of future events. For example, if you were asked to predict how often, in the next month, you would arrive home from work at a certain time, you would probably base your answer on how often that had happened to you in the recent past (as adjusted, of course, for exceptional circumstances). Indeed, it seems difficult to imagine how one can make predictions on the basis of cues that are not available to you!

On the other hand, the environment and/or specific occurrences can increase the salience of certain cues thereby making them more 'available'. An interesting phenomenon in this respect is the extent to which people are influenced by the number of occurrences of an event (i.e. frequency) rather than the relative number of occurrences (i.e. relative frequency). For example, imagine that you have been asked which of two groups in your work organization is smarter, for instance in a business setting accountants or market researchers. How would you answer this question? You might well try to think of the smart accountants and the smart market researchers you know and base your intuitive estimate on this comparison. However, in doing so, you would ignore an important element of the problem: the total numbers of accountants and market researchers. Your comparison should

54

not be based on the absolute but rather the relative number of smart persons in both groups. Research, however, indicates that people often base estimates of proportions (or probabilities or relative frequencies) on the basis of their experience of absolute as opposed to relative frequencies.[26] In a sense, this is another instance of the failure to relate judgement to some base-line considerations.*

**Anchoring and adjustment**

One commonly used judgemental strategy that is highly dependent on information presented or available to a person has been named 'anchoring and adjustment'.[27] An example serves to illustrate. Imagine that as a manager you have been asked to forecast next year's sales of your company (or division). How would you do it? A common strategy is to take a cue such as this year's sales, or perhaps next year's budgeted sales, as a starting point—or 'anchor'—and then to make adjustments to that figure according to anticipated changes in conditions (for example due to differences in pricing or advertising strategy, competitive reactions, etc.). That is, you would adjust the anchor by amounts representing these factors. If one accepts that in many time series the sheer inertia of human activity is such that each observation closely resembles the one preceding it (see Chapter 1), such a strategy has much to recommend it. However, even in situations where you are making predictions across time, events can take sudden, sharp turns. Furthermore, not all important predictive activity is of this nature.

The dangers of the anchoring and adjustment strategy lie mainly in the way the original anchor is generated. This has been dramatically demonstrated in experiments where people were asked to make judgements about uncertain quantities. The experimenter artificially generated an anchor point by spinning a random device (a so-called 'wheel of fortune') and asking subjects to make judgements once they had observed the number generated by the wheel of fortune. Results indicated significant effects in judgements due to the anchor.[27]

There is reason to believe that many intuitive anticipations are based on anchoring and adjustment strategies; for example, sales forecasts expressed as a percentage increase (or decrease) of budget, judgements about other people ('how do you rate him compared to ... ?'); there is also evidence that anchoring and adjustment techniques are used in many industries for price setting (e.g. as a percentage of cost). Indeed, the writer knows of one case where a company had serious financial difficulties precisely because of this. The anchor used as the basis for the price mark-up was totally inappropriate.

---

* Incidentally, I found myself falling precisely into this trap when asked which of two schools in which I taught had the brighter students. In making my judgement, I forgot that there were twice as many students in one school compared to the other.

Anchoring and adjustment seems to be a judgemental strategy that is almost as necessary as availability. That is, predictions are made by reference to cues that are available, adjustments are then made concerning the particular case to be predicted relative to the available cues. Furthermore, availability and anchoring and adjustment are strategies that both depend heavily upon the initial point in the judgemental process: the information that is available and which forms the anchor.

### Effects of data presentation

The manner in which information is presented can also affect its salience and thus importance as a predictive cue. For example, many studies have shown that the order in which information is presented can produce so-called 'primacy' or 'recency' effects.[28] That is, when presented with a sequence of informational inputs, sometimes the earlier items dominate the individual's final opinion (a 'primacy' effect) and sometimes the latter (a 'recency' effect). From a normative viewpoint, however, the order of presentation should not affect one's final opinion. Moreover, it appears that primacy and recency effects can be manipulated to some extent by task characteristics.

In addition to primacy and recency effects, giving too much information can reduce the consistency of a person's judgement;[29] simultaneous presentation of concrete data, e.g. figures, together with qualitative information, causes difficulty, with people tending to prefer one source to the exclusion of the other;[30] people find information presented with the use of negatives (e.g. 'not', 'no', etc.) instead of positive statements more difficult to process and understand;[31] seemingly complete presentations can blind people to the fact that important aspects of a problem have been omitted;[32] even if people do have appropriate statistical information they can be misled by the labels attached to cues, etc.[33] The list of items leading to judgemental bias seem interminable.

To summarize this section, a number of features of judgemental tasks which can affect judgement have been mentioned: contextual effects, the extent to which cues are available, the order in which information is presented, whether comparative judgements involve similar or dissimilar information, qualitative and quantitative data, and other factors. In addition, two common and almost inevitably used judgemental strategies have been described, judgement by availability and anchoring and adjustment.

## AIDS FOR COMBINING INFORMATION FOR PREDICTION

Above, the difficulties of combining information for prediction have been stressed and the dangers of certain judgemental strategies emphasized. What remedies exist?

First, it is necessary to delineate those judgemental tasks that humans are, or are not, able to perform effectively. Second, means have to be found to remedy those deficiencies which largely concern assessing the predictive ability of different cues, and being able to combine several cues effectively in judgement. The apparent remedy is the use of mechanical means to assess the predictive accuracy and reliability of cues and to weight them in some form of statistical prediction. However, it could be, and indeed it has been argued that no mechanical prediction method can possibly capture the complicated cues and patterns humans use for prediction. Flair cannot be programmed into a computer.

Or at least, this is what was initially assumed. After World War II, a number of investigators started to explore the extent to which statistical analysis could be used in certain judgemental situations, mainly involving predictions in the areas of clinical psychology and academic performance.[34] To quote Dawes:

> The statistical analysis was thought to provide a floor to which the judgment of the experienced clinician could be compared.
> The floor turned out to be a ceiling.[35]

Many studies have subsequently verified this finding and have done so in a wide variety of contexts including medicine and business applications such as auditing, loan granting, and production scheduling. Indeed, exceptions where people have outpredicted statistical models are hard to find.[36] Moreover, many statistical models have been constructed to represent the judgements of people and have been found to predict uncertain events more accurately than the judgements of the people they were supposed to represent.[37]

The actual types of models used in these situations will be discussed in more detail in Chapter 9. However, it is appropriate to consider here why the above results are observed. First, as should be apparent from this chapter, statistical methods are able to weight different cues according to their predictive accuracy and reliability. Second, statistical methods are consistent. People are not. They can become tired, bored or attend to different cues at different times. Furthermore, studies have shown that people are often not aware of how they weight different cues. For example, in one study Slovic found that stockbrokers showed considerable lack of awareness of their judgemental rules and this was particularly the case for the more experienced brokers.[38] Similar observations have been made with respect to insurance underwriters.[39] Indeed, the more experienced people are with a particular cognitive task, the more they seem to lack insight into their own mental processes or strategies. One explanation of this phenomenon is that whereas one is aware of what one is doing when learning (imagine, for example, skiing or driving a car), the processes used to achieve the task become 'automatized' as one gains experience, and thus ultimately inaccessible to introspection. Clearly this process is efficient if one acquires appropriate strategies; however, it also means that, once acquired, inappropriate strategies are difficult to change.

People also tend to believe that they pay attention to many cues, although models based on only a few cues can reproduce their judgements to a high degree of accuracy. A possible explanation of this paradox has been suggested by Shepard,

> Possibly our feeling that we can take into account a host of different factors comes about because, although we remember that at some time or other we have attended to each of the different factors, we fail to notice that it is seldom more than one or two that we consider at any one time.[40]

## Statistical models: objections and advantages

It is therefore suggested that formal, statistical models should be used for prediction where possible. However, two objections can be raised to such a suggestion. First, such models only work on the basis of quantitative data; and second, to be able to derive a statistical rule one needs sufficient numbers of past instances. Furthermore, it must be assumed that 'rules' that applied in the past will apply in the future.

These objections are understandable, although far from invalidating the suggestions. First, qualitative information can be scaled and represented in numerical form. It is, of course, true that such operations transform the character of the data and certainly misrepresent them to some extent. However, the issue to be addressed here is the degree to which such operations reduce the *predictive* power of the information. Several studies suggest that the best role for people in judgement should be that of a 'measuring instrument' for data that are to be combined subsequently by mechanical means.[41] What is lost in the transformation of data from a meaningful but loose qualitative form to a rough (but overly precise) quantitative form may well be compensated by the ability to combine them consistently with other sources of data—be they quantitative or qualitative.

It is, of course, true that to build statistical models for prediction one needs adequate data sources. However, even when data sources are not rich, some means of statistical combination of data, for example taking averages, often leads to better predictions.[42]

A third and often emotional resistance to the use of predictive rules is that they introduce a certain mechanical rigidity which is, somehow, inhuman. People feel averse to having machines predict or make decisions for them. However, the counter-argument has been made by Dawes. He states that the advantage of such rules is that to create them you have to determine a *policy*; you therefore do not treat each case on an *ad hoc* basis. According to Dawes:

> Such procedures follow the categorical imperative of Immanuel Kant: Make each decision as if it were policy for everyone, or at least as if it were a policy for yourself across time.[43]

Of course, one should not become a slave to such rules. Fortunately, if good records are maintained this should not be a problem since the predictive ability of information sources can be updated according to their track records. Indeed, and as will be argued frequently in this book, good record keeping—be it by formal means or just informally in memory—is critical to developing predictive ability.

There are, of course, many situations where statistical models cannot be built and information combination must be done intuitively. For example, many actions have to be taken on the basis of so-called 'snap judgements'. What advice can be offered here? First, it is necessary to be aware of the nature of judgement and the kinds of biases that have been described in this and the preceding chapter. It is also necessary not to be under illusions about one's judgemental ability. Some guidelines for these types of judgement are provided in Chapter 9.

Second, it is unlikely that you will make good judgements unless you have thought about the process of judgement and consciously tried to avoid some of the traps discussed in this chapter. No-one expects superlative performance from athletes who are not fit. Can good judgement be expected from people with bad judgemental habits?

## SUMMARY

This chapter has been concerned with problems of combining information from several sources in order to make predictive judgements. Since this requires mental capacity that often exceeds human capabilities, people resort to the use of different strategies for combining information. When dealing with multiple information sources for prediction, the necessity to distinguish between independent and dependent (redundant) data sources was emphasized. Whereas cues to predictive confidence, such as consistency between different sources of information, are valid when these are independent, they can give rise to illusions of validity when data are redundant.

Much mental activity involves making judgements of probable cause and the conflicts inherent in reasoning in a probabilistic as opposed to causal manner were emphasized. These related specifically to issues concerning why people did or did not consider certain information as relevant for prediction, confusion in the interpretation of probabilistic statements, the tendency to overestimate the likelihood of causally coherent scenarios, and the manner in which people update their beliefs upon the receipt of new information.

The interaction of human cognitive strategies and aspects of the environment in which these are used was further illustrated by discussing both various task effects (cues defined by context and/or the manner of data presentation) as well as different strategies (differential attention to information that is 'available' and the anchoring and adjustment strategy). Undesirable aspects of these cues and strategies were discussed and illustrated.

The major suggestion made to overcome difficulties of information combination was to use decision aids, where possible. Although touched upon here, these will be explored more fully in Chapter 9. Finally, for judgements that cannot be automated, the importance of awareness of possible biases and the development of good judgemental habits were stressed.

## NOTES AND REFERENCES

1. See, for example, E. C. Webster (1964). *Decision Making in the Employment Interview*, Montreal: Industrial Relations Centre, McGill University.
2. See S. Oskamp (1965). Overconfidence in case study judgments, *Journal of Consulting Psychology*, **29**, 261–265. See also P. Slovic (1982). Toward understanding and improving decisions. In W. C. Howell and E. A. Fleishman (eds), *Human Performance and Productivity*: Vol.2. *Information Processing and Decision Making*, Hillsdale, NJ: Erlbaum.
3. See D. Kahneman and A.Tversky (1972). Subjective probability: A judgment of representativeness, *Cognitive Psychology*, **3**, 430–454. In the preceding chapter it was noted that people seek out patterns for prediction. 'Good' patterns are precisely those with a high degree of redundant information which limit psychologically the number of interpretations a person is liable to make. For an example of this principle concerning perceptual patterns, see W. R. Garner (1970). Good patterns have few alternatives. *American Scientist*, **58**, 34–42.
4. See D. Kahneman and A. Tversky (1973). On the psychology of prediction, *Psychological Review*, **80**, 273–251.
5. See P. Slovic (1966). Cue consistency and cue utilization in judgment, *American Journal of Psychology*, **79**, 427–434.
6. See, for example, N. H. Anderson and A. Jacobson (1965). Effect of stimulus inconsistency and discounting instructions in personality impression formation, *Journal of Personality and Social Psychology*, **2**, 531–539; and P. J. Hoffman (1968). Cue-consistency and configurality in human judgment. In B. Kleinmuntz (ed.), *Formal Representation of Human Judgment*, New York: Wiley. Several studies concerning the difficulty of using redundant information appropriately are reviewed by P. Slovic, B. Fischhoff, and S. Lichtenstein (1977). Behavioral decision theory, *Annual Review of Psychology*, **28**, 1–39.
7. This section draws heavily on the paper by H. J. Einhorn and R. M. Hogarth (1986). Judging probable cause, *Psychological Bulletin*, **99**, 3–19.
8. A. Tversky and D. Kahneman (1980). Causal schemas in judgment under uncertainty. In M. Fishbein (ed.), *Progress in Social Psychology*, Hillsdale, NJ: Erlbaum.
9. See, for example, Kahneman and Tversky, Reference 4; as well as D. Lyon and P. Slovic (1976). Dominance of accuracy information and neglect of base rates in probability estimation, *Acta Psychologica*, **40**, 287–298; R. E. Nisbett and E. Borgida (1975). Attribution and the psychology of prediction, *Journal of Personality and Social Psychology*, **32**, 932–943; and M. Bar-Hillel (1980). The base-rate fallacy in probability judgments, *Acta Psychologica*, **44**, 211–233.
10. For an alternative statistical analysis of this problem see M. H. Birnbaum (1983). Base rates in Bayesian inference: Signal detection analysis of the cab problem, *American Journal of Psychology*, **96**, 85–94.
11. For further discussion of this issue, see H. J. Einhorn and R. M. Hogarth (1981). Behavioral decision theory: Processes of judgment and choice, *Annual Review of Psychology*, **32**, 53–88.
12. This term is due to R. M. Dawes (undated). *How To Use Your Head And Statistics At The Same Time Or At Least In Rapid Alternation*, Unpublished

manuscript, University of Oregon, Eugene, as is much of the substance discussed in this subsection.

13. See D. M. Eddy (1982). Probabilistic reasoning in clinical medicine: Problems and opportunities. In D. Kahneman, P. Slovic, and A. Tversky (eds), *Judgment under Uncertainty: Heuristics and Biases*, New York: Cambridge University Press.

14. See P. Slovic, B. Fischhoff, and S. Lichtenstein (1976). Cognitive processes and societal risk taking. In J. S. Carroll and J. W. Payne (eds), *Cognition and Social Behavior*, Hillsdale, NJ: Erlbaum.

15. See A. Tversky and D. Kahneman (1983). Extensional versus intuitive reasoning: The conjunction fallacy in probability judgment, *Psychological Review*, **90**, 293–315.

16. For a discussion of the relation between judgemental psychology and forecasting and planning, see R. M. Hogarth and S. Makridakis (1981). Forecasting and planning: An evaluation, *Management Science*, **27**, 115–138.

17. W. Edwards (1968). Conservatism in human information processing. In B. Kleinmuntz (ed.), *Formal Representation of Human Judgment*, New York: Wiley.

18. This has been referred to as 'pseudodiagnosticity' in the literature. See M. E. Doherty, C. R. Mynatt, R. D. Tweney, and M. D. Schiavo (1979). Pseudodiagnosticity, *Acta Psychologica*, **43**, 111–121. See also B. Fischhoff and R. Beyth-Marom (1983). Hypothesis evaluation from a Bayesian perspective, *Psychological Review*, **90**, 239–260.

19. This example is due to H. J. Einhorn and R. M. Hogarth (1981). *Uncertainty and Causality in Practical Inference.* Working paper, University of Chicago, Graduate School of Business, Center for Decision Research.

20. See R. G. Lathrop (1967). Perceived variability, *Journal of Experimental Psychology*, **73**, 498–502.

21. C. R. Peterson and L. R. Beach (1967). Man as an intuitive statistician, *Psychological Bulletin*, **68**, 31.

22. See A. Tversky and D. Kahneman (1973). Availability: A heuristic for judging frequency and probability, *Cognitive Psychology*, **5**, 207–232.

23. This example is cited by P. Slovic, H. Kunreuther, and G. F. White (1974). Decision processes, rationality, and adjustment to natural hazards. In G.F.White (ed.), *Natural Hazards: Local, National, and Global*, New York: Oxford University Press. This paper contains several good examples of the operation of the availability mechanism in relation to natural hazards.

24. See S. Lichtenstein, P. Slovic, B. Fischhoff, M. Layman, and B. Combs (1978). Judged frequency of lethal events, *Journal of Experimental Psychology: Human Learning and Memory*, **4**, 551–578.

25. This observation was made by Gordon M. Kaufman.

26. See W. K. Estes (1976). The cognitive side of probability learning, *Psychological Review,* **83**, 37–64.

27. See A. Tversky and D. Kahneman (1974). Judgment under uncertainty: Heuristics and biases, *Science*, **185**, 1124–1131.

28. For a summary of this work see N. H. Anderson (1981). *Foundations of Information Integration Theory*, New York: Academic Press.

29. See H. J. Einhorn (1971). Use of nonlinear, noncompensatory models as a function of task and amount of information, *Organizational Behavior and Human Performance*, **6**, 1–27.

30. See P. Slovic (1972). From Shakespeare to Simon: speculations—and some evidence—about man's ability to process information, *Oregon Research Institute Monograph*, Vol. 12, No.12.

31. See P. C. Wason and P. N. Johnson-Laird (1972). *Psychology of Reasoning: Structure and Content*, London: Batsford.

32. See B. Fischhoff, P. Slovic, and S. Lichtenstein (1978). Fault trees: Sensitivity of

estimated failure probabilities to problem representation, *Journal of Experimental Psychology: Human Perception and Performance*, **4**, 342–355.

33. See P. M. Miller (1971). Do labels mislead? A multiple cue study within the framework of Brunswik's probabilistic functionalism, *Organizational Behavior and Human Performance*, **6**, 480–500.

34. The classic works in this area are P. E. Meehl (1954). *Clinical versus Statistical Prediction: A Theoretical Analysis and Review of the Literature*, Minneapolis: University of Minnesota Press; and J. Sawyer (1966). Measurement *and* prediction, clinical *and* statistical, *Psychological Bulletin*, **66**, 178–200.

35. R. M. Dawes (1976). Shallow psychology. In J. S. Carroll and J. W. Payne (eds), *Cognition and Social Behavior*, Hillsdale, NJ: Erlbaum.

36. See Slovic, Fischhoff, and Lichtenstein, Reference 6.

37. For overviews, see R. M. Dawes (1979). The robust beauty of improper linear models. *American Psychologist*, **34**, 571–582; and C. Camerer (1981). General conditions for the success of bootstrapping models, *Organizational Behavior and Human Performance*, **27**, 411–422.

38. See P. Slovic, D. Fleissner, and W. S. Bauman (1972). Analyzing the use of information in investment decision making: A methodological proposal, *Journal of Business*, **45**, 283–301.

39. L. D. Phillips, personal communication.

40. R. N. Shepard (1964). On subjectively optimum selection among multiattribute alternatives. In M. W. Shelly II and G. L. Bryan (eds), *Human Judgments and Optimality*. New York: Wiley, p. 266.

41. See H. J. Einhorn (1972). Expert measurement and mechanical combination, *Organizational Behavior and Human Performance*, **7**, 86–106.

42. See H. J. Einhorn and R. M. Hogarth (1975). Unit weighting schemes for decision making. *Organizational Behavior and Human Performance*, **13**, 171–192.

43. R. M. Dawes (1977). Predictive models as a guide to preference, *IEEE Transactions on Systems, Man, and Cybernetics*, Vol. SMC-7(5), p. 357.

# CHAPTER 4

# Combining information for evaluation and choice

The preceding chapter explored issues in combining different information sources for prediction. However, as emphasized in Chapter 1, decisions also depend on a person's preferences. This chapter explores issues in the assessment of preference and thus choice.

Judgements of preference, like many predictions, involve the combination of several information sources. For example, imagine that you wish to purchase a car and that within your price range there are several models. How do you choose? Each car can be characterized on a number of dimensions such as style, comfort, maximum speed, power of acceleration, etc. In your choice, you implicitly consider such factors and decide which car is best across the dimensions you value. Note that this process demands much mental effort: determining the dimensions on which you will compare the cars; assessing the relative importance of the dimensions; and finally aggregating all this information to evaluate the cars. And, as one would expect on the basis of earlier chapters, many variables can affect your judgement, for example, inability to make intuitively all the kinds of comparisons you might initially deem important, order of information presentation, uncertainty about some dimensions, missing information, and so on.

This chapter explores these issues and consists of three major sections. First, the benchmark of rational economic choice is outlined in order to assess the difficulties that people would have if they attempted to make choices in this manner. This introduces the concept of *bounded rationality* which holds that, because of information-processing limitations, people do not necessarily make 'rational' decisions (viewed from an economic viewpoint); nonetheless, their choices reflect strategies that are 'reasonable' given both their goals and inherent limitations. Second, a general description of choice as a process of *conflict* resolution is provided. In this, it is shown that conflict, in the form of alternatives with incompatible values as well as the advantages and disadvantages of expending mental effort in choice, is inherent in the expression of preferences. A model of choice as a conflict resolution process thus helps to conceptualize these issues. Third, a number of judgemental strategies for preference judgements are outlined together

*Table 4.1   A payoff matrix*

| Alternatives | Outcomes under different states | | | | |
|:---:|:---:|:---:|:---:|:---:|:---:|
| | $S_1$ | $S_2$ | $S_3$ | -------- | $S_k$ |
| A | $a_1$ | $a_2$ | $a_3$ | -------- | $a_k$ |
| B | $b_1$ | $b_2$ | $b_3$ | -------- | $b_k$ |
| C | $c_1$ | $c_2$ | $c_3$ | -------- | $c_k$ |
| D | $d_1$ | $d_2$ | $d_3$ | -------- | $d_k$ |
| E | $e_1$ | $e_2$ | $e_3$ | -------- | $e_k$ |

with brief discussion of their advantages and disadvantages. The manner in which people choose particular strategies to deal with varying amounts and complexity of information is also discussed. For expository reasons, in this chapter choice is discussed as though uncertainty about outcomes was not an important factor. Chapter 5 extends the notions developed here to the general topic of risk or how people make decisions under conditions of uncertainty.

## BOUNDED RATIONALITY

In a series of influential papers written in the 1950s, Herbert Simon pioneered the study of choice by contrasting observations of how people actually make choices with the rational model assumed by economists.[1] The gist of Simon's argument was that humans lack both the knowledge and computational skills necessary to make decisions in a manner compatible with economic notions of rational behaviour. In Simon's view, whereas human decision making is not rational from an economic standpoint, it is still purposeful. Simon's goal was therefore to describe 'reasonable' as opposed to 'rational' behaviour. Moreover, since he perceived decision making as taking place under constraints of human information-processing limitations, this has come to be known as bounded rationality.

Simon's approach first consisted of specifying what the rational economic model requires a person to know and do prior to taking a decision, and then asking how a person with limited information-processing ability could simplify and cope with such tasks. It is instructive to follow this line of reasoning.

To be specific, assume that you are about to select a job. The requirements of a rational decision process can be illustrated by the concept of a payoff matrix illustrated in Table 4.1.

The rows of this matrix represent the alternatives (i.e. different jobs); the columns represent different 'states of the world' defined by future events that could occur and affect the attraction of different jobs. For example, let $S_1$ represent a possible change in technology that could alter the prospects offered by different employers; let $S_2$ be a change in your health that would make some jobs difficult to handle; and so on. The cell entries in the matrix indicate the 'payoffs' or outcomes you would obtain for each alternative by state of the world (i.e. job × event) combination. Thus, for example, if you chose alternative $C$, your payoff would be $c_1$ if event $S_1$ occurred, $c_2$ if $S_2$ occurred, $c_3$ if $S_3$ occurred, and so on.

The rational decision maker is assumed to be able to specify and evaluate the payoff matrix. This involves: (a) identifying all possible alternatives; (b) specifiing each of the possible states of the world; (c) attaching definite payoffs to each of the outcomes (i.e. the cell entries); (d) evaluating and ordering the payoffs associated with all of the outcomes (one would not necessarily expect different people to evaluate outcomes identically); (e) specifying probabilities for each of the states of the world; and (f) selecting the alternative that maximizes 'expected utility'. By this is meant choosing the alternative with the largest average value where the averaging reflects the probabilities assigned to the different states of the world. This is calculated by weighting the values attached to each of the outcomes by the probabilities of the different states of the world, and then adding across the rows to evaluate the worth (i.e. expected utility) of each alternative.

Although difficult to represent in Table 4.1, it is worth mentioning that each of the outcomes (i.e. the cell entries) would typically need to be evaluated on several dimensions. Thus a job could be evaluated on dimensions such as pay, location, prospects, and so on. In other words, each outcome involves multiple dimensions and thus an important task underlying the construction of the payoff matrix is to determine how these should be aggregated. This particular problem is examined further below.

It should be apparent that rational choice requires having both much information at one's disposal and impressive computational capacity. In particular, note the demands placed on you in terms of examining and/or imagining all alternatives, being able to assess how you will evaluate all outcomes under different possible states of the world, and being able to specify probabilities of events even if you have little or no relevant experience. Indeed, it is instructive to note that one has probably never made a choice of any consequence involving all the elements prescribed by the rational model. However, before considering strategies people use to cope with the information-processing demands of decision making, it is important to note two assumptions underlying the rational model. The first is that one's judgements concerning the evaluation of outcomes remain stable across time. In other words, tastes and preferences are fixed; you do not anticipate that they will change across time in light of experience. Second, the decision made assumes a fixed time horizon and moment of choice. That is, you make your decision now knowing that you will have to live with the good or bad consequences that result from the combination of your action and the chance element implicit in whatever state of the world actually materializes. As will be illustrated further below, behaviour does not always accord with these assumptions, and this leads to some interesting implications.

Simon has suggested several strategies that people use to reduce the cognitive demands of decision making in order to make 'reasonable' decisions. First, people delimit the scope of the decision problem by imposing constraints that, conceptually at least, can be thought of as eliminating whole regions of the payoff matrix. In other words, people consider only part of the total decision problem. From the viewpoint of making good decisions, this naturally raises the issue of how many alternatives and states of the world one really needs to consider. As I shall argue below and elaborate in Chapter 8, one of the biggest deficiences in choice behaviour arises from failing to be sufficiently imaginative about both the possible alternatives at one's disposal and the various events that could occur in the future.

Second, people simplify the evaluation of outcomes by, in essence, seeking to characterize whether outcomes are or are not acceptable. The key concept is that of an *aspiration level*. That is, prior to learning of the levels of outcomes that can be reached by taking different actions, the decision maker is assumed to fix a level to which he or she aspires and which is acceptable. Thus, imagine that your aspiration level is a job of certain type, in a particular geographical location, and at a given level of remuneration. In addition, assume that it is also a job for which you believe *a priori* that you have a 'good enough' chance of attaining your goals. That is, once you have found this job, it is assumed that you will take it and not search further.

It is important to note that adopting aspiration levels reduces the need to search for information to evaluate alternatives and possible states of the world. In particular, the information necessary to evaluate whether or not given alternatives are acceptable is far less refined than the information needed to evaluate precisely the relative attraction of the different alternatives. This strategy therefore considerably reduces the need for and processing of information.

In Simon's concept of bounded rationality, people do not optimize (i.e. choose the best of all possible alternatives). Instead, they *satisfice*, by which is meant that they seek a satisfactory alternative. The use of aspiration levels is thus the primary mechanism by which people can reduce the costs of information processing and yet still act in a purposeful manner. However, the use of aspiration levels is not without its costs.

For example, assume that you have established an aspiration level for your job search problem. If you do find what seems to be a suitable position, use of the aspiration level strategy does not guarantee that it is the best that is potentially available to you. It is possible that you might have found a better job had you been willing to go for some additional interviews. Second, there is always a possibility that you might have started the job search process by setting an unrealistically high level of aspiration. Thus, in the early stages of your search you might refuse what amounts objectively to an excellent position, and then subsequently be forced into lowering your aspiration level such that you end up with an inferior alternative.

As these examples illustrate, it is rare that one can place all alternatives in one 'convenient' payoff matrix and then search for the best. Rather, many significant choices involve sequential processes whereby information and alternatives must be sought, rejected, or accepted across time, and frequently without recourse to previously rejected alternatives. Significant decisions of this type include job selection, marriage, or making expensive purchases such as housing or automobiles. Moreover, this implies that aspiration levels are not necessarily stable. On the contrary, they are often sensitive to the informational content of different alternatives. A classic example is provided by Simon in the context of selling a house. Before receiving bids, one may aspire to a given selling price; however, this is likely to change over time if you only receive bids that are below your aspiration level. Conversely, do you accept any bid above your aspiration level, or would a high bid cause you to raise your aspiration level because it signals the possibility that you may not have set your initial aspirations high enough?

In Simon's model, the aspiration level is a device used to simplify choice. Its use suggests a willingness to balance the quality of a decision against the cost, and frequently impossibility, of being able to engage in more extensive analysis. How people decide to set particular aspiration levels, and the extent to which they are prepared to balance the various conflicts implied by choice through different mental strategies are thus crucial areas of investigation. I now consider the latter within a framework that explicitly accepts choice as the end product of a process of conflict resolution.

## A CONFLICT MODEL OF CHOICE[2]

What determines the mental strategies people actually use in choice? A satisfactory answer to this question is lacking at present although it is clear that many diverse situational and personal factors affect both mental processes and actual choices.

To provide some perspective on different issues in the study of the processes underlying choice and their inherent complexity, this section outlines a conceptual model of choice. The scheme illustrates the point that choices do not appear in a vacuum but are the end result of a dynamic process which itself consists of a series of choices.

Central to this scheme are three notions. First, people make choices in attempts to satisfy needs. For example, you choose to eat at a certain time (as opposed to not to eat) to satisfy your hunger, and/or perhaps a social obligation. Needs are of course often expressed in the form of goals or objectives and it is these which direct choice. In Simon's terms (see above), goals may be defined operationally in terms of an aspiration level.

Second, different forms of *conflict* are inherent in choice, where by conflict is meant incompatibility, i.e. something cannot be obtained without giving up (or expending) something else. For instance, the choice of one action usually precludes others. Consider, for example, your decision to read this book. Reading this now prevents you from doing other things. Indeed, if there were no conflict, there would be no choice.

Third, conflicts are resolved by *balancing* the costs and benefits of alternative actions. However, this balancing does not necessarily involve only the costs and benefits of different alternatives. It can also represent weighing the alternatives of engaging in or withdrawing from the choice conflict itself.

A schematic representation of the conflict model of choice is outlined in Figure 4.1. An individual has needs (box 1) which become expressed in the form of goals (box 2). For example, the need of hunger leads to the goal to eat food. In a business enterprise the sales manager's need to increase sales (perhaps to ensure his promotion), leads to forming goals to increase sales, for example the goal to find means to increase sales.

However, to satisfy needs it is necessary to engage in action. Furthermore, in most choice situations, alternative actions are not necessarily given but must be sought or invented. For example, if because of dissatisfaction with your present job you need to seek a new job, real or hypothetical alternatives have to be sought or created by you. Thus, imagination is crucial to choice.

Box 3 in Figure 4.1 represents a preliminary choice point. Do you wish to engage in the mental effort of analysing your problem, which will lead to conflict (box 5), or simply to opt out of the situation (box 4) and thus preserve the *status quo* by choosing not to choose? (This, of course, leaves your needs unfulfilled.)

Two important aspects of box 3 require elaboration. First, the choice to accept or reject the potential conflict in the situation takes place in a specific environment. Consequently, the way the environment is perceived at this early stage in the overall choice process can affect whether or not the individual will even attempt to make a choice. For example, if in our job selection example the person perceives the employment market as hopeless, the *no-choice* option will be selected almost immediately and any potential choice conflict avoided. Janis and Mann have documented many instances of just this type of behaviour which, as they point out, can have disastrous consequences.[3] For example, they illustrate how Admiral Kimmel and several other US military commanders and personnel refused to consider the option of preparing Pearl Harbour adequately just prior to the Japenese invasion in December 1941, and this despite the fact that warning signals could have been perceived. Their general expectations and perceptions of the environment did not make the signals sufficiently salient for them not to continue with the no-choice option. The importance of the manner in which the task is initially perceived by the individual is thus emphasized and is indicated in Figure 4.1 by the dotted box enclosing box 3. Note that a no-choice option can be taken at a stage well before the choice situation itself is well defined. Indeed, box 3 can be thought of as a 'pre-decision' choice.

More generally, Corbin has suggested three types of no-choice option: refusal, delay, and inattention.[4] Included in refusal is the notion that remaining with the *status quo* has two psychological advantages: first, it involves

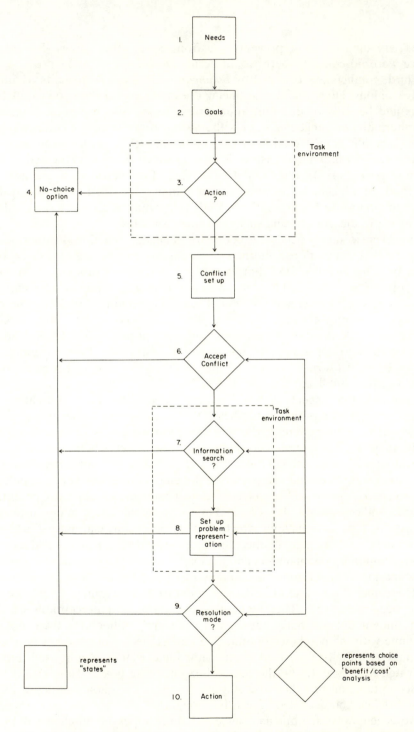

Figure 4.1   Schematic representation of a conflict model of choice

less uncertainty than other alternatives; and second, there may also 'be less uncertainty associated with the effects of "doing nothing" than with some conscious choice'. An important aspect of the *status quo* is that it often acts as an aspiration level. Thus, no action is precipitated unless alternatives are definitely perceived as better (witness the common saying 'if it works, don't fix it'). Moreover, this strategy is particularly likely to be followed under conditions of high uncertainty when unknown alternatives are difficult to evaluate. Indeed, Corbin has also argued that before deciding, a person's subjectively perceived state of uncertainty must fall below a certain threshold.

The second key point concerns the basis on which a person decides whether or not to face the conflict. It is argued here that this choice is made by an estimation of the benefits and costs involved in the conflictual situation. Since these benefits and costs can be involved to a greater or lesser extent at each of the choice points indicated in Figure 4.1, i.e. boxes 3, 6, 7, and 9, they are now discussed in some detail.

### The benefits and costs of thinking

What are the *benefits* of engaging in mental effort (i.e. thinking) in order to resolve the conflict inherent in choice? First, at a general level thinking helps the individual control actions and thus to have some control over the environment. Indeed, without control over one's actions, life would be intolerable.

Second, thinking helps clarify goals and preferences. Although one feels needs, frequently the goals by which those needs can be expressed are not evident. For example, you may feel dissatisfied with your present job and feel the need for a change. However, your preferences concerning the type of change could be quite vague. Indeed, failure to think deeply about goals often leads people to make choices without strong preferences and it is only subsequent experience with given alternatives that determines preference.

One way of avoiding thought in choice is to rely on habits acquired through past experience. However, whereas past experience may have led to satisfactory outcomes, these may have been based on poor cognitive strategies (an issue that is explored further in Chapter 6). For example, consider a housewife who buys a certain product on impulse. She likes the product and repeats her purchases over time, thus developing 'brand loyalty' toward the product. However, had her choice process been more discerning at the outset, she might never have bought the product. Instead, her preferences have been formed by chance and habit. Many of us have used similar 'unthinking' strategies concerning, for example, choice of vacation ('We liked it last year'), form of travel, and probably even more important decisions. Habitual choice is prevalent, requires little mental effort and is easy to justify to oneself ('After all, it worked last time'). However, habitual choices are not necessarily the best and even if they were successful in the past, continued success depends upon a stable environment (i.e. that the conditions under which the choices were successful have not changed).

Third, a further benefit of thinking lies in the creation of the habit of thinking and of effective ways of thinking, i.e. the more one engages in thinking the greater are the possibilities of developing mental strategies for handling complex tasks and in being able to face problems that would otherwise cause excessive conflict. Decision makers who do not bother to think about relatively easy problems stand little chance of being able to handle difficult ones. There are long-term benefits to be gained by thinking hard in the short term. Indeed, I believe it is significant that the late Lord Thomson (the Canadian-born newspaper magnate), when asked the secret of his success, once replied, 'Think 'til it hurts'.

Fourth, thinking can lead to reformulating a problem and discovering alternatives that were not evident in the original perception of the task. Task variables, for example the way information is presented, also affect judgement (see Chapters 3 and 5 as well as the next section of this chapter). Effort expended in thinking can overcome such effects and help restructure problems.

Fifth, thinking about a problem can lead to seeking ways for finding information that will help resolve the choice conflict (see box 7 in Figure 4.1).

These five benefits of thinking are of a fairly general nature and apply across all types of consequential choice. Furthermore, implicit in each there is a short-term versus long-term trade-off. Continued short-term investment in the effort of thinking has long-term benefits in the form of more control over one's actions and a greater propensity for handling choice situations adequately. A sixth major benefit of thinking, which is more situation-specific, is that it can minimize a person's *psychological* regret if the chosen alternative turns out unfavourably. The meaning of psychological regret implied here is closely linked to the responsibility inherent in choice. That is, for important issues people feel responsibility for choice, to others and/or to themselves. For example, it is hard to live with yourself if you take an important decision casually and it backfires. Consider, for instance, the purchase of a house or car. Thinking hard about a choice can, therefore, even in the event of an unfavourable outcome, minimize possible accusations of irresponsibility. In particular, it can alleviate a sense of personal blame due to the failure to think.

What are the *costs* of thinking? First, it can highlight the uncertainties in a choice situation. For example, an advantage of thinking cited above was that it could help clarify a person's preferences. However, in thinking about your preferences you may in fact realize that you do not know what you want, a realization that can be most uncomfortable. For instance, a traumatic experience for many middle-aged managers attending executive training programmes is the participation in exercises to determine their 'life goals'. These objectives have been implicitly determining their actions for years. However, in carrying out such exercises managers often discover that they are not too sure what those objectives really are, and furthermore, they find that they do not like several of their own objectives that are revealed through the exercises. Toda has made the point that at various points in life one makes so-called *meta-decisions* which determine behaviour for long periods of time and which are also 'cost-effective' in that they subsequently avoid the mental effort involved in raising fundamental questions.[5] Smoking is a case in point. People decide at a young age, perhaps not too consciously, that they will smoke. Subsequently, on each occasion that could involve smoking a cigarette, they do not engage in mental effort to determine the advantages and disadvantages of smoking. Meta-decisions (which might also be called 'strategies') are cost-effective in terms of subsequent mental effort. However, they presuppose that conditions do not change as long as they are in force. For many decisions, and particularly smoking, this supposition is not well founded (witness the number of elderly persons who regret having started to smoke when young).

A further source of uncertainty that can be accentuated by thinking concerns the structure of the choice situation itself. Careful consideration of a problem can lead to a greater appreciation of the uncertainties. For example, imagine that you are considering a number of candidates for a job. A deep analysis of the situation can lead you to realize that there are an enormous number of uncertainties involved in the choice. For example, people can develop in ways that are not easy to predict; the nature of the job itself could also change. Furthermore, these sources of uncertainty are not necessarily independent. However, people frequently suppress such uncertainties in order to simplify the choice process.

A second cost of thinking is that it makes explicit the 'trade-offs' implicit in choice. That is, even if you are aware of the uncertainties and your goals, it is uncomfortable to have to face trade-offs. For example, in considering the incorporation of safety features in cars, manufacturers usually have a direct trade-off to make between profits, on the one hand, and numbers of lives lost by the public at large because of mechanical failures on the other. When such trade-offs are made explicit, however, people baulk at the notion.[6]

Third, in order to think one has to process information. However, given that people have limited processing capacity, there are costs associated with the operations of acquiring, processing and outputting information. Although these costs are different from the preceding ones in the sense that they are not emotional, there may often be an interaction between emotional and processing costs. This issue will be considered again below.

The above discussion of the benefits and costs of thinking serves to illustrate the types of consideration that are involved at each of the choice points in Figure 4.1, i.e. boxes 3, 6, 7, and 9. In the previous discussion of that figure, the explanation had only reached box 4 (the 'no-choice' option) and box 5 where the individual had, after a preliminary screening (box 3), decided to face the conflict implicit in choice (box 5). Once the conflict has

*Table 4.2  Four job alternatives*

| Alternatives | Dimensions | | | |
|---|---|---|---|---|
| | Pay per annum* | Location | Career prospects | Job security |
| A | 20 | Paris | High | Low |
| B | 18 | Chicago | High | High |
| C | 10 | London | Low | High |
| D | 15 | San Francisco | Medium | Medium |

*To avoid problems of comparability of currencies, etc., imagine that pay per annum has been reduced to a common scale.

been created, the figure again allows the individual to opt out (box 6) before searching for information (box 7) in order to reach a representation of the choice situation (box 8). Indeed, the figure shows that prior to choosing a conflict resolution mode (box 9) leading to action (box 10), the individual can cycle back and forth between boxes, 6, 7, 8, and 9 and take the 'no-choice' option (box 4) at any point. Indeed, although the choice processes of Admiral Kimmel and his staff were described as indicating the 'no-choice' option at box 3, this could have been taken at other boxes. The diagram is only meant to be indicative. Choice is represented as a dynamic process involving constant interactions between the person and the situation as it evolves.

## STRATEGIES FOR CHOICE

Consider again the example of choosing a job illustrated in Table 4.1 and imagine that you have narrowed your choice to four jobs, A, B, C, and D. Assume further that you do not think that uncertainty concerning possible outcomes is an important issue, and that you can characterize the jobs on four dimensions: pay, location, career prospects, and job security. The alternatives are described in Table 4.2. The different strategies or 'decision rules' you could employ to reach a decision based on this information can be classified into two groups:[7] (1) strategies that *confront* the conflicts inherent in the choice situation; and (2) strategies that *avoid* the conflicts. Conflict-confronting strategies are compensatory. That is, they allow you to trade off a low value on one dimension against a high value on another. For example, if you used a compensatory strategy, you would be prepared to balance the low job security of alternative A against its high career prospects and pay. Conflict-avoiding strategies, on the other hand, are non-compensatory. That is, they do not allow trade-offs. For instance, you might decide that job security was very important to you and that you would not consider any position that was low on that dimension, no matter how attractive it was on other aspects. Thus you would eliminate job $A$.

Experimental evidence indicates a number of factors that affect the strategies people actually use in different circumstances: for example, the complexity of the task as represented by the number of alternatives and the number of dimensions per alternative; the extent to which dimensions are commensurable; order of information presentation, for instance seeing alternatives in sequence versus simultaneous presentation of all the information; missing information concerning dimensions on particular alternatives; familiarity with the kind of decision task; importance of the choice, and so on. Combinations of compensatory and non-compensatory strategies are also used.

In many situations it is difficult to evaluate alternatives characterized on several dimensions. It is therefore appropriate to consider a number of models (strategies or decision rules) and to examine them from both descriptive and normative viewpoints. This involves asking two questions. How *do* people make choices? How *should* people make choices?

### Compensatory models

*The linear model.* Conceptually, the most straightforward, and in many ways most comprehensive strategy, is the so-called linear compensatory model. In this model it is assumed that each dimension (e.g. pay, location, etc.) can be measured on a scale (implicitly at least!) and given a weight reflecting its relative importance. The evaluation of each alternative is then the sum of the weighted values on the dimensions, i.e.

value of alternative = sum of (relative weight x scale value) of all dimensions.

Choice is then made by reference to the alternative having the greatest value. Under a set of not too restrictive assumptions, this is quite a good choice model from a normative viewpoint. First, all the information concerning the alternatives is explicitly considered. Second, the decision maker has assigned weights to each dimension which, given the algebraic form of the model, reflect the extent to which he or she is willing to trade off one dimension against another. Apart from problems of measurement (and hence commensurability), the principal issue concerning the appropriateness of this model for choice is the extent to which the dimensions are 'independent' of each other. Two forms of dependence are relevant:[8] first, so-called 'environmental' correlation or the extent to which dimensions tend to occur together in the environment. For example, are jobs in Paris always highly paid and those in London lowly paid? If so, then adding the weighted dimensions of the linear model will involve double counting and be inconsistent with the scheme for weighting the dimensions. Second, dependence may exist in the sense that a combination of dimensions is more or less valuable to the decision maker than their weighted sum. For instance, a job in London with both high career prospects and high job security could be assessed as more valuable than the relative weighting scheme suggests. However, the linear model rules out such interactions.

At a descriptive level, the linear model has been shown to be remarkably accurate in predicting individual judgements in both laboratory and applied settings involving, for example, production-scheduling decisions, admitting students to university programmes, judgements by auditors, etc.[9] Linear models are remarkably insensitive to deviations from underlying assumptions and thus can reproduce judgements generated by other processes to a remarkable degree of accuracy.[10]

However, as a description of choice processes, the linear model is often inadequate. It implies a process of explicit calculations and the trading off of dimensions which, when there are many alternatives and dimensions, is not feasible for unaided judgement. Furthermore, even when the numbers of dimensions and alternatives are small, people may still avoid conflictual strategies.[11]

Whether the linear model should be used explicitly to represent a person's preferences depends, of course, on the extent to which the underlying assumptions are consistent with the individual's values and particularly in respect of independence between the dimensions. However, several reasons suggest that the linear model is well suited for preference judgements. First, when there are several alternatives, the model is able to handle all the information in a consistent manner. (It is assumed here, incidentally, that use of the linear model implies that the individual has access to some mechanical aid, be it only paper and pencil.) A number of studies have shown, for instance, that preferences based on holistic or intuitive judgement differ from those constructed by use of a linear model; however, the latter are more consistent in the sense that final judgements show less disagreement between different individuals than intuitive evaluations.[12] Intuitive judgement has two sources of inconsistency: in the application of weights attributed to dimensions, and in the aggregation of information across dimensions.

An additional reason favouring the linear model lies in its robustness to deviations from the underlying assumptions (see also previous comments). It is unlikely that dimensions will ever be perfectly independent in the sense described above. However, provided lack of independence is not too marked, the linear model is usually adequate. Techniques do exist for complicating the linear model to account for interactions between dimensions and other non-linearities; however, it is frequently unnecessary to make such adjustments. In particular, care in definition of the dimensions can often resolve many difficulties. These and related issues are reconsidered in Chapter 9 and Appendix D. Finally, a considerable practical advantage of the linear model is that it is conceptually simple and easy to explain. In one sense, however, this can also cause difficulties since decision makers often like to believe that their choice processes are more complicated than the simple algebraic formulation of the linear model.[13]

*The additive difference model.* Descriptively, the linear model assumes that people evaluate each alternative independently of the others by integrating information on each alternative across the different dimensions. Thus, the decision maker is assumed to process the information in Table 4.2 within a row (job alternative) and across the columns (dimensions). However, this is not the only way the information could be processed. Specifically, the decision maker may find it easier to first compare each alternative on each dimension prior to reaching some aggregate evaluation. This therefore implies processing information within columns (dimensions) and then across rows (job alternatives).

If there are only two alternatives, processing within dimensions and across alternatives can considerably ease information-processing demands since it involves comparing information that is commensurable. For example, imagine that you are deciding between jobs $A$ and $B$ in Table 4.2. It seems natural to examine this information by making comments and comparisons such as '$A$ pays a little more than $B$; I prefer living in Paris to Chicago; there's no difference in career prospects, but $B$ offers much more security than $A$'. This form of processing, in which like is compared to like, naturally leads to adopting a so-called *additive difference* model. In this strategy, the decision maker is assumed to evaluate the differences between the two alternatives on a dimension by dimension basis, and then to aggregate the differences to see which of the alternatives is favoured by the aggregate net difference. If the importance weights accorded to the differences between the different dimensions considered in the aggregation process are of a certain form, this model makes predictions for choosing between two alternatives that are identical to the linear model discussed above.[14] However, it is important to note that the cognitive strategy is quite different. Indeed, this raises an important difficulty of studying choice behaviour from a descriptive viewpoint. Identical outcomes can result from quite different processes.

*The ideal point model.* A model that is similar algebraically, although not conceptually, to the linear model is the so-called ideal point formulation. In this it is assumed that the decision maker has an ideal representation of what the 'perfect' (i.e. ideal) alternative would be. Imagine, for example, the ideal job. Alternatives are then evaluated by their distances from the ideal point on the different dimensions. Judgement, as noted in Chapters 2 and 3, often works by a process of comparisons with imaginary stereotypes or anchors, and thus this process can reduce mental effort. For example, given that certain alternatives are close to the ideal on some dimensions, effort only needs to be expended on considering the remaining dimensions.

76

It is important to note that the ideal point model only predicts the same choice alternatives as the linear model if the distances from the ideal point on different dimensions are evaluated in a linear manner. Ideal point models are sometimes constructed by assuming that the deviation of a dimension from its ideal level is proportional to the square of this distance. In this case, extreme deviations from the ideal are more heavily weighted than they would be in a linear model.

## Non-compensatory models

Four examples of non-compensatory models are the *conjunctive, disjunctive, lexicographic,* and *elimination-by-aspects* formulations.

The *conjunctive* model is one in which the decision maker sets certain cut-off points on the dimensions such that any alternative that falls below a cut-off is eliminated. For instance, in a job selection situation with, for example, three criteria being test scores on intelligence, motivation, and aptitude, the decision maker could decide not to hire any candidates who failed to meet certain levels on all criteria. That is, to be selected a candidate would have to reach specified levels of intelligence *and* motivation *and* aptitude. Scores below the cut-off on any of these three dimensions would disqualify a candidate. The conjunctive model implies 'satisficing' choice behaviour and, as such, has the advantages and disadvantages of this strategy that were discussed above.

In the *disjunctive* model, on the other hand, a decision maker will permit a low score on a dimension provided there is a very high score on one of the other dimensions. In other words, in the disjunctive model, the candidate would be evaluated according to his or her best attribute regardless of the levels on the other attributes. To continue the job selection example, a candidate could be very low on intelligence but the decision maker would be prepared to overlook that aspect provided he or she was very high on motivation or aptitude. In selecting a soccer team, for example, one might use a conjunctive model *vis-à-vis* certain skills and characteristics when selecting a 'utility' player, i.e. someone who can play in several positions, and therefore needs a minimum level of skills on all dimensions; however, outstanding players are hard to find and managers might well wish to select players who are outstanding in any one skill. In this case, a disjunctive model would be appropriate.

In the *lexicographic* model, the first action of the decision maker is to consider the relative importance of the dimensions and to make an initial comparison on the basis of the most important dimension. Assume, for example, that in the job selection situation this is aptitude. The decision rule is simple: select the candidate who shows the greatest aptitude. If two or more candidates are equally 'best' on aptitude, distinguish between them according to the second most important dimension; if that is insufficient, use the third criterion, and so on.

An example of the use of the lexicographic model, and its implications, was given in Chapter 1 (pages 5 and 6). There you were asked to imagine that you were shopping in a supermarket and had adopted a choice rule that involved the dimensions of price and quality, with price being considered the more important of the two. The rule was: 'if the price difference between brands is less than or equal to 5 cents, choose the higher quality product; otherwise, choose the cheaper brand'. As will be recalled, the disadvantage of this rule is that it can lead to inconsistent choices when decisions are made between pairs of alternatives. This inconsistency is of the form: $X$ is preferred to $Y$; $Y$ is preferred to $Z$; but $Z$ is preferred to $X$. This choice pattern violates commonsense notions of reasonable behaviour in that use of the rule implies that choice can be determined by the order in which options become available rather than the true preferences of the decision maker. Technically, the rule violates a tenet of rational behaviour known as *transitivity* that underlies the assumption that people can express preferences in a consistent manner, an issue that will be explored in greater depth in Chapter 5. The choice pattern expressed above in respect of $X$, $Y$, and $Z$ is referred to as *intransitive*. However, unless the decision maker is made aware of the inconsistency inherent in the lexicographic rule, he or she may adopt the habit of using it on a regular basis. In fact, I have presented this rule to many groups of MBA students and executives and asked (a) whether they had ever used rules of this type in shopping and (b) if they knew of any specific disadvantage associated with it. Whereas many readily admit to using the rule, few are aware that it can lead to intransitive choices.

The lexicographic rule is similar to the additive difference model in that it involves comparing pairs of alternatives by dimensions. Thus, an interesting issue centres on what is deemed to be a significant difference between alternatives on a particular dimension. The additive difference model requires that all differences (however small) be evaluated so that trade-offs can be made across all dimensions. In the lexicographic model, on the other hand, there is usually some threshold difference below which alternatives are considered equivalent. Thus trade-offs are avoided. Psychologically, it is difficult to make trade-offs for two reasons. The first reason is cognitive: trade-offs are difficult to execute because of information-processing limitations. The second reason is emotional: trade-offs force one to consider questions people prefer to avoid. For example, how much immediate pay is one prepared to give up in order to gain more job security? How much more are you prepared to pay for an automobile or an airline ticket to reduce the chances of an accident? Several forces induce non-compensatory strategies for choice.

The *elimination-by-aspects* model is related to the lexicographic and is also sequential in nature.[15] It assumes that alternatives consist of a set of aspects or characteristics. At each stage of the process, an aspect, i.e. dimension, is selected according to a probabilistic scheme (based on the presence of aspects among the remaining alternatives) and alternatives that do not include the aspect are eliminated. The process continues until only one alternative remains. For example:

> In contemplating the purchase of a new car ... the first aspect selected may be automatic transmission: this will eliminate all cars that do not have this feature. Given the remaining alternatives, another aspect, say, a $3000 price limit, is selected, and all cars whose price exceeds this limit are excluded. The process continues until all cars but one are eliminated.[15]

A severe limitation of strategies such as the lexicographic and elimination-by-aspects models is that they can lead to inadequate examination of the dimensions of alternatives. However, these strategies do involve a 'quasi-logic' in the sense that some ordering of the importance of dimensions is involved, and the method used seems to be intuitively justifiable. Nonetheless, they are open to severe biases. This point has been well made by Tversky in the following example of a television commercial:

> 'There are more than two dozen companies in the San Francisco area which offer training in computer programming.' The announcer puts some two dozen eggs and one walnut on the table to represent the alternatives, and continues: 'Let us examine the facts. How many of these schools have on-line computer facilities for training?' The announcer removes several eggs. 'How many of these schools have placement services that would help you find a job?' The announcer removes some more eggs. 'How many of these schools are approved for veterans' benefits?' This continues until the walnut alone remains. The announcer cracks the nutshell, which reveals the name of the company and concludes: 'This is all you need to know in a nutshell'.[15]

Note in the above example how alternatives are eliminated before consideration of their merits. For example, is a placement service really necessary in the choice of a school relative, for example, to the quality of instruction which, incidentally, is not even mentioned in the advertisement? However, the appeal of the intuitive quasi-logic of the formulation of the announcement is powerful.

### Situations and strategies

To think about what might influence the use of particular strategies for choice, consider an experimental technique exploited by Payne.[16] Payne asked a number of student subjects to engage in a task that involved choosing an apartment in which to live. The information for the choice task was presented to the students in the form of an information board, such as

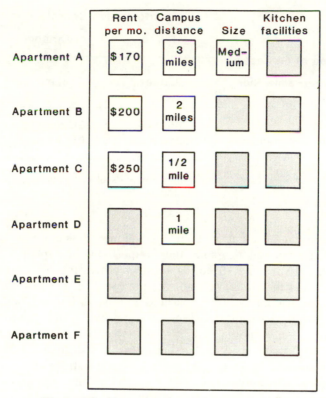

|  | Rent per mo. | Campus distance | Size | Kitchen facilities |
|---|---|---|---|---|
| Apartment A | $170 | 3 miles | Med-ium | |
| Apartment B | $200 | 2 miles | | |
| Apartment C | $250 | 1/2 mile | | |
| Apartment D | | 1 mile | | |
| Apartment E | | | | |
| Apartment F | | | | |

Figure 4.2   Example of an information board

illustrated in Figure 4.2. As can be seen, an information board is like a payoff matrix in that it can show the outcomes associated with alternatives on different dimensions. When the subject first sees the information board, it is blank. That is, he or she knows that there are a given number of alternatives (six in Figure 4.2) and that these are to be evaluated on several dimensions (in this case, rent, distance from campus, size of living and dining rooms, and kitchen facilities). However, the subject can ask for information concerning any of the cells in the matrix (i.e. concerning any of the dimensions on any of the alternatives). When this information is requested, it is shown in the appropriate place on the board. For example, in the board illustrated in Figure 4.2, the subject has requested and been provided with information about rent for three apartments. In this experimental task, the subject is told that the goal is to choose one of the apartments. To reach a decision, he or she can request any information potentially available on the information board. Note that since the subject requests the information sequentially, a researcher can follow and record the sequence of information examined by the subject thereby gaining insight into the type of choice strategy employed.

Information Search

Fixed                    Variable

| Type of processing | | |
| --- | --- | --- |
| Inter–dimensional | Linear | Conjunctive |
| Intra–dimensional | Additive–difference | Elimination–by–aspects |

Figure 4.3   Informational search demands of different strategies/models

To exploit the information board technique, Payne noted that choice strategies differ in the demands they impose on how people search for information. First, some strategies require processing all available information such that the amount of information sought is fixed or constant (this is the case, for example, of the linear and additive difference models). Other strategies, however, permit decisions based on partial information such that the amount of information sought is variable (e.g. the conjunctive and elimination-by-aspects model). Second, strategies differ on whether information is evaluated by looking at particular alternatives *across* dimensions (e.g. the linear and conjunctive models) or by examining particular dimensions *across* alternatives (e.g. the additive difference and elimination-by-aspects models). This may be referred to as the distinction between *inter-* and *intra*-dimensional search patterns. It is therefore possible to categorize strategies within the cells of a two-by-two matrix where the rows represent inter- and intra-dimensional search, and the columns represent constant and variable information search. This is illustrated in Figure 4.3 with examples of strategies in each of the cells.

In his study, Payne examined the issue of how strategies differed as the amount of information potentially available to the subjects was varied. This was achieved by requiring different groups of subjects to make choices under conditions that varied both the number of alternatives and dimensions on the information board. In addition to monitoring the choice process with the information board, Payne asked several of his subjects to verbalize their thought processes in order to provide additional evidence concerning the type of strategy they were using. Results of the study showed that subjects rarely used any single strategy in the manner defined above. Rather, combinations of strategies were used. Moreover, the following general trends emerged. For choices involving few dimensions and alternatives, subjects chose to examine almost all the information and tended to use compensatory strategies. However, as the amount of information potentially available increased (i.e. numbers of alternatives and dimensions), subjects looked at proportionally less of the information; moreover their search strategies were both more variable and involved greater intra-dimensional processing. There was a tendency initially to use non-compensatory strategies that screened out alternatives, and then to employ compensatory strategies on a subset of the available information. In a similar study involving choices made by 11- and 12-year-old children, Klayman found similar results.[17]

Payne's study raises interesting issues about choice processes. First, people do seem to be 'boundedly rational' in Simon's sense and are forced into adopting strategies that simplify tasks by reducing information-processing demands. Second, notice that Payne's paradigm could be extended by making the choice task more realistic. For example, the effects of memory could be made more salient by not displaying the information once it had been requested; costs could be imposed for obtaining information on the dimensions and/or alternatives; information about particular dimensions could be made subject to uncertainty or even be missing; choices could be subject to time pressure; and so on. Indeed, although not specifically studied within Payne's experimental paradigm, these and similar issues have been examined in the literature. It has been found, for example, that when information on a dimension is missing, people may infer a value if they believe that this is strongly related to another dimension on which they do have information. When shopping, for example, price is often used to infer quality. However, when this is not the case, the alternative with the missing information is deemed less attractive.[18] Time pressure tends to induce greater use of non-compensatory strategies as people seek to find means to process information under greater constraints.[19] Differences have also been found in the strategies used by people familiar with a task (experts) as opposed to novices, and so on.[20]

Payne's study is an important reminder that since people have limited information-processing capacity, their choice strategies reflect the structure of the tasks with which they are confronted, and in particular the informational demands that these impose. This has important implications for many aspects of choice in daily life and was dramatically illustrated in a study by Russo concerning the manner in which unit prices are displayed in supermarkets.[21] In most stores, unit prices are marked on or near the location of the brands of the different products. Thus, when shoppers compare unit prices of different brands, the manner in which they process this information depends on the sequence in which they happen to examine the different brands. Russo arranged for unit price information to be organized in a simple manner that dramatically reduced information-processing demands on consumers. Specifically, at the end of each aisle of the supermarket, unit price information was displayed in the form of lists that showed the brands ordered by their unit prices, with the most expensive at the top and the least expensive at the foot of each list. In a controlled field experiment, Russo compared how much consumers paid for food purchases in stores where unit price information was presented in the form just described as opposed to the usual format. Results showed that consumers shopped more effectively, as measured by lower average costs of shopping, in those stores where Russo had arranged the unit price information in convenient lists. In addition to showing how the 'mere' presentation of information can affect choice (an issue that is explored further in Chapter 5), Russo's results are important in that they demonstrate that choice behaviour can be helped by the simple expedient of changing the way information is presented. Moreover, the fact that managers of supermarkets do not organize information for consumers in the manner investigated by Russo, suggests that they believe that when information is difficult to process, the costs that this imposes on consumers imply greater revenues for the stores.

## SUMMARY

This chapter began with a discussion of the concept of bounded rationality introduced by Herbert Simon. In enquiring how people make decisions, Simon first considered what a person would have to do in terms of processing information if he or she were to choose according to the dictates of economic theory. He proposed that 'there is a complete lack of evidence that, in actual human choice situations of any complexity, these computations can be, or are in fact, performed'.[22] Instead, Simon suggested that, whereas humans do not take choices that are rational from the economic viewpoint, they can nonetheless act reasonably by adopting strategies that simplify information-processing demands. Critical to these strategies is the aspiration level concept which permits people both to operationalize objectives in choice and assess whether particular alternatives are 'good enough'. Simon states that people do not and usually cannot optimize; instead, limited information-processing abilities force them to satisfice.

Given limited information-processing ability, choice can be thought of as a process of *conflict resolution* where conflicts reflect not only trading off values on different dimensions of alternatives but also the mental costs and benefits of engaging in the decision process itself. In other words, the actual choice between alternatives is only part of a complex interactive process. However, although this process is complex in the sense that it can follow many paths involving a series of sub-choices, the overall organizing principle may be quite simple, namely the comparison of costs and benefits of mental effort relative to the person's emotional state *vis-à-vis* the choice situation.[23]

The third section of the chapter examined a number of potential strategies people could use when confronted with choosing between given alternatives. These strategies can be classified as to whether people confront or avoid the conflict inherent in choice. Conflict-confronting or compensatory strategies have the advantage of considering all relevant information and should lead to the same choice no matter how information becomes available to the decision maker. On the other hand, these strategies are difficult to execute from a cognitive viewpoint, and they highlight the emotional conflicts of choice. Conflict-avoiding or non-compensatory strategies have the advantage of being easier to execute cognitively and may even allow the decision maker to avoid any direct conflicts involved in considering difficult emotional aspects of choice. The main disadvantage of these strategies, however, is that they interact with the manner in which the decision maker acquires information and can thus induce people to make choices that do not reflect their true preferences (often without conscious awareness of this fact). In general, non-compensatory strategies are particularly sensitive to the manner in which choice tasks are structured. In many situations, people employ combinations of non-compensatory and compensatory strategies with the former being used to reduce information-processing demands to manageable size, and the latter to make more fine grained analyses of the remaining information.

Because the environment in which people must make decisions is far more complex than the human mind, people are forced to adapt their limited abilities to the structure of the problems they face. Thus, the key to understanding people's choice behaviour lies in understanding how they have come to represent the choice task in their minds. This means that possible alternatives for consideration, as well as the relative importance of different dimensions on the alternatives can be manipulated by task variables including, for example, order of information search or presentation, and response mode (i.e. the manner in which the individual is required to indicate choice). Further examples of these phenomena will be discussed in Chapter 5.

To summarize, a key aspect in choice is limited human ability to process information. We simply cannot handle all the information inherent in complex decision problems and, in particular, to make the many kinds of trade-offs implied by choices involving several conflicting dimensions. Intuitive judgement is deficient and requires 'decision aids', some examples of which will be discussed in Chapter 9.

## NOTES AND REFERENCES

1. See, in particular, H. A. Simon (1955). A behavioral model of rational choice, *Quarterly Journal of Economics*, **69**, 99–118, and H. A. Simon (1956). Rational choice and the structure of the environment, *Psychological Review*, **63**, 129–138.
2. The conceptual scheme developed in this section (which can clearly make no claim to empirical verification), was developed jointly by the author and H. J. Einhorn in August 1978. Subsequent to that date, it was discovered that similar ideas had been proposed by I. L. Janis and L. Mann (1977). *Decision Making: A Psychological Analysis of Conflict, Choice, and Commitment*, New York: The Free Press.
3. See Janis and Mann, Reference 2.
4. See R. M. Corbin (1980). Decisions that might not get made. In T. S. Wallsten (ed.), *Cognitive Processes in Choice and Decision Behavior*, Hillsdale, NJ: Erlbaum.
5. See M. Toda (1981). *Man, Robot, and Society: Models and Speculations*, The Hague: Martinus Nijhoff, Chapter 10.
6. As many readers will recall, there was an important public controversy about this matter in respect of the Ford Pinto.

7. For a rather complete discussion of different rules, see O. Svenson (1979). Process descriptions of decision making, *Organizational Behavior and Human Performance*, **23**, 86–112.

8. For a more complete discussion of this issue, see W. Edwards (1977). How to use multi-attribute utility measurement for social decision making. In D. E. Bell, R. L. Keeney, and H. Raiffa (eds), *Conflicting Objectives in Decisions*, Chichester: John Wiley & Sons.

9. See the reviews by P. Slovic and S. Lichtenstein (1971). Comparison of Bayesian and regression approaches to the study of information processing in judgment, *Organizational Behavior and Human Performance*, **6**, 649–744; and P. Slovic, B. Fischhoff, and S. Lichtenstein (1977). Behavioral decision theory, *Annual Review of Psychology*, **28**, 1–39. For a review of studies specifically related to accounting, see R. Libby and B. L. Lewis (1982). Human information processing research in accounting: The state of the art in 1982, *Accounting, Organizations and Society*, **7**, 231–285.

10. See R. M. Dawes and B. Corrigan (1974). Linear models in decision making, *Psychological Bulletin*, **81**, 95–106; and H. J. Einhorn and R. M. Hogarth (1975). Unit weighting schemes for decision making, *Organizational Behavior and Human Performance*, **13**, 171–192.

11. See Slovic, Fischhoff, and Lichtenstein, Reference 9.

12. See, for example, H. J. Einhorn (1972). Expert measurement and mechanical combination, *Organizational Behavior and Human Performance*, **7**, 86–106; and K. M. Aschenbrenner and W. Kasubek (1978). Challenging the Cushing syndrome: Multiattribute evaluation of cortisone drugs, *Organizational Behavior and Human Performance*, **22**, 216–234.

13. For an illuminating discussion of how cognitive processes relate to linear models, see H. J. Einhorn, D. N. Kleinmuntz, and B. Kleinmuntz (1979). Linear regression *and* process-tracing models of judgment, *Psychological Review*, **86**, 465–485.

14. See A. Tversky (1969). Intransitivity of preferences, *Psychological Review*, **76**, 31–48.

15. See A. Tversky (1972). Elimination by aspects: A theory of choice, *Psychological Review*, **79**, 281–299.

16. See J. W. Payne (1976). Task complexity and contingent processing in decision making: An information search and protocol analysis, *Organizational Behavior and Human Performance*, **16**, 366–387.

17. See J. Klayman (1985). Children's decision strategies and their adaptation to task characteristics, *Organizational Behavior and Human Decision Processes*, **35**, 179–201.

18. See for example, J. Huber and J. McCann (1982). The impact of inferential beliefs on product evaluations, *Journal of Marketing Research*, **19**, 324–333; and R. J. Meyer (1982). A descriptive model of consumer information search behavior, *Marketing Science*, **1**, 93–121.

19. See P. Wright (1974). The harassed decision maker: Time pressures, distractions, and the use of evidence. *Journal of Applied Psychology*, **59**, 555–561.

20. See, for example, H. A. Simon and W. G. Chase (1973). Skill in chess, *American Scientist*, **61**, 394–403; and J. H. Larkin, J. McDermott, D. P. Simon, and H. A. Simon (1980). Expert and novice performance in solving physics problems, *Science*, **208**, 1335–1342.

21. See J. E. Russo (1977). The value of unit price information, *Journal of Marketing Research*, **14**, 193–201.

22. See H. A. Simon, Reference 1.

23. For further perspectives of how choice may result from an over-riding cost-

benefit analysis, see L. R. Beach and T. R. Mitchell (1978). A contingency model for the selection of decision strategies, *Academy of Management Review*, **3**, 439–449; and E. J. Johnson and J. W. Payne (1985). Effort and accuracy in choice, *Management Science*, **31**, 395–414.

# CHAPTER 5

# Choice under uncertainty

The treatment of choice in Chapter 4 did not emphasize the role of uncertainty. However, since uncertainty adds greatly to the conflict people experience in choice, this chapter is devoted to the issue of how people react to and cope with this source of conflict.

To examine how uncertainty affects choice, the organization of the present chapter follows a strategy similar to that used in Chapter 4. It contains four main sections. In the first, the principles underlying the model of rational choice under uncertainty espoused by economists are presented. This serves two goals: (1) it illustrates how some commonsense principles are made operational in a model that prescribes the decision-making behaviour of rational economic agents; and (2) it provides a base-line for considering how people actually do make decisions. The second section presents a number of so-called 'paradoxical' decision problems that highlight differences between the prescriptions of rational models and actual choice behaviour. An interesting aspect of these paradoxes is that deviations from choices assumed to be rational cannot necessarily be traced to deficiencies in human information processing ability, i.e. bounded rationality. The third section introduces several descriptive principles of choice that have been used to model choice under uncertainty. The fourth section explores implications of these descriptive models.

The chapter concludes by noting the importance of three different phases of the choice process. These are: (1) the manner in which problems are *encoded* or represented in the minds of decision makers; (2) factors affecting how outcomes of actions and their associated probabilities are *evaluated*; and (3) the way in which choices are *expressed*, e.g. as prices people are prepared to pay, preferences stated between alternatives, and so on.

## EXPECTED UTILITY AS THE CRITERION OF RATIONAL CHOICE

The theory of rational choice outlined here can be thought of as describing the behaviour of an idealized person. It is known as expected utility or decision theory.[1] It argues that if people are willing to accept a number of basic principles or axioms of sensible behaviour, then these logically define a unique criterion for rational choice. In particular, it assumes that people are capable of expressing both consistent beliefs (predictive judgements) and consistent preferences (evaluative judgements). Moreover, beliefs and preferences should be independent of the other in the sense that you should not allow what you think is going to happen (beliefs) to affect what you would like to happen (preferences) or vice versa. In other words, independence of beliefs and preferences is a statement for realism, for warning people against engaging in 'wishful thinking' or conversely 'persecution mania'.

The statement that people should have consistent beliefs can be made operational in the following manner. Predictive judgements can be formulated as probabilities and these probabilities should conform to the rules of probability theory. For instance, if you assign the probability of 0.4 to a particular event (e.g. rain today), then to be consistent you should assign the probability 0.6 to its complementary event, i.e. no rain today (see Appendix A). An operational test of the consistency of your beliefs is that, when translated into probabilities on which you should be prepared to bet, no one can make a so-called 'Dutch book' against you, i.e. create a series of bets such that you would lose whatever the outcome.

To say that someone has a set of consistent preferences can be made operational by saying that he or she is capable of expressing a consistent order of preference over a set of outcomes. In other words, the person knows what he or she wants. For example, consider the four job alternatives shown in Table 4.2 (page 72). Somebody who has a consistent preference order is capable of ranking the four jobs in order of their relative attraction to him or her (i.e. from most to least). This statement is not as innocuous as might first appear since it has three important implications. First, a consistent preference order implies *transitivity*. The meaning and importance of this concept were explored in Chapter 4. Applied to the alternatives in Table 4.2, it means that if, for instance, job A is preferred to job C, and job C is preferred to job D, then job A is preferred to job D. Whereas transitivity is attractive at a commonsense level, recall too from Chapter 4 that conflict-avoiding cognitive strategies such as the lexicographic can lead to violating this principle.

The second implication following from a consistent preference order is known as *dominance*. This principle applies to cases where alternatives are represented by several dimensions and where you are able to order your preferences on each of the dimensions. Consider, for example, the four jobs in Table 4.2 and imagine that you prefer more pay to less as well as greater amounts of both career prospects and job security. Furthermore, your preference for job locations (most to least) is Paris, Chicago, London, and San Francisco. Assume further that although you have these preferences for the dimensions, you have not yet determined your preference order for the actual jobs. What is this?

From the information given, it is not possible to say. However, given that you are consistent it should be noted that you can immediately reject one alternative, *D*. Why?

Compare *B* and *D* and note that on pay, career prospects, and job security, *B* is better than *D*. Furthermore, your preference order over locations implies (by transitivity) that you prefer Chicago over San Francisco. Alternative *B* therefore dominates alternative *D* which can consequently be excluded from consideration. That is, because each dimension of *B* is preferred to each dimension of *D*, no consistent way of combining dimensions can make you prefer *D* to *B*. Dominance has important practical implications. For example, whereas one can often express preferences over dimensions, determining preferences over alternatives is far more difficult. Thus, dominance (when it exists) can be used to reduce a set of alternatives and thus simplify choice. Note, however, that it is important to look for dominance between all possible pairs of alternatives. For instance, although alternative *C* may subsequently be shown to be less preferred than *D*, *D* does not dominate *C*.

Dominated alternatives are easily eliminated once they have been recognized. However, in many problems the structure of the task is such that dominance is not evident. Indeed, even experienced decision theorists find when they have completed a complicated analysis that a number of alternatives were effectively dominated and could have been eliminated earlier in the analysis (and at great savings in cost and difficulty of analysis!).

The third implication following from a consistent preference order is that of *invariance*. This means that your preference for one outcome as opposed to another (e.g. job *A* over job *B*), should not be affected by the manner in which you are confronted with the alternatives. In other words, your choices should be invariant with respect to either how you are required to make your choice or the manner in which the alternatives have been presented to you. Your preference, for example, between two jobs should not be affected if you were asked to choose one over the other in a direct comparison or by means of expressing how much each job was worth to you. That preferences should be invariant in the manner described certainly makes good sense.

In decision theory, relative preferences for outcomes of actions taken under uncertainty are expressed on a numerical scale called a utility function. However, before discussing how this is interpreted, note that the rational criterion for choice under uncertainty is to *choose the alternative with the largest expected utility*, a notion introduced in Chapter 4 with respect to the payoff matrix in Table 4.1. The expected utility of an alternative is calculated by taking a weighted sum of the utilities associated with the outcomes of the alternative under the different possible (uncertain) states. The weights are the probabilities associated with each of the states. It is important to note that, in expected utility theory, the criterion of maximizing expected utility is the rational course of action whether the decision concerns something that is done repeatedly (as, for example, when goods are purchased or sold in a business), or whether the decision is a one-shot or unique case such as building a huge power plant.[2]

A further principle of decision theory, known as the 'sure-thing principle', also needs to be stated. An example will probably best serve to illustrate.

> A businessman contemplates buying a certain piece of property. He considers the outcomes of the next presidential election relevant to the attractiveness of the purchase. So to clarify the matter to himself, he asks whether he would buy if he knew that the Republican candidate were going to win, and decides that he would do so. Similarly, he considers whether he would buy if he knew that the Democratic candidate were going to win, and again finds that he would do so. Seeing that he would buy in either event, he decides that he should buy, even though he does not know which event obtains, or will obtain, as we would ordinarily say.[3]

The seemingly innocuous principle in the above example is the following: if a person prefers one action (e.g. invest in property) to another (do not invest), and this preference is unaffected by the manner in which a particular uncertainty is resolved (in this case whether the Republican or Democrat wins the election), then the resolution of the uncertainty (i.e. the result of the election) should not affect the choice.

## Interpreting utility functions

A utility function describes how a person evaluates the outcomes of choice alternatives under uncertainty. In essence, the function maps objective values of possible outcomes on to a subjective scale of utility. The three panels of Figure 5.1 illustrate different types of utility functions. In each panel of the figure, the horizontal axis represents dollars ($) since it is assumed, for illustrative purposes, that money is the single relevant dimension for the decision under consideration. The vertical axis represents utility. The shape of the utility function is important in that it indicates the nature of a person's attitude toward risk.

In panel (a), the relation between dollars and utility is represented by a straight line. This means that the subjective value the person places on dollars when taking a decision under uncertainty increases linearly with the objective amount of dollars involved. Thus, a person with this utility function would be indifferent, for example, between taking an action leading to a sure $500 and playing a gamble characterized by a 50% chance of gaining $1,000 and a 50% chance of gaining nothing. A person with a linear utility function is said to be risk-neutral.

In panel (b), the utility curve is concave and lies above the diagonal line that represents a risk-neutral attitude. A person with a concave function is said to be risk-averse. Thus, faced with a choice between taking an action leading to a sure $500 and playing a gamble with a 50% chance of gaining $1,000 (and a 50% chance of gaining nothing), the person would take the $500.

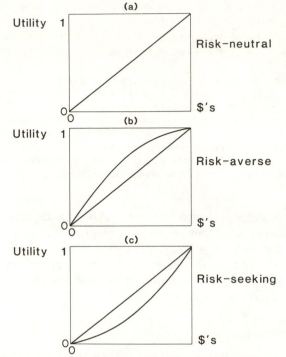

Figure 5.1   Different types of utility functions. The function in panel (a) is described as risk-neutral, that in panel
(b) as risk-averse, and that in panel (c) as risk-seeking

In panel (c), on the other hand, the utility curve is convex and lies below
the diagonal. A person with this type of utility function is said to be risk-
seeking. Thus, faced with a choice between taking an action leading to a
sure $500 and playing a gamble with a 50% chance of gaining $1,000 (and
a 50% chance of gaining nothing), the person would take the gamble.

Note that expected utility theory does not state what a person's risk
attitude should be. It simply states that the objective value of outcomes can
be translated on to a scale that reflects a person's attitude toward risk and
thus can be used for evaluating the outcomes of decisions under uncertainty.
A method for constructing a person's utility function from responses to a
hypothetical set of gambles is presented in Appendix C.

Expected utility theory can be said to describe how a rational person
decides between uncertain options. However, it is important to emphasize
that the theory can be used in different ways. On the one hand, the theory
can be used normatively or prescriptively to advise a person how to take
decisions, and as such has been adopted within statistical decision theory
(see Chapter 9). On the other hand, it can also be used in a predictive
fashion under the assumption that people are rational. As such, it forms a
cornerstone of economic theory and also provides a base-line for descriptive
studies and models of decision making under uncertainty.

## WHAT IS YOUR ATTITUDE TOWARD RISK?

To summarize, the expected utility model states that one should choose by selecting the alternative with the greatest expected utility. However, the model does not state what your risk attitude should be, i.e. risk-averse, risk-seeking, or risk-neutral. Within the theory individuals can exhibit their own attitudes toward risk. In light of the expected utility model, it is therefore instructive to explore (a) whether people do always choose according to the expected utility criterion, and (b) attitudes toward risk. To do this, I will now ask you to consider your responses to several problems.

*Problem 1*   Imagine that you are required to play one of the two gambles in each of the two situations shown below.
   *Situation 1*
         Gamble *A* has a 100% chance of winning $1,000,000.
         Gamble B has a 10% chance of winning $5,000,000,
                  an 89% chance of winning $1,000,000, and
                  a 1% chance of winning nothing.

   *Situation 2*
         Gamble *C* has an 11% chance of winning $1,000,000, and
                  an 89% chance of winning nothing.
         Gamble *D* has a 10% chance of winning $5,000,000, and
                  a 90% chance of winning nothing.

*Questions:* 1. Which gamble do you prefer in Situation 1? *A* or *B*?
         2. Which gamble do you prefer in Situation 2? *C* or *D*?

*Problem 2*   Imagine a lottery with 100 numbered tickets, one of which will be drawn at random to determine the prize. There are two situations of the same type and you are required to indicate which of the two gambles you would prefer in each situation. The ticket numbers and corresponding prizes (in units of $1 million) are as indicated below.

|  | Ticket Numbers | | |
| --- | --- | --- | --- |
|  | 1 | 2–11 | 12–100 |
| *Situation 3* | | | |
| Gamble *E* | 1 | 1 | 1 |
| Gamble *F* | 0 | 5 | 1 |
| *Situation 4* | | | |
| Gamble *G* | 1 | 1 | 0 |
| Gamble *H* | 0 | 5 | 0 |

*Questions*: 1. Which gamble do you prefer in Situation 3? *E* or *F*?
         2. Which gamble do you prefer in Situation 4? *G* or *H*?

What were your responses to Problems 1 and 2? In Problem 1, most people choose Gamble *A* in Situation 1 and Gamble *D* in Situation 2. However, this pair of choices is inconsistent with the expected utility principle.[4] To show this, let the values of $1,000,000 and $5,000,000 be written as *u*($1 mil.) and *u*($5 mil.) so that one can refer to the 'utility of $1,000,000' and the 'utility of $5,000,000' respectively. (This is done since for most people the subjective value under uncertainty of $5,000,000 is not necessarily five times that of $1,000,000). With this convention, note that choosing Gamble *A* in Situation 1 implies the condition

$$u(\$1 \text{ mil.}) > 0.10 \ u(\$5 \text{ mil.}) + 0.89 \ u(\$1 \text{ mil.})$$

where '>' means 'is greater than' and (for example) '0.10 *u*($5 mil.)' means a 10% chance of winning $5,000,000. Similarly, the choice of Gamble *D* in Situation 2 implies

$$0.10 \ u(\$5 \text{ mil.}) > 0.11 \ u(\$1 \text{ mil.}).$$

The inconsistency in the above two choices can be demonstrated by noting that the first condition (of Situation 1) can be re-expressed as

$$u(\$1 \text{ mil}) - 0.89 \ u(\$1 \text{ mil.}) > 0.10 \ u(\$5 \text{ mil.})$$

or

$$0.11 \ u(\$1 \text{ mil.}) > 0.10 \ u(\$5 \text{ mil.})$$

which is a direct contradiction of the implication of Situation 2.

Many people object to this demonstration and still feel attached to the original choices even after the inconsistencies have been indicated to them. Several explanations have been advanced to account for why people tend to violate the expected utility criterion in these circumstances. One explanation centres on the distinction between deciding between certain (Gamble *A*) and uncertain outcomes (Gambles *B*, *C*, and *D*). In particular, it has been noted that people often judge certain outcomes as being disproportionally more valuable than uncertain outcomes. As a further illustration of this phenomenon, consider the following thought experiment. Imagine that you are being forced to play Russian roulette with a six-shooter.[5] The person holding the gun to your head offers you the following deal: instead of playing the game with two of the six chambers loaded, you can buy one of the two bullets. Now consider how much you would pay for the bullet? Next, imagine that you have purchased one of the bullets and the game is about to start with only one chamber loaded. However, once again you can make a deal, this time by buying the last bullet. How much would you pay for the last bullet?

It is difficult in the abstract to imagine how much one would be willing to pay for the two bullets. However, consider an easier question: Would you be willing to pay more, less, or about the same for the last as opposed to the penultimate bullet? Informal surveys show that most people would be prepared to pay more for the last than for the penultimate bullet. In other words, people are prepared to pay more to reduce the chances of death from 1/6 to zero than they are to reduce the chances from 2/6 to 1/6. That is, the same amount of reduction in the probability of death (i.e. 1/6) is deemed more valuable when this leads to the certainty of not dying as opposed to a shift to a lower but still positive chance. However, this 'certainty effect' violates the expected utility model and specifically the notion that beliefs and preferences (in this case the value one puts on one's life) should be assessed independently of the other.[6]

A second explanation for choosing A and D in Problem 1 centres on the notion of psychological regret discussed in Chapter 4. That is, when making choices people often act to minimize possible regret they might experience after the decision has been taken. It is hard to face the accusations of others (and perhaps yourself) that you acted in an irresponsible manner. Thus, if this hypothesis is adopted, it is easy to empathize with the views that: (a) in Situation 1 it would be foolish to forego the chance of a certain $1,000,000 in the hope of gaining $5,000,000, but with a 1% chance of ending up with nothing; and (b) that in Situation 2, the difference between a 10% and 11% chance is so small that it would not be imprudent to go for the $5,000,000 payoff.

What was your answer to Problem 2? If you did not notice, you should be aware that Problem 2 is identical in structure to Problem 1.[7] The information has only been rearranged in a slightly different manner. Had you chosen A and D in Problem 1, the corresponding choices would have been E and H in Problem 2. An interesting aspect of the structure of the problem in the second formulation is that if you cover the right-hand column concerning tickets numbered 12–100, the situations are identical. Furthermore, the outcomes of the gambles in respect of tickets 12–100 *within* Situations 3 and 4 are the same. For tickets 12 to 100 Gambles E and F have the same prize in Situation 3, and Gambles G and H the same prize in Situation 4. Consequently, the sure-thing principle applies and both sets of gambles should only be evaluated by reference to tickets 1–11. This being the case, consistent choice patterns are E and G or F and H in Problem 2, and A and C or B and D in Problem 1.

There has been considerable controversy about the above issues and the so-called sure-thing principle in the literature. People tend to accept this principle when it is explained to them (as in the case of the Republican and Democrat discussed above) but to resist it in certain types of choice situations. More generally, it appears that although we are ready to accept certain principles when they are expressed in either abstract or simple terms, we fail to realize their implications for other logically equivalent situations.

Let us now consider some more problems. In Problems 3 through 5 you are asked to imagine that you work in the purchasing department of a large corporation.

*Problem 3*   Imagine you have just learned that the sole supplier of a crucial component is going to raise prices. The price increase is expected to cost the company $6,000,000. Two alternative plans have been formulated to counter the effect of the price increase. The anticipated consequences of these plans are as follows.

If plan *A* is adopted, the company will save $2,000,000.

If plan *B* is adopted, there is a 1/3 probability that $6,000,000 will be saved, and a 2/3 probability that nothing will be saved.

*Question*: Do you favour plan *A* or plan *B*?

*Problem 4*   Imagine that you are trying to arrange a contract with a supplier. The deal essentially consists of two parts. Prior to negotiating with the supplier, you consider the estimated consequences of different strategies for negotiating the two parts of the contract. These can be described as follows.

*Part 1*: This can be summarized as a decision between

      *A*. A sure gain of $240,000; and

      *B*. A 25% chance to gain $1,000,000, and
      a 75% chance to gain nothing.

*Part 2*: This can be summarized as a decision between

      *C*. A sure loss of $750,000; and

      *D*. A 75% chance to lose $1,000,000, and
      a 25% chance to lose nothing.

*Questions*: 1. What would you choose for Part 1? *A* or *B*?

             2. What would you choose for Part 2? *C* or *D*?

Having decided your strategy for the problem just described, consider what strategy you would adopt in a negotiation that could be summarized as a decision between:

      *E*. A 25% chance to win $240,000, and
      a 75% chance to lose   $760,000;
      and

      *F*. A 25% chance to win $250,000, and
      a 75% chance to lose   $750,000.

*Question*: What would you choose? *E* or *F*?

*Problem 5*   Imagine that you have just learned that the sole supplier of a crucial component is going to raise prices. The price increase is expected to cost the company $6,000,000. Two alternative plans have been formulated to counter the effect of the price increase. The anticipated consequences of these plans are as follows.

If plan *C* is adopted, the company will lose $4,000,000.

If plan $D$ is adopted, there is a 1/3 probability that there will be no loss, and a 2/3 probability that the company will lose $6,000,000.

*Question*: Do you favour plan $C$ or plan $D$?

Consider first your responses to Problems 3 and 5. As you probably realized, these problems are identical from a logical viewpoint in that plan $A$ in Problem 3 corresponds to plan $C$ in Problem 5, and $B$ in 3 corresponds to $D$ in 5. Thus, by invariance, responses should be identical to the two versions. The fact, however, is that when Problems 3 and 5 are given to different groups of people (such that people are not aware of the alternative formulations), responses are not invariant to the form of the question.[8] Specifically, when faced with the version embodied in Problem 3, most people choose plan $A$, the safe alternative. The majority choice for Problem 5, however, is action $D$, the risky alternative.

What underlies this choice pattern? Problems 3 and 5 differ in that whereas the outcomes in Problem 3 are expressed as gains (or savings) relative to the expected cost of $6,000,000, the outcomes in Problem 5 are expressed in terms of losses. Thus, if people have different risk attitudes toward potential gains and losses, choices would not necessarily be invariant to the manner in which the alternatives are presented.

Responses to Problems 3 and 5 suggest that people do not have consistent attitudes toward risk (i.e. they are not necessarily always risk-averse, risk-seeking, or risk-neutral). Instead, the way a problem is formulated can have significant effects on choice thereby raising the issue of whether people do have 'true' attitudes toward risk. These findings also suggest that inconsistent risk attitudes can be manipulated in particular situations, both willingly and unwillingly.

Now consider Problem 4. Typical responses to this are $A$ in Part 1 and $D$ in Part 2.[9] Note that this pattern also corresponds to that exhibited in Problems 3 and 5, namely: choosing the safe option when dealing with gains, and the risky alternative when confronted with losses. In dealing with the second negotiation, most people express little hesitation. $F$ is preferred to $E$. Indeed, $F$ dominates $E$ in that a 25% chance of winning $250,000 is better than a 25% chance of winning $240,000, and a 75% chance of losing $750,000 is better than a 75% chance of losing $760,000. However, what most people do not realize is that choosing $A$ in Part 1 and $D$ in Part 2 of the first negotiation is equivalent to choosing $E$ (the dominated alternative) in the second. How is this possible?

Consider the first negotiation. The objective here is to obtain the best contract. However, since your final outcome depends on the combined results of both parts of the contract, your evaluation should take into account all combinations of choices. Thus your real options are to choose between $A$ and $C$, on the one hand, versus $B$ and $D$, on the other; or $A$ and $D$ versus $B$ and $C$.

To evaluate options $A$ and $D$ as a single choice, sum their expected outcomes. In doing this, note that option $A$ implies a sure $240,000 whatever the outcome of option $D$. Thus, the combined evaluation of $A$ and $D$ involves a 75% chance of losing $760,000 (i.e. loss of $1,000,000 and gain of $240,000) and a 25% chance of gaining $240,000 (i.e. no loss and gain of $240,000). Moreover, these are exactly the outcomes of option $E$ in the second negotiation. Similarly, note that when options $B$ and $C$ are summed, these become a 25% chance to gain $250,000 (i.e. gain of $1,000,000 and loss of $750,000) and a 75% chance to lose $750,000 (i.e. no gain and loss of $750,000). Thus options $B$ and $C$ are equivalent to $F$ in the second negotiation. In other words, selecting actions $A$ and $D$ in the first negotiation leads to choosing a set of options (summarized by E) that are dominated by another set of available options ($F$). Why does this occur?

Two factors contribute to selecting a dominated alternative in Problem 4. First, there is the natural tendency to evaluate the choice options in the form provided. People typically consider the first negotiation in terms of choosing between two sets of options, $A$ and $B$ on the one hand, and $C$ and $D$ on the other. The failure to consider the choice options within a wider framework (i.e. $A$ and $C$ versus $B$ and $D$, etc.) is understandable given limitations on human information-processing ability. Even if one realizes what should be done, it takes much cognitive effort to calculate the outcomes of all combinations of alternatives. Second, the tendency noted in respect of Problems 3 and 5 for people to be inconsistent in their attitudes toward risk is highlighted by the form of the choices. Part 1 is formulated entirely in terms of gains (where people tend toward the safe option) whereas Part 2 is described in terms of losses (where people tend toward the risky option). What people fail to realize is that, by allowing these different risk attitudes to determine choices in a sequence of small or 'local' problems, they can end up selecting a set of options that is dominated by other options available to them. In other words, the combination of limited information-processing ability and inconsistent attitudes toward risk can have important dysfunctional consequences.

Before discussing models that are more descriptively accurate than expected utility theory, consider one more problem.

*Problem 6*  An urn is known to contain 90 balls of which 30 are red and the other 60 black and yellow in unknown proportions. One ball is to be drawn at random from the urn and your reward depends on the colour of the ball drawn. You must choose between the two acts described below which have consequences as indicated (in $).

|  | 30 balls | 60 balls | |
| --- | --- | --- | --- |
|  | Red | Black | Yellow |
| *Situation 1* | | | |
| Act 1. Bet on red | 100 | 0 | 0 |
| Act 2. Bet on black | 0 | 100 | 0 |

Now, under the same general conditions, which act would you choose in this second situation?

| | 30 balls | 60 balls | |
|---|---|---|---|
| | Red | Black | Yellow |
| *Situation 2* | | | |
| Act 3. Bet on red and yellow* | 100 | 0 | 100 |
| Act 4. Bet on black and yellow | 0 | 100 | 100 |

*Questions*: 1. Which act would you take in Situation 1? 1 or 2?
2. Which act would you take in Situation 2? 3 or 4?

Typical answers to these situations are Act 1 in Situation 1 and Act 4 in Situation 2.[10]

Respondents often reason along the following lines. In Situation 1, 30 of the 90 balls in the urn are red. Thus, you know there is a 1/3 chance of gaining the $100 if you select Act 1. On the other hand, the number of black balls in the urn can vary from 0 to 60. In selecting Act 2, therefore, the chances of obtaining the $100 reward vary from 0 to 2/3. Lacking precise knowledge about the actual chances, one is better off sticking to the chances one knows, i.e. the 1/3 probability of drawing a red ball. Therefore, select Act 1. Similarly in Situation 2, one knows the chances of winning $100 if one takes Act 4 (i.e. 2/3); however, the chances of winning with Act 3 vary between 0 and 2/3. Once again, stick with the chances you know and select Act 4.

Selection of Acts 1 and 4 in Problem 6 illustrates that people are sensitive to knowledge about the precise probabilities that link actions to outcomes. In this example, as in many other cases, people's actions imply the avoidance of ambiguity, that is uncertainty about their level of uncertainty. Moreover, whereas choosing the actions in Problem 6 that avoid the uncertain probabilities may seem sensible, it is important to realize that this pair of choices violates the sure-thing principle. To see this, note in Situation 1 that if a yellow ball is drawn from the urn, the same outcome (0) results from choosing either Act 1 or Act 2. Similarly, both Acts 3 and 4 in Situation 2 lead to the same outcome ($100) if yellow is drawn from the urn. Therefore, by the sure-thing principle, uncertainty about the number of yellow balls is irrelevant to choosing in both situations and should be ignored. Note that if the outcomes associated with the yellow balls are ignored (e.g. by covering over the right-hand or 'Yellow' column in Problem 6), Situations 1 and 2 are identical such that consistency implies choosing either Act 1 and Act 3 or Act 2 and Act 4.

---

* That is, you win $100 if either a red or yellow ball is drawn. The interpretation of Act 4 is similar

To summarize this section, we have considered six problems each of which shows how the principles of expected utility theory can be violated. In Problem 1, the source of the violation was traced to the certainty effect (where obtaining $1,000,000 for sure was to be compared to taking a gamble) as well as the notion of psychological regret. The principle of invariance (that responses to choices should not depend on how these are formulated) was violated in comparisons between two sets of problems, Problems 1 and 2 on the one hand, and Problems 3 and 5 on the other. In Problems 3 and 5, simply wording the same problem in terms of losses or gains was shown to lead to contrary attitudes toward risk. Specifically, people are more conservative in their risk attitudes when faced with gains as opposed to losses. This tendency was also demonstrated in responses that are typically obtained to the first two parts of Problem 4. Moreover, Problem 4 also illustrated that if one exhibits inconsistent attitudes toward risk across a series of situations, one can end up with a combination of outcomes that are inferior to (indeed, dominated by) other combinations available to you. Finally, Problem 6 showed that ambiguity about probabilities is an important factor in decision making. However, taking account of ambiguity can induce choices that are inconsistent with the sure-thing principle.

All of these problems demonstrate that people violate the principles of expected utility theory in specific circumstances. However, it is important to note that, with the exception of Problem 4, the source of the deviations from expected utility theory cannot be explained by notions of bounded rationality introduced in Chapter 4. The problems are not complicated in terms of the demands they place on information-processing ability *per se*. On the other hand, some of these phenomena may be explained by the fact that the human information-processing system operates in specific ways due to its general limitations; moreover, these mechanisms induce responses that are independent of the level of information-processing demands of particular situations. Whether the resulting violations of expected utility theory are errors one would want to avoid is an issue that will be addressed below.

## SOME DESCRIPTIVE PRINCIPLES

Expected utility theory provides a useful benchmark for considering how people make choices under uncertainty. For example, people are clearly sensitive to both the probabilities of events and the outcomes contingent on these events. Where expected utility theory differs from actual human choice behaviour is in how outcomes and probabilities are evaluated and combined in assessing the relative attraction of different courses of action. In this section, two descriptive theories of choice under uncertainty are presented and discussed. The first, known as 'prospect theory', was formulated by Kahneman and Tversky and deals with the type of phenomena exemplified in Problems 1 through 5 above.[11] The second is a model of how people assess uncertainty in ambiguous circumstances (as in Problem 6) and was developed by Einhorn and Hogarth.[12]

## Prospect theory

Prospect theory has two components, a value function that plays the role of the utility function in expected utility theory, and a decision weight function that captures the weights attached to probabilities in choice. Uncertain options are evaluated in a manner similar to expected utility theory. Outcomes evaluated by the value function are weighted by the decision weights characterizing the probabilities that link actions to outcomes.

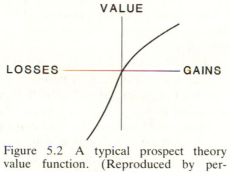

Figure 5.2 A typical prospect theory value function. (Reproduced by permission of The Econometric Society)

A typical value function is graphed in Figure 5.2 and shows how people evaluate subjectively outcomes that can be measured on some objective scale, such as dollars or units of effort. The value function has three characteristics. First, people are assumed to encode outcomes as deviations from a reference point. That is, people think in terms of gains or losses. The key psychological insight behind this principle is that, given limited information-processing ability, people are sensitive to differences. Thus, it is natural to think of outcomes in terms of deviations. However, by definition deviations only exist in reference to some norm, e.g. as potential increases or decreases from the *status quo* or some other reference point. Note that evaluating outcomes as deviations from a reference point is conceptually similar to the use of the aspiration level concept discussed in Chapter 4. There it was noted that considering outcomes in terms of whether they met a given level of aspiration was a useful heuristic for handling the information-processing demands of complex decision problems. As with the aspiration level concept, however, to understand behaviour it is necessary to know how specific reference points are established in particular cases. Unfortunately, prospect theory does not enlighten us on this topic. Nonetheless, in many cases (e.g. some of the problems discussed above), a person's *status quo* often provides a natural reference point.

The second characteristic of the value function is that its shape captures the notion that people are more sensitive to differences between outcomes the closer these are to the reference point. For example, consider how you would react to winning (or losing) the difference between $10 and $20, on the one hand, and between winning (or losing) the difference between $110 and $120, on the other. For most people, the difference between $10 and $20 is evaluated subjectively as larger than the difference between $110 and $120. Note that such relative evaluations of monetary quantities are also congruent with many different aspects of sensory experience, e.g. temperature, taste, and more generally aspects involved in experiencing both pleasure and pain. Small absolute differences in temperature, for example, can often be noticed if they involve minor adjustments to one's current conditions. (Imagine adding water when taking a bath.) The same absolute difference in temperature, however, will typically escape notice if experienced at levels that are far from one's current state. Mathematically, this insight is translated on to the graph of the value function by requiring the function to be concave over gains, and convex over losses.

The third characteristic of the value function is that it is steeper for losses than for gains. This translates the notion that people experience losses and gains with different levels of intensity. Specifically, 'losses loom larger than gains'. To illustrate, imagine that you have just been informed that one of your investments has made you $10,000 richer, and consider how happy you would feel about this event. Next imagine that you have just learned that you have lost $10,000 and consider how unhappy you would feel about this. Now try to compare the intensities of your feelings in both cases. Is a gain of $10,000 experienced more intensely than a loss of $10,000 or vice versa? For most people the displeasure of a loss is experienced more intensely than the pleasure of an objectively equivalent gain.

When considered individually, each of these characteristics has a direct intuitive appeal. However, their joint properties have important implications for choice. In particular, consider Problems 3 and 5. In Problem 3, the options are 'framed' (following the expression used by Tversky and Kahneman) in terms of gains: a sure $2,000,000 for option $A$, and a 1/3 chance of saving (gaining) $6,000,000 and a 2/3 chance of gaining nothing for option $B$. Note that the shape of the value function implies that the subjective value of $2,000,000 is greater than one-third of the subjective value of $6,000,000. Thus option $A$ is preferred. In Problem 5, on the other hand, option $C$ (i.e. $A$ in Problem 3) is framed as a loss of $4,000,000 (relative to a reference point of zero), whereas option $D$ (i.e. $B$) involves a 1/3 chance of no loss and a 2/3 chance of losing $6,000,000. Moreover, the shape of the value function implies that the subjective value of a loss of $4,000,000 is greater in absolute terms than the subjective value of two-thirds of $6,000,000. Hence, option $D$ (i.e. $B$) is preferred. The reversal in preference typically exhibited in this problem can therefore be traced to the joint effects of two characteristics of the value function—the encoding of outcomes relative to a reference point and the specific shape of the function.

There are many implications of the prospect theory value function, some of which will be explored below. To anticipate, however, note that by shifting the reference point, the same uncertain outcomes can be framed in ways that accentuate either the perception of gains or losses. These different perceptions can, in turn, induce different choices.

The decision weight function in prospect theory depicts the manner in which people are assumed to weight the probabilities linking choices to outcomes. Briefly stated, this function overweights small probabilities and underweights larger probabilities thereby also affecting, for example, responses to Problems 3 and 5 discussed above. That is, if probabilities of 1/3 and 2/3 are both underweighted, the decision weight function will further reduce the attractiveness of option $B$ in Problem 3 (over and beyond the factors discussed above) and increase the relative attraction of option $D$ in Problem 5.

An additional feature of the decision weight function is that it is only defined for probability values between 0 and 1. Probabilities of 0 and 1 are given, respectively, weights of 0 and 1 such that certainty attracts special weight. This captures the certainty effect discussed in relation to Problem 1.

**The ambiguity model**

Prospect theory assumes that people know the precise probabilities linking options to outcomes. However, as illustrated by Problem 6, choice is sensitive to ambiguity. Moreover, in many—if not most—realistic situations, people are ambiguous concerning the probabilities of events that can affect outcomes. When considering the decision to insure against theft of one's automobile, for example, how many of us know the precise probability of theft occurring in a given period?

In the Einhorn–Hogarth ambiguity model, people are assumed to assess ambiguous probabilities by first anchoring on some value of the probability and then adjusting this figure by mentally simulating or imagining other values the probability could take. The net effect of this simulation process is then aggregated with the anchor to reach an estimate. The assessment of uncertainty in conditions of ambiguity therefore involves a compromise between 'what is' (i.e. the anchor which could be data-based) and 'what might or could be' (i.e. the product of imagination). In practical situations, the anchor could be a figure suggested by experience, a third party (e.g. an expert), or simply one that is available (e.g. based on media reports). In Problem 6, for example, the anchor for assessing the probability of drawing a black ball could be 1/3. In this problem, 1/3 is a kind of default value that corresponds to the probability of drawing a red ball and is also the mid-point of the range between 0 and 2/3. As a further example, the anchor used in assessing the risk of a new technology could be the probability of failure provided by a technical expert.

Two factors are assumed to affect the mental simulation process: (a) the amount of perceived ambiguity; and (b) one's attitude toward ambiguity in the circumstances. Situations likely to be perceived as ambiguous are those where, for example, there is little causal knowledge about the process

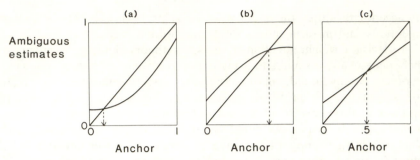

Figure 5.3 Different ambiguity functions. In panel (a), values of the probability below the anchor are weighted more heavily in imagination than those above; in panel (b) values above are weighted more heavily than those below; and in panel (c) values above and below are weighted equally. Copyright (1985) by Americn Psychological Association. (Reprinted by permission)

generating outcomes, data are scarce, or opinions conflict. Attitude toward ambiguity in the circumstances is reflected in the mental simulation process by the extent to which probability values greater than the anchor are weighted in imagination more or less than those below. This attitude could, in turn, reflect personal factors, such as tendencies towards optimism or pessimism, as well as situational variables, e.g. the sign and size of outcomes or whether the context of the choice situation induces caution (as in insurance) or playfulness (as in some forms of gambling).

The manner in which imagination affects the anchor values in the ambiguity model can be shown by depicting the judgemental compromise that results from the anchoring and adjustment process as a function of the anchor probability. This is illustrated in the three panels of Figure 5.3.

In interpreting these graphs, recall that two forces cause the final judgement to deviate from the anchor. These are the amount of perceived ambiguity and the person's attitude toward ambiguity in the circumstances. The former determines the amount of mental simulation and thus affects the extent to which the ambiguity function deviates from the diagonal (45°) line in the panels; the more the perceived ambiguity, the greater the deviation. The latter determines the direction of the adjustment and thus the point at which the ambiguity function crosses the diagonal. In panel (a), for example, values of the probability below the anchor are weighted in imagination more heavily than those above, and the crossover point lies below the .5 value on the anchor scale (the horizontal axis); in panel (b), values above the anchor are weighted more heavily than those below. Here the crossover point lies above .5; and in panel (c), values above and below the anchor are weighted equally such that the crossover occurs at .5.[13]

In general, the ambiguity function shows overweighting of small anchor values but underweighting of larger ones (like the decision weight function of prospect theory discussed above). The point at which the function changes from over- to under-weighting depends on the person's attitude toward ambiguity in the circumstances. For example, assuming that ambiguity induces caution on the part of the decision maker, the ambiguity function would resemble that shown in panel (a) if the decision maker is concerned with the chances of obtaining a positive outcome. On the other hand, when faced with the possibility of a loss (e.g. assessing the risk of a new technology), the function would be better represented by panel (b). This is because caution induces greater concern for possible values of the probability lying below rather than above the anchor in the case of potential gains, whereas the contrary holds for losses. In assessing the risk of a new technology, for example, one can imagine anchoring on the probability of failure provided by an expert and then adjusting upwards by imagining what else could occur. On the other hand, when faced with a possible $100 reward as in Problem 6, one could well imagine anchoring on 1/3 when assessing the chances of drawing a black ball from the urn, but then adjusting downwards to allow for the ambiguity.

An important implication of the ambiguity model is that, relative to anchor probabilities, it does not predict that people will always avoid situations characterized by ambiguous probabilities. Indeed, in some cases it predicts that people will prefer ambiguity, specifically when faced either with a small probability of a gain or a large probability of a loss. To illustrate, consider a situation where there are two urns each containing 1,000 balls. In Urn 1, the balls are numbered consecutively from 1 to 1,000. In Urn 2, all the balls are numbered but the distribution of numbers is unknown except that numbers are limited to lie within the 1 to 1,000 range. Thus, for example, the number 687 could appear on any number of balls from 0 to 1,000. Now imagine that you are allowed to draw a ball at random from either urn and that if you draw the number 687 you win $100. From which urn would you choose to draw, or would you be indifferent between the urns? For many people, Urn 2 (the ambiguous urn) is the most attractive choice.[14] Incidentally, many state lotteries have precisely this kind of structure. Most people playing the lotteries do not know the probability of winning other than having a general notion that it is small. However, it is easy to imagine scenarios in which they win (often reinforced by media reports or advertisements) thereby inducing a net positive adjustment to their low anchors.

## SOME IMPLICATIONS

Both prospect theory and the ambiguity model have implications for understanding how people make decisions under uncertainty in a wide range of situations. From the viewpoint of prospect theory, many interesting phenomena relate to whether options are framed as losses or gains. This, in turn, depends on the reference point or level of aspiration adopted in particular decisions.

One principle from prospect theory is that 'losses loom larger than gains'. It therefore follows that if the same amount (in economic terms) is framed

104

as either a loss or a gain, people will evaluate its impact differently. Several examples illustrate this point. One concerns how credit card charges are borne by consumers and merchants. There are two economically equivalent ways. One is for the merchant to add a surcharge to prices when goods are bought using credit cards. The other is to allow a discount to consumers who pay in cash. Assume that, from the viewpoint of the consumer, the store price provides the reference point. In this case, a consumer contemplating the use of a credit card will view the surcharge as a loss. On the other hand, a cash discount will be viewed as a potential gain (or foregone loss if a credit card is used). Since losses loom larger than gains, it is more attractive from the consumers' viewpoint if the cost of using a credit card is not framed as a surcharge. Indeed, it is significant to note that the credit card industry typically refers to differences between cash and card prices as cash discounts rather than credit card surcharges.[15]

Other examples show how subtle changes in wording can affect people's intuitive evaluation of issues. One concerns taxation. In advocating a reduction in taxes, different intensities of attitude can be induced if the proposed cut is framed as a 'gain' rather than 'less of a loss'.[16] Proponents of tax reform clearly favour the latter. In controlling energy expenditures, appeals to 'save resources' are weaker than those aimed at 'avoiding waste'.[17]

A particularly striking demonstration of the effects of problem formulation was obtained in an experiment of stated preferences between surgery and radiation therapy for the treatment of lung cancer. One group of subjects was given information about the alternative treatments in the form of survival statistics that showed the percentages of patients surviving at different times after treatment. A second group was given the same information in the form of mortality statistics, i.e. expressed in terms of the percentages of patients who had died. Answers differed strikingly between the two groups. The percentage of respondents favouring radiation therapy in the 'survival' frame was 18%. However, this figure rose to 44% when the same choice was offered in the 'mortality' frame. The advantages of radiation therapy relative to surgery clearly loomed larger in the minds of respondents when phrased in terms of reducing the chances of death as opposed to increasing the chances of survival. It is of interest to note that this effect was observed not only among groups of clinic patients but with experienced physicians as well.[18]

As noted in the previous sections, people tend to be risk-averse when problems are framed in terms of gains; however, the predominant attitude is risk-seeking when the same problems are framed in terms of losses. Moreover this reflection of risk attitudes follows directly from prospect theory.

The above problems have shown that the manipulation of reference points by framing can lead to different risk attitudes. Moreover, the possibility of such manipulations suggests mechansims for motivating specific types of behaviour. One situation, studied by Payne and his colleagues, concerns means of inducing people to become more aggressive or risk-seeking. Payne reasoned that the target rates of return that firms set for managers when evaluating investment proposals essentially become reference points or levels of aspiration against which proposals are compared. Thus, if two groups of managers were given the same set of investment proposals to evaluate, but provided with different target rates of return, those managers for whom higher rates had been set would choose a more risky set of investments. That is, since failure to achieve a given rate of return would be viewed as a loss, managers facing the higher required rates would be motivated to choose more risky investments in order to meet their targets. This hypothesis was convincingly supported by experimental data collected from both student subjects and businessmen.[19]

The examples given above, as well as Problems 3 and 5, all involved cases where one person could view the same problem from different perspectives or frames. However, there are many decision-making tasks where perspectives or frames are implied by the role a person brings to a situation. This is particularly the case in conflicts where a loss to one person is a gain for another. To illustrate, consider the different attitudes of a plaintiff and a defendant in a court case, and to simplify matters, ignore legal costs. The plaintiff's position can be thought of as involving a choice between accepting an out-of-court settlement (i.e. a sure thing), or going to court to face a chance at gaining a larger amount accompanied by a complementary chance of gaining nothing. The defendant faces the mirror-image of this situation, i.e. a choice between paying a sure amount (an out-of-court settlement), or a chance of losing a larger amount together with a complementary chance of losing nothing by going to court. Assume further that (a) both parties assess the chances of the plaintiff winning the case to be the same, and (b) the expected value of going to court represents both the maximum the defendant is prepared to pay to settle out of court and the minimum the plaintiff is prepared to accept. In this situation, the plaintiff's decision is framed in terms of gains, whereas that of the defendant is framed in terms of losses. Prospect theory therefore predicts that whereas the plaintiff would settle out of court (i.e. take the safe option), the defendant would prefer to go to court (i.e. the risky alternative). In realistic settings, of course, few cases would be as simple as this example. Plaintiffs, for example, might be concerned with non-monetary aspects of litigation; the different parties might not agree on the chances of the plaintiff winning the case in court; and so on. However, it is still true that defendants and plaintiffs would approach the case from different perspectives and, if unaware of the phenomena discussed in this chapter, might still view the case with asymmetric attitudes toward risk. Awareness of such asymmetries and the ability to exploit them could well lead to competitive advantages.[20]

More generally, the roles of levels of aspiration and reference points have been well documented in studies of bargaining. Some early studies showed that negotiators who adopt high aspiration levels make better deals than

CONSUMERS

|  | Non-ambiguous | Ambiguous |
|---|---|---|
| **Non-ambiguous** | Well-known processes (1) | Typical situation (2) |
| **Ambiguous** | New technologies–inside information for consumers (3) | New technologies–processes poorly understood (4) |

FIRMS

Figure 5.4 Classification of insurance situations. (Reproduced by permission of The University of Chicago Press)

opponents who set lower levels. The general principle here (as in the study discussed above concerning managers' risk attitudes) is that settling below aspiration level is experienced as very costly. Higher aspiration levels therefore lead to tougher bargaining behaviour.[21] More recently, a series of studies have examined the issue of what happens when agents in a bargaining situation are instructed to bargain with perspectives that imply loss or gain frames. Results, consistent with prospect theory, show that loss frame bargainers are motivated to achieve more for their principals. This, however, can have both costs and benefits. In situations where a single deal must be made, a loss frame can be beneficial. However, in situations where profits also depend on the number of deals that are consummated with different parties in a given period of time (as in trading), people with gain frames do better by completing more deals.[22]

In bargaining the objective is not necessarily to gain the best deal at the expense of one's opponent (as in so-called zero-sum games), but to make both parties better off through the bargaining process (i.e. by reframing the problem as to how the pie can be increased as opposed to shared). Thus, it follows that the two parties will probably do better and come to an acceptable agreement if the deal is framed as a gain for both. Indeed, framing issues in this manner is precisely what is required of mediators.

The Einhorn–Hogarth ambiguity model also has interesting implications for behaviour where people consider situations from different perspectives. The purchase and sale of insurance provides a case in point. Estimating the chances that a possible mishap (e.g. an automobile accident, a house fire, etc.) does or does not occur is a critical input to insurance decisions. However, what happens when insurers (i.e. firms) or consumers are ambiguous about these probabilities?

To simplify the analysis, imagine that firms and consumers either are or are not ambiguous about the relevant probability. These possibilities can be

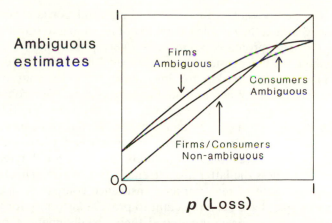

Figure 5.5 Ambiguity functions for insurance decision making: firms and consumers. Note that when firms and consumers are not ambiguous, their ambiguity functions coincide on the diagonal (45°) line. Copyright (1985) by American Psychological Association. (Reprinted by permission)

represented in the form of a 2 x 2 matrix as shown in Figure 5.4 together with examples illustrating each cell.[23] Next assume that both firms and consumers have the same anchor probability but that firms exhibit greater caution in their attitude toward ambiguity than consumers. The rationale for the latter assumption is that there is an important asymmetry in attitude between accepting and transferring a risk. Specifically, compared to the person transferring risk, one would expect the person accepting risk (e.g. an insurer) to give more weight in imagination to possible values of the probability of loss that are greater than the anchor value.[24] This asymmetry can be translated within the ambiguity model by showing different ambiguity functions for consumers and firms as illustrated in Figure 5.5. Note from the figure that the ambiguity function for firms lies uniformly above that of consumers thereby indicating a more cautious attitude in the presence of ambiguity. When neither consumers nor firms are ambiguous, their respective ambiguity functions coincide with the diagonal (45°) line.[25]

Figure 5.5 suggests several implications. First, consider situations where consumers are ambiguous. In this case, the probability of loss is overweighted relative to the anchor for low but not for high values. Thus, comparing what consumers would be willing to pay in ambiguous as opposed to non-ambiguous situations, one would expect willingness to pay additional premiums under conditions of ambiguity for low probability events (i.e. to avoid ambiguity) but less willingness to buy insurance for high probability of loss events (i.e. exhibiting preference for ambiguity). Second, for firms one would expect a desire to charge higher premiums for ambiguity across most of the probability range. Indeed, in a series of experimental studies these implications have been verified.[26]

Third, consider possible cases where firms' and consumers' ambiguity functions suggest that they would or would not be willing to transact business. For firms, the most profitable segment is where probabilities are low, they are not ambiguous but consumers are. Indeed, this type of situation characterizes much of the market for insurance. Consider your own life or automobile insurance. Whereas you may guess that the probability of a mishap is low, you are likely to be vague as to just what this is. Your insurance company, on the other hand, has good statistics concerning these issues. As noted in Figure 5.4, there are also cases where firms can be ambiguous. In these cases, it seems unlikely that they could agree on prices with consumers unless the latter are extremely risk-averse. This too is borne out by the experience of real markets. Insurance companies in the United States, for example, have been reluctant to provide insurance for the nuclear industry and have specifically attributed their unwillingness to problems of estimating risk probabilities accurately.[27]

Ambiguity affects many types of decisions involving risk, e.g. investments, technology, negotiations, purchases of major household items, and so on. By definition, it is particularly likely to affect decisions where there is little previous experience. This, in turn, suggests important asymmetries in how ambiguity might affect the assessments made by substantive experts, on the one hand, and novices on the other. Studies of risk perception, for example, have consistently shown that members of the public (as opposed to technical experts) overestimate the risks associated with possible hazards such as nuclear power that are unfamiliar and poorly understood while underestimating familiar but statistically more dangerous technologies such as X-rays.[28] Similarly, many people buy flight insurance even though the rates are far higher than readily available life insurance.[29] Note particularly that in the cases of nuclear power and flight insurance, it is easy for those unfamiliar with these technologies to imagine scenarios where mishaps occur such that anchor estimates are subject to considerable upward adjustments.

This section has illustrated several implications of both prospect theory and the ambiguity model. From an economic viewpoint, these implications—as well as several examples presented earlier in the chapter—represent violations of the expected utility model and thus could be considered 'irrational' behaviour. However, to what extent is such irrational behaviour *unreasonable*? Consider first the finding from prospect theory that different frames can induce different responses. I personally believe that it is difficult to justify a decision process as rational if it can be manipulated by simple rewording of the way a problem is posed, and particularly if the situation is not complex. If a decision maker allows the manner in which a problem is framed to affect the selected alternative, then part or even total control over choice has been effectively delegated to the manner in which the problem was worded. At best this implies yielding control over one's own choices to random factors in the environment; at worst, it means allowing oneself to be exploited by others. On the other hand, I also believe that the psychological principles that underlie framing are powerful and that it would be unwise to ignore them.

The economic prescription is to frame problems in terms of wealth as opposed to changes in wealth. To illustrate, imagine that your present wealth level is $50,000 and you are faced with evaluating a choice between, on the one hand, a sure $500, and on the other a gamble with a 50% chance of winning $1,000 and a 50% chance of nothing. From the normative economic perspective, you should think about this as a choice between having $50,500 versus accepting a gamble with a 50% chance of ending up with $51,000 and a 50% chance of remaining at your present level of $50,000.

In many practical situations, however, it is difficult to follow the economic advice to frame problems in terms of wealth. (How many people, for example, know what their wealth level is?) Thus, the major implication of prospect theory is that one should be active in how problems are framed. In other words, actively seek to frame problems from multiple perspectives in order to avoid being overly influenced by any particular one. Seeing problems from many perspectives can, of course, add to the conflict of choice. However, such conflict is usually preferable to being manipulated. Put succinctly, the advice is 'Frame, or be framed!'

The ambiguity model suggests that there are economic consequences associated with not being able to assess probabilities accurately. Moreover, these consequences can be exploited as when insurance companies take advantage of their customers' ambiguity. However, it is also true that in many cases there can be considerable information-processsing costs associated with making precise probability estimates such that it is not evident whether ignoring ambiguity is or is not 'reasonable'. The general issue of whether or not violations of expected utility theory are both 'irrational' and 'unreasonable' is thus quite complicated. It will be discussed further within a broader context in Chapter 10.

## SUMMARY AND GENERAL DISCUSSION

This chapter has outlined several issues concerning decision making under uncertainty. The first section discussed a number of principles of rational choice that are embodied in expected utility theory, the 'rational' benchmark for evaluating choice under uncertainty. Perhaps the most striking feature of these principles is that, whereas they are accepted as reasonable when stated in abstract form, their implications are often violated in actual choices. Indeed, this was illustrated in several problems discussed in the second section.

The third section discussed several psychological principles underlying the evaluation of risky actions that have been made explicit in both prospect theory and the ambiguity model. These included the notions that people encode the outcomes of choice as deviations (losses and gains) from reference points or levels of aspiration and that losses loom larger than gains. Taken together, these two particular principles imply that the manner in which decision alternatives are framed can have considerable impact on choice. The role of imagination in the assessment of uncertainty was highlighted by the ambiguity model which depicted these judgements as resulting from a compromise between data and the outcomes of a mental simulation process ('what is with could be'). In the fourth section, many implications of the principles underlying prospect theory and the ambiguity model were discussed.

In the phenomena illustrated above, the manner in which people's choices deviate from the prescriptions of the expected utility model can be largely traced to how outcomes and probabilities are evaluated. Consider, for example, the decision weight function of prospect theory or the ambiguity function. Moreover, evaluation depends on the manner in which choice alternatives have been framed or encoded. Thus, to understand how people choose, it is necessary to understand the different stages of the process in which options are (1) *encoded*, and (2) *evaluated*. In addition, choice can also depend on a third stage which is defined by the mode people use to (3) *express* preference. To illustrate, consider the following problem.

Imagine that you are standing beside a roulette wheel and you are playing a game involving the numbers 1 to 36. You are shown two possible bets.

In Bet *A*, you win \$4 if the ball finishes in numbers 1 through 35 (inclusive). If the number is 36, you lose \$1.

In Bet *B*, you win \$16 if the ball finishes in numbers 1 through 11 (inclusive), and you lose \$1.50 if the ball ends up in numbers 12 through 36 (inclusive).

Now imagine you are told you have to play one of the bets. Which would you choose? *A*? *B*? Perhaps you would be indifferent between them?

Next, imagine that you have been given tickets which give you the right to play both Bet *A* and Bet *B*. Now, instead of playing the bets, you have a chance of selling the tickets. What is the *smallest* price at which you would be prepared to sell Bet *A*? What is the *smallest* price at which you would be prepared to sell Bet *B*?

Given that you have been asked the above series of questions one after the other, there is a good chance that your answers will be consistent in the sense that the bet you prefer to play is also the one to which you accord the higher selling price. However, had this not been the case (for example, if you had received the above problems among many others), it is not certain that you would have acted so consistently. Faced with a series of problems of the above nature, a majority of people who prefer Bet *A* (which emphasizes a high probability of winning a small sum), accord a higher selling price to Bet *B* (which emphasizes a larger amount but at a lower probability). The reverse phenomenon does not, however, generally occur (i.e. prefer to play *B*, but set a higher selling price on *A*). This so-called preference reversal phenomenon has, incidentally, not only been demonstrated several times in artificial laboratory situations (including experiments conducted by economists as well as psychologists), but also in an experiment in a Las Vegas casino![30]

Why does the mode of expression affect choice, even leading to reversals of preference? One hypothesis is that in making choices involving conflicting dimensions (e.g. probability vs. amount to win), people selectively attend to one or a limited number of dimensions that are highlighted by the manner in which responses are elicited. Another hypothesis suggests that the manner in which a gamble, once evaluated, is translated on to the subjective scale on which its worth is expressed, can introduce systematic distortions.[31]

In this chapter, choice processes have been discussed from a cognitive viewpoint by emphasizing the manner in which options are encoded, evaluated, and expressed. However, it is important to realize that these basic operations of information processing can be, and often are, affected by emotional factors. For example, in discussing Problem 1, where individuals frequently feel compelled to take the option yielding a certain $1,000,000, the notion of psychological regret was invoked. Further interesting phenomena have been observed in studies of insurance behaviour. People tend not to buy insurance against events that have very small probabilities of occurrence but with large possible losses (for example concerning natural hazards such as floods or earthquakes). On the other hand, they will purchase insurance for events with higher probabilities of occurrence but with lower losses (e.g. household burglary).[32] In the first example people do not seem to feel responsible for failing to protect themselves from 'acts of God'; however, failing to insure against burglary (which happens more frequently) can be considered imprudent. Emotional factors such as anxiety, for example fear of potential outcomes of one's actions, can also cause people to block out relevant arguments, overemphasize arguments in favour of preferred alternatives, fail to search for new alternatives, and even psychologically prepare themselves for negative consequences of their decisions.[33] A full understanding of choice under uncertainty will require explicating both its cognitive and emotional determinants.

## NOTES AND REFERENCES

1. By this I mean the closely related expected utility and subjectively expected utility theories formulated by, respectively, J. von Neumann and O. Morgenstern (1947). *Theory of Games and Economic Behavior* (2nd edn), Princeton, NJ: Princeton University Press; and L. J. Savage (1954). *The Foundations of Statistics*, New York: John Wiley & Sons (also Dover, 1972). See also J. Marschak and R. Radner (1972). *Economic Theory of Teams*, New Haven: Yale University Press, especially Chapter 1.
2. Many people have criticized the notion that the expected utility principle can be applied to both long- and short-run situations. For a particularly interesting analysis, see L. L. Lopes (1981). Decision making in the short run, *Journal of Experimental Psychology: Human Perception and Performance*, **7**, 377–385, as well as the response to this article by A. Tversky and M. Bar-Hillel (1983). Risk:

The long and the short, *Journal of Experimental Psychology: Learning, Memory, and Cognition*, **9**, 713–717.

3. See Savage, Reference 1, p. 21.

4. Problem 1 was originally formulated by M. Allais (1953). Le comportement de l'homme rationnel devant le risque: critiques des postulats et axiomes de l'école américaine, *Econometrica*, **21**, 503–546. See also P. Slovic and A. Tversky (1974). Who accepts Savage's axiom? *Behavioural Science*, **19**, 368–373.

5. This example is due to R. Zeckhauser as cited in D. Kahneman and A. Tversky (1979). Prospect theory: An analysis of decision under risk, *Econometrica*, **47**, 283.

6. See D. Kahneman and A. Tversky (1979). Prospect theory: An analysis of decision under risk. *Econometrica*, **47**, 263–291.

7. The form of Problem 2 is due to Savage, Reference 1, p. 103.

8. The structure of this problem was inspired by an example in A.Tversky and D. Kahneman (1981). The framing of decisions and the psychology of choice, *Science*, **211**, 453–458. When the problem is administered to groups of MBA students, typical responses for each of the options are: plan *A* 75% and plan *B* 25% for Problem 3; and plan *C* 20% and plan *D* 80% for Problem 5.

9. This example was also adapted from one given in Tversky and Kahneman, Reference 8. When the problem is given to MBA students, approximately 70% choose *A* and *D*. Almost all respondents, however, choose *F* over *E*.

10. This problem is due to Daniel Ellsberg (1961). Risk, ambiguity, and the Savage axioms, *Quarterly Journal of Economics*, **75**, 643–669. See also Slovic and Tversky, Reference 4.

11. See Kahneman and Tversky, Reference 6.

12. See H. J. Einhorn and R. M. Hogarth (1985). Ambiguity and uncertainty in probabilistic inference, *Psychological Review*, **92**, 433–461.

13. Note that even if values of the probability below the anchor are weighted more heavily in imagination than those above, there can still be overweighting of anchor probabilities when these are low. This occurs below the cross-over point because even though possible values below the anchor are weighted more than those above, they are far fewer in number. Thus, the net effect of the simulation is an upward adjustment. Similarly, even when values above the anchor are weighted more heavily than those below, there will be a downward adjustment at the upper end of the anchor probability scale.

14. For example, given the choice between Urn 1, Urn 2, or indifference, about 35% of MBA students choose the ambiguous urn. See H. J. Einhorn and R. M. Hogarth (1986). Decision making under ambiguity, *Journal of Business*, **59**(4), Part 2, S225–S250.

15. See R. H. Thaler (1980). Toward a positive theory of consumer choice, *Journal of Economic Behavior and Organization*, **1**, 39–60. For further implications and developments of prospect theory to consumer choice, see also R. Thaler (1985). Mental accounting and consumer choice. *Marketing Science*, **4**, 199–214.

16. For an interesting application of how framing affects interpretation of the tax code, see T. C. Schelling (1981). Economic reasoning and the economics of policy, *The Public Interest*, **63**, 37–61.

17. See S. M. Yates and E. Aronson (1983). A social psychological perspective on energy conservation in residential buildings, *American Psychologist*, **38**, 435–444.

18. See B. J. McNeil, S. G. Pauker, H. C. Sox, Jr, and A. Tversky (1982). On the elicitation of preferences for alternative therapies, *New England Journal of Medicine*, **306**, 1259–1262.

19. See J. W. Payne, D. J. Laughhunn, and R. Crum (1980). Translation of gambles and aspiration effects in risky choice behavior, *Management Science*, **26**, 1039–1060.

20. I have administered this legal decision-making problem to many groups of MBA students and managers. When the amount at issue is $20,000 and the probability of the plaintiff winning the case is .80, about 90% of 'plaintiffs' say they would be willing to settle out of court for $16,000 but 70% of 'defendants' state they would prefer to take the case to court. Alternatively, when subjects are asked to state minimum (for plaintiffs) and maximum (for defendant) settlement amounts, defendant subjects state amounts that are systematically lower than those of plaintiffs.
21. See C. S. Karrass (1970). *The Negotiating Game*, New York: Crowell.
22. See, for example, M. Bazerman (1983). Negotiator judgment, *American Behavioral Scientist*, **27**, 211–218; and M. A. Neale and M. Bazerman (1985). The effects of framing and negotiator overconfidence on bargaining behaviors and outcomes, *Academy of Management Journal*, **28**, 34–49.
23. See Einhorn and Hogarth, Reference 14.
24. For further evidence on the transfer of risk effect, see R. H. Thaler, Reference 15, as well as J. C. Hershey, H. Kunreuther, and P. J. H. Schoemaker (1982). Sources of bias in assessment procedures for utility functions, *Management Science*, **28**, 936–954.
25. See Einhorn and Hogarth, Reference 12.
26. See R. M. Hogarth and H. Kunreuther (1985). Ambiguity and insurance decisions, *American Economic Review (AEA Papers and Proceedings)*, **75**, 386–390, also R. M. Hogarth and H. Kunreuther (1986). *Risk, Ambiguity, and Insurance*, Working paper, University of Chicago, Graduate School of Business.
27. See US Nuclear Regulatory Commission (December 1983). *The Price Anderson Act: The Third Decade*, Report to Congress, Washington, DC.
28. See, for example, P. Slovic, B. Fischhoff, and S. Lichtenstein (1980). Facts and fears: Understanding perceived risk. In R. C. Schwing and W. A. Albers Jr. (eds), *Societal Risk Assessment: How Safe is Safe Enough*, New York: Plenum Press, pp. 181–214.
29. See R. Eisner and R. H. Strotz (1961). Flight insurance and the theory of choice. *Journal of Political Economy*, **69**, 355–368.
30. See, for example, D. M. Grether and C. R. Plott (1979). Economic theory of choice and the preference reversal phenomenon, *American Economic Review*, **69**, 623–638; S. Lichtenstein and P. Slovic (1971). Reversals of preferences between bids and choices in gambling situations, *Journal of Experimental Psychology*, **89**, 46–55; and S. Lichtenstein and P. Slovic (1973). Response-induced reversals of preferences in gambling: An extended replication in Las Vegas, *Journal of Experimental Psychology*, **101**, 16–20.
31. See W. M. Goldstein and H. J. Einhorn (in press). Expression theory and the preference reversal phenomena, *Psychological Review*.
32. See H. Kunreuther (1976). Limited knowledge and insurance protection, *Public Policy*, **24**, 227–261; and P. Slovic, B. Fischhoff, S. Lichtenstein, B. Corrigan, and B. Combs (1977). Preference for insuring against probable small losses: Implications for the theory and practice of insurance, *Journal of Risk and Insurance*, **44**, 237–258.
33. See, for example, I. L. Janis and L. Mann (1977). *Decision Making: A Psychological Analysis of Conflict, Choice, and Commitment*, New York: The Free Press.

# CHAPTER 6

# On learning relations[1]

As discussed in preceding chapters, predictive judgements are based on cues. That is, a prediction can be thought of as the extrapolation of an assumed relation (or relations) between cue(s) and a target event. For example, imagine in a business setting that the target event is the difference between this and next year's sales of a company and budgeted advertising expenses is the cue. A crucial issue is whether you believe that the level of advertising expenses is related to differences in sales, and if so, what kind of relation exists between the two variables. For example, do annual differences in sales rise or fall with the level of advertising expenditure? By how much?

The literature on judgement has documented two disturbing findings concerning people's ability to assess relations for prediction. First, people have often been found to be overconfident in judgement.[2] That is, the degree of confidence expressed in predictions is not matched by subsequent reality. The second is the so-called 'illusory correlation' phenomenon.[3] This refers to a tendency to see relations between variables where none exists. These findings are particularly disturbing if one believes that people learn from experience. That is, why is it that experience does not necessarily teach people to moderate the confidence they express in their judgement? Why do people continue to see predictive relations where none exists?

An explanation that springs immediately to mind is of a motivational nature: people selectively forget instances where their judgement was incorrect. In other words, they have a 'bad memory' for predictive failures. The second phenomenon is more problematic. It has been suggested, for instance, that illusory correlation persists in situations where people do not receive good feedback concerning their judgements and where others share the same illusions. Thus, instead of feedback concerning actual outcomes, each person both reinforces and is reinforced by the illusions of the others. In many organizations, common beliefs are precisely of this nature.

Whereas so-called 'motivated forgetting' and common illusions undoubtedly play a role in maintaining people's high confidence in fallible judgement—as well as beliefs in non-existent relations—this chapter pursues a different approach to the problems involved in learning relations for prediction. Instead, a detailed examination is made of one context in which predictive judgements are made. Although the presentation is consequently

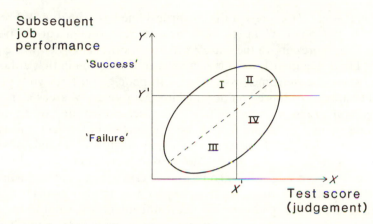

Figure 6.1   Job selection example. (Reproduced by permission of CEDEP)

specific, it raises important issues involved in the learning of relations. In particular, it illustrates the interaction between the person, judgement and the task environment in which judgement is made. The chapter concludes with a discussion of the role of experience in learning relations and the extent to which such learning is possible.

## PREDICTIVE JUDGEMENT AND DECISIONS

It is important to emphasize that predictive judgements are made for the purposes of decision.[4] For example, imagine that you are making a decision whether to employ a candidate for a particular job. The candidate is interviewed and perhaps even passes some tests. On the basis of the information collected, you judge the person to be above a certain criterion and consequently decide to hire. For expository purposes, consider that you can describe the candidate's performance on the interviews and tests by a score of some kind—to be denoted the test score.

An important issue, therefore, is the extent to which the test score—and thus by implication your judgement—is predictive of the candidate's subsequent job success.

If you were able to test and observe the results of many candidates, the relations between scores and subsequent job success could be represented by Figure 6.1. In that figure, the predictive ability of the test can be measured by the size and shape of the ellipse (cf. Chapter 2)— for a perfect test, the relation would be a straight line (i.e. the dotted line in the figure). If there were no relation between test and subsequent performance, the ellipse would become circular in appearance.

However, there is a simple reason why Figure 6.1 cannot represent the true situation. You do not hire candidates whose scores are below a certain standard on the test. To represent this, a vertical line has been drawn through the figure at the point $X'$ on the test axis to represent a cut-off point: candidates with scores above the cut-off are hired, candidates below the cut-off are not hired. Figure 6.1 misrepresents the true situation in that although you can observe the outcomes associated with people you hire, you do not know what happens to those you do not hire. Moreover, whereas a specific type of decision has been illustrated here, its structural features are common to many judgemental situations. You make a predictive judgement, this leads you to take an action, and because of the action taken you can only observe some of the outcomes related to your initial judgement. Consider, for example, decisions to engage someone in conversation, to buy a particular product, to allocate your time to one as opposed to another project, and so on. Note too that unless you believed your judgement was valid in the first place, you probably would not base your action on your judgement. This is an important point to which we shall return below.

Reconsider Figure 6.1. In addition to the cut-off on the test score ($X'$), a horizontal line has also been drawn through the line indicating the criterion of job success. There the point $Y'$ indicates the cut-off between a candidate being a success or a failure. As can be seen, the vertical and horizontal lines divide the ellipse into four quadrants which are denoted I, II, III, and IV.

Three questions are relevant to Figure 6.1: first, what information is necessary to infer the relation between judgement and outcomes; second, what information do people actually use in assessing the relation; and third, given that people usually have to identify and infer relations, what is known about this process? Cues for prediction, it should be recalled, are usually not given but have to be selected by the individual.

To assess the relation between test score ($X$) and job success ($Y$), it is necessary to have information *on all four quadrants* in Figure 6.1. Quadrants I and IV represent misclassifications—respectively, candidates who should have been offered jobs but were not (false negatives), and candidates to whom jobs were offered but who subsequently failed (false positives). Quadrants II (positive hits) and III (negative hits), on the other hand, represent correct classifications. To see why one needs to have information on all four quadrants, note that if information is missing from any quadrant, it is not possible to estimate the two ratios necessary to assess the strength of the relation. These are the number of observations in quadrant II relative to the sum of quadrants II and IV, and the number of observations in quadrant III relative to the sum of quadrants I and III.

A number of experiments have tested people's ability to assess relations in situations similar to Figure 6.1.[5] These have shown that the attention people pay to different aspects of available information is remarkably sensitive to changes in the way data are displayed and/or the manner questions are asked about the relations between variables. For example, evidence indicates that even when people receive information on all four quadrants, they do not necessarily weight all the information equally in inferring the relation. Rather, the strength of the assessed relation is heavily influenced by the number of observations in quadrant II. This is particularly the case when, as in real life, people receive the information sequentially (i.e. over time). On the other hand, when people are presented with all the information in 'intact' displays (i.e. simultaneous presentation of the information in all four quadrants), attention is more evenly spread across all the information. These findings are important for several reasons. First, they suggest that people have strong habits to look for certain kinds of information (i.e. positive hits in quadrant II) when inferring relations from data generated across time. Second, in such circumstances other data that are necessary to infer relations may be downplayed or even ignored. Note, however, that the data ignored are frequently unavailable in real life, i.e. information in quadrants I and III. And third, despite the two preceding points, people are nonetheless capable of assessing relations using all the data when these are made salient for them, as in intact displays. This latter point, incidentally, suggests that intact information displays alleviate the strain of remembering outcomes in all four quadrants, an issue that is reconsidered later in the chapter.

To summarize, these studies—as well as the kinds of situation depicted in Figure 6.1—indicate both the impossibility and difficulty of learning relations between variables in many situations: impossibility because certain information is not available, difficulty because even when it is available, it may be ignored. Note, however, this does not mean that judgements will always be followed by unsuccessful outcomes. As will be demonstrated below, the situation is more complicated.

## Testing one's hypotheses

An important issue related to the above is evidence concerning how people acquire both concepts and test ideas. As an example, consider the following problem:[6]

> You are told that the numbers '2, 4, 6' conform to a rule and your task is to discover what the rule is. To do so, you may generate sequences of three numbers and ask whether the sequences either conform or do not conform to the rule. That is, the person who knows the rule will simply tell you whether the sequence you generate does or does not exemplify the rule. You can continue generating numbers until such time as you believe you have inferred the rule.

There are two kinds of evidence you can seek in this kind of situation: first, evidence that is consistent with a hypothesis (e.g. you think that the rule might involve increments of +2, so you ask '8, 10, 12'); and second, evidence that disconfirms. For example, you believe that the rule might involve increments of +2 (as above) so you generate a series which does not correspond to your hypothesis, e.g. '8, 11, 12'. Both forms of information are necessary to infer the validity of a rule: evidence that is consistent with (or confirms) the rule, and evidence that could disconfirm the rule. However, the second form of information (disconfirming evidence) is often more powerful in that it allows you to eliminate invalid hypotheses.

What do people do in this kind of task? Most use each trial in attempts to confirm their current hypothesis. That is, few generate a sequence in order to see whether their hypothesis would be disconfirmed. Indeed, people show a strong tendency to accumulate several instances of confirming evidence. However, since this additional information is redundant, it can induce unwarranted confidence in people's hypotheses.[7]

The difference between this experiment and the job selection situation described previously is that no actions are involved. Thus, it is not the fact that a person takes an action that inhibits the search for disconfirming evidence. However, in the job selection situation, there is a direct relation between the employment decision and the evidence that can be observed concerning the validity of the prediction that led to the decision. Indeed, if for reasons to be enumerated below, there is a high probability that people who are selected for the job turn out to be successful, then the situation becomes a self-reinforcing cycle. That is:

(1) you believe there is a relation between the test (i.e. your judgement) and job success;
(2) you therefore select according to your judgement;
(3) most of the people you select turn out to be successful;
(4) you conclude your judgement is accurate.

In other words, your initial belief in the accuracy of your judgement has set in motion a sequence of events that reinforces the notion that your judgement is accurate. Your judgement might not, of course, be accurate, or at least, as accurate as you think; however, because of the structure of the task you cannot determine this. You could, of course, have tested your judgement but to do so would have implied hiring candidates you believed unsuitable for the job! Consequently, there is little motivation to test the validity of your judgement.

Incidentally, in their classic study of how people acquire concepts, Bruner, Goodnow and Austin also noted what they termed a 'thirst for confirming redundancy'.[8] This means that once people have acquired a concept, they continue to test it several times in order really to confirm it to themselves, and often redundantly. Bruner *et al.* also point out that people have greater difficulty in acquiring concepts defined in terms of the presence of *either* one, two *or* several traits as opposed to concepts defined by the simultaneous presence of several traits (i.e. so-called disjunctive and conjunctive concepts). Conjunctive concepts are easier because they are defined by the presence of several traits; disjunctive concepts, on the other hand, can be characterized by the absence of traits. Since concepts can be considered cues for prediction, these findings suggest that people will have differential confidence and difficulty in prediction depending on the form or kind of 'concepts' used.

A further problem that tests your ability to seek the appropriate information in learning relations is the following:

It is claimed that when a particular consultant says the market will rise (a so-called favourable report), the market always does rise.

You are required to check the consultant's claim and can observe any of the outcomes or predictions associated with:

(1) favourable report;
(2) unfavourable report;
(3) rise in the market;
(4) fall in the market.

What is the minimum evidence you would need to check the consultant's claim?

In a formal test of this problem,[1] a majority of analytically sophisticated subjects failed to make the appropriate response of *both* item 1 (to confirm that when the consultant makes a favourable report the market does rise) and item 4 (to verify that falls in the market were not preceded by favourable reports). Note that selecting item 1 alone (a confirmatory piece of evidence) would be insufficient to uphold the consultant's claim. To test the rule, you not only need evidence confirming the claim, but also to be able to observe possible disconfirming evidence.

## Syllogistic slips

Related to the above example are problems arising in 'syllogistic' reasoning (where people draw conclusions from premises). In this process, it is easy to make slips, a classical example being: 'All women are human; therefore, all humans are women'. Whereas most people can see the logical error in this statement, where the meaning is clear, in many inferential situations logical inconsistency is not evident. Consider the following scenario, the elements of which were first introduced in Chapter 2:

You are a businessman facing a highly competitive marketing situation. In fact, you are aware that the next move by you or your competitor could well be crucial in determining who establishes the larger market share. One of the possible weapons open to both of you is price reduction. However, given rates of profitability in the present market, this is something you would be loath to do unless forced by competition. Nonetheless, you feel that there is a fair chance (say evens) that your main competitor will reduce prices within the next week.

You receive a message from one of your field salesforce that your competitor has just booked large amounts of advertising space to go out in the next few days. If this report were true, you estimate that it is a near certainty that the advertising space has been booked to announce a reduction in prices. Therefore, you had better act fast since the first company to lower prices will gain an important competitive edge. However, before you act, you wisely stop to question the credibility of the salesman's report, since this is crucial to your decision. You clearly cannot know whether this particular report is true, so you think back on the times he has made reports to you in the recent past. His track record, it turns out, is impressive. On five occasions that you can recall within the last year, he has passed confidential information on to you. Every time he was right. You know this because just before you received each of his reports, you had also learned the same things for sure from other sources. Indeed, you were surprised that the salesman had been able to obtain the information in those cases and pleased that he had taken the initiative to approach you directly. In your view, the salesman's reports have high credibility. Consequently, you immediately order a reduction in prices. Events vindicate your action: two days after your price drop, your main competitor follows suit. However, since he followed your lead, it is you who gained the competitive edge in the 'price-war.'[9]

(Reproduced by permission of CEDEP)

The structure of the price-warfare scenario is fairly subtle and it is therefore helpful to decompose it. The following elements are involved:

(1)   One of your field salesforce reports that the main competitor has ordered a large amount of advertising space.
(2)   You estimate that if your main competitor has in fact ordered a large amount of advertising space, a price reduction is a near certainty.
(3)   You question the credibility of your salesman and find it satisfactory.
(4)   You order an immediate drop in prices.
(5)   Your competitor follows your drop in prices, albeit with a small delay.

The crucial judgement in this chain is at (3): your questioning of your salesman's credibility. Here a logical error was made. That is, the estimation of the salesman's credibility was done by considering instances where you already knew the truth of something he reported to you, and then checking his reports against this knowledge. However, what is of concern here is estimating the salesman's credibility in cases where you do not have knowledge concerning the validity of his report. This is not the same thing. What you did was to use the information about the salesman's credibility that was readily available to you (look carefully at the wording of the scenario), and to verify the salesman's credibility using instances of the form 'given that I know the competitor has booked advertising space, how likely is my salesman to report this as going to happen?' However, the appropriate question is: 'Given that the salesman has reported that the competitor has booked advertising space, what is the probability that the competitor has indeed booked advertising space?' Note that the manner in which you questioned yourself about the salesman's credibility does not correspond to this kind of statement at all. Furthermore, to assume that both statements represent the same estimate of the salesman's credibility is to commit a logical error of the form 'All women are human; therefore all humans are women'. In other words, whereas the salesman might be perfectly credible *vis-à-vis* the manner in which you posed the question, (i.e. where you knew the outcome for sure), this tells you nothing about his credibility concerning events about which you do not know the result. It is quite possible that in this 'direction' the salesman is totally unreliable.

The next judgemental error in the scenario is to assume that your competitor's decision to reduce prices is independent of yours. In this kind of situation, your competitor's price reduction may well be in retaliation to yours. The source (i.e. cause) of his reduction is your logical error concerning your salesman's credibility! Events appear to vindicate your judgement; but they are the result of errors in your judgement.

## FACTORS AFFECTING FEEDBACK

The main arguments presented so far in this chapter can be summarized as follows: people learn from what they are able to observe. However, judgemental situations are often structured in a manner such that people cannot observe the information necessary to assess relations. Furthermore, even when such information is available, people do not necessarily use it. In particular, they have a tendency to seek information that confirms existing notions rather than to seek information that could disconfirm their hypotheses.

The preceding section highlighted the important role of feedback in judgement. Generally speaking, people will continue to take actions which are positively rewarded and cease activities which lead to negative feedback. In the judgemental situation depicted in Figure 6.1, the extent of positive and negative feedback can be assessed by the relative numbers of observations falling in quadrants II and IV, which we shall simply denote as successes and failures. Since feedback is critical to what people learn, factors affecting the relative numbers of successes and failures observed are now considered in the context of the job selection task introduced above.

### The four factors

The relative numbers of successes and failures observed depends upon four factors. First, there is the 'true' relation between judgement (i.e. test scores) and outcomes. This is represented by the shape of the ellipse (covering the full range of both the test and job outcomes). As noted above, the narrower the ellipse, the greater the predictive accuracy of the test.

Second, the location of the cut-off on the test also affects the relative number of successes observed. Specifically, the more stringent the cut-off

122

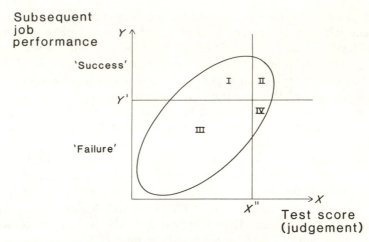

Figure 6.2   Effects of being more stringent on the test ($X$) relative to Figure 6.1. Note how feedback appears better. The ratio of quadrant II to IV has increased considerably. The number in quadrant I has also increased, but this is unobservable. (Reproduced by permission of CEDEP)

on the test, the greater is the relative number of successes to failures. This can be observed in Figure 6.2, where the cut-off $X''$ is more stringent than that shown in Figure 6.1, i.e. it is placed further to the right. Note that the ratio of successes to failures is greater in Figure 6.2 than in Figure 6.1, even though 'true' judgemental ability (as measured by the shape of the ellipse) is identical. Thus, the existence of the cut-off on the $X$-axis not only precludes one from assessing the relation between test and job outcome across the range of test scores, its location affects the relative numbers of successes and failures that can be observed.

The third factor is similar to the second: it concerns the location of the cut-off on the axis measuring the job outcomes. The lower the criterion of success, the more successes will be observed irrespective of predictive ability and the location of the cut-off on the test. This third factor, known as the base-rate of success, is most important but usually unknown. For example, suppose you observe an 80% success rate in judgement. Does this mean that your predictive ability is good? (Recall Chapter 3.) Unless you know the base-rate, it is impossible to make an assessment. For instance, if the base-rate is 70% (meaning that 70% of candidates would succeed in the job had there been no test procedure, i.e. judgement, on your part), your inherent judgemental ability does not add much. On the other hand, if the base-rate is 20%, an observed 80% success rate is good.

The relations between predictive ability, cut-off on the test and base-rate are important in determining the final ratio of successes to failures observed. Furthermore, even when true predictive ability is low, feedback from judgement as indicated by the observed ratio of successes to failures can be quite high.[10]

The fourth factor is more subtle. In the model of job selection described above, there is an implicit assumption of no relation between the judgement that someone is above the cut-off on the test score and subsequent job performance. In other words, the act of judging that a candidate will succeed is assumed not to affect subsequent job success.

This assumption can be challenged on several grounds. Indeed, the mere fact that someone has been selected for a job can set in motion a series of events that ensures subsequent success. For example, the candidate may receive 'on the job' training from experienced colleagues; the person who selected him or her may do things to ensure the candidate's success (intentionally or unintentionally). In sport, for instance, the judgement that one player is better than another and thus is selected for the first team instead of the reserves can mean that, in addition to obtaining a chance denied the other, the performance of the former is raised by the standard of the other players in the first team. And so on. In some situations it is almost impossible to separate the effects of judgement from the outcome: for example, in medicine the judgement that a person needs and receives a particular kind of therapy. Consider the following (horrific) example provided by Lewis Thomas in describing the diagnostic activities of an early twentieth-century physician:

> This physician enjoyed the reputation of a diagnostician, with a particular skill in diagnosing typhoid fever, then the commonest disease on the wards of New York's hospitals. He placed particular reliance on the appearance of the tongue, which was universal in the medicine of that day (now entirely inexplicable, long forgotten). He believed that he could detect significant differences by palpating that organ. The ward rounds conducted by this man were, essentially, tongue rounds; each patient would stick out his tongue while the eminence took it between thumb and forefinger, feeling its textures and irregularities, then moving from bed to bed, diagnosing typhoid fever in its earliest stages over and over again, and turning out a week or so later to have been right, to everyone's amazement. He was a more effective carrier, using only his hands, than Typhoid Mary.[11]

The fourth factor will be denoted a 'treatment effect' to indicate that some form of treatment intervenes between judgement and outcome. The consequences of a positive treatment are illustrated in Figure 6.3. Note that all observations to the right of the cut-off on the test, i.e. judgement, receive an upward impetus thereby distorting the feedback concerning the person's judgemental ability.

Figures 6.4(a) and 6.4(b) show a further form of treatment effect. In Figure 6.4(a) the 'true' relation between judgement and outcomes is indicated. As can be seen, there is no relation. Now assume that those accepted receive positive treatment effects and those rejected negative effects. If it were also possible to observe the outcomes of those rejected, the situation would

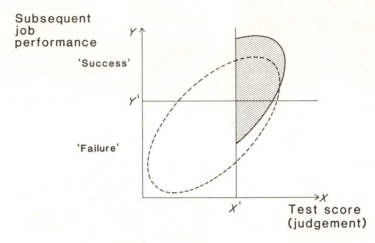

Figure 6.3   Job selection situation when judgement leads to those selected receiving special treatment, thus inflating apparent judgemental ability relative to the 'true' relation represented by the dotted ellipse. (Shaded section reflects actual observations.) Copyright (1978) by American Psychological Association. (Reprinted by permission)

subsequently appear as in Figure 6.4(b). 'Worthless' judgement apparently shows high predictive validity. Note well, however, that treatment effects need not be biased in favour of the person making the judgement. They could have negative or so-called 'boomerang' effects. For example, true judgemental ability could be as represented in Figure 6.4(b). With negative treatment effects for those accepted and positive effects for those rejected, the observed situation could be that depicted in Figure 6.4(a).

The combined effects of the four factors of the model considered here are complex. They also illustrate that there are situations where people imagine relations that do not exist—the so-called 'illusory correlation' phenomenon— and where good judgement does not appear to be vindicated. The results are consequently quite disturbing in terms of what they imply concerning human ability to learn relations for predictive purposes.

The model, however, has additional implications. How does a person know whether he or she is accurate at making judgements and the level of confidence that is appropriate in judgement? The answer to this question will be affected by the extent to which the person receives positive or negative feedback from the environment and the attention that is paid to such positive or negative feedback.

These issues were specifically explored in a simulation study of the above model by Einhorn and Hogarth.[1] The results indicated that if a person has only a modest degree of judgemental ability, then positive feedback and high confidence in judgement will often be the result of predictive activity. However, the interesting aspect of the Einhorn and Hogarth analysis is the

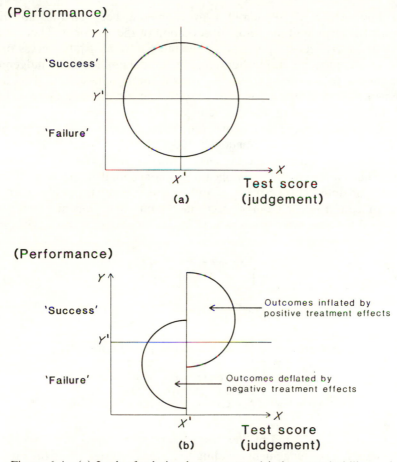

Figure 6.4 (a) Lack of relation between 'true' judgemental ability and performance; (b) observed relation between judgement and performance. (Reproduced by permission of CEDEP)

demonstration that overconfidence in judgement is not necessarily due to emotional factors, for instance so-called 'motivated forgetting' where people selectively forget instances when their judgement was incorrect. The phenomena can be accounted for simply by the structure of the judgemental task, although, as remarked at the beginning of the chapter, motivated forgetting undoubtedly also occurs.

## CONDITIONS FOR LEARNING RELATIONS

Above I have indicated some difficulties of learning relations in judgement. The model used to explain the difficulties is, of course, oversimplified in that the environment of judgement is more complex than illustrated here.

126

For example, there is frequently a large time-lag between the moment a judgement is made and the actual observation of the outcome. There is also usually no precise cut-off point on either the criterion of job success or the test score, i.e. judgement. Furthermore, the model implies many judgements of the same type whereas real life is probably better characterized by many judgements of different types (i.e. in different situations). On the other hand, the basic model of a judgement leading to an accept/reject decision which can subsequently result in observed successes and failures is common.

In Chapter 1, the point was made that judgemental accuracy is a function of both the task environment and the characteristics of the person. Subsequent chapters have allowed us to complicate this conceptualization by noting the dynamic and interactive aspects of judgements, actions, people, and situations. Indeed, it would be more accurate to state that judgement should be understood within a framework where individual, actions and environment

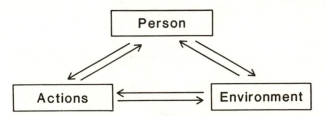

Figure 6.5 Reciprocal effects of person (judgements), actions, and environment.[12] Copyright (1978) by American Psychological Association. (Reprinted by permission)

all affect and are affected by the other, as illustrated in Figure 6.5.[12]

Individuals make judgements leading to actions, actions affect the environment, the environment affects individuals who consequently form new judgements, and so on. A good example of this kind of interaction has been suggested by Bandura:

Television-viewing behavior provides an everyday example. Personal preferences influence when and which program, from among the available alternatives, individuals choose to watch on television. Although the potential televised environment is identical for all viewers, the actual televised environment that impinges on given individuals depends on what they select to watch. Through their viewing behavior, they partly shape the nature of the future televised environment. Because production costs and commercial requirements also determine what people are shown, the options provided in the televised environment partly shape the viewers' preferences. Here, all three factors— viewer preferences, viewing behavior, and televised offerings— reciprocally affect each other.[12]

The above is an example of judgemental behaviour at an aggregate level which has implications for thinking about important aggregate behaviours

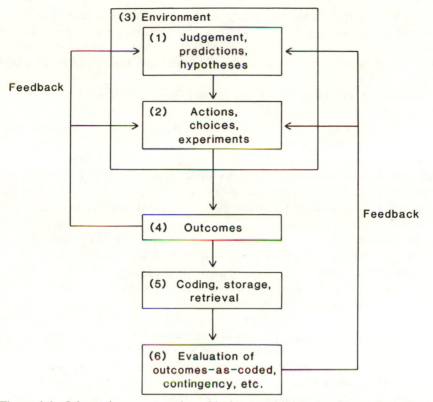

Figure 6.6   Schematic representation of judgement–action situation at the individual level. Copyright (1978) by American Psychological Association. (Reprinted by permission)

in, for example, marketing. A more detailed individual model is provided by Figure 6.6.[1]

The main differences between Figures 6.5 and 6.6 are that in the latter the individual has been 'decomposed' (as will be explained below) and the importance of feedback has been stressed. First, note that the individual forms judgements (predictions or hypotheses) leading to actions *within* a task environment. Outcomes (box 4) are a function of boxes 1 to 3, i.e. environment, judgement, and actions, and feed back into the environment (see the left-hand side of the diagram). Outcomes, however, are also observed by the individual, coded in memory (box 5) and evaluated (box 6). For example, on observing an increase in sales following an increase in advertising expenditure, a manager might attribute a causal relation. This would then feed back into formulation of hypotheses and judgements relating to future actions—and so on. Observe the feedback loops on the right-hand side of the diagram. How outcomes are coded in memory is, of course, also an important issue (box 5). For example, several experiments indicate that for predictive purposes the frequency of an event is more salient in memory than relative frequency.[13] Furthermore, the relative weight given to the observation of successful outcomes exceeds that given to failures. Indeed, in the learning of relations, some studies indicate that no weight is accorded to negative feedback.[13]

In short, an understanding of the learning of relations used in predictive judgement necessitates an understanding of the task environment, actions, outcomes, coding of outcomes in memory, interpretation of outcomes, and the different feedback loops.

Given the complexity of the above processes, what are the conditions necessary to learn predictive relations. Estes has emphasized the need for both what he calls the 'alternative event' to occur (e.g. the outcome in the personnel model associated with the reject decision), and for people to pay attention to and encode 'all the alternative events with equal efficiency'.[13] He points out that such conditions probably apply in situations such as weather forecasting, and indeed considerable evidence indicates that weather forecasters have impressive track records in prediction.[2] However, Estes' conditions cannot apply in situations where judgement leads to actions which preclude observation of the alternative event.

In addition to the fact that many judgemental situations have this feature, two reasons suggest that people will not attempt to change situations so that they are able to observe outcomes of the so-called alternative event. First, on economic grounds people will often not wish to test their judgement. That is, taking the job-hiring situation as an example, the cost of hiring a candidate judged to be unsuitable is deemed to be greater than the potential benefit of assessing the validity of one's judgement. Although, it should also be pointed out that not many organizations make efforts to find out what happened to candidates they rejected! In other situations, for example in medicine, ethical considerations are important. Does one withhold treatment from a patient deemed to be in need simply to observe what would happen? The second reason is that people frequently do not feel the need to test their judgement. The results of the simulation performed by Einhorn and Hogarth (see above) indicated that in many situations people do receive positive feedback in respect of their judgements and even when true predictive accuracy is low; consequently, there is little motivation to question predictive ability.

Some situations are, however, structured in such a manner that people have to consider the alternative event. For example, executives in the pop record business perceive the prediction of 'hit' records to be extremely difficult, even though the records they do select as promising are given elaborate and expensive publicity.[14] (This is, of course, an explicit 'treatment' effect—see Figure 6.3.) A major reason for lack of confidence is induced by the fact that records that were initially rejected can, and do sometimes, become hits with rival companies. These mistakes are made salient publicly in the 'charts' and cannot be ignored. Thus, attention is paid to the alternative event. Note, however, that it is the structure of the environment that causes negative feedback to become salient rather than an inherent desire to test and improve predictive ability.

Based on extensive work in prediction in clinical psychology, Goldberg[15] has listed three conditions for learning predictive relations : (1) feedback— which is necessary but not sufficient; (2) ability to re-arrange cases so that hypotheses can be verified or discounted. As Goldberg puts it, 'it does little good to formulate a rule for profile Type A, only to wait for another 100 profiles before an additional manifestation of Type A appears; what one must do is group together all Type A profiles in order to be able to verify one's initial preference.'[15] However, this condition is of limited practical value to decision makers faced with a range of essentially non-repetitive predictive situations; and (3) ability to keep a record of one's predictions and their outcomes. As noted earlier in the chapter, memory is important in predictive activity, and methods of bolstering this and the nature of feedback are key elements. However, as Figure 6.5 indicates, feedback has to be understood within the context in which it appears—and its interpretation is not evident. Indeed, much research indicates that feedback based on the observation of outcomes in learning situations is ineffective.[16]

What kind of feedback is likely to be effective? Some studies have shown that feedback that emphasizes the process, i.e. the structure of the judgemental task, is more effective than mere 'outcome' feedback.[17] Given what has been said above, this appears reasonable. However, the evidence on this issue is not conclusive, although it should be said that the role of memory (box 5 in Figure 6.6) has not been explicitly considered. My suggestion is that when making predictions people should be encouraged to record in writing not only their predictions (for comparison with subsequent results) but also the bases of their predictions—i.e. the cues they used in judgement, causal assumptions, and so forth. Such notes would be useful for two reasons: first, they would act as a means of bolstering memory; and second, taking notes would force people to consider both the bases of their judgement and the structure of the task. For example, experimental studies have shown that overconfidence in predictive judgment can be reduced when subjects are explicitly instructed to generate reasons that run counter to their opinions.[18]

Finally, what kinds of relations do people find more or less easy to learn? Experimental evidence indicates that linear (i.e. straight line) relations are easier to acquire than non-linear relations. Furthermore, positive relations are more readily recognized than negative ones. However, consistent with evidence in Chapter 2, when learning relations people tend to assume that such relations are less subject to random fluctuations than is, in fact, the case.[16]

## SUMMARY

This chapter has discussed problems involved in learning relations for predictive purposes. A number of points have been stressed: first, people learn primarily on the basis of what they can observe. However, many judgemental situations are structured in such a manner that one cannot observe the data necessary to infer relations; second, people have a tendency to seek information to confirm their ideas rather than to look for possible disconfirming evidence; third, positive feedback is weighted more heavily in memory than negative feedback; and fourth, the outcomes of judgement are the result of actions taken in specific environments. Furthermore, people are frequently unaware of the structure of the environment in which such actions take place and thus how to interpret outcomes.

In many situations it is not possible to untangle the different task and individual variables which cause the relation between judgements and outcomes to be complex. However, the individual can do two things over and above understanding the kinds of issues discussed in this chapter. First, an attempt can be made to bolster memory by recording both predictions and the bases of prediction. This should lead to heightened self-awareness of one's own judgement and of the nature of judgemental situations. Second, a rather special attitude of mind needs to be adopted. This is to accept the view that one does not necessarily learn from experience and, indeed, often cannot. As aptly summarized by the American humorist Will Rogers: 'It's not what we don't know that gives us trouble. It's what we know that ain't so.'

## NOTES AND REFERENCES

1. This chapter is largely based on H. J. Einhorn and R. M. Hogarth (1978). Confidence in judgment: Persistence of the illusion of validity, *Psychological Review*, **85**, 395–416.
2. See, for example, S. Lichtenstein, B. Fischhoff, and L. D. Phillips (1982). Calibration of probabilities: The state of the art to 1980. In D. Kahneman, P. Slovic, and A. Tversky (eds), *Judgment under Uncertainty: Heuristics and Biases*, Cambridge: Cambridge University Press, pp. 306–334.
3. See L. J. Chapman and J. P. Chapman (1969). Illusory correlation as an obstacle to the use of valid psychodiagnostic signs, *Journal of Abnormal Psychology*, **74**, 271–280.
4. See A. S. Elstein (1976). Clinical judgment: Psychological research and medical practice. *Science*, **194**, 696-700; and H. J. Einhorn and S. Schacht (1977). Decisions based on fallible clinical judgment. In M. Kaplan and S. Schwartz (eds), *Judgment and Decision Processes in Applied Settings*, New York: Academic Press, pp. 125–144.
5. For a review of these studies, see J. Crocker (1981). Judgment of covariation by social perceivers, *Psychological Bulletin*, **90**, 272–292; also H. J. Einhorn and R. M. Hogarth (1986). Judging probable cause, *Psychological Bulletin*, **99**, 3–19.
6. The example is taken from P. C. Wason (1960). On the failure to eliminate hypotheses in a conceptual task, *Quarterly Journal of Experimental Psychology*, **12**, 129–140. This, and some other interesting and related experiments are

summarized and discussed in P. C. Wason and P. N. Johnson-Laird (1972). *Psychology of Reasoning: Structure and Content*, London: Batsford.

7. For an illuminating discussion of this problem and, in particular, the conditions under which searching for confirming as opposed to disconfirming evidence is an appropriate strategy, see J. Klayman and Y.-W. Ha (in press). Confirmation, disconfirmation, and information in hypothesis testing, *Psychological Review*.

8. J. S. Bruner, J. J. Goodnow, and G. A. Austin (1956). *A Study of Thinking*. New York: Wiley. See also, B. Brehmer (1980). In one word: Not from experience, *Acta Psychologica*, **45**, 223–241.

9. This scenario was suggested by Hillel J. Einhorn, albeit in a different context. See R. M. Hogarth (1979). How valid is your judgement? *CEDEP Journal*, **3**, 47–56; also H. J. Einhorn (1980). Overconfidence in judgment. In R. Shweder (ed.), *New Directions for Methodology of Social and Behavioral Science: Fallible Judgment in Behavioral Research*, (Vol. 4), San Francisco, CA: Jossey-Bass.

10. This has been well known in industrial psychology for some time. See H. C. Taylor and J. J. Russell (1939). The relationship of validity coefficients to the practical effectiveness of tests in selection: Discussion and tables, *Journal of Applied Psychology*, **23**, 565–578. For a more recent discussion see Einhorn and Schacht, Reference 4.

11. L. Thomas (1983). *The Youngest Science: Notes of a Medicine Watcher*, New York: Viking, p. 22.

12. The figure is inspired by one in A. Bandura (1978). The self system in reciprocal determinism, *American Psychologist*, **33**, 344–358.

13. See W. K. Estes (1976). The cognitive side of probability learning, *Psychological Review*, **83**, 37–64; also W. K. Estes (1976). Some functions of memory in probability learning and choice behavior. In G. H. Bower (ed.), *The Psychology of Learning and Motivation*, Vol. 10, New York: Academic Press, pp. 1–45.

14. See P. Hirsch, (1969). *The Structure of the Popular Music Industry*, Ann Arbor, Michigan: Institute for Social Research, University of Michigan; and P. Hirsch (1972). Processing fads and fashions: An organization-set analysis of cultural industry systems, *American Journal of Sociology*, **77**, 639–659.

15. See L. R. Goldberg (1968). Simple models or simple processes? Some research on clinical judgments. *American Psychologist*, **23**, 483–496.

16. See Brehmer, Reference 8 above.

17. See, for example, K. R. Hammond, D. A. Summers, and D. H. Deane (1973). Negative effects of outcome-feedback on multiple-cue probability learning, *Organizational Behavior and Human Performance*, **9**, 30–34.

18. See A. Koriat, S. Lichtenstein, and B. Fischhoff (1980). Reasons for confidence. *Journal of Experimental Psychology: Human Learning and Memory*, **6**, 107–118; also S. J. Hoch (1985). Counterfactual reasoning and accuracy in predicting personal events, *Journal of Experimental Psychology: Learning, Memory, and Cognition*, **11**, 719–731.

# CHAPTER 7

# The role of memory in judgement

In the seventeenth century, the French nobleman and social critic La Roch-efoucauld said: 'Everybody complains about the badness of his memory, nobody about his judgement'. This statement has proved to be remarkably pertinent for at least two reasons: first, whereas judgement is still accorded a certain mystical status in our society, memory is not so revered; second, research on judgement points to the crucial role of memory in this process. Indeed, a good memory can be considered necessary although not sufficient for good judgement.

Memory affects judgement in several ways: the manner in which judgemental tasks are structured; cues that are selected, either from the environment and/or from the person's memory; the 'rule' used to process the information assessed to make the judgement; and the interpretation and 'coding' of the outcome of judgement. Consider, for example, the difference between a familiar and unfamiliar judgemental task (for instance, judging the distance needed to slow down your car in traffic as against predicting the date at which oil products will no longer be necessary for motor transport). In the former case, your memory of similar situations triggers responses which, in the past, have allowed you to cope with the situation. In the second task, however, most people would have trouble in even starting to think about the problem.

Memory affects the cues you use in prediction. You might remember, for example, that there is a relation between the level of economic activity in the country as a whole and your particular industrial sector. Thus when the general economic trend is up (or down) you would make a corresponding prediction for your own sector. At a more everyday level, you learn (and remember) that there is a relation between the external temperature and how warm or cold you feel. This leads you to predict what clothes will be suitable on a particular day, and so on.

Memory also affects the rules you use to process information. For example, when choosing between two candidates for a job you might well prefer the one whose profile reminds you most of a person who is now successful.[1] That is, you process the information concerning the candidates by comparison with some ideal. Your predictive judgement is then based on the degree of similarity between the profile you observe and the ideal profile you keep in memory. Finally, and as discussed in Chapter 6, memory of the outcomes of previous predictions affects expectations concerning the future.

This chapter contains three main sections. The first introduces the concepts of short- and long-term memory, discusses how these differ, and suggests that much of memory works by a process of active reconstruction rather than passive recall achieved in a manner similar to a tape- or video-recorder. Given the limited nature of human memory, the second section considers how particular information is selected for input to memory as well as processes and variables that affect the recall of specific information from memory. These themes are considered further in the third section which examines difficulties people have in attempting to recall past events accurately as well as some implications of these difficulties.

## SHORT- AND LONG-TERM MEMORY

Memory is the store that provides many if not most of the inputs to decision making. It is therefore important to understand how this store is organized and, in particular, the manner in which information can become distorted.[2]

In thinking about memory, the analogy of a computer or a video-recorder often springs to mind. In some respects, the analogy is appropriate in that these devices emphasize functions of information input, storage, and output or retrieval. Thus in conceptualizing how memory works, it is useful to ask: (a) How does information enter memory? (b) How is information stored in memory? and (c) How do people access and retrieve the contents of memory? The computer analogy, however, breaks down when we examine how human memory deals with each of these tasks.[3] In particular, and as already emphasized in Chapter 1, restrictions on memory capacity are an important aspect of human information-processing ability.

Psychologists typically make a distinction between two types of human memory. One of these, called *short-term memory*, refers to our memory for information that has just been received and on which operations are still being performed. The critical feature of short-term memory is that it is limited in capacity. In other words, one can only operate on a relatively small number of items of information at a given time. To illustrate, how many of the last words that you have just read can you recall accurately ? Most people, cannot recall *verbatim* more than one or two sentences. In fact, in many experiments psychologists have measured short-term memory capacity by a technique similar to the above example by asking people to remember strings of numbers or letters. Although limited, short-term memory can be thought of as the active part of our working memory. Moreover, it seems to work like a limited-capacity computer in that operations take place on information as it is read into or recalled from storage.

The second type of memory, called *long-term memory*, is the repository of our knowledge and corresponds to what most people think of as memory.

The operation of long-term memory also poses a paradox. That is, whereas we know that we cannot recall accurately words read more than a few sentences ago, we also know that we have immediate access to a multitude of facts and can remember details and events that occurred many years ago. Thus, perhaps memory is not that limited after all. To explain the paradox, we need to consider how long-term memory works.

To illustrate the operation of long-term memory, allow yourself limited exposure (say 20 seconds) to the letters written below, cover them up, and then see if you can recall them accurately.

N B R R Y N L G P T V C

Most people have great difficulty in recalling the above letters accurately after brief exposure. However, I can guarantee that you will be able to recall the above letters accurately long after you have finished reading this chapter, or indeed the whole book, and even if you never look at the letters again.

The preceding statement raises the important issue of what is meant by accuracy of recall. In operational terms, accuracy of memory is defined by the degree to which what is recalled matches the original information. However, note that since we cannot observe what happens to information in the human mind, accuracy of recall does not guarantee that a person actually 'remembers' the information to which he or she was exposed. To illustrate, there is a simple way to recall the above letters that does not involve rote memorization. This is to note that the letters represent the third letters of the months of the year written in order; thus, JaNuary, FeBruary, MaRch, ApRil, and so on. In other words, accurate recall does not necessarily depend on accurate memorization of the original information, but on knowing a 'code' that allows you to construct what you were supposed to remember.[4] In other words, if you know a code for 'encoding' information, you can greatly increase memory. Indeed, in listening to a lecture, or reading a book, hardly anyone tries to remember the text verbatim. Instead, one attempts to pick out the central ideas, and if asked to recall the content, will construct a representation of the text by building on the central ideas which are used as 'markers'. In recalling a joke, for example, one typically only needs to remember the initial conditions, some markers, and the 'punch line'. Thus when recounting the story, one starts from the initial conditions and constructs the story that leads to the (hopefully) amusing conclusion.

Although there is some controversy in the literature, most theorists now agree that, at the moment of recall, long-term memory works largely by a process of reconstruction. In other words, the paradox of memory is that long-term memory does not work by remembering what is actually recalled, but rather by remembering fragments of information that allow one to construct more complete representations of the information. Moreover, these fragments of information can be thought of as being linked in a net-like collection of associations. The richer the associations triggered by specific information, the more likely people are to be able to recall that information. Over time, people construct their own informal 'codes' for remembering information of importance to them. This means that they are often able to display great feats of memory in respect of information that is personally relevant to them. On the other hand, they have little memory for information drawn from areas that are novel to them and for which they have not yet constructed means of organizing such knowledge. Students, for example, often display impressive memory for facts of long-standing interest to them such as data concerning their favourite sports; but, to their instructors at least, the same students seem incapable of remembering a few stylized facts about subjects taught in class. On considering the implications of memory for the accuracy of information used in judgement and choice, therefore, it is important to understand what affects the encoding, and thus selection of information, as well as the process of decoding via reconstruction.

## SELECTION AND PROCESSING OF INFORMATION

Given limitations on human information-processing capacity, an important issue in the link between memory and judgement centres on why people implicitly construct their memories by focusing on particular pieces of information. A related issue concerns why some items are weighted more heavily in memory, and thus subsequent judgement, than others.

### Selective perception

As noted in Chapter 1, perception of information is not comprehensive but *selective*. First, anticipations of what we expect to see play a great role in what we do see and thus of what we remember. Second, the mind is not a vacuum. It not only receives information but actively seeks information which it attempts to incorporate within existing notions and thought patterns. Through experience, people develop an understanding of the world. Furthermore, they use that understanding to select information, to interpret it (i.e. give it 'meaning') and to anticipate events.

To illustrate, consider Figure 7.1. What do the drawings *A* and *B* mean to you? For most people, these figures are at first a meaningless series of

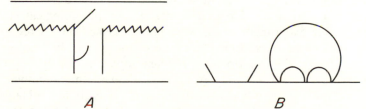

*A*                    *B*

Figure 7.1   From *Method and Theory in Experimental Psychology* by Charles E. Osgood. Copyright © by Oxford University Press Inc. (Reprinted by permission)

lines. However, if you are told that *A* represents 'A soldier and his dog passing by a hole in a picket fence' and *B* 'A washerwoman cleaning the floor', both series of lines take on a meaning of their own. Indeed, once you have been told what they represent, it is difficult not to see both the soldier and his dog and the washerwoman.

These illustrations, as well as the series of letters shown previously, emphasize that the efficiency of memory depends on being able to encode information in a way that it can subsequently be recalled and decoded in detail. Moreover, the key to efficient decoding depends on associating some form of meaning with the items or units to be remembered. Memory can and does work by reconstructing fragments of information into a whole that makes sense to the individual. Second, meaning guides our interpretation of what we see. For example, lines such as those in *A* and *B* of Figure 7.1 can be interpreted and take on a significance of their own. Indeed, newspaper cartoonists exploit precisely this feature of the human information-processing system by exaggerating particular characteristics of public figures in their drawings. Furthermore, anticipations of patterns a person expects to see (i.e. based on memory) can interfere quite strongly with what one does see.

A striking example of this latter phenomenon was provided in an experiment by Bruner and Postman.[5] Subjects were asked to recognize and name playing cards presented to them in conditions allowing only brief exposure. Included among the playing cards were several incongruent cards, such as a red ace of spades or black ace of hearts. Results of the experiment indicated that subjects both took longer to recognize and name incongruent cards and made more mistakes in doing so. For instance, on one occasion 27 of the 28 subjects made what the experimenters called a 'dominance' reaction: for example, red spades were reported as black or simply as hearts ( dominance was of both colour and shape); several subjects also sometimes reported 'compromise' colours, e.g. red spades were reported as brown; and so on. In short, when perception was incongruent with expectations, distortions occurred. If you believe, *a priori*, that hearts are red, the perception of black hearts is difficult and can even be stressful.

The implications of this admittedly artificial situation involving incongruity between memory of what one feels one should perceive and what is actually there are important. Moreover, it should be emphasized that this kind of distortion can also occur due to changes in our physiological state. For example, in one experiment words were briefly flashed on a screen in front of two groups of subjects. Subjects in one of the groups had not eaten for some time prior to the experiment, whereas subjects in the other group had eaten normally. Results of the experiment showed that members of the former ('starved') group reported having seen many more food-related words than those in the latter group. It has also been shown that witnesses in legal proceedings are often unable to report what they claim to have seen. Instead, they reconstruct what they think they should have seen. Furthermore, people can be quite confident in their mistaken memory.[6] All people who work in organizations are familiar with the occurrence of misunderstandings. The same facts can be remembered quite differently by different parties such that each comes to different conclusions concerning action.

To summarize, experience with the world teaches us to see certain things in given situations. Such expectations can be thought of as being embedded in memory which represents a network of associations related to particular objects or situations, etc. However, memory is not a complete record of all our experience. You cannot re-access all past processing in the same manner as a computer. Rather, it is fragments of experience which are remembered and the recall of total experiences takes place by reconstructing fragments in a manner that is coherent to the individual. The 'glue' used to reconstruct and make associations between fragments is the meaning people attach to fragments and their possible associations.

### Availability

Memory plays an important role in predictive judgement. In particular, Tversky and Kahneman argue that people use the ease with which they can imagine or recall instances from memory as a cue in determining intuitive judgements of frequency.[7] They term this judgemental rule the 'availability' heuristic (see also Chapter 3).

For example, consider the following questions:[7]

(1)   How familiar are you with the letter $k$? If you sample a word at random from a text in English, is it more likely that the word starts with a $k$ or that it has $k$ as its third letter?
(2)   Are words beginning with $re$ more or less frequent than words ending with $re$?
(3)   If there are 10 people from whom a committee can be formed, how many different committees of size 2 can be formed. How many different committees of size 8 can be formed? How do your answers to these questions differ?

The answers to the questions are as follows: (1) $k$ is more likely to be the third letter of a word than the first; (2) more words end with $re$ than begin with $re$, and (3) the number of committees of size 2 that can be formed from 10 people is 45. This is the same as the number of committees of size 8. How did these answers compare with yours?

Most people tend to answer these questions incorrectly. Why? Tversky and Kahneman argue that in answering these questions a plausible judgemental strategy is to think of instances with the requisite characteristics, for example words with $k$ as the first or third letter, words beginning or ending with $re$, and how many 2- or 8-person committees can be formed from groups of 10 people. Words that begin with $k$ do seem easier to recall than those with $k$

as the third letter (consider *king* as opposed to *acknowledge*); similarly it is easy to think of words beginning with *re*, such as *remember, recall, return*, but the fact that several common words end with *re* is not recalled so easily, viz, *there, therefore, were, are*. The committee problem is more subtle. It is somehow easier to imagine more arrangements of 2 out of 10 as opposed to 8 out of 10. However, it should be noted that for every arrangement of 2 people in the committee, there is a corresponding arrangement of 8 people outside the committee. Thus, if you realize that the definitions of being in and out of the committee can be switched, the number of possible arrangements of 2 clearly equals that of 8.[7]

The availability heuristic can therefore lead to bias in judgement if one always assumes correspondence between the ease with which a cue or event can be recalled or reconstructed from memory and its relative frequency.

As indicated in Chapter 3, the presence of bias due to using the availability heuristic has also been documented outside the artificial tasks considered above. Experiments have tested, for example, people's intuitive notions concerning the relative frequency of diseases or causes of death. The relative frequencies of diseases or causes that receive much publicity, for example homicide, cancer or tornadoes, tend to be overestimated, whereas other less newsworthy causes such as asthma and diabetes are underestimated.[8] Clearly the 'evidence' with which we are confronted in daily life plays a major role in determining—through memory—our anticipations of the relative frequency of events. Furthermore, such evidence is often incomplete. For example, when an aeroplane crashes or is hijacked the event is newsworthy and people are made aware of the occurrence. Furthermore, over time one can become aware of increasing trends of crashes or hijackings. However, since flights that occur without incidents are not reported in the media, people cannot know differences in the *relative* frequencies of crashes or hijacks across time. Thus if the total number of flights increases across time, the rate of the relative frequency of incidents could, in fact, decrease.

The availability heuristic can also induce bias in judgements of relative frequency even when people are aware of non-occurrences. For example, in a study of assessments of mortality rates following surgery, two groups of surgeons working in specialties characterized by high (2.42%) and low (0.44%) mortality rates were asked to assess different mortality rates. Whereas surgeons from both specialties correctly estimated that the mortality rate was higher in one group than in the other, assessments of the overall service mortality rate was biased by group membership. Specifically, surgeons in the high mortality group estimated the overall rate to be double that estimated by the low mortality surgeons.[9]

The above result is, of course, a case of 'professional deformation'. People have a natural tendency to interpret their own experiences and corresponding anticipations as normal. This leads to underestimating the extent to which the experiences of others can imply different sets of expectations. Since people usually interact largely with those of similar backgrounds and inclinations, such assumptions are often quite functional. However, when dealing with people (or problems) of other cultures, or even professional backgrounds, expectations based on 'inappropriate' memory can be dysfunctional.

## Concrete information

In Chapter 3, it was noted that people often fail to take account of so-called 'base-rate' information in judgement.* Recall, for example, the problem involving the Green and Blue taxi cabs where it was argued that failure to use base-rate information in judgement was due to its lack of causal significance. That is, if base-rate data were not seen to be causally relevant, they were ignored or down-played. Another, and not exclusive hypothesis, is that base-rate data are typically of an abstract, pallid and statistical nature and lack the vivid, concrete impact of specific information in memory. That is, whereas base-rate data can be comprehended, and possibly remembered, at an unemotional, cognitive level, concrete, specific case-data are frequently emotionally loaded and thus encoded and remembered on several dimensions with a correspondingly rich set of meaningful associations.[10] And indeed, experiments on memory do show that people are more likely to remember information that has been encoded on several sensory dimensions[11] (for example, information presented in the form of words and images is more easily and accurately recalled than information presented only in verbal form).

The hypothesis of the salience of concrete over abstract information dates back to at least 1927 when Bertrand Russell noted that 'popular induction depends upon the emotional interest of the instances, not upon their number'.[12] The following example serves to illustrate the point.

Let us suppose that you wish to buy a new car and have decided on grounds of economy and longevity that you want to purchase one of those solid, stalwart, middle class Swedish cars—either a Volvo or a Saab. As a prudent and sensible buyer, you go to *Consumer Reports*, which informs you that the consensus of their experts is that the Volvo is mechanically superior, and the consensus of the readership is that the Volvo has the better repair record. Armed with this information, you decide to go and strike a bargain with the Volvo dealer before the week is out. In the interim, however, you go to a cocktail party where you announce this intention to an acquaintance. He reacts with disbelief and alarm: 'A Volvo! You've got to be kidding. My brother-in-law had a Volvo. First, that fancy fuel injection computer thing went out. 250 bucks. Next he started having trouble with the rear end. Had to replace it. Then the transmission and the clutch. Finally sold it in three years for junk'. The logical status of this information is that the $N$ (i.e. number)† of several

---

* The distinction was made in Chapter 3 between 'base-rate' and 'specific' (or case) data. In predicting a target event, base-rate data should be moderated by specific data. Consider, for example, the prediction of whether someone (specific data) with a given type of qualification (base-rate data) will be successful in a particular job.
† Parentheses added.

140

hundred Volvo-owning *Consumer Reports* readers has been increased by one, and the mean frequency of repair record shifted up by an iota on three or four dimensions. However, anyone who maintains that he would reduce the encounter to such a net informational effect is either disingenuous or lacking in the most elemental self-knowledge.[13]

The effects of concrete over abstract information, such as in the above 'thought experiment', have been demonstrated in a number of experiments performed by Borgida, Nisbett and their colleagues as well as being evident in several real-life incidents. In one experiment, Borgida and Nisbett tested the extent to which students' choices of courses were affected by statistical base-rate data (statistical summaries of course appreciation forms) on the one hand, and the live comments of individual students who had taken the courses, on the other.[14] It was found that the comments of single individuals concerning their experience with courses had greater effects on choice than the more representative statistical data. Real life analogues of this experiment include: the observation that in the 1930s American farmers did not adopt early techniques of the Green Revolution after receiving pamphlets and other such information about the new procedures. However, they were converted when they observed the successful use of new procedures by a neighbour; the dramatized increase in waiting lists at cancer detection clinics following the highly publicized mastectomies performed on Mrs Ford and Mrs Rockefeller; the discounting of results of public opinion polls by members of the press following McGovern's presidential campaign in 1972 who were used to observing McGovern being acclaimed by large, enthusiastic crowds;[13] the reluctance of small businessmen who, despite apparently full information from governmental sources, are reluctant to effect necessary relocations on planned industrial sites until they observe other businessmen moving to the site;[15] and physicians' tendencies to discount treatment reports in the medical literature if they have already had a successful experience with a different treatment.[16] Information that involves personal experience or observation of incidents remains salient in memory. Indeed, this phenomenon is frequently exploited in different forms of propaganda. Consider, for example, the use of single examples, personal testimonials and vignettes in advertising. Opponents and proponents in debates on social issues such as abortion, capital punishment and nuclear power will argue with incidents or statistics as it suits them. For instance, if people living within a certain radius of the proposed site of a new nuclear power plant are told that it is possible that the construction will involve a miniscule reduction in life expectancy for the community, no alarm will result. However, if the same information is translated into, say, the expectation of two additional cancer-induced deaths, results are likely to be quite different.[17] During a period of public debate concerning, for example, capital punishment, it is well known that an incident involving a single person (e.g. a 'lifer' who escapes and commits another crime), can have a most dramatic effect.

In one study, an article from the *New Yorker* which detailed the pathology of a single 'stereotypic' welfare case had greater effect on people's attitudes toward welfare than more appropriate data summarizing overall welfare use.[18] In another experiment, it was shown that vividness of information can have a delayed effect on judgement. Subjects in this study were required to read a brief transcript of a legal case in which the vividness of the arguments for the prosecution and the defence were experimentally manipulated. After reading the case, subjects initially judged the defendant no more harshly whether the arguments for the prosecution or defence had been presented more vividly. However, a second set of judgements made 24 hours later revealed a different picture. Subjects' judgements swung to the side (i.e. prosecution or defence) for which the arguments had been presented more vividly.[19]

People remember *incidents* and these weigh heavily in judgement.

## INTERPRETING THE PAST

Our memories can be thought of as providing our private records of the past. However, as noted above, memory is not only a record of what one may have actually experienced; it can also reflect anticipations of what one thought one was going to experience prior to the event. Similarly, to what extent can memory be affected by information acquired *after* the event being recalled?

### Eyewitness testimony

Imagine that a person has witnessed an event and is subsequently asked to recall what happened. If the process of recall is based on reconstruction, it follows that the person's memory can also be affected by what happens *after* the critical event. Indeed, research shows that recall can be influenced by post-event information and particularly by the manner in which questions are asked to elicit information about the event.[20]

One form of 'misleading' question involves logical presuppositions. To illustrate, subjects in an experimental situation witness a film of a car accident and are then questioned about certain details. Questions can, however, be asked in two ways, one of which directly challenges the subject's ability to remember specific details, and the other which does not. As examples, consider 'Did you see *a* broken headlight?' as opposed to 'Did you see *the* broken headlight?' Whereas the first question implies doubt about the presence of a broken headlight, note that the second presupposes the existence of a broken headlight and simply asks whether or not the subject saw it. For someone who was unable to attend to all details when witnessing the event, the broken headlight suggested by the second question can easily become integrated into memory. This kind of effect has been demonstrated in several studies and can operate in quite subtle ways. For example, consider the following question: 'About how fast were the cars going when they *smashed* into each other?' When the word *smashed* is replaced by *bumped, collided, contacted*, or *hit*, quite different 'memories' for the speed at which the cars were travelling are obtained. Studies also show that people are particularly prone to the effects of misleading questions when there is a long delay between the occurrence of the event and the moment of recall as well as when the misleading presupposition is contained in complex as opposed to simple language. It is thought that complex language can divert a person's attention from the presupposition implanted within it. Warning people ahead of time of the possibility of misleading questions does, however, help them from falling prey to these effects.

Given limited information-processing ability, people use whatever cues are available to them to help them recall events. Unfortunately, these cues may be based on information received after the event and are not necessarily valid. For example, one may initially have only vague memories of an event, but the very act of recounting the incident to another person, and particularly many times, can change one's impression of a vague memory to that of a precisely recalled event. Many people, for example, have precise memories for incidents that occurred when they were young children. Typically, however, these memories have been reinforced through the years by recounting stories at different family gatherings. In similar manner, a witness can become artificially more certain of his or her testimony simply by recounting it on several occasions.

These findings have important implications for gathering evidence in decision making situations. Specifically, one should avoid asking witnesses too many direct questions. Instead witnesses should be asked to recount what they know in as open a way as possible. If one does ask direct questions, and this is often necessary, it is important not to bias these using logical presuppositions. Moreover, one should empathize with the witness and realize that in many cases it is simply not possible to recall all details.

### Hindsight bias

Was World War II inevitable? Was Neville Chamberlain deluding himself about the relative possibilities of peace and war when he returned from his historic discussions with Adolf Hitler in Munich? Was the Japanese attack on Pearl Harbour predictable? Should the West have foreseen the possibility of an Arab oil embargo (not to speak of its economic consequences) prior to 1973? Should the United States have realized the consequences of its initial engagement in Vietnam as early as 1964?

With the benefit of hindsight, the answer to these questions is a definite 'yes.' Yet how is it that people failed to make the appropriate predictions in all these cases? Furthermore, why is it that the erroneous judgements that were made or preceded the above events were (with only a few exceptions) not called into question?

One way of thinking about this issue is to put yourself in a situation which involves making a prediction about the future. Consider the following passage which describes a historical situation in the early nineteenth century with which most people are unfamiliar.

> For some years after the arrival of Hastings as governor-general of India, the consolidation of British power involved serious war. The first of these took place on the northern frontier of Bengal where the British were faced by the plundering raids of the Gurkhas of Nepal. Attempts had been made to stop the raids by an exchange of lands, but the Gurkhas would not give up their claims to country under British control, and Hastings decided to deal with them once and for all. The campaign began in November 1814. It was not glorious. The Gurkhas were only some 12,000 strong; but they were brave fighters, fighting in territory well suited to their raiding tactics. The older British commanders were used to war in the plains where the enemy ran away from a resolute attack. In the mountains of Nepal it was not easy to find the enemy. The troops and transport animals suffered from the extremes of heat and cold, and the officers learned caution only after sharp reverses. Major-General Sir D. Ochterlony was the one commander to escape from these minor defeats.[21]

Now would you be surprised to learn after the event that it was the Gurkhas who won the above war and who were subsequently able to negotiate a satisfactory (for them) peace treaty with the British? The terrain in which the Gurkhas were able to take the battle was, after all, better suited to their tactics and experience than to the British. A modern equivalent in differences in tactics and conditions is provided, for example, by certain aspects of the Vietnam war. Re-read the passage and think carefully about the significance of the different statements for predicting the outcome of the war.

Once you have been told the outcome of an uncertain situation, two things seem to happen. First, the outcome seems, with hindsight, to be inevitable. For example, Chamberlain should have realized the true nature of Hitler's intentions. Second, one can see a direct relation between certain other events or 'cues' and what actually happened: for instance in the Chamberlain case the growing strength of the German armed forces, the attitudes and acts of the Nazis towards Jews, and so on. Indeed, after the event, we can easily interpret why things happened as they did. There seems to have been a kind of 'creeping determinism'—that is, what happens seems to flow on naturally from the preceding events.

Fischhoff and his colleagues have tested people's so-called 'hindsight' biases in a number of ways. First, Fischhoff presented subjects with unfamiliar passages such as the description of the British–Gurkha war given above. He then asked them to make probabilistic predictions concerning several possible outcomes.[22] He also gave different groups different information about the actual outcome: correct information concerning the outcome of the event; false information concerning the outcome; and no information about the outcome. Subjects were also asked to indicate which items of information in the passages were particularly relevant to their judgements. Results of the experiment indicated: (1) outcome 'knowledge' affected subjects' responses in that those events which were announced as actually having occurred were judged as more likely to occur (recall false as well true outcome information was given to different groups of subjects concerning the same events); and (2) the relevance attributed by subjects to particular pieces of information was related to the outcomes they had been given.

In another study (not conducted with historical scenarios), subjects were asked to make probabilistic predictions concerning current affairs.[23] This took place on the eve of President Nixon's visits to China and the USSR in 1972. The kinds of events for which subjects were asked to assess probabilities were of the form:

China: (1) The USA will establish a permanent diplomatic mission in Peking, but not grant diplomatic recognition;
(2) President Nixon will meet Mao at least once;
(3) President Nixon will announce that his trip was successful.

USSR: (1) A group of Soviet Jews will be arrested attempting to speak with President Nixon;
(2) The USA and the USSR will agree to a joint space program.[23]

Subjects made their probabilistic predictions before Nixon's visits and, some time after the visits, were unexpectedly asked to recall what their probabilistic predictions had been. In addition, they were asked to indicate whether they thought the actual events had occurred. Results showed that subjects' recollections of the probabilities of events that had occurred were larger than the probabilities they assigned before the events did occur. There was also a tendency for the recalled probabilities of events that did not occur to be lower than the probabilities initially assigned. With hindsight, the subjects were apparently not too 'surprised' by what did and what did not happen.

The knowledge that an event has occurred seems to restructure memory. Our memory of the past is not a memory of the uncertainties of the past, rather it is a reconstruction of past events in terms of what actually occurred. Furthermore, the past is structured in a way that makes coherent sense to the individual, for example concerning the relation between what actually happened and particular (but not all) antecedent events.

### Hindsight versus foresight

What is the difference between foresight (i.e. predicting into the future) and hindsight (i.e. looking backwards)? When we look forward it is not clear what particular events or chain of events will or will not lead to the occurrence or non-occurrence of the event of interest to us. Many different paths could lead, or fail to lead, to the uncertain outcome. Furthermore, 'unexpected' events occur with an alarming frequency. Who, for example, a year before the event, would have predicted the election of a Polish Pope in 1978? However, in the mid-1980s this event seems in retrospect to have been almost inevitable given both apparent disagreements among Italian cardinals and the role of the Catholic Church in Poland. Prediction requires considerable powers of imagination and both the ability and willingness to entertain several hypotheses simultaneously. Keeping one's options open is not a tidy exercise and can induce considerable anxiety.

Postdiction, or hindsight, on the other hand, requires little imagination and is an invitation to impose a causal structure on a sequence of past events. Furthermore, subjectively there is less uncertainty than in prediction problems concerning the events that 'caused' what happened. One can believe any chain that seems plausible since it was seen to precede the event.

## Implications of hindsight bias

The marked presence of hindsight biases in the studies by Fischhoff and his colleagues raises a number of important issues concerning: (a) judgements of the apparent failures (and successes) of others; (b) distortions in memory; (c) overcoming bias; and (d) learning from experience.

### Judging others

History will undoubtedly remember Chamberlain as the person who failed to understand Hitler's true intentions in 1938. With the benefit of hindsight, we all condemn Chamberlain for his lack of foresight. Furthermore, Chamberlain-like incidents and corresponding condemnations occur with alarming frequency in most organizations. Comments are commonly heard such as 'Surely Bill must have known that our competitors were going to start a rival campaign at that time. All indications pointed to just that.'* However, it is not necessarily true that Chamberlain's judgement was any more defective than that of many other people of his day. But his judgement was made public and events proved him wrong. In the same vein, Fischhoff cites the case of what happened when a certain 'life' prisoner absconded from the Oregon State Penitentiary when released on an overnight social pass.[22] The warden of the prison promptly came under heavy fire from both the local newspaper and the Governor of the State of Oregon. It should have been known, it was said, that in the light of the particular prisoner's criminal

---

* The writer recalls an incident in an organization known to him where no-one made any comment on certain predictions inherent in the annual budget. However, when it became clear that a particular source of funds would fail to materialize, many people wanted to indict the person responsible for his lack of 'judgement'.

record, there was a high probability he would abscond. However, in defence of the prison warden, it should be added that the man with the bad criminal record had also been a model prisoner. Perhaps, as Fischhoff suggests, the only way to test whether the warden should be blamed for his decision to issue a passs, would be to ask wardens of other prisons to examine the records of several prisoners (including that of the absconding prisoner presented in anonymous form), and to see what their predictions would have been. With hindsight, the decision to issue a pass seems to have been a terrible mistake. At the time the decision was taken it might have been reasonable, given what was known.

*Distortions in memory*

Memory plays tricks with judgement in allowing rationalizations after the event. Above I have indicated cases where we are quick to blame others for apparently avoidable errors. However, it also follows that people may take the wrong decision and yet get away with it in that history—i.e. our hindsightful judgement—does not blame them. Indeed, given the above results, one should ask whether attributions of foresight with which many 'great' men have been credited may have had fortuitous origins. For example, was Lord Nelson just lucky in the decisions he made in his crucial naval battles?

Hindsight bias implies distortion in memory. However, one should also note that in many circumstances this can be functional for the individual. Most of our learning about the environment (see Chapter 6) is based on observing or experiencing relations between events that occur. Furthermore, given the limited capacity of memory, it is important to store and organize events in a coherent manner that allows recall. Our environments are characterized more by the lack than the presence of useful relations and thus it is clearly economical (in terms of memory) to concentrate and remember those that work. Similarly, forgetting relations that you tried but that did not work is also 'cost-effective'.[24] For example, when you drive a car you learn a relation between turning the steering wheel and your position on the road. You do not need to learn that depressing the clutch pedal in a certain way will not cause the car to move to the right. Many relations which we use in daily life can be comprehended by observation or experience of the occurrence of two events. Indeed, it could be said that the majority of our judgements—which involve mainly short-term physical actions (e.g. judging distance when walking so as not to bump into objects or people)—are of this nature. Restructuring one's understanding of the world in terms of what is observed to happen is useful, adaptive behaviour. Furthermore, we are so proficient at doing this that it is carried out continuously at an unconscious level.

However, as noted in Chapter 6, learning relations only by what is observable can lead to biases. Noting non-occurrences is often also necessary for inferring relations. In particular, prediction problems which are difficult in the sense that outcome feedback is either delayed or biased by the environment, require observation of non-occurrences to validate relations (see Chapter 6). These problems typically involve conceptual rather than physical relations (for example, predicting a candidate's future success in a particular job as opposed to avoiding the tea-trolley in the corridor), and can have important consequences. As discussed briefly in Chapter 1, the nature of the human environment is changing in the sense that conceptual skills are becoming more important than physical skills. Use of higher mental processes places great demands on memory (e.g. requiring that attention be directed to non-occurrences as well as occurrences of events as discussed in Chapter 6). Distortions in memory induced by knowledge of outcomes are therefore not only an important source of bias. They are becoming increasingly important as demands for conceptual skills grow.

### Overcoming bias

Is it possible to 'debias' distortions in memory caused by outcome knowledge? In one experiment, Fischhoff explicitly warned subjects of possible biases due to knowledge of outcomes. However, this manipulation had no effect in that the subjects warned of hindsight bias exhibited the same degree of bias as subjects who had not been warned.[25] People have a remarkable capacity for assimilating facts as being consistent with their preceding notions and thus seeming as though they 'knew it all along'. For example, how many times do people exhibit surprise when being told the result of an investigation, be it a scientific study, a market research report or a judicial enquiry? It has been said, and in the writer's experience justifiably so, that there are three stages in attitudes toward certain types of investigation. First, the investigators are told that what they propose to do is impossible.* (Imagine, for example, a study proposed in a business firm to investigate the efficiency of TV advertising.) Second, when people are told the results of the study they typically comment on how these seem evident. ('Sure, the more you advertise on TV the more you sell.') And third, when people accept the implications of findings they either say that they 'knew it all along' or that they already do it. ('Of course, that's why we advertise on TV.')

How can one overcome the biasing effect of outcome knowledge and so force people to realize the real significance of events? In the context of reporting results of scientific experiments, Slovic and Fischhoff attacked this problem by first giving their subjects false information concerning the outcomes of the experiments.[26] Once the subjects had been told and had assimilated the false outcomes they were then given the true results. This

---

* The author has had precisely this experience when starting several research projects—an attitude expressed by both scientists and laymen. Indeed, when people do not tell me a project is 'impossible' I now seriously question whether it is worthwhile!

manipulation was found to be quite successful in that it overcame 'hindsight' bias. That is, it seems that when the true experimental results were made known, subjects were forced to 'undo' the mental effort they had previously expended in assimiliating the false outcomes with their prior notions. That is, giving knowledge of the true outcomes following the false information provided a stimulus capable of overcoming hindsight bias.

Now, without looking back, do you recall who won the British–Gurkha war described earlier in the chapter? Why did the Gurkhas win?

In fact, it was the British who won that particular war. Look back at the passage. After the passage, I deliberately gave you false 'outcome feedback' in order to illustrate the point made above concerning means to debias the effects of outcome feedback.

*Learning from experience*

The experiments on hindsight bias raise a number of questions concerning both people's ability to learn from experience and to make predictions. Consider, for example, the fact that outcomes fail to surprise people as much as they should. This has several implications: first, failure to be surprised implies that people apparently thought they had little to learn in the first instance. In other words, outcomes are not instructive. However, predictive 'track records' often indicate considerable inconsistencies (as documented throughout this book) and the expression of excessive confidence in predictive judgement is a common human failing. Learning from experience (as also discussed in Chapter 6) is thus not evident, and memory distortions may also often be functional for the individual. It would seem that nature has determined a trade-off between two kinds of costs: storage in memory and learning from experience. A real issue to be faced is whether that trade-off is appropriate in today's world.

A second implication of lack of outcome surprise concerns people's ability to construct causal explanations. There can be little doubt that the ability to construct good causal explanations is important in prediction, since accurate prediction depends on identifying key variables in the environment and their relation to the event predicted. However, if people are unduly influenced by knowledge of outcomes in explaining the past, this means that they will accept sufficient (although not necessary) explanations too easily. For example, if increases in TV advertising appear to precede increases in the sales of the product advertised, it is easy to adopt a causal model that advertising leads to sales. However, other explanations are possible, for example corresponding availability of products at points of sale, salesmen being told to make special efforts at the time of advertising campaigns, and so on. A major problem of many *post-hoc* explanations is that they are not, and indeed often cannot be, put to predictive test. If people accept outcome explanations too easily, this reduces the discipline of seeking alternative explanations for phenomena observed in the past and, as a consequence, the ability to imagine and create alternative causal scenarios for predicting the future. As discussed in Chapter 6, people rarely seek information that could negate their preconceptions, rather they look for possible confirming evidence. This tendency clearly interacts with the fallibility of memory discussed here in producing biased conceptions of the world.

A further important source of bias in interpreting outcomes arises from the fact that outcomes result from both actions people take and chance occurrences in the environment. As discussed in Chapter 2, people do not have good intuitions concerning the nature of randomness, and this can lead to errors in interpreting events. In particular, people are remarkably insensitive at determining whether outcomes should be attributed to their skill in a particular situation or to chance factors. Indeed, factors of chance and skill are closely intertwined in people's experience. For example, to what extent is your present job due to skill on your part or some combinaton of chance factors or both? This is a difficult question. However, there is disturbing evidence from psychological experiments that even in situations which people know have been governed by chance mechanisms (e.g. coin tossing), observations of success at a task are followed by attributions of skill. Furthermore, attempts to debias the supposed causes of observed phenomena fail. It seems that once memory of an outcome has been assigned a cause, it is extremely hard to erase that cause–effect relation in the person's mind. In particular, in chance–skill situations there is a strong tendency to assign the observation of success to skill, and the observation of failure to chance.[27]

What remedies exist to correct the judgemental fallibilities noted above? I can only repeat what has been said in earlier chapters: first, an attitude of mind which is prepared both to admit the operation of chance factors and the possibility of multiple explanations; and second, to bolster memory by record-keeping. People should be encouraged to record both their predictions and the bases on which predictive judgements are made.

## SUMMARY

This chapter has considered the role of memory in predictive judgement. Discussion of memory as an integral part of intuitive judgement has not, however, been restricted to this chapter since it also affects the topics treated in other chapters.

It was emphasized at the outset that memory is not like the dump store of a computer where all past experience exists and can be referenced intact. Rather, human memory is limited and would seem to depend on two basic principles. First, information can be encoded in more or less efficient ways and this acts to increase or decrease what is recalled, i.e. memory capacity. Second, the coding process itself depends upon the meaning attached to information. This meaning both holds information and associations together in memory and permits recall of events. However, recall is based on fragments of information which the mind construes as a coherent whole according to the meaning attached to the particular fragments recalled and their associations. Perception of events, their interpretation, and extrapolation to future events (i.e. prediction), thus depend crucially on a limited, fallible, incomplete system which is held together by the meaning given to events in the environment, such meaning itself being a function of previous perception and experiences. Although deficient in many respects, people's memories usually work remarkably well for a wide variety of tasks. And forgetting can often be as adaptive and functional as remembering. Indeed, mnemonists (people with phenomenal memory) indicate considerable dysfunctional aspects of 'excessive' memory—inability to infer useful rules from the environment, for example, or in more familiar terms incapacity to 'see the wood for the trees'.[28] On the other hand, in a world that places increasingly greater demands on conceptual skills, deficiencies in ordinary memory become more critical.

Why is some information more salient in memory and thus weighed more heavily in judgement than other data? The chapter explored and discussed the 'availability' heuristic whereby estimates of frequency are related to the ease with which specific instances can be imagined or recalled. The fact that vivid, concrete 'case data' often outweigh more representative, but abstract and pallid statistical data was also discussed and illustrated. Incidents, which can be encoded on several sensory dimensions (e.g. sight and sound) and which relate to one's experience with the world, weigh heavily in memory and thus in subsequent judgement.

The chapter also discussed the fallibilities of eyewitness testimony and explored people's hindsight bias or the phenomenon of 'creeping determinism' whereby, in retrospect, past events seem to have been inevitable. Once the outcome of an event is known, memory of events that preceded the outcome are reconstructed in a manner that distorts prior perceptions. Hindsight bias has important implications for how people judge others, the ability to learn from experience and to imagine, construct, and entertain alternative explanatory hypotheses. Finally, to improve predictive ability the necessity to bolster memory by good record-keeping was again emphasized.

## NOTES AND REFERENCES

1. This would be an example of the 'representativeness' heuristic. See D. Kahneman and A. Tversky (1972). Subjective probability: A judgment of representativeness, *Cognitive Psychology*, **3**, 430–454.
2. It should be pointed out that the interpretation given here to how memory 'works' is personal. Memory is, in fact, a hotly disputed and actively researched area in psychology. My own views on the topic have been heavily influenced by A. Baddeley (1976). *The Psychology of Memory*, New York: Basic Books.
3. See, for example, W. K. Estes (1980). Is human memory obsolete? *American Scientist*, **68**, 62-69.
4. The classical reference concerning the use of coding systems in memory is G. A. Miller (1956). The magical number seven, plus or minus two: Some limits on

our capacity for processing information. *Psychological Review*, **63**, 81–96.

5. See J. S. Bruner and L. J. Postman (1949). On the perception of incongruity: A paradigm, *Journal of Personality*, **18**, 206–223.

6. See, for example, R. Buckhout (1974). Eyewitness testimony, *Scientific American*, **231**, 23–31; and E. F. Loftus (1979). *Eyewitness Testimony*, Cambridge, MA: Harvard University Press.

7. See A. Tversky and D. Kahneman (1973). Availability: A heuristic for judging frequency and probability, *Cognitive Psychology*, **5**, 207–232.

8. See S. Lichtenstein, P. Slovic, B. Fischhoff, M. Layman, and B. Combs (1978). Judged frequency of lethal events, *Journal of Experimental Psychology: Human Learning and Memory*, **4**, 551–578; also B. Combs and P. Slovic (1979). Newspaper coverage of causes of death, *Journalism Quarterly*, **56**, 837–843; 849.

9. See D. E. Detmer, D. G. Fryback, and K. Gassner (1978). Heuristics and biases in medical decision-making, *Journal of Medical Education*, **53**, 682–683.

10. See R. P. Abelson (1976). Script processing in attitude formation and decision making. In J. S. Carroll and J. W. Payne (eds), *Cognition and Social Behavior*, Hillsdale, NJ: Lawrence Erlbaum, pp. 33–45.

11. See, for example, A. Paivio (1969). Mental imagery in associative learning and memory. *Psychological Review*, **76**, 241–263.

12. B. R. Russell. (1927). *Philosophy*, New York: Norton, p. 269.

13. R. E. Nisbett, E. Borgida, R. Crandall, and H. Reed. Popular induction: Information is not necessarily informative. In Carroll and Payne, Reference 10, p.129.

14. See E. Borgida and R. E. Nisbett (1977). The differential impact of abstract vs. concrete information on decisions, *Journal of Applied Social Psychology*, **7**, 258–271. Whereas I argue quite strongly here for the effects of concrete information, it should also be pointed out that these effects have not always been observed in experimental studies. See the review paper by S. E. Taylor and S. C. Thompson. (1982). Stalking the elusive 'vividness' effect, *Psychological Review*, **89**, 155–181.

15. See R. M. Hogarth, C. Michaud, and J.-L. Mery (1980). Decision behavior in urban development: A methodological approach and substantive considerations, *Acta Psychologica*, **45**, 95–117.

16. See K. Knafl and G. Burkett (1975). Professional socialization in a surgical specialty: Acquiring medical judgment, *Social Science of Medicine*, **9**, 397–404.

17. See P. Slovic, B. Fischhoff, and S. Lichtenstein. Cognitive processes and societal risk taking. In Carroll and Payne, Reference 10, pp. 165–184.

18. R. Nisbett and L. Ross (1980). *Human Inference: Strategies and Shortcomings of Social Judgment,* Englewood Cliffs, NJ: Prentice-Hall, p. 57.

19. See R. M. Reyes, W. L. Thompson, and G. H. Bower (1980). Judgmental biases resulting from differing availabilities of arguments *Journal of Personality and Social Psychology*, **39**, 2–12.

20. For highly readable accounts of research on eyewitness testimony, see Loftus, Reference 6; also G. L. Wells and E. F. Loftus (eds) (1984). *Eyewitness Testimony: Psychological Perspectives,* Cambridge: Cambridge University Press.

21. E. L. Woodward (1938). *Age of Reform*, London: Oxford University Press, pp. 383–384.

22. See B. Fischhoff (1975). Hindsight ≠ foresight: The effect of outcome knowledge on judgment under uncertainty, *Journal of Experimental Psychology: Human Perception and Performance*, **1**, 288–299. For a replication of this type of experiment in a business setting, see T. A. Buchman (1985). An effect of hindsight on predicting bankruptcy with accounting information, *Accounting, Organizations and Society*, **10**, 267–286.

23. See B. Fischhoff and R. Beyth (1975). 'I knew it would happen'—Remembered

probabilities of once-future things, *Organizational Behavior and Human Performance*, **13**, 1–16.

24. For a fascinating discussion on this topic, see M. Toda (1962). The design of a fungus-eater: A model of human behavior in an unsophisticated environment, *Behavioral Science*, **7**, 164–183.

25. See B. Fischhoff (1977). Perceived informativeness of facts, *Journal of Experimental Psychology: Human Perception and Performance*, **3**, 349–358.

26. See P. Slovic and B. Fischhoff (1977). On the psychology of experimental surprises, *Journal of Experimental Psychology: Human Perception and Performance*, **3**, 544–551.

27. See the instructive paper by E. J. Langer (1977). The psychology of chance, *Journal for the Theory of Social Behaviour*, **7**, 185–207.

28. See S. R. Luria (1968). *The Mind of a Mnemonist*, New York: Basic Books.

# CHAPTER 8

# Creativity, imagination, and choice

Imagination and creativity play key roles in judgement and choice. For example, predictive judgement requires the ability to imagine possible outcomes, or at least to assess the relative likelihood of different outcomes. Similarly, in many choice situations alternatives are not given but must be created. Furthermore, in the act of choice the ability to imagine how one would like different alternatives is crucial (i.e. in the expression of preference). Indeed, it can be said that a person who exhibits neither creativity nor imagination is incapable of expressing 'free' judgement or choice. Such a person would have no control over his or her behaviour, which would be determined entirely by the whims of the environment.

In making choices, therefore, people use imagination. It also follows that to the extent that a person has large powers of imagination, the more rich and varied are his or her choice alternatives. This point has already been mentioned in preceding chapters. It was pointed out, for example, that one cause of poor predictive performance was failure to conceive of different possibilities in the environment. In addition, reliance on habit in choice (for example, when shopping) can both restrict the range of a person's experience and opportunities for exercising imagination through choice.

Imagination and creativity are invariably linked. People thought to be creative are imaginative, and vice versa. My own view is that imagination is a necessary but not sufficient condition for creativity, a viewpoint that is elaborated below. However, like judgement, both creativity and imagination are subject to popular misconceptions. For example, creativity is often considered to be a gift which people either do or do not have. This is particularly the case when creativity is thought of in relation to scientific, musical, artistic, or literary genius. Einstein, Mozart, Rembrandt, and Shakespeare, for example, were creative geniuses. However, and as stated above, whenever a person makes a conscious judgement or choice some degree of imagination and/or creativity is involved. What distinguishes the genius from the ordinary person, therefore, is not the act of creation or imagination itself, but its degree and scope. Imagination and creativity should be thought of as varying on continua as opposed to being categoric qualities.

This chapter aims to stress the importance of imagination and creativity in judgement and choice. Indeed, the central thesis is that the quality of judgement and choice depends crucially upon these variables. The chapter begins with a discussion of the nature of creativity and characteristics of creative people. It is argued that given even a minimal level of intelligence, most people are both creative and imaginative and, furthermore, are capable of becoming even more so—although not without limit and with little probability of achieving acts of genius. The benchmark of creativity people should use to calibrate their own creative performance is not that of geniuses, but rather their own habitual level. Most people are capable of increasing their own levels of creativity. Indeed, one clear finding that emerges from the literature is that relative creativity and imagination are a function of the amount of mental effort people are used to and willing to expend. Several devices or techniques for increasing creativity have been proposed (e.g., brainstorming, synectics, morphological analysis). These are briefly examined and discussed.

## CREATIVITY AND THE CREATIVE

What is a creative act? A dictionary definition refers to the verb 'create' as the act of bringing something 'into existence'. By this definition, therefore, the use of almost all language is an example of creativity in the sense that almost all sentences are unique. However, ordinary speech is usually not considered creative in that almost everyone can speak. Furthermore, few people would characterize a nonsensical sentence as a creative act even though it might be original. Creativity, as generally understood, therefore has more meaning ascribed to it than simply bringing into existence something that did not exist previously.

Jerome Bruner argues that a creative act is one 'that produces effective surprise'.[1] He further specifies three kinds of 'effectiveness':

(1) *Predictive effectiveness*. This is exemplified by the discovery of laws in science which allow the prediction of certain phenomena. Consider, for example, the discovery of the law concerning the speed of falling bodies.

(2) *Formal effectiveness* by which Bruner means 'an ordering of elements in such a way that one sees relationships that were not evident before, groupings that were before not present, ways of putting things together not before within reach'. In this domain he cites works in mathematics, logic and, perhaps, music.

(3) *Metaphoric effectiveness* which is also 'effective by connecting domains of experience that were before apart, but with the form of connectedness that has the discipline of art'.

In fact, what Bruner—and indeed many other writers on creativity—are saying amounts roughly to the following. Creativity occurs when ideas, 'things' or associations are produced in some new combination that is either useful or appropriate for a particular problem or purpose, and/or is aesthetically pleasing. Studies show that people can agree whether certain acts or people are more or less creative, although there is less agreement about the actual definition of 'creativity'.[2] The necessity for the 'appropriateness' of a creative act is nonetheless a dimension on which most people would agree, although the extent to which a single act is appropriate under particular circumstances could be the subject of debate. Originality and appropriateness are probably the two most important aspects of creativity.

Examples of great creative acts are easy to indicate and can be used to illustrate the 'definition' given above. Einstein's theory of relativity is an example of reconstructing and seeing physical reality from a new, and more 'useful' perspective. The apocryphal story of Newton asking why the apple fell is an example of a creative question that led to reconceptualizing many problems. The interesting aspect of the Newton story is that millions of people before Newton knew that apples fall from trees. Newton's genius was to ask 'why'. Creativity thus often involves questioning what one has taken for granted. And indeed, the posing of a question can be a most significant creative contribution in that it allows people to see relations in the environment from a different perspective. Keynes, for example, was a genius in that he was able to look at economic questions in a manner quite foreign to other economists of his day. Similarly, the businessman who is both imaginative and creative enough to see problems from the viewpoints of other persons in his environment (e.g. customers, suppliers, unions, etc.) is at a great advantage.

A statement was made previously that imagination was a necessary but not sufficient condition for creativity. By this I mean the following: in order to be creative, one must be able to imagine new associations between ideas, concepts or things. However, seeing novel associations does not necessarily lead to creativity. For example, one aspect of creativity that psychologists have investigated concerns the ability to produce unusual associations to given words. However, if this were adopted as a criterion for creativity, then the places with the greatest density of creative people would be mental hospitals.[2] Schizophrenics, for example, continually see relations and associations which are novel—but dysfunctional. Imagination, therefore, is necessary to generate new solutions to problems. However, there is no guarantee that the new solutions will be better than the old. We return to this point below.

Several writers have tried to identify different stages in creative activity—and many such 'schemes' are in fact quite similar.[3] Johnson, for example, identifies three stages:[4]

(1) *Preparation*, during which the individual collects material or otherwise 'prepares' for the creative activity. This stage could include reading or thinking about the problem. Consider, for example, that you are faced with a problem concerning how to handle a contract with a new

supplier. You would probably spend some time discussing issues with colleagues, considering other examples or precedents, thinking about the peculiarities of the particular case, and so forth.

(2) *Production*—at this stage ideas relevant to the problem at hand are generated.

(3) *Judgement*, by which Johnson means evaluation of the ideas prior to selecting a 'creative' solution.

Whereas different stages have been identified, it is not necessarily the case that people follow these stages in linear fashion. For example, the judgement (more precisely evaluation) of an idea could take place before other ideas have been generated. Ideas that have been suppressed could reappear, and so on.

How do people handle the above three stages of creative thinking? This question has intrigued psychologists for years and has been investigated by several methodologies.

### Introspection

One interesting approach has been to examine the thoughts and recollections of eminent creators (scientists, artists, musicians, writers, philosophers) concerning their own creative efforts.[5] Although there must be doubt concerning people's ability to report on their own mental processes[6]—and particularly after the fact—the investigations have indicated some interesting insights.

One issue concerns the role of conscious and unconscious processes in creative thought. For many creators concerned with particular problems, there seems to be a feeling that solutions appear suddenly as a result of some subliminal process. For example, the mathematician Poincaré cites a case where:

> One evening, contrary to my custom, I drank black coffee and could not sleep. Ideas rose in clouds; I felt them collide until pairs interlocked, so to speak, making a stable combination. By the next morning I had established the existence of a class of Fuchsian functions, those which come from the hypergeometric series; I only had to write out the results, which took but a few hours.[5]

Most people know the feeling where, when bothered by a problem, ideas and potential solutions suddenly seem to emerge from the unconscious. Bertrand Russell has stated that he found it fruitless to try and push his creative work to completion by sheer will power. Rather, he found it necessary to wait until his subconscious had made some further development.[5]

Mozart too reported similar subliminal experiences:

> When I am, as it were, completely myself, entirely alone, and of good cheer— say travelling in a carriage, or walking after a good meal, or during the night when I cannot sleep; it is on such occasions that my ideas flow best and most

abundantly. *Whence* and *how* they come, I know not; nor can I force them. Those pleasures that please me I retain in memory, and am accustomed, as I have been told, to hum them to myself. If I continue in this way, it soon occurs to me how I may turn this or that morsel to account, so as to make a good dish of it, that is to say, agreeably to the rules of counterpoint, to the peculiarities of the various instruments, etc.[5]

The above quotations, which seem to imply that great creative acts just happen to 'great' people, could be thought to contradict the notion expressed earlier that creativity can be achieved by most people. There is, however, no contradiction. The people cited above were preoccupied by problems and had presumably concluded the 'preparation' stage of creativity. What seems to happen, if this first stage has been adequately effected, is that the mind races on subconsciously working on the problem. Furthermore, some mechanism exists, which allows the bringing into consciousness of an adequate solution—or at least, these notable creators only report the good solutions they found in the above way. Apocryphal stories exist, for example, of people preoccupied by problems waking up in the middle of the night believing they have found a solution. However, even if they commit the 'solution' to writing, they are unable to interpret it the next morning.

### Campbell's model

Campbell has proposed a model whereby creative thought is but one aspect of a general process by which people acquire knowledge concerning the world.[7] He postulates—in somewhat abstract terms—three conditions/mechanisms: first, the production of 'variations' (for example, the generation and combination of different possible associations between elements of a problem); second, a consistent selection process, whereby particular combinations produced can be picked out; and third, a mechanism for preserving and reproducing the selected variations. That is, an ability to notice and replicate actions that have proven to be successful. These processes are, of course, precisely what occurs in trial-and-error learning. A concrete example would be the following. Imagine that you need to find the appropriate spanner with which to tighten a bolt. You try several spanners until one fits. You use that spanner and tighten the bolt. The next time you need to tighten that kind of bolt, you will know what spanner to take. As stated above, it is Campbell's thesis that creative thinking involves precisely the same principles as trial-and-error learning. However, in conceptual problems, instead of manipulating different spanners in order to find the one that fits the particular problem, the individual is involved in a series of 'thought trials', or imaginary experiences attempting to find a solution. That is, a problem presents itself to an individual, who then attempts several 'thought trials' until a satisfactory solution is obtained. Campbell terms this process 'blind variation and selective retention'—'blind' in the sense that attempts at solving problems are often made more or less at random. As he states:

... it must be emphasized that insofar as thought achieves innovation, the internal emitting of thought trials one by one is blind, lacking prescience or foresight. The process as a whole of course provides 'foresight' for the overt level of behavior, once the process has blindly stumbled into a thought trial that 'fits' the selection criterion accompanied by the 'something clicked', 'Eureka', or 'aha-erlebnis' that usually marks the successful termination of the process.[7]

(Reproduced by permission of the American Psychological Association)

This somewhat mechanical explanation of creative thought which emphasizes the role of chance both raises objections, which Campbell meets, and has many implications. Among possible objections are that: (1) Campbell's scheme would seem to make no allowance for observations of people achieving 'insightful' solutions to problems; (2) the existence of individual differences and particularly creative geniuses; and (3) the enormous amount of thought trials that are necessary to make the creative steps inherent in increases in knowledge. Campbell counters these arguments by noting, first, that the sensation of 'insightful' solutions to problems occurs *after* a problem has been solved—that is, after blind search has hit an appropriate solution. (Recall the discussion in Chapter 7 concerning how outcome knowledge seems to restructure memory and make the outcome seem inevitable after the event.) Second, trial-and-error responses refer not only to actual thought trials but classes of thought trials or responses. To make an analogy, when faced with the problem of tightening a bolt, the individual does not need to try more than one screwdriver to realize that that type of instrument will not be equal to the task. The class of instrument 'spanner' can, however, be seen or remembered to fit the type of problem. People therefore learn— through trial-and-error—approaches to classes of problems.

Third, an important implication of Campbell's model is that chance plays a crucial role in creative thinking. In this he sees no problem. Indeed, Campbell warns people against attributing special 'creative powers' to particular individuals:

Explanations in terms of special antecedents will very often be irrelevant and ... the causal-interpretative biases of our minds make us prone to such over-interpretations, to *post-hoc-ergo-propter-hoc* interpretations, deifying the creative genius to whom we impute a capacity for direct insight instead of mental flounderings and blind-alley entrances of the kind we are aware typify our own thought processes. Ernst Mach (1896) notes our nostalgia for the directly-knowing genius: 'To our humiliation we learn that even the greatest men are born more for life than for science in the extent to which even they are indebted to accident' (p. 175).[7]

(Reproduced by permission of the American Psychological Association)

The dangers of causal attributions to chance occurrences have, of course, been emphasized several times already in this book.

Campbell does not deny the importance of individual differences in creativity. Indeed, his model points to sources of differences. First, people will be more creative to the extent that they can produce a wider range and number of thought trials (hence imagination is necessary but not sufficient for creativity). In this motivation to produce thoughts and 'practice' in doing so are important. (Recall the discussion on the benefits of thinking in Chapter 4.) That is, individual 'investment' in thinking increases the probability of being creative. Second, a wider experience of life equips people with the capability of greater creativity (by increasing the range of possible thought trials they can produce). Third, living and working in an atmosphere with a wide tolerance for exploratory behaviour can liberate the mind for generating creative solutions. And fourth, people differ in their ability to seize upon solutions that are appropriate. It is insufficient merely to generate possible solutions to a problem. The individual must decide *which* solution should be implemented. Such an 'editing talent' can very considerably from individual to individual. In addition to selecting the appropriate solution to a given problem, one should also note that wide scanning of possible solutions can generate solutions to other problems. Thus, by engaging in large numbers of thought trials, the creative individual also increases his chances of solving other problems. Indeed, in science, the art of serendipity (i.e. recognizing that one has generated a solution to problem B while searching for a solution to problem A) has long been recognized—witness Fleming's 'accidental' discovery of penicillin.

Finally, Campbell's model points to the fact that to solve problems often requires what seems like a prohibitively large number of thought trials. This is indeed the case. However, Campbell points out that we only achieve satisfactory solutions to a very small number of problems facing us. We may survive without solutions but that is, of course, a different matter. Furthermore, we are usually unaware of the extent to which many of our actions are 'sub-optimal.' In addition,

> The tremendous number of non-productive thought trials ... must not be underestimated. Think of what a small proportion of thought becomes conscious, and of conscious thought what a small proportion gets uttered, what a still smaller fragment gets published, and what a small proportion of what is published is used by the next intellectual generation. There is a tremendous wastefulness, slowness, and rarity of achievement.[7]
> (Reproduced by permission of the American Psychological Association)

To sum up, Campbell's position is that the invention of creative solutions depends upon generating many thought experiments or combinations of factors possibly capable of leading to solutions. To this is added the notion that a mechanism must exist to select, test and retain 'successful' solutions. Many creativity techniques described later in this chapter depend precisely upon these kinds of notions.

**Creativity and casual thinking**

Preceding chapters have stressed the importance of understanding the manner in which people structure their understanding of the world in terms of causal relations between variables. Since much creative problem solving essentially involves generating explanations or determining causes, it is appropriate to consider this link further.

In Chapter 3, a conceptual model of the elements of causal reasoning was outlined.[8] This involved four components: (1) a background or 'causal field' which provides the context within which judgments of cause are made; (2) the specification of 'cues-to-causality' which are imperfect indicators of the presence or absence of causal relations. These cues are covariation (causes and effects tend to occur together, i.e. covary), temporal order (causes precede effects in time), contiguity (in time and space), and similarity which can involve notions of physical similarity and/or congruity between cause and effect as well as the role of metaphor or analogy; (3) judgemental strategies for combining the field and cues in the assessment of cause; and (4) the role of alternative explanations.

The causal field serves the important function of directing attention to particular causal candidates. As noted in previous chapters, cognitive processes are sensitive to differences such that the manner in which the causal field is defined, explicitly or implicitly, directs attention to particular differences as being potential causal candidates. For example, in Chapter 3 the cause of a watch face being smashed was attributed in one scenario to the force of the hammer used to hit it. However, a defect in the glass was seen to be the cause in another setting (the testing procedure in a watch factory). Similarly, when considering the cause of teenage pregnancy in the US, some people may attribute this to lack of use of birth control devices, whereas others blame promiscuity among teenagers.[9] For the first group, lack of use of birth control devices is seen as a difference against a background of sexually active people; the second group, however, considers sexual activity among teenagers to be the difference relative to other populations of teenagers in different times or places. The important point about these examples is that we cannot attend to all possible stimuli. Thus attending to differences is an effective strategy for dealing with informational complexity. We have learned over time that observed changes (effects) are typically related to other changes or differences that occurred previously. Indeed, the curiosity that leads us to seek explanations in the first place is often triggered by noting exceptions, deviations, or unusual events.[10] For example, why did a particular company make less profit than expected? Why did the favoured football team fail to win the game? The cost of this cognitive strategy, however, is that differences can only be defined relative to some background. Thus, the manner in which the background comes to be defined is crucial to how the problem is interpreted.

The cues-to-causality also serve to direct attention in causal reasoning. We assume that causes precede effects; we use evidence of covariation to suggest which variables are causally relevant; and our expectations about contiguity reinforce the notion that whereas some variables could be causally relevant, others are not. For example, in trying to determine why sales have increased sharply, we are unlikely to attribute this to an advertising campaign that has just started precisely because we know that the effects of advertising campaigns take some time to have an impact. Instead, we would search for other causally relevant variables. Similarities in the form of metaphors and analogies are also useful in causal reasoning in that they can suggest implications about the unfamiliar. Thus, in trying to understand the human brain, the metaphor of a computer suggests analogous processes of inputting information, operations on input, storage in memory, and output.

In short, both the causal field and the cues-to-causality direct attention and help us create order out of the mass of information with which we are confronted. Moreover, given the complexity of the environment relative to human information-processing ability, the advantages this brings should not be underestimated. On the other hand, since these forces also restrict our attention, they may prevent us from seeing other possible causes or ways of viewing problems that could be more productive. For example, reference was made above to the computer as a metaphor for the brain. However, this is not the only possible metaphor. One could also think of the brain as a muscle. This would direct attention to its capability of maintaining and increasing strength through use or atrophying through disuse. Alternatively, one could think of the brain as a sponge, thereby suggesting that we soak up information, and so on.[11]

The processes of causal reasoning imply a trade-off. On the one hand, use of both causal fields and the cues-to-causality help the mind establish order out of the mass of information with which it is confronted. On the other hand, this order is bought at the cost of being able to perceive alternative problem formulations (i.e. casual fields) and potential causal candidates. Creative thinking requires resisting these heavily entrenched cognitive habits and actively seeking alternative ways of viewing problems. As an example, consider the following puzzle:

> One morning, exactly at sunrise, a Buddhist monk began to climb a tall mountain. A narrow path, no more than a foot or two wide, spiraled around the mountain to a glittering temple at the summit. The monk ascended at varying rates of speed, stopping many times along the way to rest and eat dried fruit he carried with him. He reached the temple shortly before sunset. After several days of fasting and meditation he began his journey back along the same path, starting at sunrise and again walking at variable speeds, with many pauses along the way. His average speed descending was, of course, greater than his average climbing speed. Prove that there is a spot along the path that the monk will occupy on both trips at precisely the same time of day.[12]

Can you think of a solution to this problem? One way to think about it is the following. Instead of visualizing the monk ascending and descending the mountain on different days, imagine two monks where one ascends and the other descends the mountain on the same day. If both monks start their journeys at the same time, there must be a point on the path where they cross, and this point must, by definition, be at the same time of day for both monks. Now transpose the two monk version of the problem to the one monk version and you have the problem solved.

Finally, as noted in Chapter 3, the ability to *imagine* alternative explanations is critical to causal thinking. In particular, the confidence people place in explanations is reduced by the extent to which they are able to generate or imagine alternative explanations. This leads to a further trade-off. For reasons elaborated throughout this chapter, it is important to invest in imagination. However, the cost of imagination can be a heightened awareness of uncertainty which, at the limit, could reduce one's willingness to take action. It is important to learn to accept the uncertainties induced by a vivid imagination.

**Distinguishing the creative**

What distinguishes people who are creative from those who are not so creative? As would be expected from the discussion of the Campbell model, creative people tend to work hard. That is, they engage in a greater number of thought experiments than the less creative. A series of studies has examined the characteristics of creative people and particularly scientists. Although one cannot generalize from scientists, the list of characteristics of productive scientists presented in Table 8.1 is indicative.

On reviewing the list in Table 8.1, Johnson notes that what seems to emerge reads like 'a universal catalog of virtues'. However, he goes on to say that 'creative thinkers are not, as far as we know, any more agreeable, friendly, considerate, or tolerant than other people. They are seldom described as happy and well-rounded, nor are they accused, any more than others, of excessive modesty.'[4]

As stated above, the list in Table 8.1 was based on a group of scientists and thus certain traits are possibly not applicable to all types of creative people. Novelists and dramatists, for example, may well exhibit preferences for people rather than things (item 2), and they may also tend to be more interested and involved in interpersonal relationships. In another study of scientists, Roe noted important differences in these respects between physical and social scientists.[14]

Perhaps the most important traits of creative people are high autonomy (item 1) and independence of judgement (item 9). As stated above, creativity depends not only on the willingness to form new mental associations, but also judgement in selecting new combinations and the strength of character to suggest them to others, possibly at the expense of being ridiculed.[15] Independence of judgement and an ability to go against popular streams of

*Table 8.1    Characteristics of productive scientists*[13]

(1) A high degree of autonomy, self-sufficiency, self-direction.
(2) A preference for mental manipulations involving things rather than people: a somewhat distant or detached attitude in interpersonal relations, and a preference for intellectually challenging situations rather than socially challenging ones.
(3) High ego strength and emotional stability.
(4) A liking for method, precision, exactness.
(5) A preference for such defence mechanisms as repression and isolation in dealing with affect and instinctual energies.
(6) A high degree of personal dominance but a dislike of personally toned controversy.
(7) A high degree of control of impulse, amounting almost to over-control: relatively little talkativeness, gregariousness, impulsiveness.
(8) A liking for abstract thinking, with considerable tolerance of cognitive ambiguity.
(9) Marked independence of judgement, rejection of group pressures toward conformity in thinking.
(10) Superior general intelligence.
(11) An early, very broad interest in intellectual activities.
(12) A drive toward comprehensiveness and elegance in explanation.
(13) A special interest in the kind of 'wagering' which involves pitting oneself against uncertain circumstances in which one's own effort can be the deciding factor.

thought are important. Indeed, many important innovations are precisely of this nature. That is, once creative ideas have been suggested, it is not the case that everyone will necessarily accept them—witness, for example, the fact that many great authors and artists are not recognized until after their deaths, the persecution Galileo had to endure for his ideas, and so on. The ideas of creative people often lead them into direct conflict with the trends of their time and they need the courage to be able to stand alone.

The above comments apply to the world of business as much as to science and the arts. Not only do successful entrepreneurs need good insights or ideas in order to exploit commercial opportunities, they also need the ability to buck social pressures and to 'go it alone'. Anyone who has tried to bring about a social innovation in an organization will recognize both the difficulty of the task (hence the need for a wide range of productive ideas) and the problems of implementation. In *The Prince*, Machiavelli stated this point with great clarity:

> There is nothing more difficult to take in hand, more perilous to conduct, or more uncertain in its success, than to take the lead in the introduction of a new order of things, because the innovator has for enemies all those who have done well under the old conditions, and lukewarm defenders in those who may do well under the new.

Consider, for example, what would happen in your own organization if you were to introduce an important cost-saving innovation which would require, among other things, that many people alter their work habits in a way that could threaten their job security. (Such issues are, of course, the crux of the matter in many attempts to 'rationalize' certain industries or companies.)

To summarize, creativity consists of finding new combinations of ideas, concepts, or 'things' which are *appropriate*. The creative process consists of three stages: (1) preparation; (2) production; and (3) judgement (i.e. evaluation of ideas produced at stage 2). To be effective as creators, people need not only to be willing and able to invest in mental effort, but also to have *strength* of character and judgement. Creative ideas are not always immediately recognized as such and the ultimate effectiveness of creative thought depends heavily on social forces.

## CONDITIONS AFFECTING CREATIVITY

Many investigations have centred on conditions affecting the production of creative ideas. These can be considered as they affect the three stages described above (i.e. preparation, production, and judgement).

As might be expected, the amount of preparation a person has relative to a problem will affect the production of ideas. However, it is not true that more preparation necessarily leads to more creative ideas. Prior experience with the type of problem considered, or attempts at creative effort, can also cause blockages and limit the subsequent production of ideas. People can become stuck in 'cages of thought' which preclude the exploration of ideas.

Consider, for example, the experiment which consisted of asking personnel working in a plant manufacturing spark plugs to name as many different possible uses of a spark plug as they could imagine. The respondents generated fewer alternatives than people who did not work in the plant and thus who had less prior experience with spark plugs.[4]

The Germans have a word *betriebsblind* (company blind) which describes how a person who has worked in a particular company for some time fails to see problems in new ways. And indeed, the success of consultants depends precisely on this fact. A major advantage of consultants lies in seeing problems with a fresh eye. Psychological research supports this anecdotal type of evidence. For example, a number of experiments have shown how experience with a type of problem can lead to lack of success in solving it. On considering the problem, the individual can become trapped by the direction of his own thought.[4] When this occurs, the individual is best advised to leave the problem and return to it later when the force of the 'direction' has subsided.

It should not, however, be inferred from the above that experience related to a problem is a hindrance to finding novel solutions. On the contrary, experience with similar problems can facilitate solutions. Furthermore, for many problems, knowledge which comes through experience is necessary to be even able to generate a solution. What is important is that the individual be able to 'turn a problem on its head' before contemplating solutions.

In preceding chapters the importance of the role of 'availability' of information in the environment or memory was noted. This has also been documented in studies of problem solving. Subjects in problem-solving experiments have been found to be unusually sensitive to aspects of the experimental situation which emphasize certain features of the problem. By moderating instructions, or even handling elements of the problem, experimenters are able to indicate cues which help or hinder the subjects.[16] Indeed, it almost seems that experimenters can manipulate the probability that people will solve particular problems by the use of such cues. The practical implications of these findings are clear. When facing a problem with which they are not familiar, people will be considerably affected by 'chance' observations of aspects of the particular situation. To follow Campbell's model outlined above, 'blind variation' will be initiated at the particular 'chance point' on which people happen to focus. Consequently, if the problem is such that its basic structure is not apparent, solutions will not be easily achieved. People should therefore spend considerable time looking at problems from different 'angles' before beginning to 'emit thought trials' in attempts to find solutions (see also comments above).

Motivation and attitudes are most important in the preparatory stages of creative activity. Excessive motivation can be dysfunctional in that it tends to direct energy into excessively narrow thought patterns. Research indicates that more relaxed postures are called for. However, motivation must be high since persistence in mental activity is so important. The effect of attitudes was nicely illustrated in a study by Hyman.[17] Two groups of engineers were asked to examine attempts to design a system for recognizing boxes in an automatic warehouse. One group was asked to study the attempts critically and to list faults; the second group was instructed to be constructive and note the useful features of the different attempts. Subsequently the individuals in the two groups were asked to propose solutions to both this problem and a similar one. The engineers who had been asked to evaluate the earlier attempts constructively were subsequently found to generate better solutions to both problems. The implications of this and similar studies are far-reaching.[4] People who tend to examine the creative attempts of others in *constructive* rather than *destructive* ways probably stand more chance of generating creative, constructive solutions themselves.

During the actual production of ideas, two important blocks have been identified: first, the way a person conceptualizes a problem based both on prior experience and the forces of causal reasoning discussed above; and second, the criteria people use to evaluate solutions before suggesting them.

As an example of the inhibiting effects of prior 'cages of thought' on the production of ideas, consider the nine dots in Figure 8.1. Can you draw four straight lines that pass through all nine dots without lifting your pencil? Try it!

Most people assume that to solve this problem you are not supposed to allow the pencil to go outside the dots. However, to solve the problem, this

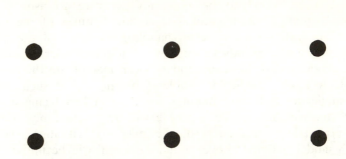

Figure 8.1 The nine-dot exercise. Can you draw four (and only four) straight lines that pass through all nine dots without lifting your pencil? (Reproduced by permission of Penguin Books Ltd)

is precisely what you must do—as illustrated in note 18. In other words, when faced with a problem, there is a natural tendency to limit one's attempts at solution within *self-imposed* constraints.[19] However, such constraints are arbitrary. The first task, therefore, is to free oneself of such constraints. Creative people tend to be remarkably unconstrained—which perhaps explains why their behaviour appears odd to other people. However, 'odd' behaviour allows one to see the world from many different vantage points and allows a greater and richer sampling of behaviour (i.e. scanning of a wider range of associations). It is, of course, also true that many uncreative people affect 'odd' behaviour patterns. Thus, it is not always easy to discriminate creative and uncreative 'odd-balls'. Constraints are not, however, only imposed internally. The conventional habits and norms of society, and industry and commerce in particular, can be a great block to the production of ideas. Furthermore, the creative person is, almost by definition, not an 'organization man'. David Ogilvy, the Scotsman who made a fortune in the advertising business on Madison Avenue, writes:

> It is sad that the majority of men who are responsible for advertising today, both the agents and the clients, are so conventional. The business community wants remarkable advertising, but turns a cold shoulder to the kind of people who can produce it .... Albert Lasker made $50,000,000 out of advertising, partly because he could stomach the atrocious manners of his great copywriters ....[20]

Ogilvy's comments on his own creative processes and life-style are also worth reproducing:

The creative process requires more than reason. Most original thinking isn't even verbal. It requires 'a groping experimentation with ideas, governed by intuitive hunches and inspired by the unconscious'. The majority of businessmen are incapable of original thinking, because they are unable to escape from the tyranny of reason. Their imaginations are blocked.

I am almost incapable of logical thought, but I have developed techniques for keeping open the telephone line to my unconscious, in case that disorderly repository has anything to tell me. I hear a great deal of music. I am on friendly terms with John Barleycorn. I take long hot baths. I garden. I go into retreat among the Amish. I watch birds. I go for long walks in the country. And I take frequent vacations, so that my brain can lie fallow—no golf, no cocktail parties, no tennis, no bridge, no concentration; only a bicycle.

While thus employed in doing nothing, I receive a constant stream of telegrams from my unconscious, and these become the raw material for my advertisements. But more is required: hard work, an open mind, and ungovernable curiosity.[20]

(Reproduced by permission of John Farquhason Ltd. Bell House, Bell Yard, London WC2)

Anyone who reads Ogilvy's book, *Confessions of an Advertising Man*, will find it hard to believe that he is 'almost incapable of logical thought'. However, what is being stressed above is the necessity not to allow the constraints of 'logic' to interfere with the generation of ideas.

As also discussed previously, willingness to invest in mental activity is a prerequisite for creativity. Indeed, a number of studies show that simply instructing people to think and produce ideas can have quite important effects. Whereas the 'quality' of ideas tends to decrease as the number increases, people are capable of generating many ideas about a variety of subjects provided, of course, that they are motivated to make the effort.[4] In producing ideas, however, people are best advised not to evaluate them too quickly, since the criteria used for evaluation can have important effects on the range and quality of ideas produced.[4]

To summarize, research shows that given the knowledge necessary either to solve problems or to be creative in a particular field, people need: (1) preparation that does not block possible channels of thought. Much time needs to be spent in reconstructing and conceptualizing problems from different viewpoints. Furthermore, motivation needs to be high to ensure persistence. However, a relaxed attitude is conducive to emitting productive 'thought trials'; (2) conditions that allow the production of ideas to range as freely as possible; and (3) the ability to postpone evaluation (or judgement) of ideas as long as is feasible.

In the next section several techniques for stimulating creativity are considered.

## CREATIVITY TECHNIQUES

As should be apparent from the preceding pages, 'effective' creativity requires free-wheeling, 'imaginative' (or even 'irrational') thought processes as well as logical structures to be able to evaluate the potential usefulness of ideas and solutions. These different types of thought processes have been described in the literature as *divergent* and *convergent*, respectively.[3] Once a problem has been perceived, convergent thinking is necessary to define it; divergent thinking is then needed to play with the problem structure and to seek new and possibly unusual associations; convergent thinking is subsequently required to evaluate the appropriateness of different solutions, and so on. Creativity techniques tend to emphasize these different stages in the problem-solving process by providing means: (1) to structure problems from different possible associations; and (2) to evaluate the range of possible associations in a systematic manner.[21]

*Brainstorming* is probably the oldest and best-known creativity technique.[22] This is a group technique where several people are encouraged to work together on a problem. The group is encouraged to generate ideas, recording them, for example, on a flip-chart, under the following guidelines:

(1)   All ideas are acceptable no matter how outrageous they might seem.
(2)   Criticism or judgement of ideas is not permitted until all ideas have been generated.
(3)   The greatest number of ideas is encouraged.
(4)   The group members should use the ideas of others to spark off or cue ideas of their own.   In this way it is hoped the process will induce a 'chain reaction'.

Brainstorming is now used a great deal and there can be little doubt that with a group of people who are prepared to cooperate it can be a most useful exercise. There is, however, no evidence that brainstorming in groups is necessarily more fruitful than individual brainstorming.[3,4] Both procedures can generate many ideas. The essential aspect, as stated previously, is individual investment in mental effort. If the social pressures of a group facilitate such effort, then so much the better. My own view is that one should not expect too much of brainstorming—or indeed of most creativity techniques—but it is often a useful starting point. One possible advantage of a group technique concerns situations where the group may subsequently be responsible for implementing a solution. If group members have participated in the solution-generating process, there is a greater possibility that they will regard it as their own and be willing to implement it.[23]

Synectics is another group creativity process.[24] The word 'synectics' comes from the Greek and implies the joining together of elements that were apparently unconnected. Stages in the process of the synectics method are:

(1)   A common definition of the problem by different members of the group. People in a group will often have different viewpoints on a problem and a simple, but systematic exploration of the different definitions and viewpoints is frequently most revealing. The result of

this stage is to define and select one viewpoint which is to be developed further.

(2)  At this stage synectics differs from other methods in that the method deliberately involves taking a 'vacation' from the problem by a free discussion on a subject unconnected with the original problem. The purpose of the discussion (which to be effective typically requires considerable skill on the part of the discussion leader), is to help the group find analogies that could be useful in solving the problem.

Gordon, the originator of synectics, sees analogy as a powerful means of problem solving and a stimulus to creativity. Three kinds of analogy are advocated: (a) Analogy with *biology* (i.e. nature). Natural evolution has developed fantastic 'solutions' to many problems which can also inspire human solutions. For example, the organization of colonies of ants or bees has shown what and how coordination among parts of a society can achieve; similarly one can admire and be inspired by the beaver's ability to build dams or the intricacies of the spider's web. Nature is full of elegant solutions to difficult problems; (b) *Personal* analogy can be most revealing. In this mode, members of a synectics group are asked to imagine that they are something, for example a certain type of bridge over a river or some kind of container. In 'role playing' the object the individual can often achieve insights which were not otherwise apparent; and (c) *Symbolic* analogy, whereby individuals are asked to symbolize the problems faced by the group by a single word or phrase. For example, the member of a group faced with a problem of transporting goods across the Atlantic might symbolize the problem as a need for a 'bridge'. In symbolic analogy, it is hoped that the evocation of a symbol can help restructure the problem in a way that triggers more creative solutions and further ideas. Other analogies, for example, social or historical, can also be useful.

(3)  The third stage of a synectics discussion consists of applying to the problem ideas gained during the previous divergent 'vacation', evaluating the ideas, etc. In other words, the third stage is convergent. The whole process can, of course, also be restarted from this point.

As with the brainstorming method, synectics is highly dependent upon group process, and skilled intervention in this is necessary for most groups. Some writers have suggested certain ground rules to avoid negative criticisms from spoiling the internal dynamics, for example 'before a member criticizes the idea of another, he or she must state three aspects of it which are good'.[25] Another specialist suggests that the group should be composed of people with different levels of involvement and expertise in the problem. Such heterogeneous groups, it is claimed, are more likely to hit on unusual and probably appropriate solutions.[26] Clearly there is a great deal of artificiality in these kinds of rules and discussions. However, before all such methods are dismissed out of hand, the reader should consider the alternatives. In many cases, the alternatives consist of haphazard attempts by individuals or, what is even worse, they just do not exist.

*The K-J method* is an intriguing methodology for structuring problems that has been suggested by a leading Japanese cultural anthropologist, Kawakita Jiro.[27] It is a method for grouping and synthesizing observations and concretizing and facilitating the generation and use of 'thought trials'. Its aim is to produce a useful structure from a series of seemingly unrelated observations. It is based on the notion that the appropriate structure yields the appropriate solution. There are several phases.

(1)   Observations concerning the problem or phenomenon of interest are recorded on separate pieces of paper. Consider, for example, observations concerning different aspects of, say, aviation technology, or of a consumer product in a particular market. The observations could be in the form of single words, phrases or short sentences. From the separate pieces of paper, full sentences are written to be entered on punched cards (which can subsequently be coded and sorted by dimenions). The problem area is thus represented by a series of such cards.

(2)   The data on the cards are then shuffled so that their ordering is random. The cards are then examined by the person (or people) concerned to see if there are associations linking observations. This iterative process continues until the total set of observations has been classified into groups within which items are linked in some way. For instance, observations in the consumer–product example could be linked within one group by the fact that they all relate to the habits of a certain type of consumer. The groups of items found at the first stage are then given names or appropriate phrases.

(3)   The next stage consists of trying to arrange the different groups of observations into some meaningful patterns. Many patterns are, of course, possible, and the investigators have to play with different possibilities at this stage. The patterns of groups can also be hierarchical in nature and in a really successful application a 'meta-concept' can be found from which the other classifications can be derived.

Proponents of the K-J method see its use in creativity as a step beyond brainstorming. Brainstorming generates data in the form of items that can be entered on cards. The K-J method then permits the raw data to be structured in a pattern. In other words, the K-J method is a classification procedure which uses a deliberate random mechanism to induce blind variation (cf. Campbell's model above) into the forming of associations between elements. The K-J method has, apparently, been used with some success in Japanese industry.

*Morphological analysis* is also based on the notion that systematic blind variation has great creative potential. The method was invented by the Swiss astronomer and aero-engine specialist, Zwicky. It 'concerns itself with the development and practical application of basic methods that will allow us to discover and analyze the structural or morphological interrelationships among objects, phenomena and concepts and to explore the results obtained for the construction of a sound world.'[28] Basically, Zwicky advocated:

(1) An explicit formulation and problem definition. Consider, for example, attempts to think about or create new forms of human transportation.[29]

(2) Identification of the fundamental dimensions or parameters of the problem. To continue the transportation example, there are (a) the type of carrier, (b) the medium of support for the carrier, and (c) the source of power for the carrier. In addition, within each dimension there are various possibilities, for example: for (a) cart, chair, bed, etc., for (b) water, ground, air, oil, rails, wheels, and for (c) human power, steam, jet engine, electricity, oil, and so on.

(3) A so-called 'morphological box' is constructed from the parameters and dimensions identified at Stage 2. This 'box' is a multi-dimensional matrix which results from all possible combinations of parameters and dimensions. For example, if a problem were to have 6 parameters, each characterized by, say, 3 dimensions, the matrix would contain $3^6$ = 729 different combinations or 'possible solutions'.

(4) All possible solutions in the morphological box need to be scrutinized to see how they meet the specifications of the problem posed. In several instances, of course, the combinations in the box are infeasible *a priori*; however, this can be an aid in the sense that as the number of parameters and dimensions increase, so do the number of possibilities. Consequently, in practice heuristic methods have to be employed to reduce the number of possibilities examined to reasonable proportions.

(5) Analyses of the best solutions selected at the preceding steps relative to their feasibility given existing resources.

Zwicky has successfully used the technique described above in several stages of the development of jet engines and he has also developed a considerable number of patents on this basis.

The 'morphological' approach is clearly a checklist system in that it systematically structures all possible combinations of parameters. The notion of a checklist is, in fact, basic to quite a number of techniques. For example, the industrial technique of 'value analysis' consists of taking a product, e.g. a screwdriver, and asking what functions it can or should perform. The different attributes of the screwdriver can then be evaluated against such a checklist and an assessment made as to whether the features of the particular screwdriver being examined need to be modified.[26]

*Cross-impact matrices* are a further 'creativity tool' based on systematic combinatorial methods.[30] They apply to problems of forecasting and thus are particularly germane to issues treated in this book. Consider, for example, that you wish to assess the probability that oil products will no longer be necessary for motor transportation by the year 2000. This development will clearly depend upon a series of other events, for example, the development of alternative sources of energy, changes in needs for transportation (for example, people working more at home and relying to a greater extent on telecommunications), and so on. Each of these events can, in turn, impact on the others and thus an assessment of the target event depends on evaluating each of the other events and their interactions. A cross-impact matrix is a means of arranging the events in a systematic order, enumerating the different possible combinations, and subsequently assessing the possible effects of their interrelations. As pointed out in earlier chapters, human intuition is often incapable of assessing the implications of different possible combinations of future events. Cross-impact matrices can thus provide a useful aid to judgement .

## SUMMARY AND IMPLICATIONS

The purpose of this chapter has been threefold: first, to emphasize that imagination and creativity play crucial roles in judgement and choice; second, to discuss the nature of creative processes and to show that most people have the ability to be more creative than they might themselves believe; and third to illustrate the rationale behind several structured creativity techniques.

'Imagination', Napoleon is reputed to have said, 'rules the world'. Imagination affects both the predictive and evaluative aspects of judgement: the ability to conceptualize different possibilities and how one might appreciate different outcomes. Without imagination, free choice is impossible. This point is so fundamental that it has to be stated both simply and frequently.

Creativity has been shown in this chapter to be linked to imagination. More specifically, creativity has been defined as the discovery of novel associations or reconstructions of ideas, concepts or 'things' that are *appropriate* to a given situation. The notion of appropriateness is important since novelty *per se* is not necessarily useful. For example, you could make a novel association between the words 'tree' and 'potato'. However, unless this association could be turned into something 'fruitful', the association is hardly creative. For example, could potatoes be grown on trees in a way that would facilitate harvesting them? Everybody forms novel associations in, for example, everyday speech. Thus everyone has the capacity to be creative.

Campbell's model of creative thought was discussed in some detail. This is based on the notion of 'blind variation' of possible associations and 'selective retention' of certain 'thought trials'. The model emphasizes the role of chance factors in hitting upon creative solutions, but points out that the probability of reaching good solutions can be increased by (1) the sheer number of thought trials emitted, and (2) experiencing a wide range of environmental conditions which augment the possibility of setting off productive thought trials. Campbell's model emphasizes that creative people will almost necessarily be involved in behaviour that seems different from others—since they 'must' sample a wider range of experience. Furthermore, working atmospheres that demand strict adherence to social norms do not foster creative habits.

The link between causal reasoning and creative thinking was also discussed. In particular, it was noted that the forces that direct our attention in causal reasoning (the causal field and the cues-to-causality) serve the important function of limiting the number of possible interpretations we can make of the information to which we are exposed. On the other hand, by limiting the ways in which we can interpret what we observe, these forces also restrict our ability to see problems from different perspectives and thereby reduce possibilities for creative thought.

To be creative, people not only need to be willing to invest mental effort in imagination, but must also exercise considerable independence of character and judgement. Creative ideas are not always well received, particularly in the social domain. To bring creative ideas to fruition often requires considerable tenacity of purpose and an ability to withstand social pressures.

Creativity can be considered to consist of three stages: (1) preparation; (2) production; and (3) judgement. These stages require both *convergent* and *divergent* ways of thinking: convergent to define problems and evaluate possible solutions, divergent to produce associations, reformulate problems, and generate possible solutions. Creativity techniques are largely designed to prevent creative blocks and to foster the generation of large numbers of possible solutions (i.e. making blind variation systematic). For example, techniques are supposed to help people restructure problems (to escape common 'cages of thought'), generate possible associations and solutions, and to suspend judgement of solutions until many have been discovered. Whereas creativity techniques are no panacea, their utility should be compared with the *status quo*. This can often be characterized by haphazard attempts which stop at the first apparently satisfactory solution or, even worse, virtually nothing. Table 8.2 provides a brief overview of aids/barriers at the different stages of problem solving and creative processes. It also adds a fourth stage to the three discussed above, that of implementation.

Finally, whereas the level of imagination and creativity that yields acts of genius is rare, the ability to increase one's own level is available to all. The prime necessities are, as with most judgemental skills, an attitude of mind that believes in the feasibility of increased imagination, and a willingness to invest the mental effort necessary to achieve it, or as David Ogilvy put it, 'hard work'.

*Table 8.2   Aids/barriers at different stages of problem solving and creativity*

| Stages | Required | Aids | Barriers |
|---|---|---|---|
| (1) Preparation | Sufficient 'technical' expertise to define problem; analytical skills | Experience; several definitions; reconsidering problems from many angles; motivation; tolerance for ambiguity; questioning the obvious, what is given and assumptions (why? what for?) | Perceptual sets; defining problem too quickly |
| (2) Production | 'Free', unconstrained thinking; generation of associations | Luck (!); generation of sheer number of possible solutions; persistence; ability to withhold judgement; constructive framework of mind; relaxed attitude but high motivation; use of analogies; lack of experience with problem area can help; sampling of many opinions from different viewpoints; willingness to entertain 'impossible' ideas; independence of mind | Self-imposed constraints; constraints imposed by others; fear of failure; fear of ridicule; critical frame of mind; conformity; conservatism; norms of group/ organizational setting ('groupthink') |
| (3) Evaluation | Analytical ability to evaluate feasibility of alternatives | Systematic means of examining solutions, willingness to push analysis far and also to return to Stage 2; good taste, imagination, high motivation and persistence; independence of mind | Evaluation done too quickly; 'satisficing'; unwillingness to invest in mental effort; acceptance of social norms and standards |

*Table 8.2* (cont'd.)

| Stages | Required | Aids | Barriers |
|---|---|---|---|
| (4) Implementation | Belief in one's ideas | Independence of character and judgement ('guts'); ability to withstand ridicule; motivation; persistence; ability to continue after failure; supportive organizational climate | Fear of failure; social and organizational norms and pressures |

## NOTES AND REFERENCES

1. J. S. Bruner (1962). *On Knowing: Essays for the Left Hand*, Cambridge, Mass.: Belknap Press of Harvard University Press.
2. F. Barron (1965). The psychology of creativity. In T. M. Newcomb (ed.), *New Directions in Psychology*, Vol. 2, New York: Holt, Rinehart & Winston, Inc., pp. 1–134.
3. J. P. Guilford (1967). *The Nature of Human Intelligence*, New York: McGraw-Hill.
4. D. M. Johnson (1972). *A Systematic Introduction to the Psychology of Thinking*, New York: Harper & Row.
5. See the fascinating collection of personal testimonials in B. Ghiselin (ed.). (1952). *The Creative Process*, Berkeley, California: University of California Press. (Reprinted by Mentor Books, New York.)
6. See R. E. Nisbett and T. D. Wilson (1977). Telling more than we can know: Verbal reports on mental processes, *Psychological Review*, **84**, 213–259.
7. D. T. Campbell (1960). Blind variation and selective retention in creative thought as in other knowledge processes, *Psychological Review*, **67**, 380–400. The general model of trial-and-error learning espoused by Campbell is, in fact, no more than part of Darwin's explanation of the process of evolution.
8. See H. J. Einhorn and R. M. Hogarth (1986). Judging probable cause, *Psychological Bulletin*, **99**, 3–19.
9. This example is due to Ann McGill (1986). *Context Effects in Judgments of Causation*, Unpublished Ph.D. thesis, University of Chicago.
10. For a specific review of studies on this point see B. Weiner (1985). 'Spontaneous' causal thinking, *Psychological Bulletin*, **97**, 74–84.
11. See H. J. Einhorn and R. M. Hogarth (1982). Prediction, diagnosis, and casual thinking in forecasting, *Journal of Forecasting*, **1**, 23–36.
12. See A. Koestler (1967). *The Act of Creation*, New York: Dell.
13. C. W. Taylor and F. Barrron (eds) (1963). *Scientific Creativity: Its Recognition and Development*, New York: Wiley, pp. 385–386.
14. A. Roe (1952). A psychologist examines sixty-four eminent scientists, *Scientific American*, **187**, 21–25.

15. See, for example, some of the stories of industrial innovation contained in P. R. Whitfield (1975). *Creativity in Industry*, Harmondsworth, Middlesex, England: Penguin.
16. R. J. Burke, N. R. Maier, and L. R. Hoffman (1966). Functions of hints in individual problem-solving, *American Journal of Psychology*, **79**, 389–399.
17. R. Hyman (1961). On prior information and creativity, *Psychological Reports*, **9**, 151–161.
18. This problem is taken from Whitfield, Reference 15, p. 36. The solution is as shown in Figure 8.2. The trick is to allow the pencil to go beyond the limits of the dots.

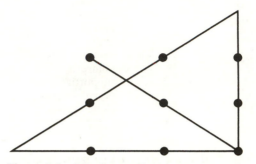

Figure 8.2    Solution to the nine-dot exercise

19. For a highly readable account of mental blocks in problem solving and how to deal with them, see J. L. Adams (1976). *Conceptual Blockbusting: A Pleasurable Guide to Better Problem Solving*, San Francisco: San Francisco Book Company.
20. D. Ogilvy (1963). *Confessions of an Advertising Man*, New York: Atheneum.
21. A short, useful, and readable overview of 'techniques' has been provided by W. E. Souder and R. W. Ziegler (1977). A review of creativity and problem solving techniques, *Research Management*, July, 34–42.
22. A. F. Osborn (1953). *Applied Imagination*, New York: Scribner.
23. N. R. F. Maier (1970). *Problem Solving and Creativity in Individuals and Groups*, Belmont, California: Wadsworth.
24. W. J. J. Gordon (1961). *Synectics*. New York: Harper & Row.
25. G. M. Prince (1969). How to be a better chairman, *Harvard Business Review*, Jan.–Feb., 98–108.
26. J. P. Sol (1974). *Techniques et Méthodes de Créativité Appliquée*, Paris: Editions Universitaires.
27. T. Hoshino and J. H. McPherson. *The K. J. Method of Creative Problem Solving*, Menlo Park, California: Stanford Research Institute.
28. F. Zwicky (1962). Morphology of propulsive power, *Monographs on Morphological Research*, No. 1, Pasadena, California: Society for Morphological Research, p. 275.
29. Example quoted by Guilford, Reference 3, p. 399.
30. See, for example, S. Makridakis and S. C. Wheelwright (1978). *Forecasting: Methods and Applications*, New York: Wiley, Chapter 14.

# CHAPTER 9

# Problem structuring and decision aids

The preceding chapters of this book have indicated a large variety of judgemental deficiencies. Indeed, they give considerable cause for concern when one considers the wide range of problems, both trivial and important, to which intuitive judgement is necessarily applied. Recent decades have, however, seen the development and growth of several 'decision aids' which range in complexity from highly sophisticated computer-based models to simple rules of thumb. The purpose of this chapter is to discuss these decision aids and how they can help counteract human fallibilities. It should be pointed out, however, that the use of decison aids has met with mixed enthusiasm. Comments will therefore also be addressed to this issue.

The most comprehensive approach to structuring decision problems is the method of *decision analysis*. Consequently, the chapter begins by outlining the steps involved in the decision analysis approach. The intention, however, is not to provide a detailed presentation of decision analysis, familiarity with which can be better gained by consulting specialized references.[1] Rather, the aim is to provide a framework within which (1) the questions that need to be asked in decision situations can be posed, and (2) procedures and aids that have been suggested for answering those questions discussed and illustrated. In many decision situations, there is insufficient time to make a thorough analysis. This discussion of relevant questions should therefore aid in the process of suggesting where available analytic effort should be spent.

## A DECISION ANALYSIS FRAMEWORK

Decision analysis recognizes that all decisions depend on the answer to two questions:[2]

(1)   What are the consequences of alternative actions? That is, what is 'at stake'?
(2)   What are the uncertainties in the environment relevant to the decision?

These questions relate, respectively, to the *evaluative* and *predictive* dimen-

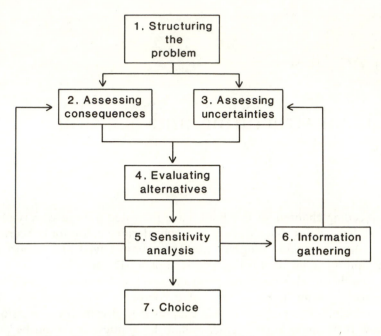

Figure 9.1  Simplified flow-chart of the decision analysis approach.

sions of judgement; i.e., how much you 'like' consequences of different alternatives, and what you expect to happen.

The steps involved in decision analysis are essentially an elaboration of these two questions and are outlined in flow-chart form in Figure 9.1. These steps and their interrelations are now briefly considered. To provide focus, consider a situation where you are hiring a candidate for your organization. Whereas this is a single example of a type of decision, it does illustrate many general points.

### 1. Structuring the problem

The key questions at this stage are:

Who is (are) the decision maker(s)?
What are the alternatives?
On what dimensions should the alternatives be evaluated?
What are the key uncertainties?
At what level of detail does the problem need to be structured? (To this there is also a subsidiary question: To what level of detail can the problem be structured?)

Determining the identity of the decision maker(s) is a necessary but not always evident step. In the job-hiring situaton, for example, lack of clarity concerning the decision maker's identity can exist with respect to whether the person is being hired for a particular department or for the firm as a whole. If this issue is not resolved, disagreements and difficulties can arise. More generally, the question of determining *the* decision maker is an important issue in instances where several people are party to a decision. Consider, for example, a corporation. The members of the board of directors may be *the* decision maker; furthermore, there may be differences between these individuals concerning particular decisions which would need to be reconciled. As further examples, consider issues involving relationships between head-office and branches or subsidiaries. What is optimal for one party may not be the best for the other, and vice versa.

A decision situation is clearly defined by the existence of alternatives. That is, with no alternatives, there is no choice. However, alternatives are not necessarily given but must also be sought and/or created. Furthermore, as illustrated in Chapter 8, imagination in the creation of alternatives greatly increases the scope for choice. In short, alternatives—in the job situation candidates—must be identified.

It is rare that an alternative, be it an investment opportunity or a job candidate, can be evaluated on a single dimension, e.g. discounted cash flow over five years in the first case, or intelligence in the second. Consequently, an important aspect of structuring problems is the specification of dimensions on which alternatives are to be evaluated; for example, intelligence, motivation, prior experience, personal compatibility with other persons in the organization, and so on. These dimensions can also be thought of as the *objectives* against which alternatives are evaluated.

'Assessing uncertainties' is given as a separate step in Figure 9.1. However, it is crucial at the outset to identify *what* the key uncertainties are. For example, is it certain that a specific candidate would accept an offer if one were made? Is there a possibility that hiring someone from outside will cause problems within the organization?

Finally, decisions can be analysed at different levels of detail. For example, one may wish to analyse the job situation in the form of a 'decision tree' as illustrated in Figure 9.2. In that figure, the decision situation represented is whether to make an offer *now* to one of two candidates, *A* or *B*. The situation is complicated by two levels of uncertainty: (1) whether *A* and *B* would accept an offer made *now*; and (2) whether if *A* or *B* rejected the offer, the other would accept an offer made *later*. The decision tree allows one to show the connections between different possible acts and events and can be represented in more or less detail.[1] An advantage of formally structuring problems is that one can see both the complexity of decision situations as well as the simplifying assumptions one has to make to deal with them (although often the latter can cause some salutary personal discomfort when the extent of simplistic assumptions inherent in intuitive judgement is realized). The level of detail at which one chooses to analyse a decision is an

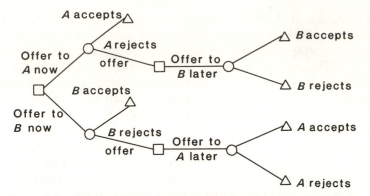

Figure 9.2 Illustrative decision tree: The decision here is whether one should make an offer first to candidate A or to candidate B in a situation where only one post is available. (The possibility of making an offer to both and hoping that one declines is excluded.) If, for example, B rejects an offer made now, then the delay in making an offer to A reduces the probability that he will accept later—the same applies to B if A rejects the initial offer. The possible decision points are represented by square boxes, □, uncertainties by circles ○.

important consideration. Decisions usually become more complex as one starts to analyse different possibilities; thus the best general advice is to start somewhat simplistically since complications will soon become apparent. In any event, the guiding principle should be an assessment of the costs and benefits of different levels of detail of analysis.

## 2. Assessing consequences

The major issues at this stage are:

How adequate are the measures of the dimensions on which the alternatives are to be evaluated?
How should the different dimensions be weighted?

The first of these issues subsumes two questions: (1) How well do the dimensions chosen represent the alternatives? In the job selection situation, for example, do the dimensions (i.e. selection criteria) cover all relevant domains? Has an important dimension, e.g. 'character,' been omitted? (2) Where and how can measures on the dimensions be obtained? That is, how do you judge a person's motivation or intelligence? In many instances it is necessary to obtain 'expert' opinion. However, which experts should you consult? What should you do if experts disagree?

The importance of identifying the decison maker(s) is emphasized by the second question. Different parties to a decision are liable to attach different 'weights' to different dimensions (or, in other words, they can have different objectives). For example, one decision maker could believe relevant prior experience to be the most important dimension in job selection. Another might believe intelligence or motivation to be more important. In situations where several decision makers are involved, the weights attached to different evaluative dimensions are the primary source of disagreement. The relative weights decision makers attach to different dimensions translate how they value the alternatives. Value, it is emphasized, therefore depends on who is making the evaluation and the purpose for which it is made. This issue is explored further below.

## 3. Assessing uncertainties

Assuming that the uncertainties have been identified (see Section 1 above), one needs to ask:

What information is relevant to the uncertainties?

As will be explained below, uncertainties should ideally be quantified in the form of probabilities. For example, one could attach, say, a 75% probability to the event that a certain candidate accepts a job under specific conditions. Sources of information, i.e. data and/or people, clearly need to be identified to make the necessary probabilistic judgements. As with assessing consequences, there are similar issues involved in consulting 'experts'.

## 4. Evaluating alternatives

The issues here can be summarized by a single question:

What criterion (i.e. decision rule) do you wish to use?

Decision theory prescribes choosing the alternative, i.e. job candidate, for whom *expected utility* is greatest.[3] That is one should weight the assessed consequences (i.e. utilities) by the assessed uncertainties (i.e. probabilities) and choose the alternative for which the weighted sum is largest (see also Chapters 4 and 5). For example, consider Figure 9.2. If one assigns utilities to the different outcomes (i.e. A accepts, B accepts, B accepts after A rejects, A accepts after B rejects, neither A nor B accepts), and probabilities have been assessed for the events (A and B accepting now or later), it is possible, by multiplying (i.e. weighting) the utilities of outcomes by the probabilities of the events upon which they depend, to assess the relative expected utilities of the strategies of offering jobs *now* to A and B. The decision is then made by choosing the action that has the larger expected utility. (Assessment of utilities is discussed further in this chapter and in Appendices C and D.)

This method of evaluating alternatives emphasizes the importance of separating Steps 2 and 3 (i.e. assessing consequences and uncertainties, respectively). In evaluating alternatives, it is crucial that the assessment of consequences (i.e. *evaluative* judgements) should not affect the assessment of uncertainties (i.e. *predictive* judgements). That is, although the relative values of actions should be calculated by combining 'preferences' and 'beliefs', the assessment of preferences should be done independently of the assessment of beliefs to avoid the pitfalls of 'wishful thinking' (or alternatively 'persecution mania').

## 5. Sensitivity analysis

Decision analysis aims to provide an explicit quantitative representation of a problem and the expected benefits of different courses of action. However, it is wise to adopt the maxim that whatever figures are used to model a situation *they must be wrong*. This therefore leads to the question:

*How* wrong are the estimated consequences and uncertainties?

This question is resolved by the technique of *sensitivity analysis*. What degree of variation in the inputs of assessed consequences and uncertainties would change the decision indicated at Step 4 above? That is, by varying both the estimated values of alternatives (e.g. by using different weighting schemes for the dimensions), and the probabilities of events, it is instructive to observe the extent to which the decision is *sensitive* to such changes.

This technique is important for two reasons. First, many inputs to a decision are necessarily subjective. Thus, if the choice between alternatives, e.g. job candidates, is relatively insensitive to ranges of such inputs as opposed to precise values, this provides some answer to the question concerning how wrong estimated consequences and uncertainties can be, and yet not affect the decision. Second, when people disagree concerning subjective inputs to a decision, disagreement does not necessarily imply different actions. Through sensitivity analysis one can test the extent to which actions (e.g. make an offer to candidate *A now*) are compatible with ranges of opinions and values (i.e. weights accorded to dimensions of consequences).

## 6. Information gathering

An important output of the preceding step can be the revelation that the decision is sensitive to lack of knowledge concerning certain variables. There is a need for more information. However, this leads to the question:

What are the costs and benefits of securing additional information?

For example, in a job selection situation one may wish, before offering a job, to obtain some information about a candidate. However, the delay incurred in obtaining the information may be more costly than the value of the information (the candidate might, for instance, accept a job from a competitor in the interim). There is often a tendency to defer taking decisions on the grounds that insufficient information is available. However, the costs of deferral and the fact that 'perfect' information is usually an unattainable goal are also frequently ignored.[4]

Information gathering is shown in Figure 9.1 after 'sensitivity analysis' to emphasize the point that the need for additional information should be undertaken only once the key aspects of the decision have been isolated. It would be wasteful to collect additional information about something that had little effect on the decision. The information-gathering step has also been shown to relate to the assessment of uncertainties since the effect of information is to reduce uncertainty. Conceptually, 'information' could, of course, also be collected to refine inputs concerning the assessment of consequences, for example by reassessing the decision maker's preferences (i.e. the relative weights attached to the dimensions used to evaluate alternatives). However, this aspect is assumed here to be covered under the heading of sensitivity analysis.

## 7. Choice

The questions posed here are simple:

Has there been sufficient analysis of the problem?

The answer to this question is invariably 'no'. However, the sufficiency of the analysis should be judged relative to the costs, benefits, and constraints of the situation. If the answer is positive, one then asks:

Which alternative has the greatest expected utility?

The decision rule is simple: Choose the alternative with the greatest expected utility.

In the above presentation, the decision analysis approach has been intentionally simplified. Prior to the more detailed discussion of different aspects below, the following points are emphasized. First, although the presentation has been made in a step-by-step fashion, in practice there is considerable recycling between steps. Indeed, the process of analysis often indicates new alternatives or dimensions of evaluation and the problem structure may go through several iterations after the first passes through Steps 4 and 5. Although the aim of the analysis is an explicit quantitative problem formulation, use of Step 5 (sensitivity analysis) enables one to see 'how quantitative' the formulation needs to be. Given that most inputs to problems are necessarily subjective, this is a particularly important consideration. Third, the theory of decision analysis strictly applies to a single decision

*Table 9.1    Summary of questions by steps in decision analysis*

---

*Step 1: Structuring the problem*
Who is (are) the decision maker(s)?
What are the alternatives?
On what dimensions should the alternatives be evaluated?
What are the key uncertainties?
At what level does the problem need to be structured?

*Step 2: Assessing consequences*
How adequate are the measures of the dimensions on which the alternatives are to be evaluated?
How should the different dimensions be weighted?

*Step 3: Assessing uncertainties*
What information is relevant to the uncertainties?

*Step 4: Evaluating alternatives*
What criterion (i.e. decision rule) do you wish to use?

*Step 5: Sensitivity analysis*
How wrong are the estimated consequences and uncertainties?

*Step 6: Information gathering*
What are the costs and benefits of securing additional information?

*Step 7: Choice*
Has there been sufficient analysis of the problem?
Which alternative has the greatest expected utility?

---

maker. However, if the analysis is carried out for several persons or groups, this can highlight the real extent of agreements and their relative importance. Fourth, by decomposing problems in the manner illustrated here, it is possible to synthesize the opinions of experts in different subject areas to the extent that their expertise relates to different aspects of the problem.

Table 9.1 summarizes the steps and the questions.

## DECISION AIDS

### Structuring the problem

There are no decision aids that can structure a problem automatically. Rather, this crucial phase must be largely achieved through unaided human judgement. Furthermore, apart from the issue of identifying the decision maker(s), it is unlikely that a first attempt at answering the subsequent questions will yield a satisfactory representation of anything but the simplest of problems. The structure of the problem typically emerges once one has grappled with the other steps outlined in Table 9.1. Nonetheless, the questions indicated at Step 1 have to be posed at the outset in order to begin the analysis.

## Assessing consequences

There has been much work involved in finding means to represent the consequences of alternatives.[5] The underlying rationale consists of decomposing the alternatives into a number of dimensions (sometimes called attributes) and then finding means to aggregate across the dimensions to find a value for each alternative.

To illustrate, consider the problems involved in evaluating alternative plans for a business organization, i.e. determining corporate strategy. Plans can only be assessed against objectives and this therefore necessitates making objectives explicit. Much clarity can be achieved by noting that objectives are often hierarchical in nature. For example, in 1972 the San Francisco-based Woodward–Clyde Consultants translated its overall *Statement of Purpose* into the 'goal hierarchy' illustrated in Figure 9.3. The *Statement of Purpose* read: 'The combined efforts of Woodward–Clyde Consultants and its affiliates are directed toward the creation and maintenance of an environment in which their employees can realize their personal, professional, and financial goals.'[6]

As can be seen in Figure 9.3, the overall objective has been broken down into two main sub-objectives, financial growth and growth in professional capabilities. These sub-objectives have also been further subdivided. When objectives are considered in this manner, what typically occurs is that a loose-sounding global objective is gradually broken down until at the base of the hierarchy it can be represented by specific items. As a further example, consider Figure 9.4, which shows part of a goal hierarchy developed for considering training plans in a company. The company's overall objective was to 'Maintain and improve training practices within the company in order to foster management development'.[7] This statement was subsequently broken down into distinct 'maintain' and 'improve' objectives. As shown in the illustration, four attributes of the 'improve' sub-objective were determined and measures of the attributes identified. As can be seen, two of the four measures required consulting experts whereas the other two could be based on 'hard' data.

How does one know whether a goal hierarchy adequately characterizes the alternatives? Although there is no blanket answer to this question, the following points are relevant. Edwards states that when first starting an analysis one should be careful not to include too many dimensions; specifically, 'As a rule of thumb, eight dimensions is plenty, and fifteen is too many'.[2] It is probable that as an analysis evolves, and the decision maker becomes more aware of the different complexities, more rather than fewer dimensions will be included in the final model. Keeney and Raiffa have suggested five criteria for considering the adequacy of dimensions chosen to

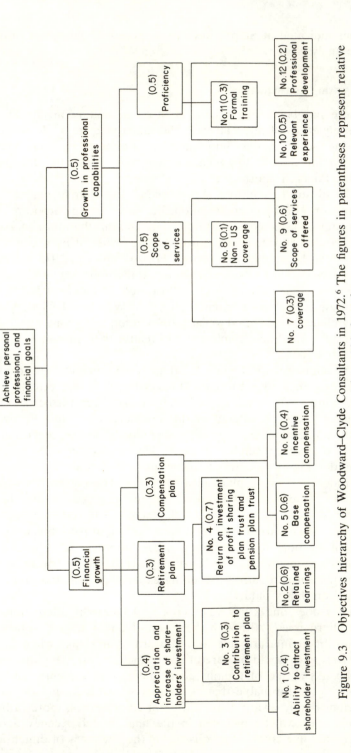

Figure 9.3  Objectives hierarchy of Woodward–Clyde Consultants in 1972.[6] The figures in parentheses represent relative importance weights within branches.

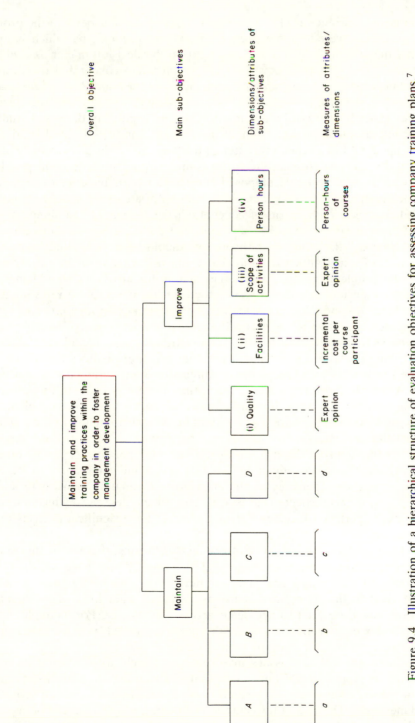

Figure 9.4 Illustration of a hierarchical structure of evaluation objectives for assessing company training plans.[7]

represent a problem:[6] (1) *completeness*, all important aspects of the problem should be covered by the dimensions; (2) *operational*, by which is meant that the attributes should be meaningful to the decision maker as well as to persons with whom he or she might communicate concerning the decision. Political considerations can play a role here. Keeney and Raiffa, for instance, cite the case of a mayor considering alternatives for handling solid wastes; they state,'It may not be possible for him, in a publicly discussed study, to include an attribute like "annual number of tons of untreated solid waste dumped into the ocean" even though this amount might be extremely important';[6] (3) *decomposable*, given the complexity of most decision problems, attributes need to be decomposed into simpler parts in order to be handled intelligibly; (4) *non-redundancy*, the final set of attributes should not contain redundancies in the form of conceptualizing/measuring the same thing by different means. Otherwise, unintentional double-counting can occur; and (5) *minimal*, the number of dimensions should be kept as small as possible.

Keeney and Raiffa point out that the actual attributes chosen for a particular problem are not unique. The search for attributes should therefore cease when it is felt that a satisfactory set has been found relevant to the problem at hand. When considering the addition of an attribute to a set, an important question to ask is how the relative attractiveness of the alternatives considered would change if the new attribute were included. If the new attribute does not induce significant changes, there is no need to add it to the set of attributes (recall the comments on *sensitivity analysis* above).

A complication frequently arises in that it is not possible to find attributes that actually measure the dimensions of concern to the problem. For example, consider Figure 9.4. It would be difficult to maintain the argument that the 'incremental cost per course participant' *is* the attribute 'facilities' under the 'improve' branch. However, the incremental cost can be taken to represent the improvement in facilities and a judgement has to be made concerning the adequacy of this measure. Fortunately, sensitivity analysis can help in this respect. That is, one can test the degree to which variations in this imperfectly measured attribute would have significant effects on the decision.

Having identified the set of attributes/dimensions, the next issue concerns how alternatives can be characterized by a single figure across all the dimensions. Two problems are involved here. First, what 'weights' should be attached to the different dimensions? Second, what kind of mathematical form should be used to aggregate across dimensions? For example, should the index of attractiveness of an alternative be based on a weighted sum of the dimensions? Or perhaps their product?

There are technical issues involved here which are discussed in greater detail in Appendix D. For conceptual clarification, therefore, concentrate on the situation where the overall index is based on a weighted sum of the dimensions. The issue thus centres on how the weights should be assessed. However, first note that the units in which the measures of the dimensions are recorded will also affect relative weighting. Thus it is essential to transform the measures to common scales (a procedure is explained in Appendix D). A second problem is the potential violation of an assumption implicit in the model known as *value independence*. Value independence means that preferences for any dimension of a particular alternative should be unaffected by its measurements on the other dimensions. For example, given that an alternative has certain locations (i.e. values) on dimensions A, B, and C, evaluation of the alternative's location on D should be independent of its location on A, B, and C. In other words, there are no strong 'interactions' between dimensions in terms of the decision maker's preferences. This kind of consideration must be examined, and if found to exist, corrected. The correction can often be achieved by redefining the attributes in such a way that the interactions no longer exist. Whereas this point is of a technical nature, it illustrates the fact that decision models can rarely be structured in their final form at the outset; rather, they must be allowed to grow out of the total process.

The actual weights assigned to attributes represent the decision maker's values. For example, the weights assigned in Figure 9.3 to the various objectives and sub-objectives of Woodward–Clyde Consultants indicate the relative importance attached to the different objectives by the company. How should one actually set about assessing such relative weights? One procedure, which is based on first ranking the attributes in importance, is outlined in Appendix D.

As stated above, different decision makers are most likely to disagree concerning the assessment of relative weights given to attributes. Thus, if agreement between parties to a decision is important, a useful procedure is to calculate relative preferences for alternatives under different possible weighting schemes and to see how this affects the ranking of alternatives. Sensitivity analysis carried out at even this early stage can be most instructive. For example, if the same action can accommodate differences in objectives this is worth knowing *before* different parties allow themselves to become involved in dispute. Experience with these types of models shows that the crux of the matter usually centres on determining the appropriate variables, i.e. attributes, rather than how they are weighted.

In this respect, extracts from a letter written by Benjamin Franklin to the British scientist Joseph Priestley in 1772 are most revealing. Franklin wrote:

In the affair of so much importance to you, wherein you ask my advice, I cannot, for want of sufficient premises, advise you what to determine, but if you please I will tell you how. When these difficult cases occur, they are difficult, chiefly because while we have them under consideration, all the reasons pro and con are not present to the mind at the same time; but sometimes one set present themselves, and at other times another, the first being out of sight. Hence the various purposes or inclinations that alternatively prevail, and the uncertainty that perplexes us. To get over this, my way is to divide half a sheet of paper by a line into two columns; writing over the one

Pro, and over the other Con. Then, during three or four days consideration, I put down under the different heads short hints of the different motives, that at different times occur to me, for or against the measure. When I have thus got them all together in one view, I endeavor to estimate their respective weights; and where I find two, one on each side, that seem equal, I strike them both out. If I find a reason pro equal to some two reasons con, I strike out the three. If I judge some two reasons con, equal to some three reasons pro, I strike out the five; and thus proceeding I find at length where the balance lies; and if, after a day or two of further consideration, nothing new that is of importance occurs on either side, I come to a determination accordingly. And, though the weights or reasons cannot be taken with the precision of algebraic quantities, yet when each is thus considered, separately and comparatively, and the whole lies before me, I think I can judge better, and am less liable to make a rash step, and in fact I have found great advantage from this kind of equation, in what may be called moral or prudential algebra.[8]

Although simplistic, Benjamin Franklin's method has much to recommend it. Indeed, it is the forerunner of many more complicated schemes that have been advocated in recent years. It concentrates on identifying the key attributes and their relative weights.

In summary, the stages involved in assessing consequences are, first, determining a set of attributes (which may often be organized in hierarchical fashion); second, finding measures of the attributes which are subsequently transformed to a common scale; and third, assigning weights to the attributes which reflect their relative importance. As indicated in the quotation from Franklin's letter to Priestley, it is not the precise figures placed on dimensions (arguments 'pro' or 'con') that are important. What is important is a procedure for bringing all important dimensions of a problem to bear on the decision. In this respect, whereas systematic methods are imperfect, they are superior to intuition.

### Assessing uncertainties

Most decision situations are subject to uncertainty. It is therefore important to identify uncertainties and quantify them. Consider, for example, the decision situation modelled in Figure 9.2. Whether a job is offered *now* to A or B clearly depends upon the assessment of the relative likelihoods of A and B accepting offers *now* and *later*. In this section, it is assumed that uncertainties in the decision situation have been identified. The focus is on the expression of uncertainty or, more accurately, *partial knowledge*.

What does it mean when someone says something is 'likely', 'possible' or 'probable'? If you were told that a price rise by one of your competitors was expected within the next 48 hours, should you take this to mean that it was certainly going to happen? Would you be prepared to bet on it? And if so, how much?

Words describing uncertainty are used frequently, although their precise meaning is often unclear. For example, groups of managers attending some

*Table 9.2   Ranking of uncertainty expressions*[9]
(Reproduced by permission of the Royal Statistical Society)

| Expression | Average rank | Range of ranks |
|---|---|---|
| Quite certain | 1.10 | 1–3 |
| Expected | 2.95 | 1–4 |
| Likely | 3.85 | 2–7 |
| Probable | 4.25 | 2–9 |
| Not unreasonable that | 4.65 | 3–7 |
| Possible | 6.10 | 3–9 |
| Hoped | 7.15 | 3–10 |
| Not certain | 7.80 | 3–10 |
| Doubtful | 8.60 | 7–10 |
| Unlikely | 8.75 | 3–10 |

Results observed when 40 managers were asked to rank ten expressions by decreasing order of certainty. The above table indicates the average ranks assigned to the expressions as well as the range of ranks accorded to each expression. As can be seen from the column on the right, the ranges are often quite wide and indicate considerable disagreement concerning the relative degrees of uncertainty implied by the different expressions. The results of this group of 40 managers represent a typical outcome from experiences with some 250 managers.

executive training programmes were asked to rank by decreasing order of certainty ten expressions used to describe forecasts made in the consumer durable field—see Table 9.2.[9] Results indicated considerable inconsistency between respondents as measured by the range of ranks observed and the fact that when a group was asked to repeat the exercise after the lapse of a month, they were unable to reproduce their original rankings. Although results of these experiments did show less inconsistency in meaning ascribed to the expressions by managers working within the same organizations, it is clear that the translation and communication of states of uncertainty by words is subject to ambiguity.[10] Uncertainty is best communicated through the medium of probability theory, that is by saying that an event has, say, a 30% chance of occurring. The quantitative form is precise and readily interpretable.

An objection to the use of probability as just illustrated is that for many events the probabilities are unknown. For example, whereas most people would readily agree that the probability of observing a 6 on the throw of a fair die is 1/6, it is more problematic in 1986 to determine the probability that, say, a given athlete will win the 1988 men's Olympic marathon race. The difficulty stems from the fact that whereas the first event can be considered 'repetitive,' the second is unique. That is, even if one did not know that the die was fair, it would be possible to throw it several times and observe the relative frequency of the outcome '6'. (Knowledge that the die

192

is fair obviates the need to conduct such an experiment.) On the other hand, in 1986 we cannot replicate the 1988 men's Olympic marathon. For unique events, therefore, a probability simply translates our subjective opinion into a number and so measures our 'degree of belief'. (This is in fact also true of repetitive events—see Appendices A and B.) Consequently, one cannot say whether a probability or opinion is wrong in any absolute sense unless a person is found to be mistaken when he or she had previously expressed total certainty or uncertainty. However, if over a series of events a person consistently over- or underestimates probabilities, for example by assessing probabilities of about 30% to events that occur 90% of the time, one can seriously question his or her sense of realism. The objection that the probabilities of specific events are unknown is not the issue since probabilities simply express one's degree of partial knowledge about an event. Nonetheless, people do have difficulty in expressing their degree of knowledge in the precise quantitative form demanded by probability theory.

Probability theory serves two purposes as a decision aid. First, and as discussed above, it is a common language for expressing states of uncertainty. Second, the rules for manipulating the probabilities of several events, the so-called 'probability calculus', provide a mechanism for determining the logical interrelations between uncertain events. Numerous studies have shown fallibilities in intuitive attempts to guess probabilistic relations from given facts. However, there is no reason that people should be constrained to guess the probabilistic relations between events. Arithmetic, to make an analogy, is not done by guesswork and few businessmen balance their books on this basis.

Expression of uncertainty in probabilistic form is not easily achieved. Moreover, and as emphasized in Chapter 2, our cultural backgrounds do not train us to distinguish consistently between situations involving certainty and belief. Sometimes we act and speak as though we were certain when, in fact, we are not too sure. On other occasions, we do not give enough weight to our opinions.[11]

In Appendix A, the rules of probability theory are briefly outlined and Appendix B offers guidelines concerning the assessment of probabilities.

There is, however, one aspect of probability-assessment techniques which deserves mention at this point. An event about which a probability, or indeed any non-quantified opinion, is expressed should be unambiguously defined. One way to think about this is to apply the so-called 'clairvoyant' test.[12] Could a clairvoyant—assuming one existed—tell you unambiguously whether the event would or would not occur? Alternatively, if a bet were placed contingent on the outcome, the event would have to be defined in such a way that the subsequent loser of the wager could not escape from his or her obligation.[13] A characteristic of much predictive activity is that we have loosely held opinions about loosely defined events. In probabilistic prediction, however, one has to be precise.

A distinction was made above concerning events that are unique and repetitive. For the latter a number of decision aids have been developed and tested.

## Repetitive predictions

There are many decision situations where predictive judgements have to be made on a repetitive basis. Consider personnel selection problems, medical prognosis, vetting loan applications, predicting expected returns of companies quoted on the stock market, production-scheduling decisions, short-term sales forecasts, and so on. The predictive activity in such situations can often be described by the relations between the outcomes (e.g. sales, job success, stock market returns, etc.) and a number of indicators or cues on which judgement is based. For example, in determining whether a loan should be granted to a company, a bank lending officer could consider, amongst other evidence, various financial ratios in the balance sheet of the company requesting the loan. Consequently, for such decisions, information on which judgement is based can be coded, either as hard data in the form of, say, a financial ratio, or by an opinion expressed on a scale—concerning, for example, the bank's assessment of the managerial competence of the company requesting the loan.

In situations of repetitive prediction such as described here, how should one proceed? The evidence overwhelmingly suggests that statistical methods should be used instead of intuitive judgement. That is, more accurate predictions can be achieved by using statistical rules to predict outcomes as opposed to relying on intuitive judgement.[14] An instructive example is provided by a study done at A T & T in the late 1970s to determine which new customers should not be required to make deposits when applying for telephone service.[15] An extensive statistical survey was conducted to determine characteristics that distinguished good from bad credit risks. The results of this survey were then implemented in a set of decision rules which were to be applied in making future credit decisions. Two features of this study are noteworthy. First, when determining the decision rules, A T & T accepted that to validate the results the company would have to go through a period of time during which it would grant credit to all customers thereby enabling it to distinguish accurately the characteristics of those who did or did not pay their subsequent bills (see Chapter 6). Second, whereas no data have been made public concerning the cost of the study, it is hard to believe that it could have been anything but a fraction of the estimated annual savings of $ 137,000,000 attributed to the project.

In the A T & T study, criteria were available to build statistical models and then to validate them. However, what can one do in circumstances where information about the subsequent criterion is hard to come by or might even be misleading? Consider, for example, trying to pick students for a new school, or selecting recruits into a firm where performance data will not be available for several years. In these cases, statistical models can still be built. However, instead of trying to build models relating available predictors to the criterion, it is the judgemental processes of the persons who normally make such decisions or predictions that are modelled. Moreover, in cases where criteria have been subsequently available, these models have generally been found to outpredict the people on whose judgements they were originally based. In other words, models of judges have been shown to be more accurate predictors than the judges whose processes have been modelled. This procedure, known as 'bootstrapping', has been found to hold in situations as diverse as admissions to graduate school, loan-granting and predicting returns on stocks.[16]

The counter-intuitive aspect of these findings is that one could suppose that through intuitive judgement people are able to capture important information which escapes codification and is thus not amenable to statistical analysis. Indeed, intuitive judgement does capture much information; however, it is inconsistent. Moreover such inconsistency necessarily attenuates human predictive validity. In other words, although humans may on occasion exhibit high accuracy in judgement, inability to apply judgemental rules consistently across a series of cases means that *on average* models outpredict people.

One may also ask why the question has been posed in a manner whereby either a person or a model is better. Surely a combination of person and model should be preferred to either alone? And indeed, some work has been pursued along these lines in respect of repetitive predictions[17] (see also below). Perhaps the reason that this approach has not been investigated more fully to date is that human pride has taken (and is still taking) some time to appreciate the notion that intuitive judgement can be improved by simple statistical models. Once this is fully realized, use of combination models can be expected to follow. On the other hand, it should also be recognized that, in bootstrapping situations, there could be no models without humans to model in the first place and, in this sense, these models do combine the benefits of both human intuition and statistical aggregation. In other models, humans are also needed in the critical task of selecting the information thought to be relevant to the task at hand.

Inconsistency is a major source of human judgemental fallibility. One way to reduce inconsistency is to take averages (see also Chapter 2). This can be done in two ways. Either one can average a person's past judgements to predict the future, or the judgements of several persons can be averaged. Although the first suggestion might initially seem counter-intuitive, it has much to offer in situations where the system of which the outcomes are being predicted is not subject to important changes. Bowman, for example, tested this notion in settings involving production-scheduling decisions and found that managers' past average decisions were in fact superior to their actual decisions. He explained his findings in the following way:

> It seems useful to attempt an explanation of why decision rules derived from management's own average behavior might yield better results than the aggregate behavior itself. Man seems to respond to selective cues in his environ-

ment—particular things seem to catch his attention at times (the last telephone call), while at other times it is a different set of stimuli. Not only is this selective cueing the case, but a threshold concept seems to apply. He may respond not at all up to some point and then over-respond beyond that. It is this type of behavior which helps explain the variance in the organization's (or its management's) behavior.

Departures of the decision making behavior of management from the preferred results, in this sense then can be divided or factored into two components, one which in the manner of a grand average departing from some preferred figure, we call bias..., and one which representing individual occurrences of experience departing from the grand average, we call variance.... It is the latter and more important component which seems to offer the tempting possibility of elimination through the use of decision rules incorporating coefficients derived from management's own recurrent behavior.[18]

(Reprinted by permission from E. H. Bowman, Consistency and optimality in managerial decision making, *Management Science*, 9(2), Jan. 1963. Copyright 1963 The Institute of Management Sciences)

To paraphrase Bowman, there are two kinds of error: bias, which represents systematic error, and *variance* which results from inconsistency. Averaging acts to reduce the variance and bias is usually only of secondary importance. Moreover, it is relatively easy to remove bias from judgement by a statistical adjustment.

The use of an average of the judgements of several persons raises the whole issue of how to combine several judgements for prediction.[19] Consider, for example, economic forecasters. The empirical evidence indicates that averages have remarkably good predictive performance. However, two remarks should be made. First, although the average stabilizes the variability in individual judgements, one has to be aware of the fact that judgements between individuals are likely to be correlated. Thus one is often averaging redundant information with the result that beyond a certain point gains in adding experts to a group are small. Indeed, it has been estimated that in most predictive situations involving the use of experts there is little point in averaging more than about ten persons and that six or seven will often be sufficient.[20] Second, there is something to be gained by weighting experts in a prediction group differentially, e.g. proportionally to their expertise. However, if this is done the penalty for assessing relative expertise incorrectly is high. Given that people are inconsistent in judgement, the use of averages is therefore often to be preferred even when one suspects differential expertise among members of a group.[21]

## Delphi and other methods

A method for aggregating group opinion which has attracted much attention in recent years is the so-called Delphi procedure.[22] This method, which is usually employed for predicting unique as opposed to repetitive events, relies on the fact that statistical aggregates of opinion must, by definition, be more accurate than a large proportion of the opinions aggregated. Another tenet is that interaction between people in groups is often dysfunctional. Consequently in the Delphi procedure face-to-face interaction between group members is avoided with communication being handled by anonymous statistical summary measures of the opinions of others administered by a third party. There have been some interesting Delphi applications. However, the reader should be warned that merely aggregating opinion through a Delphi-like procedure implies no guarantee of predictive validity.

Other aids have also been suggested for the prediction of unique events. One such system named PIP—an acronym for probabilistic information processing—decomposes the probabilistic prediction task in a way that allows humans to give inputs to a model that can then be aggregated mechanically.[23] This system has been experimentally tested in laboratory simulations with a view to potential military applications, but has not, to my knowledge, been applied in actual business situations. On the other hand, similar models for evaluating probabilities in underwriting (i.e. in the insurance business) have been developed and there have been several applications in medicine.[24]

In many situations assessing uncertainties is extraordinarily difficult since there are many different sources of uncertainty and it is unclear what combinations of contingencies might prevail. Such situations can often be usefully explored by *simulation* techniques. This involves modelling the decision by a series of equations in a computer and then observing what happens under a range of different possibilities. Furthermore, since inputs to such models are uncertain, the models can be run many times to assess the effects of the uncertainties empirically by observing simulated distributions of outcomes. Clearly the output of such models is conditioned by the quality of the input and the assumptions underlying the design of the model. However, they do provide powerful means to extend intuition and explore the implications of one's assumptions. In fact, many people now have the ability to do this kind of analysis using electronic spreadsheets that have become popular with the widespread adoption of microcomputer technology.

Further decision aids that have been fostered by the availability of microcomputers are so-called 'expert systems' that have grown out of work in artificial intelligence.[25] These systems are conceptually similar to bootstrapping models in that the models are programmed to capture the knowledge of a person (an expert) in a particular domain which then becomes available to users. Contrary to bootstrapping models, that can only be used for predictive tasks, expert systems can be used for both predictive and diagnostic tasks. In essence, the expert system has available to it much of the knowledge of a substantive expert (e.g. of a medical specialty) and it is able to suggest, through an interactive question and answer session, responses concerning diagnosis and prognosis based on the characteristics of cases about which it has been informed. Expert systems have been developed, for example, to simulate physicians and geologists as well as to suggest diagnostic tests in the construction and malfunction of computers.

## Rules-of-thumb

The use of most of the decision aids mentioned above typically requires a certain degree of technical sophistication. Furthermore, decision makers need to have sufficient knowledge of their underlying assumptions in order to use them for decisions of any consequence. What is lacking are simple rules-of-thumb which can be applied with confidence under specified circumstances.

Perhaps the only rule meeting this specification is that of using average judgements as described above. On the other hand, several useful checklist approaches have also been suggested. Kahneman and Tversky, for example, have proposed a five-step procedure for intuitive prediction which focuses on aspects of prediction which are often overlooked.[26] In particular, they point out that the major error in predictive judgement is to treat each case as unique. Although, every future event is, by definition, *unique* (i.e. it has never occurred before), it should be recognized that most events can be considered to belong to a 'reference class' about which quite a lot is known. For example, consider estimating sales of a new book by a new author. Whereas the book must be unique, many facts are also known about new authors publishing similar books. Furthermore, even if no similar books exist, other book analogies exist with which the new author's work can be categorized. In Kahneman and Tversky's procedure, it is suggested that information about the particular book (so-called 'singular' data) used for prediction be modified by 'distributional data' (i.e. information concerning the reference class). In this manner, Kahneman and Tversky suggest that intuitive prediction will not ignore relevant 'base-rate' data when predicting a 'target' event. Kahneman and Tversky also suggest a procedure for moderating intuitive predictions to allow for 'regression' effects (see Chapters 2 and 3).

In earlier chapters, several deficiencies in probabilistic thinking were noted. However, since probability theory itself is difficult to learn and apply, Table 9.3 outlines eight key points. These are provided as a checklist to avoid probabilistic traps and review many of the points made earlier in the book.

In summary, I have argued that the most appropriate way to express uncertainties is through the language of probability. This avoids the ambiguity inherent when ordinary language is used to express degrees of uncertainty and also provides a logic for structuring the relations between uncertain events. Second, I have discussed problems of prediction for repetitive and unique events. For the former, a number of decision aids have been developed which show great promise, although human reluctance to entrust predictive activity to mechanical aids does not favour the widespread adoption they merit. Some devices also exist for structuring intuitive prediction of unique events; however, these are not easily accessible to most decision makers. Nonetheless, the widespread introduction and growing use of mic-

*Table 9.3   Eight key points for probabilistic thinking/prediction*

---

(1) Think in terms of variation around the arithmetic average. The amount of variation depends upon (a) the 'true' variation of the phenomena and (b) lack of reliability/measurement error (see also point (5) below).

(2) Averages of data show less variation than the data averaged. Furthermore, variation of averages is reduced as the number of observations averaged increases. (Variation of averages is affected both by the amount of variability in the data averaged—*upwards*—and by the number of items of data averaged—*downwards*.

(3) What is the *base-rate*? (Recall Thurber's: 'Compared to what?')

(4) What is the *validity* of the information source? How does it relate to the predictive target?

(5) What is the *reliability* of the information source? Recall that imperfect reliability implies lowered predictive validity, e.g. measurement error in economic statistics. Assess the 'signal/noise' ratio (margin of error). Avoid extreme predictions based on extreme observations from data sources that are not perfectly reliable (the 'regression' fallacy).

(6) When predicting from several items of information, distinguish between:
   (a) *redundancy* (extent to which different sources overlap/can be predicted from each other); and
   (b) *validity* of different data sources *vis-à-vis* the target.
   Remember, consistency between data sources is only a valid cue to confidence in prediction to the extent that sources are not redundant/overlapping.

(7) To what extent could a 'random hypothesis' account for your data?

(8) Is it possible to test your predictions?

---

rocomputers may well accelerate the adoption of many such decision aids in the near future.

**Aids for other steps**

Structuring a problem and assessing consequences and uncertainties are the major aspects of decision analysis. The other steps indicated in Figure 9.1 and Table 9.1 are simply refinements of the former. Indeed, it is often the case that once a decision problem has been structured, many of the other steps become superfluous. However, as pointed out above, the actual structure will frequently only emerge once detailed work has been attempted on other phases. In most problems, several starts and blind alleys are inevitable.

## CONCLUDING REMARKS

This chapter has outlined some of the principles and problems of applying aids for structuring decisions. The approach taken was based on the so-called decision analysis methodology, although other valuable methods also exist. Decision-makers understandably ask for concrete examples when decision methodology is discussed. Many can now be given and cover a wide range of applications in science, medicine, the public sector and industry. Note 27 provides references to a cross-section of such applications.

Several decision makers reading this book will have had some, even minimal, contact with decision aids derived from disciplines with such esoteric names as 'operations research', 'management science' or even 'decision analysis'. Furthermore, many decision makers have opinions concerning the practical usefulness of these disciplines, often of a sceptical nature. To place this chapter in perspective, therefore, it is necessary to clarify several issues.[28]

First, when evaluating decison aids it is crucial to specify a basis of comparison. The base-line is usually unaided, intuitive judgement. However, as illustrated in this book, intuitive judgement does not have an impressive track record. One way to think through this issue is to consider the following analogy: 'When driving at night with your headlights on you do not necessarily see too well. However, turning your headlights off will not improve the situation.' Decision aids do not guarantee perfect decisions, but when *appropriately* used they will yield better decisions on average than intuition. The choice of a decision aid or procedure is itself a decision. Therefore one should not necessarily expect perfection, but rather strive to find the best available procedure.

Second, the decision aids discussed in this chapter all involve the translation of a problem into a mathematical model, which is subsequently manipulated to produce a 'decision'. There are a number of resistances to such quantification. The first concerns the ability to translate the problem situation into mathematical terms. The issue that should be addressed here is that a trade-off is involved between, on the one hand, having the problem loosely but perhaps veridically represented in its complexity in the decision maker's mind,* and on the other representing it simplistically, over-precisely and probably somewhat inaccurately in a form that is open to scrutiny. In the former case, one leaves oneself open to the deficiencies as well as the capabilities of the human information-processing system. And in many cases, it is not clear that capabilities dominate deficiencies. In the latter, the defects of the mode of analysis are exposed. For example, assumptions which may be hidden in intuitive reasoning are made explicit and thus questioned. One of the great strengths of decision aids is their 'public' nature. You know what you are doing with them. However, this strength can also reveal weaknesses which lead paradoxically to their rejection in favour of the hidden weaknesses of intuitive processes. (This is a good example of the 'out-of-sight, out-of-mind' phenomenon.) A further problem with quantification is lack of understanding of mathematical manipulations. People naturally resist the analysis of a problem in a 'language' they do not fully comprehend. Furthermore, this attitude can be aggravated by the failure of the mathematically inclined to empathize sufficiently with those lacking their skills. Common sense dictates that a decision-maker is ill-advised to delegate his

---

* Although intuitive capacity to do this must be doubted for problems of any complexity.

responsibilities to a model he or she does not understand. On the other hand, even a little analysis can go a long way toward generating insight about a problem and it is foolish to dismiss all formal modelling.[29]

Third, there seems to be a belief that the use of models somehow diminishes the role of the decision-maker who ends up relinquishing control to an 'algorithm' which, as noted above, he or she may not fully understand and is therefore unable to trust. However, decision aids are not to be 'believed'; they are to be used. Furthermore, the person using a decision aid has no lesser role to play. On the contrary, it is the decision-maker who must recognize and structure the problem as well as provide many of the subjective inputs necessary for the analysis. In this sense, decision aids should be considered a mental 'crutch' that allow operations which are often lost in intuitive processes to be made explicit. This does not, of course, mean that no part of the analysis will be intuitive; much will inevitably remain so. However, it does mean that certain intuitive operations which the human mind performs ineffectively (e.g. aggregating across data sources), can be avoided. Furthermore, it implies that the decision-maker probably has to think a lot harder about many of the issues involved. It is my view that many decision-makers avoid using decision aids precisely because these imply greater investment in mental effort as well as the necessity to face squarely the fact that we lack the means to deal with complex problems.

Fourth, a real problem arises in many applied settings where the decision-maker is under pressure and has no time to use a formal decision aid. What can be done in such circumstances? In one sense intuitive judgement is the only resort. However, I submit that if intuitive judgement has been trained in the use of formal aids, there is a greater probability that, under pressure, more appropriate questions will be asked. Structuring and taking decisions is highly dependent upon formulating questions pertinent to the situation. Indeed, this is probably one of the most important aspects of decision making. Therefore, if the use of aids does enhance this aspect of intuitive judgement, it should lead to improved decision performance in situations where aids cannot be formally applied. For example, simply posing the questions in Table 9.1 and 9.3 might clarify several issues in a decision taken under pressure.

There are costs and benefits associated with using decision aids. Furthermore, they are no panacea; nor, however, is unaided intuition. Writing several centuries ago, it is Francis Bacon who has best encapsulated my own view: 'Neither hand nor mind alone, left to themselves, amounts to much; instruments and aids are the means to perfection.'

## NOTES AND REFERENCES

1. See, for example, R. L. Keeney (1982). Decision analysis: An overview. *Operations Research*, **30**, 803–838; R. L. Keeney and H. Raiffa (1976). *Decisions With Multiple Objectives: Preferences and Value Tradeoffs*, New York: Wiley;

P. G. Moore and H. Thomas (1976). *The Anatomy of Decisions*, Harmondsworth, England: Penguin; D. V. Lindley (1985). *Making Decisions* (2nd. edn), Chichester, England: Wiley; and H. Raiffa (1968). *Decision Analysis*, Reading, Mass: Addison-Wesley.

2. W. Edwards (1977). Use of multiattribute utility measurement for social decision making. In D. E. Bell, R. L. Keeney, and H. Raiffa (eds.), *Conflicting Objectives in Decisions*, Chichester, England: Wiley, pp. 247–275.

3. Indeed, it can be shown under a set of not too restrictive assumptions that maximizing expected utility is the only decision criterion that should be considered by a 'rational' person. See for example, J. Marschak and R. Radner (1972). *Economic Theory of Teams*, New Haven: Yale University Press, Chapter 1.

4. For an analysis of the personnel decision situation along the lines indicated here, see R. M. Hogarth and H. J. Einhorn (1976). Optimal strategies for personnel selection when candidates can reject offers, *Journal of Business*, **49**, 478–495.

5. See, for example, Keeney and Raiffa, and Bell, Keeney, and Raiffa, References 1 and 2.

6. Keeney and Raiffa, Reference 1.

7. This example is taken from R. M. Hogarth (1979). *Evaluating Management Education*, Chichester, England: Wiley, Chapter 12.

8. J. Bigelow (ed.) (1887). *The Complete Works of Benjamin Franklin*, Vol. 4, New York: Putnam, p. 522. My attention to this reference was drawn by R. M. Dawes and B. Corrigan (1974). Linear models in decision making, *Psychological Bulletin*, **81**, 95–106.

9. P. G. Moore (1977). The manager struggles with uncertainty, *Journal of the Royal Statistical Society, Series A (General)*, **140**, 129–148.

10. See also R. Beyth-Marom (1982). How probable is probable? A numerical translation of verbal probability expressions. *Journal of Forecasting*, **1**, 257–270.

11. L. J. Savage (1971). Elicitation of personal probabilities and expectations, *Journal of the American Statistical Association*, **66**, 800.

12. C. S. Spetzler and C.-A. S. Staël von Holstein (1975). Probability encoding in decision analysis, *Management Science*, **22**, 340–358.

13. This point has been made many times by B. de Finetti.

14. See the considerable evidence reviewed by P. E. Meehl (1954). *Clinical versus Statistical Prediction: A Theoretical Analysis and Review of the Literature*, Minneapolis: University of Minnesota Press; P. Slovic and S. Lichtenstein (1971). Comparison of Bayesian and regression approaches to the study of information processing in judgment, *Organizational Behavior and Human Performance*, **6**, 649–744; and J. Sawyer (1966). Measurement *and* prediction, clinical *and* statistical, *Psychological Bulletin*, **66**, 178–200.

15. See J. L. Showers and L. M. Chakrin (1981). Reducing uncollectible revenue from residential telephone customers, *Interfaces*, **11**(6), 21–31.

16. R. M. Dawes (1971). A case study of graduate admissions: Applications of three principles of human decision making, *American Psychologist*, **26**, 180–188; R. M. Dawes (1979). The robust beauty of improper models in decision making, *American Psychologist*, **34**, 571–582; L. R. Goldberg, (1976). Man versus model of man: Just how conflicting is that evidence? *Organizational Behavior and Human Performance*, **16**, 13–22; and the review provided by C. Camerer (1981). General conditions for the success of bootstrapping models. *Organizational Behavior and Human Performance*, **27**, 411–422.

17. H. J. Einhorn (1974). Cue definition and residual judgment, *Organizational Behavior and Human Performance*, **12**, 30–49; and L. D. Pankoff and H. V. Roberts (1968). Bayesian synthesis of clinical and statistical prediction, *Psychological Bulletin*, **70**, 762–773.

18. E. H. Bowman (1963). Consistency and optimality in managerial decision making, *Management Science*, **9**, 316.
19. See the review by R. M. Hogarth (1977). Methods for aggregating opinions. In H. Jungermann and G. de Zeuuw (eds.), *Decision Making and Change in Human Affairs*, Dordrecht, Holland: Reidel, pp. 231–255; also J. S. Armstrong (1985). *Long-Range Forecasting: From Crystal Ball to Computer* (2nd edn), New York: Wiley.
20. R. M. Hogarth (1978). A note on aggregating opinions, *Organizational Behavior and Human Performance*, **21** 40–46.
21. H. J. Einhorn and R. M. Hogarth (1975). Unit weighting schemes for decision making, *Organizational Behavior and Human Performance*, **13**, 171–192.
22. H. A. Linstone and M. Turoff (1975). *The Delphi Method: Techniques and Applications*, Reading, Mass: Addison-Wesley.
23. See the fascinating literature on this topic in W. Edwards (1962). Dynamic decision theory and probabilistic information processing, *Human Factors*, **4**, 59–73; W. Edwards, H. Lindman, and L. D. Phillips (1965). Emerging technologies for making decisions. In *New Directions in Psychology II*, New York: Holt, Rinehart & Winston; W. Edwards and L. D. Phillips (1964). Man as transducer for probabilities in Bayesian command and control systems. In M. W. Shelly and G. L. Bryan (eds.), *Human Judgments and Optimality*, New York: Wiley; W. Edwards, L. D. Phillips, W. L. Hays, and B. C. Goodman (1968). Probabilistic information processing systems: Design and evaluation, *IEEE Transactions on Systems Science and Cybernetics*, Vol. SSC-4, pp. 248–265.
24. B. H. Beach (1975). Expert judgment about uncertainty: Bayesian decision making in realistic settings. *Organizational Behavior and Human Performance*, **14**, 10–59.
25. See R. O. Duda and E. H. Shortliffe (1983). Expert system research, *Science*, **220**(4594), 261–268.
26. D. Kahneman and A. Tversky (1979). Intuitive prediction: Biases and corrective procedures. In S. Makridakis and S. C. Wheelwright (eds), *TIMS Studies in Management Science*, **12**, 313–327.
27. The works cited above in Note 1 as well as the book by Bell, Keeney, and Raiffa in Reference 2 indicate many empirical examples as well as discussing theoretical issues. Another useful source of decision analysis readings is R. A. Howard, J. E. Matheson, and K. E. Miller (1976). *Readings in Decision Analysis*, Menlo Park, CA: Stanford Research Institute. A compendium of medical decision making applications can be found in J. P. Krischer (1980). An annotated bibliography of decision analytic applications to health care, *Operations Research*, **28**, 97–113. For a discussion of business applications, see J. W. Ulvila and R. V. Brown (1982). Decision analysis comes of age, *Harvard Business Review*, **60**(5), 130–141. Some fascinating studies have also been done from the viewpoint of social judgement theory. See W. M. Balke, K. R. Hammond, and G. D. Meyer (1973). An alternative approach to labor-management negotiations, *Administrative Science Quarterly*, **18**, 311–327; K. R. Hammond, T. R. Stewart, B. Brehmer, and D. O. Steinmann (1975). Social judgment theory. In M. F. Kaplan and S. Schwartz (eds), *Human Judgment and Decision Processes*, New York: Academic Press, pp. 271–312; K. R. Hammond, and L. Adelman (1976). Science, values and human judgment, *Science*, **194**, 389–396; K. R. Hammond, J. Rohrbaugh, J. Mumpower, and L. Adelman (1977). Social judgment theory: Applications in policy formation. In M. F. Kaplan and S. Schwartz (eds), *Human Judgment and Decision Processes in Applied Settings*, New York: Academic Press; and K. R. Hammond, J. L. Mumpower, and T. H. Smith (1977). Linking environmental models with models of human judgment: A symmetrical decision

aid, *IEEE Transactions on Systems, Man and Cybernetics*, Vol. SMC-7, pp. 358–367.

28. Useful discussions on this issue are contained in B. Fischhoff (1977). Cost-benefit analysis and the art of motorcycle maintenance, *Policy Sciences*, **8**, 177–202; B. Fischhoff, (1980). Clinical decision analysis, *Operations Research*, **28**, 28–43; C. J. Grayson, Jr (1973). Management science and business practice, *Harvard Business Review*, July–Aug. 41–48; and M. Zeleny (1975). Managers without management science? *Interfaces, 5*, 35–42.

29. See the excellent book by R. D. Behn and J. W. Vaupel (1982). *Quick Analysis for Busy Decision Makers*, New York: Basic Books.

# CHAPTER 10

# Human judgement—an overview[1]

In many ways, this book can be considered a 'catalogue' of human judgemental fallibilities. Chapter 1 set the scene by stressing the limitations of human information-processing capacity. It was pointed out that whereas human conceptual skills may have served us well to date, they are no longer adequate to meet the needs of the 'information revolution'. Furthermore, in today's world, the consequences of judgement are more far-reaching than was ever the case in the past. Consider, for example, the complexity of judgemental issues involved in the use of atomic power or genetic engineering, the multiple contingencies that need to be monitored in running an organization of any size, and the rapidly changing nature of the environment as evidenced, for example, by changes in social and demographic trends, technological advances, and so on.

Chapter 2 discussed human difficulties in dealing with uncertainty, and particularly in distinguishing systematic trends from random fluctuations. The attribution of *causes* to *random* occurrences was shown to be a common source of erroneous judgement. Recall, for instance, the so-called regression phenomenon. When observations, for example, sales or job performance, oscillate irregularly around a trend or level, extreme observations (large or small) are usually followed by less extreme observations, i.e. there is *regression* toward the mean or trend level of the series. However, people's intuitions frequently fail to realize the nature of this phenomenon.

Chapters 3 and 4 considered the combination of information sources for predictive and evaluative judgements, respectively. Here it was shown that difficulty in processing information leads people to adopt mental 'strategies' that simplify the tasks of judgement and choice. These strategies are often effective but can sometimes lead to systematic biases. In combining information for predictive purposes, for example, the power of causal thinking to structure how the mind seeks and interprets information was particularly noted. In choice, whereas the adoption of aspiration levels or reference points considerably simplifies assessing alternative decisions, this may be at the cost of failing to make the best decision. This was further emphasized in Chapter 5 which explored the topic of decision making under uncertainty. Here several examples showed that how problems are encoded or framed can interact both with the way alternatives are evaluated and the manner in which people are required to express preferences, e.g. by placing values on alternatives or choosing between them in a direct comparison.

In Chapter 6, the difficulties of learning relations for prediction were described. It was shown that the structure of many judgemental tasks often inhibits efficient learning. Consider, for example, judgements made in job selection. In this task, one typically never learns the outcomes associated with candidates who either decline offers or are rejected. Thus, judgemental relations and their corresponding accuracy can often only be assessed on partial information. This is further compounded by the human tendency to seek information that supports one's hypotheses rather than information that could challenge them.

Chapter 7 emphasized the role of memory in judgement recalling La Rochefoucauld's apt comment that although people tend to complain of the badness of their memory, nobody complains about their judgement. It was pointed out that memory is not a faithful reproduction of the past. Rather people reconstruct the past from fragments of items remembered, the reconstruction being heavily dependent on the meaning attached to ideas, incidents, associations, and so on. The prevalence of 'hindsight' biases was also stressed. The past seems inevitable in retrospect. It holds few surprises and people have considerable facility in constructing causal explanations to account for past occurrences. Moreover, people exhibit excessive confidence in judgement. They are quick to forget how uncertain they were in the past and they are far from proficient at inventing causal scenarios for predicting the future accurately.

The ability to 'create' scenarios and explanatory models capable of yielding accurate predictions about the future is highly dependent upon powers of imagination and creativity, the subject of Chapter 8. Indeed, without imagination there can be no 'free' choice. In Chapter 8, creativity— defined as the reconstruction of ideas, concepts, associations, 'things' etc., in a manner that is novel and appropriate to a given situation — was shown to be dependent on a willingness to invest in mental effort (by emitting many 'thought trials') and an ability to retain and test novel associations. It was also shown that 'creativity techniques' are based on these principles; furthermore, most people are capable of being both more imaginative and creative than they are at present. Creative ideas are, however, exposed to social pressures and thus considerable independence of character and judgement is necessary to implement such ideas effectively.

The fallibility of human judgement was further accentuated in Chapter 9, where various means of aiding judgement were illustrated and discussed.

The purpose of this chapter is to provide an overview of human judgement in a manner that synthesizes the various findings reported in the book. The plan of the chapter is as follows. First, a conceptual model of judgement is outlined. This shows, *inter alia*, that judgemental biases can be thought of as occurring at different stages of information processing. The subsequent section of the chapter reviews biases associated with these different stages. Next, some issues involved in determining whether or not particular acts or judgements are rational are discussed as well as conditions under which judgements and choices are likely to be accompanied by good outcomes. This is followed, prior to a conclusion, by some speculative comments on the origins of judgemental bias.

On considering the synthesis presented here, it is important to emphasize that human judgemental activity is proficient in a wide range of demanding tasks. However, judgemental abilities have developed in circumstances of relatively slow evolutionary change. As increasing technological development acts to accelerate change, the deficiencies of human judgement are inevitably accentuated. Nonetheless, technology can be adapted to complement human judgement rather than expose its weaknesses. However, to accept such aids, people must first be willing to admit their own deficiencies.

In many ways this chapter presents ideas at a conceptual, and sometimes abstract level which exceeds that of other chapters. This results from the intent to provide a more general framework within which the reader can examine his or her own judgemental activity, and perhaps that of others. Despite the more abstract nature of the chapter, I believe it should still be accessible to those who understood the preceding chapters.

## A CONCEPTUAL MODEL OF JUDGEMENT

The conceptual model presented here conceives of judgement taking place within a system composed of three elements. First, there is the person; second, the task environment within which the person makes judgements; and third, the actions that result from judgement and which can subsequently affect both the person and the task environment (cf. Chapter 6). To be specific, consider a waiter in a restaurant who believes that young people do not tip generously.[2] Consistent with his belief, he concentrates attention on older customers. The result is that younger customers receive poor service to which they react by giving small tips. This in turn reinforces the waiter's belief.

A schematic, and more detailed, representation of this model is presented in Figure 10.1. Judgement occurs within a so-called task environment—box 1. Within the task environment is what we shall call the person's *schema*—box 2. This symbolizes the person's beliefs concerning the task environment and his or her representation of it; that is, how he or she perceives the judgemental task. For example, part of the schema of the waiter described above is the belief, 'Young people do not have the means to tip well. Thus efforts in service directed at younger customers are unlikely to be rewarded.' In any given situation, therefore, the schema is created both by the person's memory and characteristics of the judgemental task (e.g. the age distribution of customers in the restaurant at a particular time).

The actual processing of information, that is the operations that lead to judgement, can be decomposed into: (a) *acquisition* of information—box 3; (b) *processing* of information—box 4; and (c) *output*—box 5. To continue

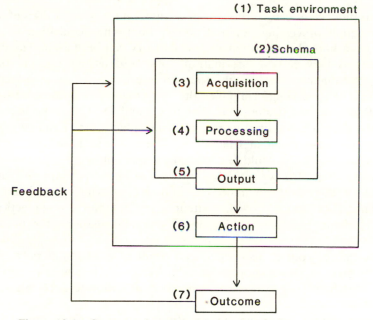

Figure 10.1   Conceptual model of judgement (refer to text as well as Table 10.1)

the example of the waiter, when deciding how much attention to give to different customers, he first accesses information both from memory (i.e. beliefs concerning tipping habits and age), and the environment (the age distribution of customers); second, this information is processed; and third, the result of processing is the waiter's judgement as to how much attention should be devoted to different customers. In this example, the 'output' is probably internal to the waiter. However, in other situations the output could be expressed externally. Consider, for instance, a salesman giving an estimate of sales in his region for the next quarter.

Output (box 5) has been drawn at the interface of the schema and the task environment to emphasize the location of its occurrence. However, frequently—and this is true of the waiter example—the output is indistinguishable to a third party from the *action* (box 6) which occurs within the task environment. (The waiter's judgement is reflected in the quality of service he actually gives to different customers.) Subsequently the action leads to an *outcome* (box 7)—in this case the tips given by the different customers. These outcomes can then feed back into the person's schema (e.g. reinforcing the notion that younger customers do not tip generously), and may even affect the environment in which the action takes place. For example, if young people receive poor service at the restaurant they may cease to frequent it and thus affect the subsequent age distribution of customers.

Bias in judgement can be thought of as intervening at the different stages of information processing outlined above. First, the acquisition of information from both the environment and memory can be biased. The crucial issue here is how certain information does or does not become *salient*. Second, the manner in which information is processed can be biased; for example, if the individual simplifies the judgemental situation by using an inappropriate mental strategy (cf. Chapters 3 and 4). Third, the manner in which the person is required to respond can induce bias. Examples of this kind of bias were given in Chapter 5, where it was noted that relative preferences for gambles could be reversed when people were asked to express choices in different ways. Finally, and as outlined in Chapters 2 and 6, outcomes of judgement can induce bias in both (1) the interpretation of their significance (For example, is the outcome attributable to one's actions or simply a chance fluctuation?), and (2) learning relations for predictive activity.

Biases can, of course, also occur as a result of interactions between the different stages of information processing. For example, the requirement to make a particular type of response can direct attention to accessing specific information.

However, prior to reviewing these different sources of judgemental bias, it is appropriate to recall the relevant features of the human information-processing system.

As stated in Chapter 1, although people have limited information-processing capacity, they are adaptive. The nature of a judgemental task determines to a large extent how people can and do deal with the task. For example, if information is presented sequentially, this can induce a judgemental strategy that is different from that used when all information is presented simultaneously. Consider, for instance, the difference between selecting one of several products on a supermarket shelf as opposed to being given a complete information display indicating the different attributes of the alternatives.

There are four major consequences of limited human information-processing capacity (cf. Chapter 1): (1) perception of information is not comprehensive but *selective*; (2) since people cannot simultaneously integrate a great deal of information, they process information in a predominantly *sequential* manner; (3) information processing is necessarily dependent upon the use of operations that *simplify judgemental tasks* and *reduce mental effort*; and (4) people have *limited memory* capacity. It is important to add, however, that people do not submit passively to their environment. On the contrary, in order to meet their needs people require some degree of control over the environment. Behaviour is thus purposeful and characterized by people *acting on* the environment.

In summary, the conceptual model of human judgemental activity described here is the following: The context of judgement is that of a three-element system involved in mutual interaction. There is the person, actions

*Table 10.1   Key issues in judgemental biases*

(1) *Characteristics of human information-processing system*
   (a) Selective perception
   (b) Sequential processing
   (c) Limited 'computational' ability
   (d) Limited memory
   (e) Dependence on task characteristics—'adaptiveness'

(2) *Need to understand, control, and master the environment*

(3) *Location of judgemental bias*

| | Key questions |
|---|---|
| (a) Information acquisition | Salience of information |
| (b) Processing | Choice of decision/processing rule |
| (c) Output | Response mode |
| (d) Feedback | Interpretability of outcome feedback |

that result from judgements made by the person, and the environment in which judgements, actions and their outcomes take place and are interpreted by the individual—see Figure 10.1. It is important to emphasize that each of the elements affects and is affected by the others as illustrated, for instance, in the example of the waiter given above. When one considers the information-processing capacity of the person within the three-element system, the picture is one of a selective, essentially sequential information processor with limited powers of 'computation' and memory. Although limited, however, people have the ability to be creative and do seek to understand, control and master their environments. Indeed, understanding and control of the environment are essential to survival. Nonetheless, in these tasks unaided human judgement is often deficient in a number of important respects.

Table 10.1 summarizes the above and indicates the key issues involved in judgemental bias.

## SOURCES OF BIAS

### Information acquisition

The issue of bias in information acquisition can be conceptualized by enquiring when and why information becomes *salient* to an individual. This question can be further broken down by noting that information can be accessed from two sources: (1) the individual's memory; and (2) the task environment. Consequently the relative salience of information can be a function of memory, features of the task environment, or both. A related point is that the mind is not a vacuum. It actively seeks and selects information.

Several sources of memory bias in information acquisition were noted in earlier chapters:

(1) The ease with which information can be recalled from memory is a clue people use to predict the frequency of an event (the 'availability' heuristic). Thus people may believe, for example, that events that are well publicized (such as tornadoes or certain causes of death), are more frequent than is in fact the case. There is also a tendency to consider one's own range of experience as 'normal' and thus to make erroneous attributions in judging the 'deviant' behaviour of others. People's jobs can also induce so-called 'professional deformation,' evidenced in tendencies to perceive problems in ways related to specific experience. More generally, this is known as *selective perception*. The same administrative problem, for instance, can be perceived as an 'accounting' problem by accountants, a 'personnel' problem by personnel officers and a 'marketing' problem by marketing managers.[3]

(2) The mind does not register what it does not or cannot perceive. Judgements of likelihood are thus not influenced by what might have happened but did not. To clarify these apparently obscure statements, consider what happens when a candidate is rejected for a job. A judgement has been made. However, that judgement will (usually) produce no feedback, since the rejected candidate can neither be a success nor failure in the job.

(3) Related to the preceding point is the tendency for people to judge strength of predictive ability by frequency rather than relative frequency. For example, if you have been told that company A has successfully marketed 12 innovations in the last 3 years while company B has only marketed 6, there is a tendency to believe that company A has been more successful in this area. However, one should also ask how many innovations—in total—both companies have attempted!

(4) Information that is *concrete* is more salient in memory than information that is *abstract*. That is, information that is vivid, e.g. describing an experience or perhaps involving a personal incident, is more easily recalled than, for example, statistical summary data. Furthermore, this tendency can have important effects on judgement. For instance, if you are contemplating buying a car, witnessing the positive or negative experience of a neighbour with a particular model is liable to be recalled more vividly in your memory—and thus weigh more heavily in judgement—than more extensive data published about that model in a consumer or motoring magazine. Data coded in memory by images and through several associations can become disproportionately salient.

The physical structure of a judgemental task can also bias information acquisition:

(1) Order effects have been noted. Sometimes the first in a series of items dominates (a primacy effect), sometimes the latter (a recency effect).

(2) As with acquisition from memory, the 'availability' heuristic can play an important role. In problem solving and creative thinking, for example, hints can exert subtle effects on how problems are perceived thereby affecting

subsequent solutions. Consider, for instance, the 'Eureka' effect, on the one hand, or the difficulty in solving a problem when one has a negative 'set,' on the other (i.e. you only see one side of a problem and this inhibits you from solving it). Other biases can be induced by the simple absence of some data and the presence of other information. As attested by the adage 'out of sight, out of mind', data that are physically 'available' somehow seem more important than those that are missing.

(3) As noted in several chapters, the mind is sensitive to deviations or exceptions. Thus, in casual reasoning the adoption of particular 'causal fields' or backgrounds can determine what is perceived to be a difference, and thus which variables are deemed to be causally relevant. Similarly, in choice the attributes of alternatives are evaluated as deviations from reference points or levels of aspiration. Thus, since losses are generally weighted more heavily than gains, the selection of particular reference points can exert important influences on choice.

(4) Information is typically not 'given' but must be sought. Consequently, when information is presented to a person in a readily accessible form this can have important consequences. Russo's study of the effects of different presentations of 'unit-price' information in supermarkets attests precisely to this point (see Chapter 4).[4] Task variables, such as manner and order of presentation, context effects, and so on, contribute to how a person perceives a situation, and consequently how he or she makes judgements. Other task variables include (a) data displays that seem so logical and complete that important omissions are overlooked, (b) information overload—there is so much information present that the individual is unable to discern the important variables—and (c) redundant information displays. All information presented seems so consistent that the individual is only able to come to one, possibly erroneous conclusion.

The interaction of memory (i.e. a person's schema) and features of the task environment can also bias judgement:

(1) What a person expects to see affects what a person does see. This effect was dramatically illustrated in Bruner and Postman's playing-card experiment (see Chapter 7).[5] People had extraordinary difficulty recognizing red spades and often distorted their perceptions to concur with what they expected to see. More generally, taking expectations for reality can have serious dysfunctional consequences.

(2) The meaning people attach to information can produce serious distortions in omitting to consider certain information. Several studies show that even when so-called base-rate data are available, people will ignore them in the presence of 'specific' data. When the latter are missing, however, base-rate data do become salient in judgement.

(3) A related issue concerns the biases involved when people seek information in judgemental activity. People have a strong tendency to seek

information that is consistent with their hypotheses rather than information that could cause them to reject a hypothesis. Consider the employment interview. Evidence indicates that once an interviewer has formulated an impression (e.g. the person will be successful or unsuccessful in the job), the rest of the interview is spent seeking information consistent with this hypothesis. Little weight or thought is given to information that could be inconsistent. Some studies also show more general evidence of tendencies to ignore, or at least discount, conflicting evidence.

(4) A person's causal framework or schema for thinking about a situation guides his or her interpretation of information. If the schema is biased, it follows that the acquisition of particular information can also be biased.

## Processing

The key question identified in Table 10.1 relating to the 'processing' stage is the individual's choice of a decision/information-processing rule. That is, what is the series of mental operations the person applies to the information that has been accessed? Furthermore, from a perspective of bias, what is the relative effectiveness of different types of operations? As in information acquisition, bias in processing can be induced by both memory and task characteristics.

Memory biases in processing include the following:

(1) Recalling that a particular choice/judgement worked well in the past. Habit in judgement and choice is important. However, the fact that a previous choice or choice rule was successful in the past carries no guarantee of future success.

(2) Effects of the 'availability' heuristic can also operate in the choice of a decision rule. That is, certain 'rules' may be more available to a person than others because of specific personal experience. For example, a common human fallibility is to assume that because one is an expert in a particular domain, expertise also 'generalizes' to other areas. However, processing rules that operate well in, say, financial decision making, do not necessarily carry over to problems of general management.

The bulk of processing biases noted in the literature, however, result from (1) effects of task variables, (2) unwillingness to expend mental effort, and (3) inconsistency in applying judgemental rules.

(1) Task variables that bias processing include: amount of information, time pressures, sequential vs. intact data presentation formats, inconsistent or missing values in information.

(2) People adopt processing strategies to reduce mental effort and these can often lead to bias. There is a general preference to avoid direct comparisons or trade-offs among different information sources. Over-reliance on

subsets of the information, can, however, lead to choices that are inconsistent with a person's preferences, as when subsets of information are eliminated in a sequential manner. Furthermore, several strategies discussed in Chapters 3 and 4 seem to be based on a potentially misleading 'quasi-logic'. Thus, although easy to use, the 'representativeness heuristic' leads to underestimating the extent of variation in the environment. With an anchoring and adjustment strategy, adjustments away from the anchor are often insufficient.

(3) A major source of processing bias is lack of consistency in judgement. People do not seem capable of applying judgemental rules consistently across a series of cases. Indeed, several studies show that the validity of judgement is considerably attentuated by this particular fallibility.

## Output

'Output' biases appear to be triggered by the way in which people express judgement or choice (i.e. the 'response mode'—see Table 10.1). There are many examples:

(1) Estimates of probabilities have been found to differ according to the method with which people have been asked to respond as well as the scale used to measure responses.[6]

(2) People evaluate risky prospects (and even change their preferences) according to the basis on which they are asked to evaluate them (e.g. playing a bet versus setting a minimum selling price).

(3) As most market researchers know, responses to questions can vary under the variety of possible methods used to elicit responses (e.g. open interviews, different types of questionnaires, and so on).

(4) In choice situations, response modes can accentuate different aspects of alternatives and, in some circumstances, even lead people into making *intransitive* choices. The ubiquity of 'response mode bias' is a problem that has and will cause problems for both social science and its users for many years.[7]

## Feedback

The importance of feedback in judgement relates to its effects on learning. If a person's judgement is not accompanied by some form of feedback, learning cannot occur. For example, consider what happens when you make a judgement in a situation where feedback is not possible—concerning, for example, the ability of a person to do a job for which he or she was rejected. Bias in feedback, caused either because it is not 'possible' to observe outcomes associated with the total range of judgements (as in the job selection example), or for other reasons (e.g. feedback is delayed inordinately, other events affect outcomes, and so on), is one of the most important sources of difficulty in judgement. Consider the following:

(1) Misinterpretation of 'chance' and 'cause.' As noted in Chapter 2, people have great difficulty in distinguishing whether particular outcomes (for example, the result of a sales campaign), are due to a specific cause (e.g. a special advertising effort), or to chance factors (e.g. a freak combination of circumstances increasing demand). That people should confound 'chance' and 'cause' is, of course, understandable, since they both occur simultaneously in experience. Furthermore, 'chance' is an artificial concept in the sense that everything must have some causal agent, or combination of such agents. 'Chance' thus refers to a combination of unidentifiable causes, and to state that something occurs 'by chance' is necessarily an admission of ignorance (to which, of course, no negative connotation need be associated). The misinterpretation of chance and cause leads to *erroneous causal attributions*, instances of which are exemplified by the failure to understand the effects of regression.

More generally, in tasks involving both skill and chance, it is difficult to disentangle the relative contributions of both factors. Furthermore, there is a tendency for people to attribute 'good' outcomes to skill and 'bad' outcomes to chance. Langer has further demonstrated what she has called the 'illusion of control'.[8] Either through observing a sequence of successful outcomes or spending time analysing a situation, people can acquire the impression of having more control over outcomes than is justified by a more objective appraisal of the circumstances. This bias has important implications for decision makers when considering their track records of past successes and failures, as well as their efforts to plan for the future.

(2) A second bias arising from observation of chance occurrences is the so-called 'gambler's fallacy'. After seeing a sequence of successes or failures in a situation known to be random in nature, people tend to believe that the event that has not appeared recently becomes more probable.

(3) From early childhood people learn predictive relations by observing the joint occurrence of events, for example reducing the sensation of hunger by eating. However, even if memory were perfect, use of the observation of the joint occurrence of events as a clue to predictive relations could lead to systematic bias. First, to infer predictive relations, it is necessary to have information concerning non-occurrences (consider again the missing outcome concerning the rejected job candidate). However, even when such information is available, people tend to ignore it unless it is made salient for them. Second, ideas of association based on the observation of a few joint occurrences can take on a life of their own and become resistant to disconfirming evidence.[9] Consider, for example, the case of a manager observing an increase in efficiency in a troublesome department after placing it under the control of a new supervisor. The 'joint occurrence' of (a) the increase in efficiency and (b) the appointment of the new supervisor can lead to a more general belief in the supervisor's competence which can be upheld even if negative evidence about the supervisor's competence subsequently becomes available.

(4) An effect of the knowledge of an 'outcome' noted in Chapter 7 was the creation of *hindsight* bias. Cognizance of an outcome can restructure memory in a way that makes the presumed causal links leading to the observed outcome seem inevitable. People have short memories concerning their prior uncertainties. This, in turn, can lead to a diminished ability to imagine alternative explanatory schemes for the past, and by extension for the future.

(5) Misplaced confidence in judgement is another possible feedback bias which was explored in some depth in Chapter 6. Because people are unaware of the characteristics of the task structure in which they make judgements, interpretations that lead to misplaced confidence (usually overconfidence) are common.

In Table 10.2 the main sources of bias reported in the literature, together with brief descriptions and examples, are summarized according to the stages of information processing indicated in Figure 10.1.[10]

## ON GOOD AND BAD DECISIONS[11]

As noted previously, this book has emphasized information-processing biases in judgement and choice. This, in turn, could lead to an impression that people are totally incompetent at making decisions. However, this impression is inconsistent with everyday experience in which we typically encounter both good and bad decision making as well as the fact that the human mind is capable of impressive intellectual achievements. Therefore, in evaluating the more general question of whether people are or are not good at making decisions, it is necessary to consider (a) the criteria by which decisions are judged, and (b) the conditions which hinder or facilitate good decision making.

### Criteria for good decisions

The statement that a judgement or choice is biased cannot be made without reference to a standard. Typically, the standard is the output of some optimal model of the situation such as those prescribed by the laws of probability or expected utility theory. For example, the claim that people often fail to recognize regression effects when making probabilistic predictions rests on the assumption that the underlying process generating the events to be predicted can be modelled by a particular class of statistical models. However, there can be no assurance that this is the case.

In determining the 'correct' decision in any given situation, one needs to consider characteristics of two models of the task with which the person is confronted. These are, first, the model of the situation as perceived by the person making the decision (i.e. his or her understanding of the task), and second, that of a third party (perhaps a researcher) who has chosen an

216

*Table 10.2   Biases in information processing[10]*

(Reprinted by permission from R. M. Hogarth and S. Makridakis, Forecasting and planning: an evaluation, *Management Science,* **27**(2), Feb. 1981. Copyright 1981 The Institute of Management Sciences)

| Bias/source of bias | Description | Example |
|---|---|---|
| **ACQUISITION** | | |
| Availability | – Ease with which specific instances can be recalled from memory affects judgements of frequency. | – Frequency of well-publicized events is overestimated (e.g., deaths due to homicide, cancer); frequency of less well-publicized events is underestimated (e.g., deaths due to asthma and diabetes). |
| | – Chance 'availability' of particular 'cues' in the immediate environment affects judgement. | – Problem-solving can be hindered/facilitated by cues perceived by chance in a particular setting (hints set up cognitive 'direction'). |
| Selective perception | – People structure problems on the basis of their own experience. | – The same problem can be seen by a marketing manager as a marketing problem, as a financial problem by a finance manager, etc. |
| | – Anticipations of what one expects to see bias what one does see. | – Identification of incongruent objects, e.g. playing cards with *red* spades, is either inaccurately reported or causes discomfort. |
| | – People seek information consistent with their own views/hypotheses. | – Interviewers seek information about candidates consistent with first impressions rather than information that could refute those impressions. |
| | – People downplay/disregard conflicting evidence. | – In forming impressions, people underweight information that does not fit a consistent profile. |

*Table 10.2   Cont'd.*

| Bias/source of bias | Description | Example |
|---|---|---|
| Frequency | – Cue used to judge strength of predictive relations is observed frequency rather than observed relative frequency. Information on 'non-occurrences' of an event is often unavailable and frequently ignored when available. | – When considering relative performance (of, say, two persons), the absolute number of successes is given greater weight than the relative number of successes to successes *and* failures (i.e. the denominator is ignored). Note, however, that the number of failures is frequently unavailable. |
| Concrete information (ignoring base-rate, or prior information) | – *Concrete* information (i.e. vivid, or based on experience/incidents) dominates *abstract* information (e.g. summaries, statistical base-rates, etc.). | – When purchasing a car, the positive or negative experience of a *single* person you know, is liable to weigh more heavily in judgement than available and more valid statistical information, e.g. in *Consumer Reports*. |
| Illusory correlation | – Belief that two variables covary when in fact they do not (possibly related to 'Frequency' above) | – Selection of an inappropriate variable to make a prediction. |
| Data presentation | – Order effects (primacy/recency). | – Sometimes the first items in a sequential presentation assume undue importance (primacy), sometimes the last items (recency). |
|  | – Mode of presentation. | – Sequential vs. intact data displays can affect what people are able to access. Contrast, for example, complete listed unit-price shopping vs. own sequential information search. |

218

*Table 10.2   Cont'd.*

| Bias/source of bias | Description | Example |
|---|---|---|
|  | – Mixture of types of information, e.g. qualitative and quantitative. | – Concentration on quantitative data, exclusion of qualitative, or vice versa. |
|  | – Logical data displays. | – Apparently complete 'logical' data displays can blind people to critical omissions. |
|  | – Context effects on perceived variability. | – Assessments of variability, of say a series of numbers, is affected by the absolute size (e.g. mean level) of the numbers. |
| Framing | – Outcomes are evaluated as deviations from reference points or levels of aspirations. This can interact with the way people evaluate outcomes that are 'framed' as losses or gains. | – Loss versus gains frames can induce reversals in expressed choices. |

PROCESSING

| Inconsistency | – Inability to apply a consistent judgemental strategy over a repetitive set of cases. | – Judgements involving selection, e.g. personnel/graduate school admissions. |
| Conservatism | – Failure to revise opinion on receipt of new information to the same extent as Bayes' theorem. (Note this may be counterbalanced by the 'best-guess' strategy and produce near optimal performance in the presence of unreliable data sources.) | – Opinion revision in many settings, e.g. military, business, medicine. |

Table 10.2 Cont'd.

| Bias/source of bias | Description | Example |
|---|---|---|
| Non-linear extrapolation | – Inability to extrapolate growth processes (e.g. exponential) and tendency to underestimate joint probabilities of several events. | – Gross underestimation of outcomes of exponentially increasing processes and overestimation of joint probabilities of several events. |

*'Heuristics' used to reduce mental effort:*

| | | |
|---|---|---|
| – Habit/'rules of thumb' | – Choosing an alternative because it has previously been satisfactory. | – Consumer shopping; 'rules of thumb' adopted in certain professions. |
| – Anchoring and adjustment | – Prediction made by anchoring on a cue or value and then adjusting to allow for the circumstances of the present case. | – Making a sales forecast by taking last year's sales and adding, say, 5%. |
| – Representative-ness | – Judging the likelihood of an event by estimating degree of *similarity* to the class of events of which it is supposed to be an exemplar. | – Stereotyping, e.g. imagining that someone is a lawyer because he exhibits characteristics typical of a lawyer. |
| – Law of *small* numbers | – Characteristics of small samples are deemed to be representative of the populations from which they are drawn. | – Interpretation of data, too much weight given to small sample results (which are quite likely to be atypical). |
| – Justifiability | – A 'processing' rule can be used if the individual finds a rationale to 'justify' it. | – When provided with an apparently rational argument, people will tend to follow a decision rule even if it is really inappropriate. |

*Table 10.2   Cont'd.*

| Bias/source of bias | Description | Example |
|---|---|---|
| – Regression bias | – Extreme values of a variable are used to predict extreme values of the next observation of the variable (thus failing to allow for regression to the mean). | – Following observation of bad performance by an employee, a manager could attribute subsequent improvement to his or her intervention (e.g. warning to the employee). However, due to regression effects, improvement (performance closer to the mean level), is likely *without* intervention. |
| – 'Best guess' strategy | – Under conditions involving several sources of uncertainty, simplification is made by ignoring some uncertainties and basing judgement on the 'most likely' hypothesis. (Note, people simplify by ignoring uncertainty.) More generally, tendency to discount uncertainty. | – Ignoring the fact that information sources are unreliable. |
| *The decision environment*: | | |
| – Complexity | – Complexity induced by time pressure, information overload, distractions lead to reduced consistency of judgement. | – In decisions taken under time pressure information processing may be quite superficial. |
| – Emotional stress | – Emotional stress reduces the care with which people select and process information. | – Panic judgements. |
| – Social pressures | – Social pressures, e.g. of a group, cause people to distort their judgements. | – The majority in a group can unduly influence the judgement of minority members. |

*Table 10.2  Cont'd.*

| Bias/source of bias | Description | Example |
|---|---|---|
| *Information sources*: | | |
| – Consistency of information sources | – Consistency of information sources can lead to increases in confidence in judgement but not to increased predictive accuracy. | – People often like to have more information, even though it is redundant with what they already have. |

– Data presentation: See items under the ACQUISITION section.

## OUTPUT

| *Response mode*: | | |
|---|---|---|
| – Question format | – The way a person is required or chooses to make a judgement can affect the outcome. | – Preferences for risky gambles have been found to be inconsistent with the prices for which people are willing to sell them. |
| – Scale effects | – The scale on which responses are recorded can affect responses. | – Estimates of probabilities can vary when estimated directly on a scale from zero to one, or when 'odds' or even 'log-odds' are used. |
| Wishful thinking | – People's preferences for outcomes of events affect their assessment of the events. | – People sometimes assess the probability of outcomes they desire to be greater than their state of knowledge justifies. |
| Illusion of control | – Activity concerning an uncertain outcome can by itself induce in a person feelings of control over the uncertain event. | – Activities such as planning, or even the making of forecasts, can induce feelings of control over the uncertain future. |

*Table 10.2   Cont'd.*

| Bias/source of bias | Description | Example |
|---|---|---|
| **FEEDBACK** | | |
| Outcome irrelevant learning structures | – Outcomes observed yield inaccurate or incomplete information concerning predictive relations. This can lead, *inter alia*, to unrealistic confidence in one's own judgement. | – In personnel selection you can learn how good your judgement is concerning candidates selected; but you usually have no information concerning subsequent performance of rejected candidates. |
| Misperception of chance fluctuations (e.g. gambler's fallacy) | – Observation of an unexpected number of similar chance outcomes leads to the expectation that the probability of the appearance of an event not recently seen increases. | – So-called 'gambler's fallacy'—after observing, say, 9 successive Reds in roulette, people tend to believe that Black is more likely on the next throw. |
| Success/failure attributions | – Tendency to attribute success to one's skill, and failure to chance (this is also related to the 'Illusion of control'—see above). | – Successes in one's job, e.g. making a difficult sale, are attributed to one's skill; failures to 'bad luck'. |
| Logical fallacies in recall | – Inability to recall details of an event leads to 'logical' reconstruction which can be inaccurate. | – Eyewitness testimony. |
| – Hindsight bias | – In retrospect, people are not 'surprised' about what has happened in the past. They can easily find plausible explanations. | – The 'Monday morning quarterback' phenomenon. |

'optimal' model for the task at hand. However, whereas the adequacy of decisions is often judged by noting discrepancies between the outputs of the two models (i.e. Do the person's responses match those of the optimal model?), there are three ways of interpreting such discrepancies. (1) Both models could represent the task inadequately, but in different ways. (2) The optimal model respresents the task more adequately than that of the person (the assumption under which much of the research discussed in this book is predicated). (3) The person's model is more appropriate than the optimal model. In addition, there could be cases where there are no differences between the models but they both misrepresent the task. Thus before comparing discrepancies between the two models, it is important to compare each with the task at hand.

There are two important characteristics of optimal models for decision tasks. First, the definition of what is optimal is made conditionally upon both a set of assumptions about the task (e.g. one is dealing with an underlying random process) and some explicit decision criterion (e.g., maximize expected utility). Second, by definition the model is an abstraction, and thus a simplification of reality. The importance of this latter statement is that since a model is a simplification, it must—by necessity—fail to be a complete representation of the task. In this sense, therefore, outputs of optimal models must be 'wrong' to some degree. The critical question, therefore, is 'how wrong'.

Considering the complexity of decision tasks relative to the capabilities of the human information-processing system, it must also be the case that people's models (i.e. mental representations) of tasks are incomplete. However, these models often differ from the optimal models discussed above in that both underlying assumptions about the task and criteria used to evaluate decisions are often only loosely specified. Moreover, when discrepancies occur between an optimal model and that of the decision maker, a case can sometimes be made that the person's model captures the essence of the task more adequately than the optimal model. That is, it is the optimal model rather than the person that is 'wrong'. Nonetheless, care must be exercised in using this kind of reasoning when interpreting why people may have acted in particular ways. It is often not posssible to test whether rationalizations after the fact are justified, and thus easy to delude oneself that they are.

The above arguments raise an important issue. If, in any given situation, both the optimal model and that of the decision maker are inadequate, how can one tell whether a decision is or is not appropriate? At one level, it is possible to judge decisions by their outcomes, and indeed, many people only judge decisions by results. However, since outcomes depend both on actions taken by a decision maker and chance factors, this is not a satisfactory procedure. In the final analysis, we have no option but to use our admittedly fallible judgement to determine whether or not decisions have been appropriate. For example, do we believe that the assumptions of the optimal model provide an adequate representation of the task? Do we accept the axioms or principles underlying the choice rule? And so on.

An important implication of this discussion is that how a person represents a task in his or her mind is the critical determinant of the adequacy of a decision. That is, not only does this representation determine how the person sees the task, it will also determine the extent to which he or she judges other representations such as the optimal model proposed by a third party. However, since for many decisions the appropriate representation of a task is not obvious, what does this imply? My own view is that a good decision procedure involves looking at a problem from many different perspectives. One should avoid being 'framed' (cf. Chapter 5) by the first representation of the problem that one encounters or formulates. In other words, a good decision follows from considering a problem from different viewpoints and from attempting to judge which is the most appropriate. This means that to support the claim that a decision is biased, one has to show that, at the time the decision is made, other responses could have been reached through determining alternative representations of the problem; moreover, had the person considered such alternative representations, he or she would have made a different decision. For example, a person may at first deny that he or she has made an error in probabilistic reasoning by failing to take account of regression toward the mean. However, if after reconsidering the problem and being exposed to the arguments about regression, the person changes his or her response, then by the criterion given here, the first response was biased. If, on the other hand, the person persists in his or her response after seriously considering alternative representations of the problem, then it would be difficult to claim that the response was biased.

Discussion of good and bad decisions inevitably leads to considering the issue of what is or what is not rational behaviour. Without elaborating on this topic at length, it is important to emphasize that disagreement on this issue often has its roots in failing to realize the distinction between two types of rationality. The first concerns itself solely with the efficacy with which a person reaches his or her goals. This can be called the *rationality of means* and is the form of rationality embodied in the optimal models used as standards for decision behaviour in this book. The second kind of rationality concerns the goals themselves and thus could be called the *rationality of goals*. In contrast to the former, the latter asks whether the person's goals are rational irrespective of how he or she attempts to achieve them. Thus, a person could exhibit high rationality of means, but low rationality of goals, or vice versa. As an example of the former, consider a criminal who carries out a heinous crime with great efficacy. Is this person rational? If one only considers means, the answer is positive. On the other hand, few would consider that such a person had rational goals. In judging whether particular acts are rational, however, people typically (and implicitly) consider both the rationalities of means and goals. However, if people weight the two types of rationality differently in judgement, it should come as no surprise that assessing the rationality of specific acts can lead to spirited debate.

**When are good outcomes likely to occur?**

Two issues are central to whether people do or do not experience good outcomes following their decisions. The first concerns the extent to which a person's understanding of a task (or schema, cf. Figure 10.1) accurately represents relations between important variables in the environment. Simply put, the more accurate one's schema, the more likely one is to observe good outcomes following action.[12] The second issue refers to the sensitivity of outcomes to specific judgements and/or choices. Since much of this book has examined how people's perceptions of decision tasks are often distorted (both by limitations of the human information-processing system and characteristics of the environment in which decisions must be made), I will concentrate here on the latter.

In thinking about the adequacy of decision making, it is important to consider 'how good' judgements or decisions need to be in different types of tasks. To illustrate, consider the following apocryphal story. A pilot flying a Boeing 747 from Tokyo to the United States missed the runway at San Francisco International Airport by 200 yards and ditched the aircraft in the adjacent bay. Fortunately, little damage was done and neither the passengers nor crew were harmed. After the event, the pilot was besieged by journalists who asked how he came to miss the runway by 200 yards. Seemingly unconcerned by the implied criticism, the pilot responded: 'Considering that I flew from Tokyo, 200 yards is not much of a miss.'

This story highlights an important feature of much decision making activity. Many judgements—and their accompanying actions—involve sequences of judgement–action–feedback loops (cf. Figure 10.1) in tasks where the decision maker knows that even if the first judgement is inaccurate, this can be modified across time as information is received. For example, whereas a pilot would start by setting a trajectory in Tokyo with the goal of flying to San Francisco, he or she would typically expect to update the flight plan as more precise information became available on the way across the Pacific. Indeed, the degree of accuracy required of the pilot's first judgement could be quite crude, i.e. fly toward the East. Moreover, knowing this, it would be absurd for the pilot to stick rigidly to the flight plan originally established in Tokyo. In other words, two critical aspects of decision making tasks are the availability of accurate feedback and the degree of commitment implied by particular actions. Specifically, their importance lies in the fact that they can be used to reduce the extent to which particular judgements or actions need to be wholly accurate or appropriate.

It is easy to overlook the importance of feedback to behavior. As stated by one investigator:

> All behavior involves strong feedback effects, whether one is considering spinal reflexes or self-actualization. Feedback is such an all-pervasive and fundamental aspect of behavior that it is as invisible as the air we breathe. Quite literally it is behavior—we know nothing of our own behavior but the feedback effects of our own outputs.[13]

In other words, if the environment in which decisions are taken generates clear feedback, people will generally be able to adapt to the demands of the task. Moreover, this is particularly likely to be the case where sequences of decisions are taken across time (as in piloting an aircraft) and where it is possible to respond to the feedback and observe the effects of actions on outcomes. Conversely, if feedback is misleading, people may not be able to learn appropriate responses and may even be reinforced to learn wrong ones (recall Chapter 6). In particular, studies show that in trying to handle complex, dynamic decision tasks, people have much difficulty in interpreting feedback if this is received with delays (e.g. the feedback you receive does not relate to the action you have just taken, but to actions made prior to this).[14] In short, the efficacy of feedback depends on the ability to interpret it, and—unless one has a well-developed causal schema for a given task—use of cues-to-causality (Chapters 3 and 8) such as covariation and contiguity in time and space may be quite misleading in complex situations.

The second variable highlighted by the example of flying relates to the degree of commitment implied by each action. Thus, to use another analogy, consider the task of clipping an overgrown hedge.[15] One does not make complex, *a priori*, calculations involving, for instance, the cantilever characteristics of branches or differential weights of various woods. Rather, one proceeds incrementally, snipping and observing, thereby reducing the level of commitment implied by any particular action. To be sure, the final product is the outcome of all one's actions; however, provided that no single action dominates the outcome, this incremental approach to decision making takes advantage of a task that can generate useful feedback.

Two other variables discussed in previous chapters can also affect decision performance. These are the base-rate for accurate prediction and the extent to which different information sources are redundant. If the base-rate in a predictive task is high, there is little need for accurate judgement *per se*. Moreover, if information sources are redundant, the need to weight different sources accurately in accord with their relative importance or predictive ability is considerably reduced. For example, when making predictions based on two highly correlated variables, judgements—and thus predictive accuracy—will be insensitive to the relative importance given to each variable since each is, in essence, a proxy for the other.

To summarize, the need for accurate judgement and the choice of appropriate actions can be considerably reduced when there is clear feedback and decisions are taken across time in an incremental manner. This can be further facilitated when base-rates are high and there is redundancy between different sources of information. Unfortunately, not all decisions are of this type and it would be foolish to assume that since people can adapt to the demands of certain kinds of tasks they can adapt to all. In particular, many decision environments are characterized by high complexity such that it is difficult to understand the relevant causal variables. Consider, for instance, our poor understanding of how economies work. In addition, many actions cannot be implemented on an incremental basis such as those discussed above. For example, one cannot build an atomic power plant in this manner. Decision tasks vary considerably on the demands they require for accurate judgement and choice. Understanding these demands is important for understanding both the possibilities and limitations of human decision making.

## ORIGINS OF JUDGEMENTAL BIAS

Much of this section is of a speculative nature.[16] The issue is the following: Why do humans, who are capable of considerable physical and conceptual achievements, exhibit the systematic judgemental biases described in this book? The tentative answer to this question is based on an evolutionary argument. The human mind and body have evolved over millions of years. Furthermore, it is important to realize that our skills have developed to meet the challenges and needs of the environment. That is, evolution consists of adaptation to the environment, which it should be recalled is also composed of other species adapting to the environment. The consequence of ineffective adaptation is extinction of the species. Thus effective adaptation is oriented toward survival.

On considering the development of human skills from this evolutionary perspective, three points should be borne in mind. First, physical skills had to develop earlier to a greater extent than mental or conceptual skills. That is, in early human development physical skills were at a premium for survival. Second, the design of the human body that has evolved over the centuries by adaptation to environmental conditions represents a compromise between the skills necessary to perform different types of task and the coordination between such skills. For example, in some respects it would be helpful if humans were taller. However, height can also be a disadvantage—consider the force of gravity, the need to manipulate objects on the ground, and so on. Third, our human systems have not evolved in a manner that necessarily implies some 'optimal' design; rather the human species began its existence in a decidedly sub-optimal form. Since then, it has been evolving and developing through natural selection. Furthermore, it is still developing.

Below, a number of judgemental biases are considered in light of the above comments. In doing so, one point will be continually emphasized. Judgemental bias can often be considered to result from a trade-off between different types of error in the design of the human system. This point has been nicely stated by Toda:

228

To win a survival game, the subject need not be always correct, always precise, nor always very rapid in performing his individual functions, but the co-ordination of these functions should be well balanced and efficiently organized.[17]

## Failure to appreciate randomness

It has been pointed out frequently in this book that failure to distinguish random from non-random occurrences, or to confuse chance with cause, can lead to dysfunctional behaviour. People are inept at making predictions involving known random sequences (viz. the gambler's fallacy), and mis-attributions of chance fluctuations to causal mechanisms are frequent. Moreover, whereas people are motivated and need to exercise control over their environment, failure to discriminate between random fluctuations and meaningful events can lead to unrealistic attempts to control, or at least to believe that one controls, events. However, if one considers that distinguishing random from non-random occurrences cannot be perfect, which of the following two errors is more costly: excessive belief that one can control one's environment, or the belief that what happens is totally beyond one's control? The first position is characterized by excessive, and unrealistic confidence, the latter by helplessness. For creatures who need to master their environments to survive, the first form of delusion is far less costly. In the world of business, for example, it is evident that policies that consist of making the future happen are more successful than 'submitting' to the actions of others. It is true that one may deceive oneself with the first policy, but this is preferable to the latter.

A related source of judgemental bias concerns the general lack of appreciation of the concept of uncertainty. However, this too can have positive benefits. Uncertain events create anxiety and can thus inhibit action. Furthermore, avoiding uncertainty is one way of reducing the complexity of the environment.

## Inconsistency

As indicated in Chapter 9, inconsistency in judgement is one of the principal reasons that people should be replaced by models in repetitive judgemental tasks. People just do not seem to be capable of making consistent judgements across time. Indeed, behaviour itself is often inconsistent and many people even argue that they should have the right to be inconsistent. From an evolutionary perspective, a certain level of inconsistency in behaviour has advantages. Indeed, in a hostile environment, perfectly consistent behaviour is a short-cut to self-destruction. The animal that always takes the same path to the same waterhole becomes an easy prey to its enemies. Inconsistency in behaviour therefore has the functional advantage of keeping opponents in a state of uncertainty concerning your actions. In a competitive market situation, for example, companies deliberately try to 'keep their competitors guessing' about their future actions. Furthermore, as most people know, in organizational politics people frequently avoid being consistent in order to keep others in suspense concerning their beliefs and/or goals.

A parenthetical point should be made here. It is functional to be inconsistent *vis-à-vis* one's 'enemies'. However, inconsistency in behaviour with oneself or those close to one is not to be recommended.

A commonly cited cause of inconsistency in repetitive judgement is boredom. That is, one quickly becomes bored performing the same task in the same manner. Attention wanders and many different signals are picked up from the environment. However, boredom with repetitive tasks can have advantages. In a hostile environment it is necessary to keep aware of what is happening while engaged in a task, thus wandering attention can have positive value in monitoring potential sources of danger. Secondly, boredom induced through a repetitive task can lead one to question how to devise a system to do the task by other means. Necessity, induced by boredom, has been parent to many inventions.

## Learning

Learning is frequently based on noting that events occur closely together— for example, in time. However, the observation of such joint occurrences can often give misleading information in respect of true relations in the environment, and particularly when 'non-occurrences' cannot be observed. Nonetheless, the sheer power of the human body and mind to learn by noting positive covariations of events should not be underestimated. Consider, as an example, the ability of children to learn language and particularly the rules of grammar. By observation and experiment based on noting co-occurrences, children acquire schemes capable of generating quite complex behaviour. The same could be said of many motor skills, for example riding a bicycle or steering a car.

However, there are important distinctions between the learning of motor skills, the acquisition and use of language, and certain other conceptual skills, and many of the judgemental skills discussed in this book. These distinctions centre on (1) the conditions under which the skills were acquired, and (2) opportunities for testing and practising the skills. Most people underestimate the potential for learning inherent in situations where judgemental skills are acquired as well as the frequency, or more precisely lack of frequency, with which such skills are put to use.

As an example, contrast the situation where you might make a monthly forecast (in a business, say, of sales), with that of using language, or possibly making a perceptual judgement to avoid bumping into an object while walking. The frequency of the first task is clearly far less than those of the other activities. Furthermore, feedback is both less rapid and can be

230

confounded by other factors. Learning by observing or experiencing events that take place both frequently and with rapid feedback is efficient—memory, for example, does not need to be used heavily in the process. However, many important judgemental tasks of the type considered in this book are not of this nature. For example, how often do people make specific competence-based judgements (concerning, for example, revenue, personnel, administrative matters, and so on) compared to the judgements made to function simply as human beings? The proportion must be very small.

The point emphasized here is the following. Our learning processes are efficient for developing many skills necessary to our functioning as human beings. The environmental conditions for learning 'judgement' of more conceptual issues, however, are not so appropriate. In particular, although we use cues-to-causality such as covariation to infer, and 'learn' causal relations in the environment, these may be erroneous in particular instances and lead to the acquisition of superstitious beliefs that are not easily eliminated by feedback.[18] We return to this point below.

## Memory

Much has been made in this book of the deficiencies and limitations of human memory (see particularly Chapter 7). Whereas remembering is of great use in many situations, it is important not to overlook the efficiency of forgetting. The amount of information with which a person is confronted is enormous. If we had to remember all that is perceived—through all our senses—the size of human memory would have to be far greater than it is. As it is, human memory is imperfect. However, it is rapid (consider for example your ability to encode words and comprehend the meaning of speech), and it is adequate for dealing with many tasks we meet in our environment.

## Computational capacity

Bias in judgement due to the limited 'computational capacity' of the human mind has been stressed frequently throughout the book. In particular, people avoid investing in 'mental effort' when other paths are open to them. Furthermore, much mental activity consists of 'simplifying' the judgemental situation. Once again, it can be argued that the human race has developed cognitive skills such that certain types of 'computational ability' are not necessary. A good example of this is the following:

Consider the problem of predicting, before each shot, the direction of travel of a billiard ball hit by an expert billiard player. It would be possible to construct one or more mathematical formulas that would give the directions of travel that would score points and, among these, would indicate the one (or more) that would leave the balls in the best positions. The formulas might, of course, be extremely complicated, since they would necessarily take account of the location of the balls in relation to one another and of the cushions and of the complicated phenomena induced by 'english'. Nonetheless it seems not at all unreasonable that excellent predictions would be yielded by the hypothesis that the billiard player makes his shots *as if* he knew the formulas, could estimate accurately by eye the angles, etc., describing the location of the balls, could make lightning calculations from the formulas, and could then make the ball travel in the direction indicated by the formulas.[19]

It is, of course, quite clear that the expert billiard player does not and cannot make the complicated mathematical computations described above when he plays each shot. However, he does manage to coordinate his movements as though he did. (Although he would probably be incapable of telling you *how*.) The point being made here is that, despite lack of 'computational ability' people are capable of complex coordinated skills which they can achieve *without* computational ability *such as we understand it*.

### Order out of chaos versus creativity

An important function of the cues-to-causality discussed in Chapters 3 and 8 was that they direct attention to specific aspects of the environment. Given limited information-processing ability, this is an extremely important function in that it enables people to achieve order out of the potential chaos of all the information that is available in the environment. The cost of this order, however, is that if attention is always channelled in specific ways, occasions will arise when people fail to perceive new patterns or variables in the environment that could be more useful. In other words, order may be established at the expense of creativity.

### Other aspects

There are other human judgemental biases which may also be the 'reverse side' of adaptive behaviour. One concerns the phenomenon whereby once a person has decided upon a course of action, there is a tendency to ignore information indicating that the action was ill-advised. However, once action has started, it may often be more costly not to complete it. Indeed, in some cases, it may even be 'impossible' to stop an action once it has been engaged—consider a declaration of war. A second point related to the discounting of information concerns the preservation of a person's own self-image. If one allowed 'unpleasant' information to dominate one's self-image, this could be quite dysfunctional (see also comments above under 'Failure to appreciate randomness').

To summarize the above, I am suggesting the following. Many judgemental biases can be attributed to aspects of human behaviour which have provided, and still do provide adaptive responses to many situations. In the design of the present human system, nature has determined a number of trade-offs between, on the one hand, different parts of the system (in order to coordinate the whole), and, on the other, different types of error. Until recently, human evolution has adapted to the environment. But in doing so, it must be seriously questioned whether unaided judgement is sufficient to meet the needs of this changing environment. In 'designing humans', natural selection has developed trade-offs between possible errors that were appropriate to the environment humans faced. However, if humans change the environment, they must also change the apparatus (i.e. the human system) for dealing with it. Otherwise, the trade-offs developed through natural selection will no longer be appropriate.

Finally, of the many information-processing biases discussed in this book, the most important in my opinion is that induced by 'cognitive myopia' or our general unwillingness to use imagination and to invest in mental thought trials about the future.[20] In other words, the uncertainties that inevitably accompany attempts to imagine different future scenarios frequently seem, in the short run, to outweigh such exercises. However, failure to think seriously about future events can have important dysfunctional consequences. For example, in an age when the products of our past use of imagination have produced technologies capable of both great good and harm, it is ironic that society typically waits for disasters (e.g. industrial accidents) to occur before introducing means of counteracting the negative consequences of these technologies. In a sense, it seems that we are unwilling to invest in the imagination necessary to foresee the outcomes of products that owe their very existence to our having exercised imagination in the past.

## CONCLUDING COMMENTS

Despite the somewhat authoritative manner in which this book is written, it should be made clear that we know relatively little about how the human mind works and its influence on behaviour. The research done to date has only scratched the surface of these issues, and when I say 'scratch the surface', two meanings can be implied: first, existing research has, almost necessarily, dealt with surface phenomena. That is, inferences have been made about the human mind by examining behaviour (i.e. the end result of judgement) under different circumstances; and second, the range of conditions under which human judgement has been systematically examined remains small. Nonetheless, whereas the findings revealed to date do constitute a fairly coherent view of human mental capabilities, only future research will determine the adequacy of this image.

The importance of judgement on behaviour is, I believe, generally underestimated. Few people seem to be aware that they are continually making all kinds of predictive and evaluative judgements. Indeed, the activity is so common that most of us take it for granted. However, as is true in many other domains, it is precisely those things that we take for granted that should be questioned.

Underlying this book is the premise that it is important to learn the limits of one's judgemental ability. I believe this to be essential for two main reasons: first, because it helps avoid fantasies about the abilities of both oneself and others. The importance of this should not be overlooked. In their professional work, people are frequently evaluated and promoted or demoted as a consequence of actions based on judgements. If, as shown in this book, the relations between judgements and outcomes are complex, one must question the process by which some persons rise or fall within organizational hierarchies. Reputations can clearly be gained and lost through purely chance mechanisms. The moral for the individual is clear: whatever others think of you, don't fool yourself. Second, poor judgements can and do lead to disastrous outcomes. Understanding and improving judgement is consequently of great importance.

Some years ago, Paul Slovic made a comparison between a view of the human mind described by William Shakespeare, on the one hand, and that of Herbert Simon, the 1978 Nobel prize winner in economics, on the other.[21] Shakespeare said:

> What a piece of work is man! how noble in reason! how infinite in faculties! in form and moving how express and admirable! in action how like an angel! in apprehension how like a god! the beauty of the world! the paragon of animals!

Simon said:

> The capacity of the human mind for formulating and solving complex problems is very small compared with the size of the problems whose solution is required for objectively rational behavior in the real world—or even for a reasonable approximation to such objective rationality.[22]

The views, admittedly several centuries apart, are quite different. The student of human behaviour will also clearly agree with both men under different sets of conditions. Like Slovic, my own view is expressed by a contemporary of Shakespeare, Francis Bacon. He said: 'We do ill to exalt the powers of the human mind, when we should seek out its proper helps.' It is in precisely this spirit that this book has been written.

## NOTES AND REFERENCES

1. Since much of this chapter represents a review of evidence and views expressed in earlier chapters, specific reference is made only to new references.
2. This example is adapted from H. J. Einhorn (1980). Learning from experience and sub-optimal rules in decision making. In T. Wallsten (ed.), *Cognitive Processes in Choice and Decision Behavior*, Hillsdale, NJ: Lawrence Erlbaum.
3. For an empirical demonstration see D. C. Dearborn and H. A. Simon (1958). Selective perception: A note on the departmental identifications of executives, *Sociometry*, **21**, 140–144.
4. J. E. Russo (1977). The value of unit price information, *Journal of Marketing Research*, **14**, 193–201.
5. J. S. Bruner and L. J. Postman (1949). On the perception of incongruity: A paradigm, *Journal of Personality*, **18**, 206–223.

234

6. R. M. Hogarth (1975). Cognitive processes and the assessment of subjective probability distributions, *Journal of the American Statistical Association*, **70**, 271–289.
7. For a review, see R. M. Hogarth (ed.) (1982). *Question Framing and Response Consistency*, San Francisco: Jossey-Bass.
8. E. J. Langer (1975). The illusion of control, *Journal of Personality and Social Psychology*, **32**, 311–328.
9. See R. E. Nisbett and L. Ross (1980). *Human Inference: Strategies and Shortcomings in Social Judgment*, Englewood Cliffs, NJ: Prentice-Hall.
10. Table 10.2 is reprinted by permission from R. M. Hogarth and S. Makridakis (1981). Forecasting and planning: An evaluation, *Management Science*, **27**, Feb., 115–138. Copyright 1981 The Institute of Management Sciences.
11. This section owes much to two papers: H. J. Einhorn and R. M. Hogarth (1981). Behavioral decision theory: Processes of judgment and choice, *Annual Review of Psychology*, **32**, 53–88; and R. M. Hogarth (1981). Beyond discrete biases: Functional and dysfunctional aspects of judgmental heuristics, *Psychological Bulletin*, **90**, 197–217.
12. A. Tversky and D. Kahneman make the point that problems can be presented in both opaque and transparent forms. In their opaque versions, problems can induce decidedly 'irrational' behaviour; however, this is rarely the case when problems are transparent to the decision maker. Unfortunately, Tversky and Kahneman do not specify when different formulations of problems will be perceived as opaque or transparent. See A. Tversky and D. Kahneman (1986). Rational choice and the framing of decisions, *Journal of Business*, **4**(2), Part 2, S251–S278.
13. W. T. Powers (1973). Feedback: Beyond behaviorism, *Science*, **179**, 351.
14. See B. Brehmer and R. Allard (1986). *Dynamic Decision Making: A General Paradigm and some Experimental Results*, Unpublished manuscript, Department of Psychology, Uppsala University.
15. The analogy is due to T. Connolly (1980). Uncertainty, action and competence: Some alternatives to omniscience in complex problem-solving. In S. Fiddle (ed.), *Uncertainty: Social and Behavioral Dimensions*, New York: Praeger.
16. The writing of this section was stimulated by conversation with Hillel J. Einhorn. Fascinating references on the topic discussed are: D. T. Campbell (1959). Systematic error on the part of human links in communication systems, *Information and Control*, **1**, 334–369; D. T. Campbell (1975). On the conflicts between biological and social evolution and between psychology and moral tradition, *American Psychologist*, **30**, 1103–1126; and M. Toda (1962). The design of a fungus-eater: A model of human behavior in an unsophisticated environment, *Behavioral Science*, **7**, 164–183.
17. Toda, cited in Reference 16, p. 166.
18. H. J. Einhorn and R. M. Hogarth (1982). Prediction, diagnosis, and causal thinking in forecasting, *Journal of Forecasting*, **1**, 23–36.
19. M. Friedman and L. J. Savage (1948). The utility analysis of choice involving risk, *Journal of Political Economy*, **56**, 279–304.
20. See Hogarth, Reference 11.
21. P. Slovic (1972). *From Shakespeare to Simon: Speculations—and Some Evidence—About Man's Ability to Process Information*, Eugene, OR: Oregon Research Institute Monograph, Vol. 12, No. 12. The quotation from Shakespeare is from Hamlet, Act II, Scene ii. Whereas one could argue that Slovic took this quotation out of context, it does help indicate the range of qualities ascribed to human mental capabilities.
22. H. A. Simon (1957). *Models of man: Social and rational* New York: Wiley, p. 198.

# APPENDIX A

# Rules of probability*

The main text argued that predictive judgement is most usefully expressed in probabilistic form. For instance, instead of saying that there is a 'good chance' of, say, next year's sales exceeding budget, such predictions should be calibrated with an explicit probabilistic statement of the form 'There is a 0.30 probability of next year's sales exceeding target.' However, this type of statement immediately raises two problems: First, what is meant by probability—in this case of 0.30? Second, how are such probabilities assessed? A response to the first question is given below in the section headed 'The meaning of probability'. The second question is the subject of Appendix B.

A further use of probability theory referred to in the text concerned the rules governing the probabilities of 'combinations' of events. For example, how should a probabilistic prediction founded on a base-rate be modified by specific data? How does one moderate the predictive validity of a data source by considerations of its reliability? The rules of probability which govern these operations are the subject of this appendix. Use of the word 'rules,' however, requires some clarification. The principles to be enumerated below should be considered rules in the same manner as the rules of logic or arithmetic. You may or may not choose to follow them. But following them guarantees that the probabilities you estimate for combinations of events will be consistent with the assessment of probabilities of the different events of which the combinations are composed. Furthermore, use of the rules allows one to deduce probabilities of single events which may not be intuitively evident.

However, first consider the 'meaning' of probability.

## THE 'MEANING' OF PROBABILITY

The 'meaning' of probability has been the subject of long debate and for many the issues are still far from settled. Nonetheless, one, and only one operational definition of probability is given here.

---

* This appendix does not claim to be a complete statement of the intricacies of the rules of probability. It simply aims to provide some basic knowledge and principles to help the reader appreciate aspects of the main text.

*Definition:* The probability a person assigns to an event represents his or her subjective degree of belief that the event will occur and is expressed on a continuous numerical scale with end-points of 0 and 1.

In other words, a probability is a quantified opinion. The actual scale used is, of course, arbitrary; however, it should be noted that there is no implication that a person's subjective degree of belief is arbitrary. Furthermore, because it is subjective, this does not mean that different people will necessarily differ.

The end-points of the probability scale, 0 and 1, represent certainty. That is, in assigning a probability of 0 to an event a person is saying that he or she is certain that the event will *not* occur; by an assessment of 1, certainty that the event *will* occur is implied. Intermediate values represent different shades of uncertainty. For example, an assessment of 0.50 implies a belief that an event is as likely to occur as not.

For *repetitive* events, most people have a good intuitive feeling for probability based on considering the ratio of so-called 'favourable' to 'possible' occurrences, i.e. the number of times an event did occur divided by the number of times it could have occurred. Familiar gambling devices, such as tossing a coin or die, or observing a roulette wheel, are cases in point. From experience one 'knows' that in tossing a fair coin the chance of observing a 'head' on any throw is about one-half. Similar statements can be made, for example, about the observation of male or female births. The relative frequency of past occurrences of an event is often a useful indicator of probability. However, it is a mistake to equate probability and relative frequency unless one is willing to make a subjective judgement that all 'possible' cases are equally likely, i.e. probable. Hence, a subjective judgement of 'degree of belief' is involved in estimating probabilities on the basis of observed relative frequencies. This issue is discussed in greater detail in Appendix B.

Many important events are, of course, not repetitive. Consider, for example, the possibility of certain types of accident in nuclear power plants or an investment in a new industry. In these cases, subjective judgement—unaided by observation of past relative frequency—is necessarily the sole basis of probability.

People often baulk at the above notions. However, they must be faced squarely. The only comfort that can be given is that the expression of opinions in the form of subjective probabilities that conform to the rules of probability theory is consistent with several intuitively appealing principles of rational behaviour. In other words, if you behave rationally, your subjective opinions can be considered probabilities that conform to the rules of probability theory.

# RULES OF PROBABILITY

## Events

Probabilities are assigned to events, for example the observation of rain at a certain place tomorrow. Consequently, it follows that an event must be precisely defined. For example, if a bet is made conditional on the occurrence of an event it should not be possible for someone to avoid paying the bet on account of a loose definition. The event, rain tomorrow in a certain town, for instance, would have to be operationally defined by a given level of precipitation at a specific point where measurements can be taken.

Events belong to a class of events which make up a range of possibilities (often technically known as a sample space). Furthermore, events might themselves be subdivided. As an example, consider assessing probabilities for the level of a company's sales next year. The range of possibilities is from a theoretical minimum of zero to some maximum value. Events can be divisions of that range, for example, all values in excess of budget. This 'event,' could be further subdivided into smaller ranges, and at the limit to actual values expressed at the level of dollars and cents.

The actual definition of events one works with in a particular problem must be made specific.

In using probability theory, people often refer to the *complementary* event. This covers all events in the range of possibilities other than the event you are considering. For example, the complementary event to sales exceeding budget is that of sales being equal to or less than budget.

In the sequel, events will be labelled by letters, for instance $A$, $B$, $E$, etc. The shorthand used to denote the probability of an event is given, for example, in the case of event $A$, by $p(A)$. Events also occur in different kinds of 'combinations'. The reader should therefore note the following:

$p(A \text{ or } B)$ : the probability that either $A$ or $B$ occurs.
$p(A \text{ and } E)$ : the probability that $A$ and $E$ occur.
$p(B|E)$ : the conditional probability of $B$ given $E$ (i.e. the probability of $B$ occurring given that $E$ has occurred or could be supposed to have occurred).

Two further points need to be made: (1) events are sometimes *mutually exclusive*, which means that if one occurs the other(s) cannot. Consider, for instance, a horse race with four horses, $A$, $B$, $C$, and $D$. The event of any one horse winning the race is mutually exclusive of the others—only one horse can win the race (excluding ties). By definition, an event and its complement are mutually exclusive; (2) events can be *independent* of each other. By this is meant that knowledge of the occurrence of one event does not affect the probability of the other, or vice versa. For example, the events of 'rain today' and 'your car breaking down tomorrow' could be independent if your assessment of the probability of both events were the same whether or not you knew the other event had occurred. That is, you assess the same probability of 'your car breaking down tomorrow' irrespective of whether it did or did not rain today. Note that although in many situations one may use data to assess whether two events are independent (for example, sunspots and stock-market prices), in the final analysis independence is a subjective judgement.

## Properties and rules of probability theory

There are four properties:

(1) For any event $A$, $0 \leq p(A) \leq 1$.

(2) If the set of all the events within a range of possibilities is denoted by $S$, then

$$p(S) = 1.$$

(3) If $A$ and $B$ are mutually exclusive, then

$$p(A \text{ or } B) = p(A) + p(B).$$

(4) $p(B/C) = \dfrac{p(B \text{ and } C)}{P(C)}$

From these four properties, all the rules of probability theory can be derived. Two rules, of 'addition' and 'multiplication,' are particularly useful in calculations.

## Addition rule

The probability of either of two events, $C$ and $D$, occurring is

$$p(C \text{ or } D) = p(C) + p(D) - p(C \text{ and } D).$$

In the special case that $C$ and $D$ are *mutually exclusive*, $p(C \text{ and } D) = 0$, and we have Property 3.

The addition rule generalizes to more than two events.

## Multiplication rule

The probability of two events, $E$ and $F$, both occurring is

$$p(E \text{ and } F) = p(E)\, p(F|E) = p(F)\, p(E|F).$$

In other words, 'the probability of both $E$ and $F$ is the probability of $E$ multiplied by the probability of $F$ given $E$, or the probability of $F$ multiplied by the probability of $E$ given $F$'. The multiplication rule also generalizes to more than two events. A special case of the multiplication rule occurs when $E$ and $F$ are independent. In this case,

$$p(E) = p(E/F) \text{ and } p(F) = p(F/E)$$

That is, knowledge of $F$ does not affect the probability of $E$, and knowledge of $E$ does not affect the probability of $F$. If this is the case, then

$$p(E \text{ and } F) = p(E) \, p(F).$$

*Examples of addition and multiplication rules*

The following example may help the reader appreciate both rules. Imagine you are attending a race meeting. You have the opportunity of betting on two horses. $G_1$ and $G_2$, running in the same race, and on two horses, $H_1$ and $H_2$, running in different races.

In the first race, what is the probability that either $G_1$ or $G_2$ wins? Second, what is the probability that both $H_1$ and $H_2$ win their respective races?

The first question is a simple application of the addition rule for mutually exclusive events: $p(G_1 \text{ or } G_2) = p(G_1) + p(G_2)$. That is, if $G_1$ or $G_2$ wins the race, no other horse can win. You clearly have a better chance of picking the winner if you can bet on both $G_1$ and $G_2$.

The second question can be answered by the multiplication rule:

$$p(H_1 \text{ and } H_2) = p(H_1) \, p(H_2|H_1).$$

That is, the probability of both $H_1$ and $H_2$ winning is the probability that $H_1$ wins multiplied by the probability that $H_2$ wins given that $H_1$ won. [If $H_1$ and $H_2$ are independent, note that $p(H_1 \text{ and } H_2) = p(H_1) \, p(H_2)$.]

It should be noted that since the probability of an event is at most 1, joint probabilities, e.g. $p(H_1 \text{ and } H_2)$ must be equal to or less than the individual probabilities of which they are composed. Thus the joint probability of several events is frequently a very small number (which, by the way, explains why race tracks can pay such large sums for naming the winners of, say, three consecutive races— in France, the so-called 'tiercé'). People, incidentally, have been shown to overestimate systematically the joint probability of several events, and to underestimate the probability of one of several events occurring. That is, people's unaided intuitions do not appreciate the properties of the multiplication and addition rules.

## Bayes' theorem

Property 4 provides the formula for calculating conditional probabilities and is known as Bayes' theorem (or rule). Recalling that

$$p(B \text{ and } C) = p(B)\, p(C|B),$$

note that Property 4 can be re-written as

$$p\,(B|C) = \frac{p(B)\, p(C|B)}{p(C)}$$

which, if both sides are multiplied by $p(C)$, reflects the fact that

$$p(B \text{ and } C) = p(C)\, p(B|C) = p(B)\, p(C|B).$$

Bayes' theorem is particularly useful for updating so-called *base-rate* probabilities by specific data. This is now illustrated with respect to the cab problem introduced in Chapter 3.

## The cab problem

The information given in the problem is as follows:

| | |
|---|---|
| $p(G) = 0.85$ | There is a base-rate or prior probability that a cab is Green. (Note, $p(B) = 0.15$). |
| $p(SG|G) = 0.80$ | When testing witnesses, 80% of Green cabs were said to be green $(SG)$. Consequently, $p(SB|G) = 0.20$. |
| $p(SB|B) = 0.80$ | When testing witnesses, 80% of Blue cabs were said to be blue $(SB)$. Consequently, $p(SG|B) = 0.20$. |

The probability that the cab involved in the accident was blue is $p(B|SB)$. This is

$$p(B|SB) = \frac{p(B)\, p(SB/B)}{p(SB)}$$

Whereas $p(B)$ and $p(SB|B)$ are given in the formulation of the problem, $p(SB)$ is not. This must be deduced from the data provided. It can be calculated by noting that a witness could say that the cab is blue under the conditions that it is either green or blue. Thus, using the addition rule, it must be the case that

$$p(SB) = p(B \text{ and } SB) + p(G \text{ and } SB).$$

By using the definition of joint probabilities, $p(SB)$ can be re-written as

$$p(SB) = p(B)\, p(SB/B) + p(G)\, p(SB/G)$$

$$= (0.15 \times 0.80) + (0.85 \times 0.20)$$

$$= 0.29.$$

Therefore,

$$p(B|SB) = \frac{p(B)\, p(SB|B)}{p(SB)}$$

$$= \frac{0.15 \times 0.80}{0.29}$$

$$= \underline{0.41}.$$

# APPENDIX B

# Notes on probability assessment

This appendix, which is written in tutorial fashion, provides guidelines to probability assessment and an introduction to some probabilistic ideas.[1] No prior knowledge of probability or statistics is assumed other than some definitions given in Appendix A.

The reader is advised to work through the appendix and, in particular *to do* the exercises which can also be supplemented by assessment tasks from the reader's own experience. The material has been found more useful if several persons work through the exercises together.

The appendix is organized in six sections:

- First experience with probability assessment.
- Graphical representation of probability assessment.
- Exercises in graphical representation.
- The method of successive subdivisions.
- Checking out probability assessments.
- Assessing probabilities from historical data.

## FIRST EXPERIENCE WITH PROBABILITY ASSESSMENT

To appreciate what is involved in the assessment of probability, it is helpful to consider a concrete example. Specifically, I asked three friends the following question:

Do you believe that the population of the greater London area is:
less than 11 million?
between 11 and 13 million?
greater than 13 millíon?

None of the three knew the answer for certain. However, note that I have defined three events which are both mutually exclusive and exhaustive (i.e. they cover the range of all possibilities). Thus one of the events must be true.

My three friends assigned probabilities—representing their *subjective degrees of belief*—to the events as given in Table B1.

* The notes are based on previously unpublished material developed by R. M. Hogarth and J. Téboul.

*Table B.1*

| Event | Probabilities | | |
|---|---|---|---|
| | Roger | Tom | Michael |
| Less than 11 million | 0.10 | 0.70 | 0.30 |
| 11 to 13 million | 0.80 | 0.20 | 0.50 |
| Greater than 13 million | 0.10 | 0.10 | 0.20 |
| | 1.00 | 1.00 | 1.00 |

First, note that my three friends had quite different opinions. Second, they are all consistent in the sense that in each case the sum of the probabilities assigned to the range of possibilities equals one.

But which of my friends was correct in his assessment? There is no answer to this since they all just said what they believed.*

The best way to consider probability assessment is to try it oneself. Therefore, please complete the following exercises:

(A) You see before you a picture of a person. How old do you think she is?

| Years | Less than 16 | _____ |
|---|---|---|
| | 16–20 | _____ |
| | 21–25 | _____ |
| | 26–30 | _____ |
| | 31–35 | _____ |
| | 36–40 | _____ |
| | 41–45 | _____ |
| | Greater than 45 | _____ |

* Problems of determining the 'validity' of probability assessments are discussed further below.

Here age has been broken down into eight mutually exclusive and exhaustive classes. Record your opinion in probabilistic form beside each age classification. For example, you think that the person is between 21 and 25 years of age with probability.... Remember that to be consistent, the sum of your probabilities must equal one.

Also, do not feel compelled to stick to your original assessments. Feel free to change assessments as you like. Simply record your opinion.

Take your time and do this task extremely carefully. Ask yourself, in particular, what knowledge you have concerning the issue at hand.

(B) You are presented with another picture. Once again, how old do you think this person is?

Do this exercise in the same manner as the last. However, whereas last time age groupings were provided, this time feel free to use whatever age grouping you deem appropriate.

(C) Why not try birth-dates of some well-known people?
  Pope John Paul II,
  Jack Nicklaus,
  Queen Elizabeth.

(In these cases it is possible to check your answers against records.)

**Evaluating the exercises**

You have now just completed a task which many people find very difficult. The difficulty you may have experienced is probably due to the fact that although the task in itself was somewhat trivial (and you had some idea of the range in which the true replies must lie), you have probably never questioned yourself so precisely concerning such matters before.

Experience indicates that the most difficult facet of probability assessment is asking yourself what you really think. As you are the only person who can judge what this is, there is no single way to determine how this should be done. You may find it useful to try out these exercises with some friends. Ask them afterwards how they went about doing the exercises and compare your different approaches.

## GRAPHICAL REPRESENTATION OF PROBABILITY ASSESSMENTS

Probablity assessments are often usefully represented in the form of graphs. This section presents some basic material concerning the representation of probability assessments in graphical form.

### 1. Histograms

Consider the distribution shown in Table B.2 of the age of a person known to be between 16 and 50 years of age, which has been assessed by considering seven class intervals of 5 years.

It is possible to represent this distribution in the form of a graph known as a *histogram*, as shown in Fig. B.1

The graph shows age on the abscissa (i.e. horizontal axis) and probability on the ordinate (i.e. vertical axis). The histogram gives a good indication of the general shape of the assessed probability distribution; however, its interpretation can be misleading in that the graph depends upon the fact that the variable—age—has been considered in seven intervals of 5 years.

*Table B.2*

| Age | Class interval (in years) | Probability |
|-----|---------------------------|-------------|
| 16–20 | 5 | 0.03 |
| 21–25 | 5 | 0.12 |
| 26–30 | 5 | 0.25 |
| 31–35 | 5 | 0.35 |
| 36–40 | 5 | 0.20 |
| 41–45 | 5 | 0.04 |
| 46–50 | 5 | 0.01 |
| | | 1.00 |

Probabilities

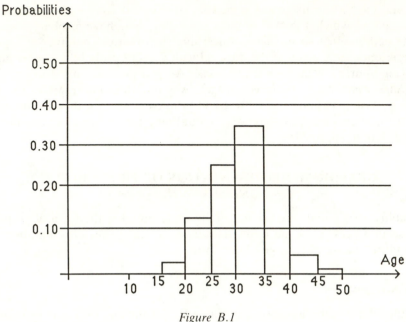

*Figure B.1*

Consider, for example, what happens if the assessed probabilities are broken down into *one* class interval of 5 years, and *three* of 10, as shown in Table B.3.

This distribution, which is entirely consistent with the preceding one, yields the histogram shown in Fig. B.2. This histogram is clearly different from the original one, a fact which is brought home when the first histogram is placed over the second (Fig. B.3).

It is evident that the form of the graph depends upon the class interval chosen, and this is a severe constraint. However, this problem can be

*Table B.3*

| Age | Class interval (in years) | Probability |
|---|---|---|
| 16–20 | 5 | 0.03 |
| 21–30 | 10 | 0.37 |
| 37–40 | 10 | 0.55 |
| 41–50 | 10 | 0.05 |
| | | 1.00 |

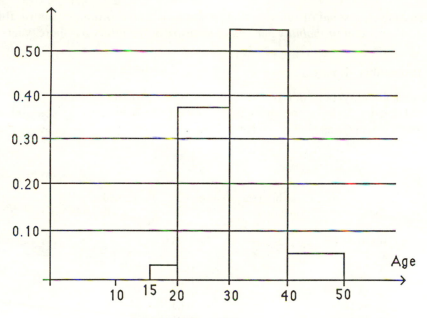

*Figure B.2*

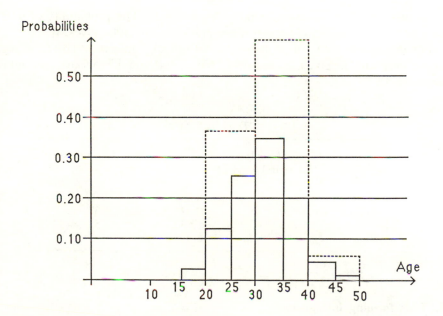

*Figure B.3*

overcome if, instead of representing *probability* on the ordinate, we use this axis to represent *probability per unit of measure* of the intervals—here 'years'.

## 2. Probability density

This probability per unit of measure is called probability density, and is calculated by dividing the probability of each class interval by the unit of measure (years), as shown in Table B.4.

*Table B.4*

| Age | Class interval (in years) | Probability | Probability density (× 1000) |
|---|---|---|---|
| 16–20 | 5 | 0.03 | 6 |
| 21–25 | 5 | 0.12 | 24 |
| 26–30 | 5 | 0.25 | 50 |
| 31–35 | 5 | 0.35 | 70 |
| 36–40 | 5 | 0.20 | 40 |
| 41–45 | 5 | 0.04 | 8 |
| 46–50 | 5 | 0.01 | 2 |

(Note that the densities have been multiplied by 1000 to avoid decimals.)

By way of example, consider the interval 16–20. The probability of 0.03 divided by 5 yields 0.006 (which when multiplied by 1000 gives 6).

For the second table of probabilities we obtain Table B.5. The resulting histograms are as given in Fig. B.4. Note that the histograms are now comparable.

*Table B.5*

| Age | Class interval (in years) | Probability | Probability density (× 1000) |
|---|---|---|---|
| 16–20 | 5 | 0.03 | 6 |
| 21–30 | 10 | 0.37 | 37 |
| 31–40 | 10 | 0.55 | 55 |
| 41–50 | 10 | 0.05 | 5 |

## 3. Transforming histograms

In the example of the assessment of age considered here, it is difficult to ask someone to assess a probability for *each* age—i.e. the probability of 16, 17, 18, etc. It is far easier to consider intervals of age—in the example, seven

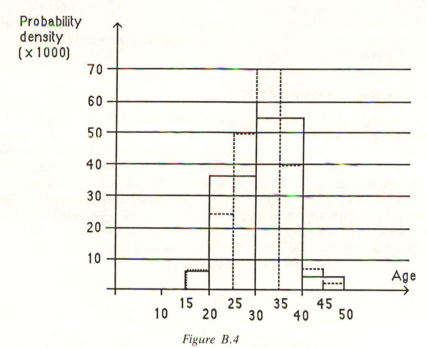

*Figure B.4*

intervals of 5 years. However, often what is ultimately desired is a more refined distribution than that given by the class intervals. This may be achieved by simply drawing a smooth line through the mid-points of the class intervals at the tops of the rectangles forming the histogram.

The second graph in Fig. B.5 is a subjective extrapolation by the assessor of his initial assessment. It may be considered as the graph he would have

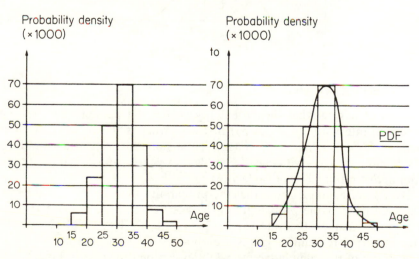

*Figure B.5*

obtained had he been able to decompose the variable considered (age) into infinitely small subdivisions. It is known as the assessor's *probability density function*—or, for short, *PDF*.

## 4. Measuring probability by a PDF

On the graph of the *probability density* function (PDF) given in Fig. B.5, probability density is given on the ordinate (i.e. vertical axis), and the variable—age—on the horizontal axis (i.e. abscissa). How does one therefore measure the probability for a given interval of age—say, 29–33 years?

By the manner in which the graph of the *PDF* was constructed, the total area between the *PDF* and the horizontal axis *must* be equal to 1. Therefore, the probability of any given interval—in this case 29–33—must be the area under the *PDF* between the limits of the interval considered. An example is given in Fig. B.6. However, calculating or measuring such areas is not easy. Therefore, consider an alternative route.

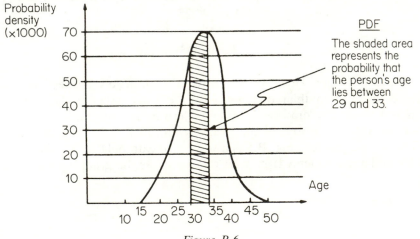

*Figure B.6*

## 5. Cumulative probabilities

Instead of asking what the probability is that the person's age lies within a certain interval (e.g. 29 to 33) first ask 'what is the probability that the person is younger than a given age?' To answer this, reconsider the original distribution of age—with class intervals of 5 years—and construct a table of *cumulative* probabilities (Table B.6).

By way of example, note that the probability that the person is less than or equal to 25 is the probability of the age being in the interval 16–20, i.e. 0.03, *plus* that of the interval 21–25, i.e. 0.12: 0.03 + 0.12 = 0.15 as indicated; the remaining figures are obtained in analogous manner.

A graph of the cumulative probabilities can be drawn as in Fig. B.7. Next 'smooth' the graph by drawing a curve through the tops of all the lines. (Once again, this is a subjective extrapolation of the original probability

Table B.6

| Age | Probability | Age | Probability that person is less than or equal to the given age |
|---|---|---|---|
| 16–20 | 0.03 | 20 | 0.03 |
| 21–25 | 0.12 | 25 | 0.03 + 0.12 = 0.15 |
| 26–30 | 0.25 | 30 | 0.15 + 0.25 = 0.40 |
| 31–35 | 0.35 | 35 | 0.40 + 0.35 = 0.75 |
| 36–40 | 0.20 | 40 | 0.75 + 0.20 = 0.95 |
| 41–45 | 0.04 | 45 | 0.95 + 0.04 = 0.99 |
| 46–50 | 0.01 | 50 | 0.99 + 0.01 = 1.00 |

assessment.) The graph so obtained (Fig. B.8) is known as a *cumulative distribution function* or, for short, *CDF*.

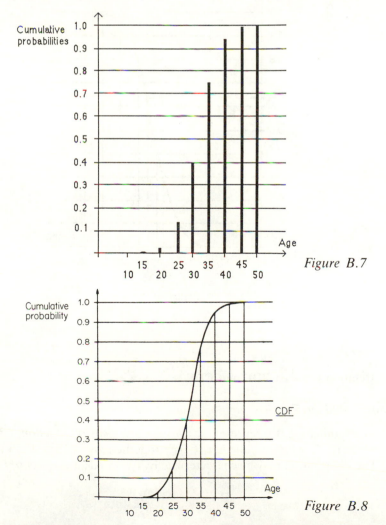

Figure B.7

Figure B.8

## 6. Measuring probabilities with a CDF

The *cumulative distribution function (CDF)* permits easy calculation of any given interval of the variable. For example, consider the interval 29–33. From the *CDF* we can read:

(1)  The probability that the person is younger than 33 is 0.64.
(2)  The probability that he is younger than 29 is 0.30.

Thus the probability that the person's age lies in the interval 29–33 is 0.64 − 0.30 = 0.34.

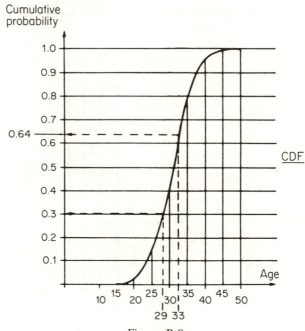

*Figure B.9*

## 7. Relation between PDF and CDF

*Mode–Median–Fractiles*

It is illuminating to represent a *probability density function (PDF)* and *cumulative distribution function (CDF)* together, as in Figs. B.10 and B.11.
The distribution may be characterized by two measures of *central tendency*.

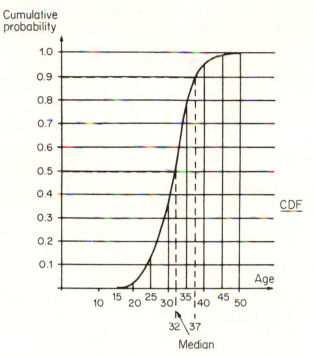

*Figure B.10*

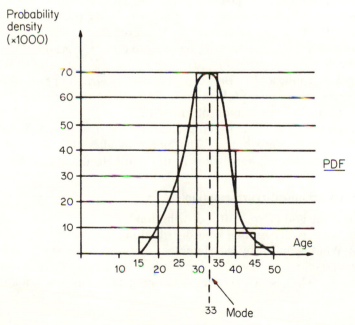

*Figure B.11*

The *mode* is the value which corresponds to the greatest probability density—i.e. to the highest point on the *PDF*. In the example (Fig. B.11) this is 33.

The *median* is the value for which there is as much probability that the person's age is equal to or less than this figure, as that it is above it. It thus corresponds to the 0.50 point on the ordinate of the *CDF*. In the example considered here (Fig. B.10), therefore, the median is 32. The median is the value which cuts the range of possible values of the variable into two equally likely subdivisions.

In fact, the *median* is a special case of any point on the scale of the variable (here age) corresponding to a point of the cumulative probability scale known as a *fractile*. The age 37, for example, is the 0.90 *fractile* (see previous CDF). Thus the median is the 0.50 *fractile*.

## 8. Summary

The key points to note from this section are:

(1)   A *probability density function (PDF)* shows the relation between probability density and the variable studied. (Probability density is probability per unit of measure and is thus independent of the size of class intervals considered initially.)

(2)   The area under the graph of a *PDF* is equal to 1 (reflecting allocation of probabilities to all possible values of the variable).

(3)   The point corresponding to the highest point of the *PDF* is known as the *mode* of the distribution. It is *the most likely value*.

(4)   Cumulative probabilities may be represented by a graph of the *cumulative distribution function (CDF)*.

(5)   The points indicated on the vertical axis of the graph of the *CDF* (which show the cumulative probabilities) determine—through the CDF—the *fractiles* of the distribution of interest.

(6)   The value of the variable represented by the 0.50 fractile is called the *median* of the distribution. This point signifies that one half of the assessed probability lies below it and one half above it.

## Exercises on graphical representation

(A)   (i) What is the *mode* of a distribution?
        (ii) What is the *median* of a distribution?
        (iii) What is meant by the statement: 'the median is the 0.50 fractile'?

(B)   The variable 'age' considered in the text is an example of a continuous variable. That is, a variable which may take any one of an infinite number of values: for example, 25 years, 10 months, 5 days, 4 hours, 3 minutes, 10 seconds, 12 milliseconds, etc., is one possible value and there is an infinite number of these. A *discrete* variable, on the other hand, is one that may take only a certain given number of values; for example, the number of goals scored in a soccer match (0, 1, 2, 3, 4, 5, 6, etc.). Whether we are dealing with *discrete* or *continuous* variables the principles enumerated above remain exactly the same, but with one exception: since we no longer have probabilities for intervals of the variable, we talk of probability *mass* instead of probability *density*. Draw the probability *mass* function (*PMF*) and cumulative distribution function (*CDF*) for the assessed distribution shown in Table B.7.

(Note: Since discrete variables can often be treated as *though* they were continuous, in the rest of this appendix all variables are treated as continuous.)

Table B.7 Probability of the number of goals that will be scored in a certain soccer match

| Number of goals | Probability |
| --- | --- |
| 0 | 0.30 |
| 1 | 0.20 |
| 2 | 0.20 |
| 3 | 0.10 |
| 4 | 0.10 |
| 5 | 0.05 |
| 6 | 0.05 |

(C) Take one of the distributions you assessed at the last exercise and draw both the *PDF* and *CDF* of this distribution. Try and do this in a manner such that you have a continuous distribution which satisfies you. To do this, you may be forced to modify your opinion concerning the characteristic studied. This does not matter so long as you still express your opinion.

(D) *Reading graphs.* Try to have a friend work through this appendix with you. Exchange the graphs of your *CDF*s. These graphs represent your assessed opinions concerning the characteristics of interest—in the present example, ages of different persons. Read and try to understand the graph of your friend. In particular, ask your friend questions concerning the probabilities of events and see to what extent his or her answers agree with the opinions previously assessed on the graphs. For example, ask what the probability is that the girl in the picture is less than 31. Or, that she is between 21 and 23? Your friend has already implicitly given an answer to these questions in the graphs. See to what extent his or her opinions still agree with the graphs.

## ANSWERS TO EXERCISES ON GRAPHICAL REPRESENTATION

(A)    (i)    The *mode* is the point of the abscissa of a *PDF* corresponding to the highest point of that graph. It is the most probable value.
    (ii)   The *median* is the point which divides all possible values of the variable into two equally likely subdivisions.
    (iii)  The median is a specific fractile, namely the 0.50 *fractile*.
(B)    See Figs. B.12, B.13.

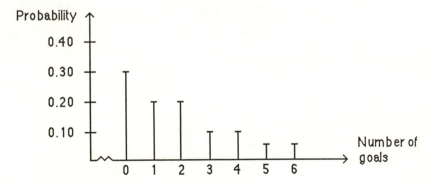

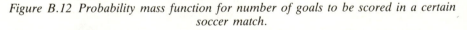

*Figure B.12 Probability mass function for number of goals to be scored in a certain soccer match.*

## THE METHOD OF SUCCESSIVE SUBDIVISIONS

### 1. Methods of probability assessment

So far you have assessed probability distributions by considering fixed intervals of the variable under study and then allocating probability to the intervals. For example, fixed intervals of five years were considered and

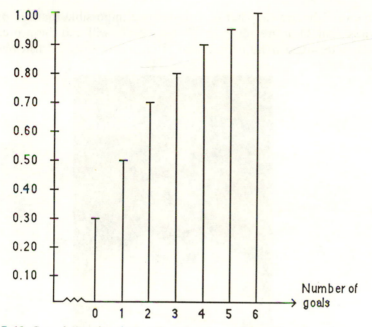

Figure B.13 Cumulative distribution function for number of goals to be scored in a certain soccer match.

then the likelihood of each of the intervals was estimated. This approach is called the *variable fixed* method.

It is, however, also possible to attack probability assessment from another angle: specifically to consider *fixed intervals of probability* and then ask what values of the variable are covered by these fixed probability intervals. These methods represent the *probability fixed* approach. One such method is presented here.

## 2. The method of successive subdivisions

Once again, age is used as an example. Consider the accompanying picture of a person for whose age you are asked to assess a probability distribution.

The method presented is known as the method of successive subdivisions, for reasons that will become evident. This method enables one to record the assessed distribution directly on to a graph of the *CDF (cumulative distribution function)*.

Age is recorded on the abscissa and cumulative probabilities on the ordinate. In the present example, assume that the person's age is assessed to lie between 20 and 45. That is, it is deemed impossible that the person's age is less than 20 or greater than 45. The reader will find the presentation easier to understand if he or she also attempts to assess a distribution as illustrated here.

The method of successive subdivisions consists of asking questions to determine particular fractiles of the distribution being assessed. The procedure is as follows:

## Question 1

For which age do you deem it is equally likely that the person's age is above that age as it is below it? In other words, can you determine an age for which you deem there is as much probability that the person *is* that age, or *younger*, than that she is *older* than the given age? Another way of saying this is: Can you divide the range of possible ages into two equally likely subdivisions? What is the age which separates these two subdivisions?

On the abscissa of your *CDF* place a mark beside this age. Recall, however, what this age means for you. It means that you consider it equally likely that the person's age lies between 20 and the indicated age, as that it lies between that age and 45.

As you have no doubt already noticed, the point you have just determined is the *median* or 0.50 *fractile* of your distribution.

In short, *M*—the median—is the point for which you should be prepared to bet that there is an equal chance that the person is older or younger than that age—*M*. For example, the median age, *M*, was assessed by the author to be 29, and is marked as shown in Fig. B.15.

259

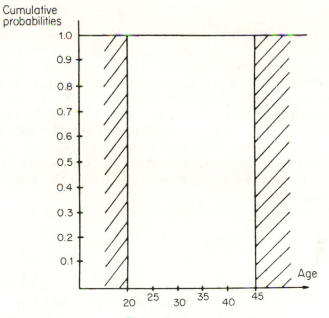

*Figure B.14*

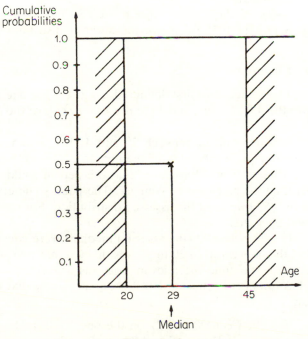

*Figure B.15*

## Question 2

Now consider only ages below the median—*M*—you have just assessed. Can you determine a point on the interval from 20 to your previously assessed median—*M*—where you consider that it is equally likely that the person's age lies below that point (i.e. age) as above it? In other words, can you divide the interval from 20 to your previously assessed median into two intervals which have equal probability? When you find this point, mark it on the abscissa (i.e. age axis) of your *CDF*. To make this assessment, it may help you *to imagine that you have been told that the person is under M years of age*. Under this hypothesis, proceed exactly as in the first question.

The author considered the relevant age to be 27. This is marked on the graph of the *CDF*.

As you will have noticed, the age 27 is the 0.25 *fractile* of the author's distribution.

## Question 3

Now consider possible ages *above* the median of your distribution—*M*. Can you find a point between your 'median' and 45 years for which you consider it equally likely that the person is under that age as older than it? That is, can you divide the interval from the median to 45 into two equi-probable sub-intervals? Please mark the point which separates these sub-intervals on the abscissa of your *CDF*.

The author assessed the relevant age to be 33. This is marked on the graph in Fig. B.17. The 0.75 *fractile* of the author's distribution is 33.

## 3. Summary of questions

The range of possible ages was first delimited: 20 to 45. The age 20 therefore corresponds to the 0.00 *fractile*, and 45 to the 1.00 *fractile* of the distribution.
   Then:
(1)   A point was determined between 20 and 45 below and above which there was an equal probability of the person's true age being in either interval. That is, it was considered that the person could equally well be older than the given age as younger. The point so determined is the *median* or 0.50 *fractile* of the assessed distribution. For the author, this point was 29 years.
(2)   Next, only ages below 29 (the assessed median) were considered possible, and the interval from 20 to 29 was divided into two equally likely subdivisions. This time the relevant age was assessed to be 27. Note that it has in effect been said that it is equally likely that the person's age lies:

between 20 and 27 on the one hand, and
between 27 and 29 on the other.

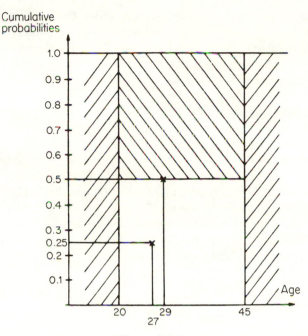

*Figure B.16*

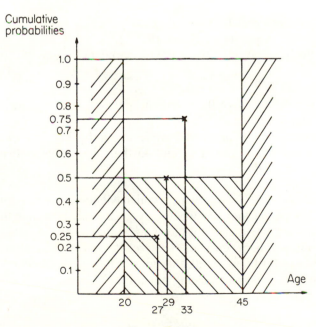

*Figure B.17*

(3)   Next, attention was restricted to ages above the median, 29; and the interval from 29 to 45 was divided into two equally likely subdivisions. On this occasion the assessed age was 33. This means that it is considered equally likely that the person's age lies between 29 and 33 as that it lies between 33 and 45.

Note that whereas the author assessed certain values for the different fractiles of the distribution, it does not follow that these figures should be the same as those you assessed.

Reconsider the assessed points. The age of 29—the first point assessed— was seen to be the *median* or 0.50 *fractile* of the distribution. The age 27 divided the interval between 20 and 29 into two equally likely subdivisions. Hence, since 29 was the 0.50 *fractile*, 27 must be the 0.25 *fractile*.

Similarly, the interval between 29 and 45 was divided into two equally likely subdivisions at the age of 33. Thus as 29 is the 0.50 *fractile* and 45 marks the maximum possible age, 33 must be the 0.75 *fractile*.

### 4. Checking the points

Having marked these points on the graph (Fig. B.18), recall for a moment what they mean. For illustrative purposes, this is done using the figures assessed here. Your own figures will probably be different.

(1)   It is considered equally likely that the person is above 29 years of age as that she is equal to or below that age.
(2)   The following age intervals are considered to be equally likely:

   20–27      27–29      29–33      33–45.

   There is probability of 0.25 that the person's true age lies in each of these intervals.
(3)   Furthermore, it is considered twice as likely that, for example, the person's age lies between 29 and 45 than that it lies between 20 and 27 or 27 and 29.

Reconsider the three points which you have just assessed for the 0.25, 0.50 and 0.75 *fractiles* and see whether you are satisfied that the kinds of relations discussed above also hold for your figures. For example, check that *for you* the interval between your 0.75 *fractile* and 45 is really only *half* as likely as the interval between 20 and your 0.50 *fractile* (median).

When you have finished checking out these relations mark any necessary changes on your *CDF*.

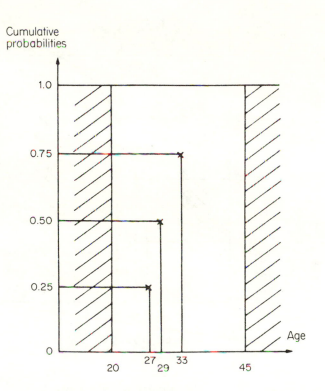

Cumulative
probabilities

1.0

0.75

0.50

0.25

0

Age

20    27  33    45
      29

*Figure B.18*

## 5. Drawing the CDF

There are now five points on the *CDF* and a line can be smoothed through the points to give an estimation of the *CDF* (Fig. B.19). Of course, there is no rule as to the number of points which are necessary to do this. One simply assesses as many points as are deemed necessary to estimate the distribution.

## 6. Summary

The method of successive subdivisions consists of six steps:

(1) Determine the range of possible values the variable can take (i.e. the *fractiles* 0.00 and 1.00 of the distribution). In fact, to save yourself from

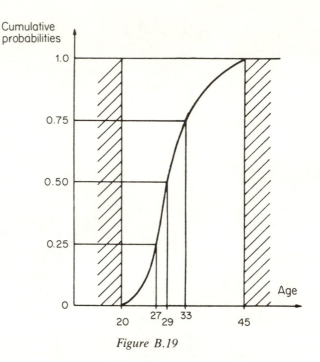

Cumulative
probabilities

*Figure B.19*

too many 'surprises' (or the occurrence of events deemed *impossible*) it is often wiser to start out by assessing the 0.01 and 0.99 *fractiles* of the distribution. Delimiting the 0.00 and 1.00 *fractiles* may be too categoric.

(2)   Determine the median or 0.50 *fractile*.
(3)   Determine the 0.25 *fractile*.
(4)   Determine the 0.75 *fractile*.
(5)   Question yourself as to whether you are really satisfied with the assessed *fractiles*, and if so,
(6)   Draw a smooth line through the assessed *fractiles*.

**7. Exercises**

Use the method of successive subdivisions to assess probability distributions for:

the population of your town;
the revenue of your organization next year;
the height of the building in which you work.

If you are working through the appendix with a friend, check out your distributions by exchanging graphs and asking questions.

# CHECKING OUT PROBABILITY ASSESSMENTS

## 1. Summary

Up to this point probabilities have been estimated by two methods:

(i)   Where intervals of the variable are fixed, viz.:

*Table B.8*

| Age | Class intervals (in years) | Probability | Probability density (× 1000) | Cumulative probability |
|---|---|---|---|---|
| 16–20 | 5 | 0.03 | 6 | 0.03 |
| 21–25 | 5 | 0.12 | 24 | 0.15 |
| 26–30 | 5 | 0.25 | 50 | 0.40 |
| 31–35 | 5 | 0.35 | 70 | 0.75 |
| 36–40 | 5 | 0.20 | 40 | 0.95 |
| 41–45 | 5 | 0.04 | 8 | 0.99 |
| 46–50 | 5 | 0.01 | 2 | 1.00 |

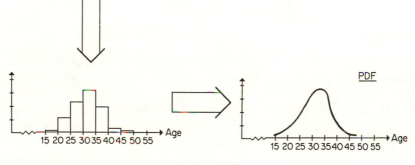

*Figure B.20*

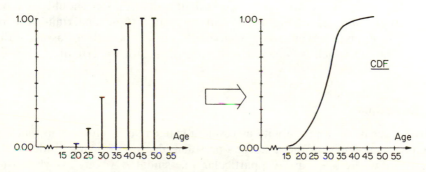

*Figure B.21*

266

(ii) Where intervals of probability are fixed, viz.:

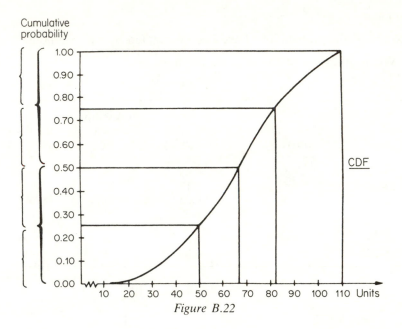

*Figure B.22*

## 2. Coherence

The basic requirement of a probability assessment is that it should be coherent, and more specifically, *coherent* in *two* respects:

(1) The assessed distribution should be coherent with the laws of probability, e.g. the probabilities assigned to a set of mutually exclusive and exhaustive events should sum to 1.
(2) The assessed distribution should also be *coherent* with the assessor's state of uncertainty. For example, if we are fairly certain concerning the age of a person we might assign a *tight* distribution, as in Fig. B.23. However, if we are very uncertain, the distribution should be more spread out, as in Fig. B.24. But no matter *how* uncertain you are concerning a given event, you should always be able to assess a distribution which is *coherent* with your degree of uncertainty.

## 3. Evaluation

Strictly speaking, a probability assessment cannot be 'evaluated' in that it is simply a statement of the assessor's personal 'degree of belief'. Indeed, the only case where one can say a particular assessment is 'wrong', is when after

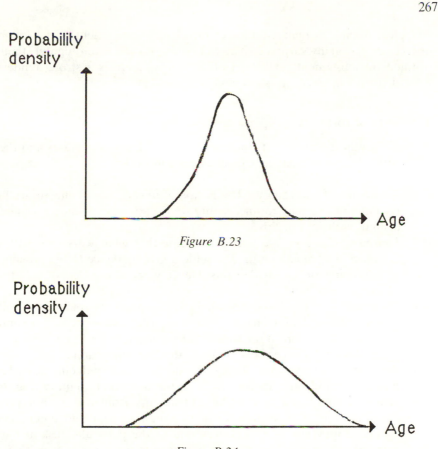

Figure B.23

Figure B.24

a categoric assessment (i.e. probability of 0 or 1), the 'impossible' happens.

However, in predictive situations it is legitimate to assess the extent to which a person's assessments are realistic. This may be done by considering, over a series of assessments, the degree to which the person's assessments are matched by the empirical relative frequencies of the events assessed. For example, events for which probabilities of 0.60 are assessed should occur about 60% of the time. Occasionally, an assessor who is well *calibrated* should observe surprises.

However, actual and expected surprises should be roughly equal. That is, in 100 assessments, a well-calibrated assessor should experience about:

- 2 true values falling outside the assessed 0.01 and 0.99 fractiles;
- 20 true values falling outside the assessed 0.10 and 0.90 fractiles;
- 40 true values falling outside the assessed 0.20 and 0.80 fractiles;
- 50 true values falling outside the assessed 0.25 and 0.75 fractiles; and so on.

A typical finding in many studies of probability assessment is that people experience too many surprises. Their distributions are often 'tighter' than is justified by subsequent reality. In other words, there is a strong tendency toward overconfidence in assessment.

### 4. Sources of surprises

As indicated in the main text, there are many judgemental biases and these affect probability assessment. Consider the following:

(a)  *Avoidance of uncertainty*   The notion of uncertainty is uncomfortable. By failing to face up to uncertainty we do not acquire mechanisms for dealing with it explicitly.

(b)  *Representativeness*   We tend to imagine that what we see or will see is *typical* of what can occur. We seldom give credence to the possibility of 'surprising' or 'unusual' events. Hence we tend to assess distributions which are too 'tight'.

(c)  *Availability*   When imagining what could happen, we remember similar past situations. Unfortunately, our memory search process for similar instances often stops after superficial recollection and may tend to be overly biased by recent events (e.g. the last sales campaign).

(d)  *Anchoring and adjusting*   In making any particular judgement, we tend first to 'anchor' on a specific value of the uncertain quantity (e.g. last year's revenue) and then make adjustments from this anchor point. Unfortunately, the anchor tends to dominate our judgement even though it may not be entirely relevant to the particular task at hand.

(e)  *Internal coherence*   We like our judgements to be coherent with facts we have observed. Thus, if we do know of events which are inconsistent with our beliefs we tend to diminish their importance in formulating our judgements.

(f)  *Unstated assumptions*   Our judgements are often made against a background of assumptions which are not made explicit (for example, our stated probability distribution may be conditional upon the premise that our competitors *will* not undertake a certain action).

### 5. Methodology bias

Different methods of assessing probabilities induce different stated probability distributions.

### 6. Avoiding surprises/biases

(1)  Be sure that the variable for which you are to assess a distribution is unambiguously defined. What are your implicit and explicit assumptions concerning the task at hand?

(2)  Ask yourself what you *know* about the task at hand and not just what you *think* you know.

(3)  Is the judgemental 'heuristic' you are using susceptible to bias? Check the following:

(a)  Are you avoiding uncertainty?

(b)  Try to think in terms of ranges of values and not just one *typical* value (i.e. fight 'representativeness').

(c)  Have you considered *all* the information *available* to you and not just that which comes first to your mind?

(d)  To what extent does/did the first number you thought of determine your entire assessment?

(e)  Have you considered all *conflicting*—as well as coherent—evidence?

(4)  Check out your distribution by different assessment methods:

- Assess your distribution by probability fixed and variable fixed approaches.

- Reconcile the sources of differences (don't just split the difference unless you know why!).

- Have someone question you concerning the implications of your assessment.

- In actually making an assessment, use *external random processes* in order to calibrate your judgements. For example, consider an example of age:

(a)    When assessing the median a useful reference is to consider the probability of observing, say, heads on the toss of a fair coin.

(b)    For assessing extreme fractiles, consider the possibility of randomly drawing, say, one black ball out of an urn containing 98 white and 2 black balls.

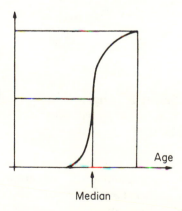

There is an equal chance that the person's age is above the median as below it

Age less than the median

*Figure B.25*

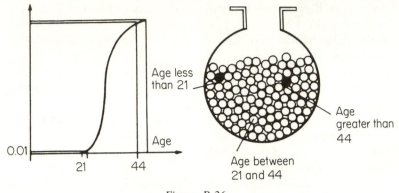

*Figure B.26*

(c)     One may also usefully consider a roulette wheel to assess the chances of an event occurring.

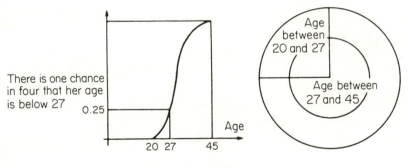

*Figure B.27*

## 7. Summary

Probability assessment is difficult. It is open to biases and there is *no one true method*. To be effective, we need to ask ourselves searching questions and to avoid biases. In practice, this means:

(1)  use *different* methods for the same assessment task;
(2)  develop means for questioning ourselves concerning our judgements, i.e. beware of human biases; have others question us; compare our judgements to external random processes, and so on.

### ASSESSING PROBABILITIES FROM HISTORICAL DATA

#### 1. Definitions of probability

(a)   Probability has been defined here as *a measure of a degree of belief* (see Appendix A).

(b)   Another commonly used definition is the ratio of favourable to possible cases, i.e.

$$p = \frac{\text{number of 'favourable' cases}}{\text{number of possible cases}}$$

(where *p* stands for 'probability').

This is the so-called objective definition, although as will be shown below, it is but a *special case of the subjective view*.

#### 2. Establishing the ratio *p*

A machine produces plastic caps for bottles at the rate of 200 per hour. In every hour, the machine produces a number of *defective* caps, and thus it is uncertain how long the machine should be run in order to produce 200 *good* caps. To answer this question, it would be useful to know the probability that any given cap produced by the machine is defective, and thus, how many good caps one could *expect* the machine to make in a given period of time.

One way to estimate the probability that a cap produced by the machine is defective is empirical observation. Assume, therefore, that you have observed the machine for a period of *five* hours during which time it produced 1000 caps. In Table B.9, column (1) records the hour of observation; column (2) records the number of caps produced per hour; column (3) the number of good caps produced each hour; and finally column (4) shows the number of defective caps produced each hour.

Table B.9   Caps produced by machine in 5-hour period

| (1) Hour | (2) Total number of caps produced | (3) Good caps | (4) Defective caps |
|---|---|---|---|
| 1 | 200 | 190 | 10 |
| 2 | 200 | 185 | 15 |
| 3 | 200 | 170 | 30 |
| 4 | 200 | 195 | 5 |
| 5 | 200 | 187 | 13 |
| Total: | 1000 | 927 | 73 |

From that table note that

(1)  Although the total number of caps produced per hour is constant (200), the number of defective caps produced per hour varies. For example, in hour 3 there were 30 defectives, but only 5 in hour 4.
(2)  In total there were 73 defectives among the 1000 caps produced.

We now ask: What is the probability that a given cap produced by the machine is defective?

### 3. Assumptions: identical and independent trials

The question is answered in the following manner. *First*, assume that each cap was produced *under identical circumstances*. For example, the machine was not adjusted or changed in any way during the time the caps were produced. *Second*, assume that the production of a given defective (or good) cap has no effect upon the fact that another cap produced is either good or defective.

In these circumstances—of *identical and independent* trials—it can be assumed that the proportion of defective to total caps produced by the machine is a fair estimate of the probability that the machine will produce a defective cap.

### 4. Ratio of favourable to possible cases

That is, *in circumstances which are deemed to be independent and identical*, ask how many times the event of interest—a defective cap—appears in the number of trials or occasions observed, i.e. the number of caps produced.

In the example, there are 73 defective caps on 1000 occasions when defective caps could have been produced, thus, it can be said that the probability of the machine producing a defective cap is 73/1000 or 0.073.

### 5. Definition

The argument implied by the example of the machine producing plastic caps leads to a definition. This is: the probability of an event may be taken to be equal to the ratio

$$\frac{\text{number of times the event occurs}}{\text{number of times the event could occur}}$$

or

$$\frac{\text{number of 'favourable' cases}}{\text{number of possible cases}}$$

when all *possible* cases have an *equal chance* or *likelihood* of occurring. Note, however, that this definition of probability is circular in that the words *chance* and *likelihood* (which are synonyms for probability) have been used to define probability.

In order to use the definition, a *subjective* judgement must be made that all cases are *equally probable*. In this sense, therefore, the so-called *objective* definition is but a special case of the *subjective* definition.

## 6. Long-run relative frequency

As you might already have observed, the estimation of probability in the above example was made by equating *probability* with the *relative frequency* of the event of interest in a given number of trials. In the case under consideration, the *relative frequency* of defective to total caps is defined by the ratio 73/1000 or 0.073. Note, however, that had we observed only the first hour of the machine, the relative frequency would have been 10/200 or 0.05. Thus, for the definition of probability adopted above to be useful, we should really think in terms of *long-run relative frequency*, which implies that we must observe a great number of trials. We could always *estimate* a probability based on a few trials. However, we will have greater *confidence* in our estimate the greater the number of trials. In many practical situations it is not possible to observe a large number of trials; nonetheless it can often be useful to consider the relative frequency of past events in order to *estimate* probabilities.

## 7. Estimating probabilities of sales

Imagine you are the manufacturer of a product for which the selling season is about to begin. You are uncertain as to how many units of your product will be demanded but have no reason to believe that the forthcoming season will be any different from its ten predecessors (for each of which, you had no reason to believe that any one would be different from the others). In the ten preceding seasons you sold your products in the quantities given in Table B.10. On the basis of these figures, and assuming that you have no other information, how would you assess demand for the forthcoming season?

One approach would be to calculate the relative frequencies of the observed quantities. Notice that a demand of:

- 17,000 occurred 2 times in 10 seasons;
- 18,000 occurred 4 times in 10 seasons;
- 19,000 occurred 3 times in 10 seasons;
- 20,000 occurred 1 time in 10 seasons.

*Table B.10*

| Seasons | Sales in 000's of units |
|---------|-------------------------|
| 1 | 19 |
| 2 | 18 |
| 3 | 18 |
| 4 | 20 |
| 5 | 19 |
| 6 | 17 |
| 7 | 18 |
| 8 | 19 |
| 9 | 17 |
| 10 | 18 |

Therefore, the relative frequencies of occurrence are given in Table B.11. (Recall that relative frequency is defined as the ratio of observed to total cases. Thus, for example, the relative frequency of 17,000 units is 2/10 or 0.20.)

These relative frequencies can, of course, also be represented in graphical form as in Fig. B.28, where relative frequency has been recorded on the

*Table B.11*

| Demand in 000's of units | Relative frequency |
|--------------------------|--------------------|
| 17 | 0.20 |
| 18 | 0.40 |
| 19 | 0.30 |
| 20 | 0.10 |
| Total | 1.00 |

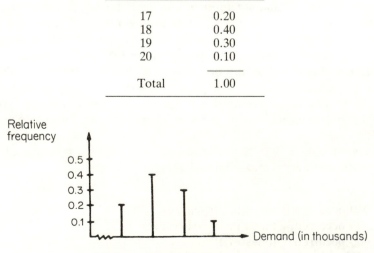

*Figure B.28*

ordinate and demand in thousands of units on the abscissa. In the absence of further information, this graph could well be used to represent a probability distribution over future demand. This could be done by simply replacing the words *relative frequency* by *probability*.

## 8. Estimating demand

It is unlikely that in practical situations demand for a given product would behave as 'nicely' as in the above example. Therefore, consider the following more complicated case.

A retailer wishes to assess his probability distribution for the demand of a certain product. He decides to examine demand for the product during the last 20 days. He considers that the pattern of demand observed during these 20 days will persist into the future and does not feel that on any one of the days there was any particular reason why demand should have been larger or smaller than demand on any other day.

He summarized demand in the preceding 20 days as shown in Table B.12. In column (1) of the table, he records the different quantities that could have been demanded each day: from 0 to 10 or more. In column (2), he records the number of times different numbers of items were demanded during the 20-day period. For example, on only *one* occasion were two items demanded, but *three* items were demanded on three occasions. In column (3), the retailer notes the *relative frequency* with which each event—i.e. number of items demanded—occurred. For example, in 20 days 6 items were demanded on three occasions and thus the relative frequency of the event

*Table B.12*

| (1) Number of items demanded | (2) Number of occasions | (3) Relative frequency |
|---|---|---|
| 0 | 0 | 0 |
| 1 | 1 | 0.05 |
| 2 | 1 | 0.05 |
| 3 | 3 | 0.15 |
| 4 | 5 | 0.25 |
| 5 | 4 | 0.20 |
| 6 | 3 | 0.15 |
| 7 | 0 | 0 |
| 8 | 2 | 0.10 |
| 9 | 1 | 0.05 |
| 10 or more | 0 | 0 |
|  | 20 | 1.00 |

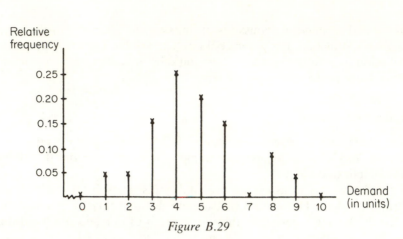

*Figure B.29*

'6 items demanded' is 3/20 or 0.15. As you can see, the entries in column (3) are obtained by dividing the corresponding entries of column (2) by 20.

Our retailer may also represent his table of relative frequencies in the form of a graph, as shown in Fig. B.29, where the relative frequency is shown on the ordinate, and demand on the abscissa.

The graph shows a fairly symmetric pattern of demand, with one exception. In the 20-day period analysed, there was *no* day on which 7 items of the product were demanded. However, there were 3 days on which 6 were requested, and 2 days when 8 were requested. Does it seem reasonable, therefore, that in assessing his probability distribution over future demand the retailer should equate probability with relative frequency—that is, to have *zero* probability of having 7 units demanded but to have *non-zero* probability of having 6 and 8 units of demand? Given the present pattern of demand, and bearing in mind that the distribution is based on only 20 observations, equating probability blindly with relative frequency in the observed sample seems unreasonable.

## 9. General Principle

This example of estimating demand leads to the following general principle:

> *When using relative frequencies of past observations as a guide to assessing probabilities, past historical data should not be followed blindly. Rather, we should blend such past data with our own opinions and common sense.*

The use of relative frequencies as probabilities is only really justified when there is a large number of observations. The retailer in the present example, for instance, finally assessed his distribution in a manner which allowed for what he considered to be an anomaly in the past data—i.e. no demand for

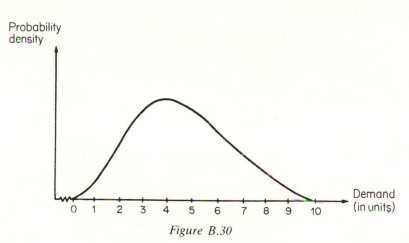

Probability density

Demand (in units)

Figure B.30

7 units of his product. Note that the retailer finally assessed what one could describe as a 'smooth' distribution (Fig. B.30). That is, he deemed it wiser to smooth out irregularities in the sample data on the grounds that although the sample was useful to him, the number of observations (20) was limited.

## 10. Summary

(1) A commonly used defintion of probability is the ratio of so-called 'favourable to possible cases', i.e.

$$\frac{\text{number of favourable cases}}{\text{number of possible cases}}$$

Estimating probabilities in this manner in practical situations frequently amounts to equating the relative frequencies of observations in a sample with probabilities. It was noted, however, that this procedure was only justified when

(a)  all possible events (i.e. cases) are deemed to have an equal probability of occurring; and
(b)  the total number of events under consideration is large.

(2) When other information is lacking, it is often possible to use historical data as a basis for estimating probabilities. When the sample size is small, however, the observed relative frequencies will only give a rough approximation of probabilities and the assessor may well prefer to smooth empirical distributions to account for irregularities in the observed data.

# APPENDIX C

# Assessing a utility function under uncertainty

It is possible to assess a person's utility function under uncertainty by asking a number of hypothetical questions. In doing so, it is assumed that the person's responses are consistent with expected utility theory. A particularly useful procedure, known as the *lottery equivalent* method, involves the notion of an *elementary lottery* and is based on the following logic.[1]

Delimit the variable over which utility is being assessed by *maximum* and *minimum* plausible values for the application under consideration. Let the maximum plausible value have a utility of 1, and the minimum a utility of 0. For example, if utility is being assessed over dollars with maximum and minimum plausible values of $1,000 and $0, respectively, then let $u(\$1,000) = 1.0$ and $u(\$0) = 0$.

Consider an elementary lottery that gives you a $p$ chance of gaining $\$X$ and a $(1-p)$ chance of gaining nothing, where $0 < X < 1000$. For example, imagine a lottery that gives you a .5 chance of winning $500. Now imagine a second elementary lottery that gives you a $q$ chance of winning $1,000 and a $(1-q)$ chance of nothing, and consider your attitudes toward the two lotteries. In particular, ask yourself what value of $q$ would leave you indifferent between the two lotteries. In other words, what value of $q$ would leave you indifferent between having a .5 chance of winning $500 and a $q$ chance of winning $1,000?

By the manner in which this question is posed, note that you are being asked to assess a value $q$ such that

$$q\ u(\$1,000) = p\ u(\$X).$$

However, since $u(\$1,000) = 1.0$, this in turn implies that

$$q = p\ u(\$X)$$

so that

$$u(\$X) = q/p.$$

278

Thus in the example given, $u(\$500) = q/.5$. In other words, by asking people to estimate probabilities that leave them indifferent between two lotteries, utility values can be directly obtained from the ratio of $q$ to $p$. This reasoning leads to the following procedure for assessing a utility function over a variable $X$ that has a maximum plausible value of $X^*$ and a minimum plausible value of $X_*$.

(1)  Set $u(X_*) = 0$ and $u(X^*) = 1.0$.
(2)  Choose a convenient value of $p$ such as .5 to ask in all questions.
(3)  Divide the range from $X_*$ to $X^*$ into a number of points $X_i$.
(4)  Obtain the lottery equivalent $q_i$'s for all the $X_i$'s.
(5)  Plot the $q_i/p$ values directly on to a graph of the utility function.
(6)  Draw the utility function over the whole range of $X$ by interpolating between the assessed values. (Note that in practice one would want to return and check responses to certain questions if the assessed utility function does not seem reasonable to the persons concerned.)

An example of a utility function assessed by this method is given in Fig. C.1. In eliciting this utility function over the range of $0 to $1,000, $p$ was set at .5, and the $X_i$ values used in the questions were $200, $400, $600, and $800. The $q_i$'s given by the respondent were .20, .32, .40, and .45, respectively.

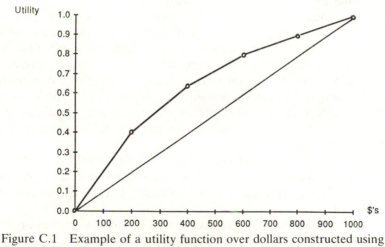

Figure C.1  Example of a utility function over dollars constructed using the method of lottery equivalents

## REFERENCE

1. This procedure was proposed by Mark McCord and Richard de Neufville (1986). 'Lottery equivalents': Reduction of the certainty effect in utility assessment, *Management Science*, **32**, 56–60.

# APPENDIX D

# Notes on multi-attribute utility assessment[1]

These brief notes are intended to supplement the discussion of 'assessing consequences' presented in Chapter 9.

The basic question addressed is how to assess *relative preferences* for possible outcomes of a decision that can be represented on several dimensions. Consider, for example, the selection of one of several job candidates who are evaluated on dimensions of, say, intelligence, motivation, and relevant prior experience. As further examples, Figure 9.3 of the text illustrated the dimensions by which Woodward–Clyde consultants intended evaluating different possible corporate strategies, and Figure 9.4 that of a company's scheme for evaluating training plans.

Several methods for assessing relative preferences for multi-dimensional outcomes have been suggested in the literature. The basic features of these methods involve: (1) selecting dimensions on which the alternatives are to be evaluated; (2) determining the adequacy of the set of dimensions (see discussion in Chapter 9); (3) measuring each of the alternatives on scales which are comparable across dimensions; (4) weighting the dimensions according to their relative importance; (5) aggregating across dimensions to find a 'score' for each of the alternatives; and (6) choosing the alternative with the largest 'score'.

It should be noted that although the word *dimension* is used here to describe a given aspect of an alternative, the word *attribute* is frequently used in the literature. *Attribute* and *dimension* should therefore be considered interchangeable.

Edwards has presented a 10-step procedure for *multi-attribute* utility assessment.[2] This method is presented here for two reasons: first, it is a method that is both easy to understand and apply; and second, such 'simple' methods have often been found to give results that are satisfactory when compared to theoretically sounder but more complex methodologies.

In following the presentation, the reader is asked to imagine a choice between alternatives with multi-dimensional outcomes: for example, job candidates, different possible locations of a site for a new factory, alternative training plans for a company (cf. Figure 9.4), and so on. One alternative which should also be kept in the set under consideration is that of not taking any action, i.e. the *status quo*.

Edwards' 10-step procedure can be subdivided into four phases:

(1)  structuring the problem;
(2)  determining the importance of dimensions;
(3)  measuring alternatives on the dimensions; and
(4)  choice.

A linear presentation of the Edwards procedure is now made, although in practice there would be considerable 'recycling' between phases—in the same manner as the general decision analysis model presented in Chapter 9.

## Structuring the Problem

As discussed in Chapter 9, this is the most important phase. Indeed, in many cases it may not even be necessary to go beyond it since the best alternative could become evident simply by structuring the problem. There are four steps which are also covered by the general model indicated in Chapter 9.

### Step 1

Identify the decision maker(s). Where an organization is *the* decision maker, it is particularly important to identify people who can speak for the organization.

### Step 2

Identify the decision. It is important to note that value (i.e. relative preference for outcomes) depends not only upon (a) the identity of the decision maker, but also on (b) what is being evaluated, and (c) the purpose for which it is being evaluated.

### Step 3

Identify the alternatives to be evaluated.

### Step 4

Identify the dimensions on which the alternatives are to be evaluated (cf. Tables 9.3 and 9.4).

Issues relevant to structuring problems, e.g. selection of a set of dimensions, were discussed in some detail in Chapter 9 and are therefore not considered further here.

**Determining the importance of dimensions**

The object of this phase is to determine the decision maker's attitudes toward the relative importance of the dimensions.

*Step 5*

Rank order the dimensions in terms of their importance. If there is more than one decision maker, Edwards recommends attempting to gain consensus on the rank ordering through group discussion. Consensus gained at this level can greatly facilitate the subsequent process.

*Step 6*

Translate the rankings to ratings. Edwards suggests that the lowest ranking dimension be given a score of 10. The next lowest dimension is then considered and it is asked how much more important it is than the lowest. This is then assigned a number to reflect its importance and one works one's way up the list of dimensions. In doing so, it is important to preserve ratios in the sense that if a dimension is allotted a score of 30, it should be considered three times as important as a dimension with a score of 10, but only half as important as a dimension with a score of 60, and so on. In assigning numbers, one should not be reticent about changing previous assessments, rearranging, etc. It is unlikely that the final assessments will be achieved at a first attempt and even more unlikely that a group will succeed in doing so.

*Step 7*

This is a computational step to convert ratings to numbers that sum to 1. Simply add the weights assessed in Step 6, and divide each dimension's Step 6 assessment by the sum of all assessments to obtain a 'normalized' weight for each dimension.

Note that it is possible to go directly from Step 4 to Step 7. The intermediate steps simply serve to systematize the process.

**Measuring alternatives on the dimensions**

*Step 8*

Each alternative must now be measured on each of the dimensions. However, there is a problem in that the dimensions themselves are not expressed in commensurable units. Consider, for example, the dimensions/attributes at the base of the hierarchies in Figures 9.3 and 9.4. Rescaling is necesssary.

Associate with each dimension a possible worth or value scale which goes from 0 to 100 and where the end-points represent minimum and maximum plausible values. (Note *plausible*, not possible. The minimum plausible value does not necessarily indicate total absence of an alternative on a dimension.) Given these comparable worth scales, the problem now consists of measuring the location of each alternative on the scales—for each of the dimensions. In some cases, all one can do is have an expert assess a value for each alternative. Consider, for example, dimensions such as Quality in Figure 9.4. In other cases, one may wish to define a relation between a physical measurement, e.g. Person-hours in Figure 9.4, and a worth scale. Once again, such relations would typically be assessed by substantive experts. Indeed, most evaluations of dimensions will require a high degree of subjective expert judgement. However, an advantage of this methodology is that one can obtain, and combine, assessments on the different dimensions by experts in ,each of their respective domains. For example, an expert in dimension A can assess all alternatives on this dimension; an expert in dimension B can make similar judgements in respect of dimension B; and so on.

*Step 9*

The overall worth of each alternative is calculated by summing each alternative's scores on the dimensions as weighted by the appropriate importance weights determined in Step 7.

**Choice**

*Step 10*

Step 9 yields a list of alternatives accompanied by their measures of relative worth. The normative rule is to choose the alternative with the largest assessment of worth.

**Additional considerations**

Chapter 9 discussed some important issues and assumptions involved in determining the set of dimensions (attributes) on which the mathematical operations are to be performed. In particular, for the procedures outlined here to be used with confidence, the assumption of value independence should be checked. Chapter 9 also considered the technique of sensitivity analysis. One should not believe the figures that emerge from an analysis. They are bound to be wrong. However, it is important to discover how wrong they are relative to the problem at hand. This can be achieved by varying the quantitative inputs to the problem and observing the extent of changes in overall preferences for alternatives to such variations.

Another important point is that there is no need to follow slavishly through the 10-step procedure outlined above. In some applications, it might be advisable to avoid Steps 5-7 (i.e. determining the relative importance of dimensions) since these value judgements can cause conflicts. It may be possible to wait until the measurement procedure has been completed (Step 8) and then to see how the weights that might be given by different parties to the decision would affect the final rank-ordering of alternatives. This is also important in that the analysis of alternatives often takes place concurrently with policy formulation and the importance weights might simply not be available when the alternatives are first compared. In addition, it might be possible to eliminate some alternatives at an early stage of the analysis if it can be shown that no set of weights, or at least no reasonable set of weights, could ever make the alternatives acceptable. Assigning equal weights to the dimensions can also be a satisfactory procedure in many situations.[3]

Situations arise where the decision maker chooses between alternatives against a budget constraint. Consider, for example, the allocation of funds to different projects in R & D, differential allocation of resources in advertising or training and development, and so on. Since alternatives usually vary in cost, it is important to bring cost into the model. The simplest procedure is to calculate benefit-to-cost ratios for each of the alternatives. That is, divide the overall worth of each alternative (as determined by the model) by its cost and re-rank the alternatives by the resultant benefit-to-cost ratios. The optimal choice is reached by allocating the budget to the alternatives with the largest benefit-to-cost ratios, since these yield the greatest benefit per unit of cost.

People sometimes feel diffident about bringing cost directly into an analysis, for example by treating it as a dimension with a negative value. Thus, although scaling a worth function for cost is not conceptually different from scaling worth functions for other dimensions, the following ploy of evaluating alternatives relative to the *status quo* can be useful.

Let $b_i$ denote the benefit of alternative $i$ and $b_{sq}$ that of the *status quo*; represent the cost of alternative $i$ by $c_i$ and that of the *status quo* by $c_{sq}$. Calculate the index:

$$\frac{b_i - b_{sq}}{c_i - c_{sq}}$$

This ratio gives a notion of the incremental benefit of alternative $i$ over the *status quo* relative to the additional cost, i.e. incremental benefit per unit of cost (assuming $c_i > c_{sq}$). It can be used as a measure of the efficacy, or expected efficacy, of an alternative relative to the *status quo*.

Finally, a useful user-oriented tutorial of multi-attribute assessment methods has been provided by Johnson and Huber.[4]

## NOTES TO APPENDIX D

1. These notes are based on a presentation made in R. M. Hogarth (1979). *Evaluating Management Education*, Chichester, England: John Wiley & Sons, Chapter 12.
2. W. Edwards (1977). Use of multiattribute utility measurement for social decision making. In D. E. Bell, R. L. Keeney, and H. Raiffa (eds), *Conflicting Objectives in Decisions*, Chichester, England: John Wiley & Sons, pp. 247–275. In this presentation, Edwards also indicates several empirical examples.
3. For a relevant empirical example, see H. J. Einhorn and W. McCoach (1977). A simple multiattribute procedure for evaluation, *Behavioral Science*, **22**, 270–282.
4. E. M. Johnson and G. P. Huber (1977). The technology of utility assessment, *IEEE Transactions on Systems, Man and Cybernetics*, Vol. SMC-7, pp. 311–325.

# APPENDIX E

# A guide to further reading

This appendix provides a guide to further reading. It contains eight sections:

I.   Overviews/discussions of behavioural decision theory
II.  More general approaches to the study of decision behaviour
III. Rationality and human limitations
IV.  Biases in information processing
V.   Models of decision behaviour
VI.  Risk
VII. Creativity and problem solving
VIII. Decision aids

The bibliography includes items referenced in the notes at the end of each chapter, although not all. With the exception of Section IV, the references are organized in *chronological* order so that readers can acquire an indication of the manner in which knowledge in the field has developed. Section IV is the most detailed and is divided into sub-sections corresponding to the conceptual scheme of Figure 10.1 and Table 10.2 (Chapter 10). References within sub-sections of Section IV are presented alphabetically.

## I. OVERVIEWS/DISCUSSIONS OF BEHAVIOURAL DECISION THEORY

The field now known in psychology as 'behavioural decision theory' has been reviewed periodically over the last three decades. The following books and papers are quite complete in terms of references, but readers should be aware that they were written for psychological audiences.

1. Edwards, W. (1954). The theory of decision making, *Psychological Bulletin*, **51**, 380–417.
2. Edwards, W. (1961). Behavioral decision theory, *Annual Review of Psychology*, **12**, 473–498.
3. Becker, G. M., and McClintock, C. G. (1967). Value: Behavioral decision theory, *Annual Review of Psychology*, **18**, 239–286.
4. Peterson, C. R., and Beach. L. R. (1967). Man as an intuitive statistician, *Psychological Bulletin*, **68**, 29–46.

286

5. Kleinmuntz, B. (ed.) (1968). *Formal Representation of Human Judgment*, New York: John Wiley.

6. Lee, W. (1971). *Decision Theory and Human Behavior*, New York: Wiley.

7. Rapoport, A., and Wallsten, T. S. (1972). Individual decision behavior, *Annual Review of Psychology*, **23**, 131–175.

8. Newell, A., and Simon, H. A. (1972). *Human Problem Solving*, Englewood Cliffs, NJ: Prentice-Hall. (For an overview of this book see H. A. Simon and A. Newell (1971). Human problem solving: The state of the theory in 1970, *American Psychologist*, **26**, 145–159.)

9. Rappoport, L., and Summers, D. A. (eds) (1973). *Human Judgment and Social Interaction*, New York: Holt, Rinehart & Winston. This volume includes the classic overview paper by P. Slovic and S. Lichtenstein (1971). Comparison of Bayesian and regression approaches to the study of information processing in judgment, *Organizational Behavior and Human Performance*, **6**, 649–744.

10. Rapoport, A. (1975). Research paradigms for studying dynamic decision behavior. In D. Wendt and C. A. J. Vlek (eds), *Utility, Probability, and Human Decision Making*, Dordrecht, Holland: Reidel.

11. Slovic, P., Fischhoff, B., and Lichtenstein, S. (1977). Behavioral decision theory, *Annual Review of Psychology*, **28**, 1–39.

12. Vlek, C. A. J., and Wagenaar, W. A. (1979). Judgment and decision under uncertainty. In J. A. Michon, E. G. J. Eijkman, and L. F. W. de Klerk (eds), *Handbook of Psychonomics*, Vol. 2, Amsterdam: North-Holland.

13. Einhorn, H. J., and Hogarth, R. M. (1981). Behavioral decision theory: Processes of judgment and choice, *Annual Review of Psychology*, **32**, 53–88.

14. Payne, J. W. (1982). Contingent decision behavior, *Psychological Bulletin*, **92**, 382–402.

15. Pitz, G. F., and Sachs, N. J. (1984). Judgment and decision: Theory and application, *Annual Review of Psychology*, **35**, 139–163.

16. Slovic, P., Lichtenstein, S., and Fischhoff, B. (1986). Decision making. In R. C. Atkinson, R. J. Herrnstein, G. Lindzey, and R. D. Luce (eds), *Stevens' Handbook of Experimental Psychology* (2nd edn), New York : Wiley.   Inter library

## II. MORE GENERAL APPROACHES TO THE STUDY OF DECISION BEHAVIOUR

The following references provide a broader perspective on human decision behaviour than those contained in Section I.

1. Bruner, J. S., Goodnow, J. J., and Austin, G. A. (1956). *A Study of Thinking*, New York: John Wiley.

2. Simon, H. A. (1959). Theories of decision-making in economics and

behavioral science, *American Economic Review*, **49**, No. 3.

3. Cohen, J. (1960). *Chance, Skill and Luck*, Harmondsworth, Middlesex: Penguin Books.

4. Gore, W. J., and Dyson, J. W. (eds) (1964). *The Making of Decisions: A Reader in Administrative Behavior*, Glencoe: The Free Press.

5. Kogan, N., and Wallach, M. A. (1964). *Risk Taking: A Study in Cognition and Personality*, New York: Holt, Rinehart & Winston. (One of the few studies of effects of personality on decision making.)

6. Simon, H. A. (1969). *The Sciences of the Artificial* (2nd edn 1981). Cambridge, MA: M.I.T. Press.

7. Coombs, C. H., Dawes, R. M., and Tversky, A. (1970). *Mathematical Psychology: An Elementary Introduction*, Englewood Cliffs, NJ: Prentice-Hall. (Chapters 5, 6 and 7 provide good introductions to theories of individual decision making, the theory of signal detection and game theory.)

8. Johnson, D. M. (1972). *A Systematic Introduction to the Psychology of Thinking*, New York: Harper & Row.

9. Cohen, J. (1972). *Psychological Probability: Or the Art of Doubt*, London: George Allen & Unwin.

10. Wason, P. C., and Johnson-Laird, P. N. (1972). *Psychology of Reasoning: Structure and Content*, London: Batsford.

11. MacCrimmon, K. R., and Taylor, R. N. (1976). Decision making and problem solving. In M. D. Dunnette (ed.), *Handbook of Industrial and Organizational Psychology*, Chicago: Rand-McNally.

12. Janis, I. L., and Mann, L. (1977). *Decision Making: A Psychological Analysis of Conflict, Choice, and Commitment*, New York: The Free Press.

13. Nisbett, R. E., and Ross, L. (1980). *Human Inference: Strategies and Shortcomings of Social Judgment*, Englewood Cliffs, NJ: Prentice-Hall.

14. Wallsten, T. S. (ed.) (1980). *Cognitive Processes in Choice and Decision Behavior*, Hillsdale, NJ: Erlbaum.

15. Hogarth, R. M. (ed.) (1982). *Question Framing and Response Consistency*, San Francisco, CA: Jossey-Bass.

16. Einhorn, H. J., and Hogarth, R. M. (1986). Judging probable cause, *Psychological Bulletin*, **99**, 3–19.

17. Arkes, A., and Hammond, K. R. (eds) (1986). *Judgment and Decision Making: An Interdisciplinary Reader*, New York: Cambridge University Press.

## III. RATIONALITY AND HUMAN LIMITATIONS

Much of this book is concerned with the notion that people cannot exercise rational choice because of limitations of the human information processing system. The following are pertinent to this issue.

1. Simon, H. A. (1955). A behavioral model of rational choice, *Quarterly Journal of Economics*, **69**, 99–118.

2. Miller, G. A. (1956). The magical number seven, plus or minus two: Some limits on our capacity for processing information, *Psychological Review*, **63**, 81–97.

3. Simon, H. A. (1956). Rational choice and the structure of the environment, *Psychological Review*, **63**, 129–138.

4. Toda, M. (1962). The design of a fungus eater: A model of human behavior in an unsophisticated environment, *Behavioral Science*, **7**, 164–183. [Reprinted in Toda (1982) below.]

5. Russo, J. E. (1977). The value of unit price information, *Journal of Marketing Research*, **14**, 193–201.

6. March, J. G. (1978). Bounded rationality, ambiguity, and the engineering of choice, *Bell Journal of Economics*, **9**, 587–608.

7. Simon, H. A. (1978). Rationality as process and as product of thought, *American Economic Review*, **68**, 1–16.

8. Simon, H. A. (1979). Rational decision making in business organizations, *American Economic Review*, **69**, 493–513.

9. Thaler, R. H. (1980). Toward a positive theory of consumer choice, *Journal of Economic Behavior and Organization*, **1**, 39–60.

10. Hogarth, R. M. (1981). Beyond discrete biases: Functional and dysfunctional aspects of judgmental heuristics, *Psychological Bulletin*, **90**, 197–217.

11. Cohen, L. J. (1981). Can human irrationality be experimentally demonstrated? *The Behavioral and Brain Sciences*, **4**, 317–370. (See also the commentaries on this paper in the same issue.)

12. Lopes, L. L. (1982). Doing the impossible: A note on induction and the experience of randomness, *Journal of Experimental Psychology: Learning, Memory, and Cognition*, **8**, 626–636.

13. Toda , M. (1982). *Man, Robot, and Society: Models and Speculations*, Boston, MA: Martinus Nijhoff.

14. Kahneman, D., Slovic, P., and Tversky, A. (eds) (1982). *Judgment under Uncertainty: Heuristics and Biases*, New York: Cambridge University Press.

15. Berkeley, D., and Humphreys, P. (1982). Structuring decision problems and the bias heuristic, *Acta Psychologica*, **50**, 201–252.

16. Tversky, A. and Kahneman, D. (1983). Extensional versus intuitive reasoning: The conjunction fallacy in probability judgment, *Psychological Review*, **90**, 293–315.

17. Nisbett, R. L., Krantz, D. H., Jepson, C., and Kunda, Z. (1983). The use of statistical heuristics in everyday inductive reasoning, *Psychological Review*, **90**, 339–363.

18. Christensen-Szalanski, J., and Beach, L. (1984). The citation bias: Fad and fashion in the judgment and decision literature, *American Psychologist*, **39**, 75–78.

19. Thaler, R. (1985). Mental accounting and consumer choice, *Marketing Science*, **4**, 199–214.

20. Tversky, A., and Kahneman, D. (1986). Rational choice and the framing of decisions, *Journal of Business*, **59**(4), Part 2, S251–S278.

## IV. BIASES IN INFORMATION PROCESSING

In Chapter 10, Table 10.2 lists biases in information processing indicating that bias can occur at different stages of information processing: (a) acquisition; (b) processing; (c) output; and (d) feedback. Selected (but not exhaustive) references to these biases/sources of bias are provided here and organized according to the scheme given in Figure 10.1 and Table 10.2.

### A. Acquisition

*(i) Availability*

1. Combs, B., and Slovic, P. (1979). Newspaper coverage of causes of death, *Journalism Quarterly*, **56**, 837–843; 849.
2. Lichtenstein, S., Slovic, P., Fischhoff, B., Layman, M., and Combs, B. (1978). Judged frequency of lethal events, *Journal of Experimental Psychology: Human Learning and Memory*, **4**, 551–578.
3. Maier, N. R. F. (1931). Reasoning in humans: II. The solution of a problem and its appearance in consciousness, *Journal of Comparative Psychology*, **12**, 181–194.
4. Tversky, A., and Kahneman, D. (1973). Availability: A heuristic for judging frequency and probability, *Cognitive Psychology*, **5**, 207–232.

*(ii) Selective perception*

1. Bruner, J. S., and Postman, L. J. (1949). On the perception of incongruity: A paradigm, *Journal of Personality*, **18**, 206–223.
2. Dearborn, D. C., and Simon, H. A. (1958). Selective perception: A note on the departmental identification of executives, *Sociometry*, **21**, 140–144.
3. Wason, P. C. (1960). On the failure to eliminate hypotheses in a conceptual task, *Quarterly Journal of Experimental Psychology*, **12**, 129–140.
4. Webster, E. C. (1964). *Decision Making in the Employment Interview*, Industrial Relations Centre, McGill University, Montreal.

*(iii) Frequency*

1. Estes, W. K. (1976). The cognitive side of probability learning, *Psychological Review*, **83**, 37–64.
2. Smedslund, J. (1963). The concept of correlation in adults, *Scandinavian Journal of Psychology*, **4**, 165–173.
3. Ward, W. C., and Jenkins, H. M. (1965). The display of information

and the judgment of contingency, *Canadian Journal of Psychology*, **19**, 231–241.

### (iv) Concrete information

1. Bar-Hillel, M. (1980). The base-rate fallacy in probability judgments, *Acta Psychologica*, **44**, 211–233.
2. Borgida, E., and Nisbett, R. E. (1977). The differential impact of abstract vs. concrete information on decisions, *Journal of Applied Social Psychology*, **7**, 258–271.
3. Lyon, D., and Slovic, P. (1976). Dominance of accuracy information and neglect of base rates in probability estimation, *Acta Psychologica*, **40**, 287–298.
4. Nisbett, R. E., Borgida, E., Crandall, R., and Reed, H. (1976). Popular induction: Information is not necessarily informative. In J. S. Carroll and J. W. Payne (eds), *Cognition and Social Behavior*, Hillsdale, NJ: Lawrence Erlbaum.
5. Taylor, S. E., and Thompson, S. C. (1982). Stalking the elusive 'vividness' effect, *Psychological Review*, **89**, 155–181.

### (v) Illusory correlation

1. Chapman, L. J. (1967). Illusory correlation in observational report, *Journal of Verbal Learning and Verbal Behavior*, **6**, 151–155.
2. Chapman, L. J., and Chapman, J. P. (1969). Illusory correlation as an obstacle to the use of valid psychodiagnostic signs, *Journal of Abnormal Psychology*, **74**, 271–280.
3. Crocker, J. (1981). Judgment of covariation by social perceivers, *Psychological Bulletin*, **90**, 272–292.
4. Golding, S. L., and Rorer, L. G. (1972). Illusory correlation and subjective judgment, *Journal of Abnormal Psychology*, **80**, 249–260.
5. Shweder, R. A. (1977). Likeness and likelihood in everyday thought: Magical thinking in judgments about personality, *Current Anthropology*, **18**, 637–658.

### (vi) Data presentation

1. Dickson, G. W., Senn, J. A., and Chervany, N. L. (1977). Research in management information systems: The Minnesota experiments, *Management Science*, **23**, 913–923.
2. Fischhoff, B., Slovic, P., and Lichtenstein, S. (1978). Fault trees: Sensitivity of estimated failure probabilities to problem representation. *Journal of Experimental Psychology: Human Perception and Performance*, **4**, 330–344.

3. Jenkins, H. M., and Ward, W. C. (1965). Judgment of contingency between responses and outcomes, *Psychological Monographs: General and Applied*, **79**, 1–17.
4. Keller, L. R. (1985). The effects of problem representation on the sure-thing and substitution principles, *Management Science*, **31**, 738–751.
5. Lathrop, R. G. (1967). Perceived variability, *Journal of Experimental Psychology*, **73**, 498–502.
6. Ronen, J. (1973). Effects of some probability displays on choices, *Organizational Behavior and Human Performance*, **9**, 1–15.

## B. Processing of information

### (i) Inconsistency

1. Bowman, E. H. (1963). Consistency and optimality in management decision making, *Management Science*, **10**, 310–321.
2. Brehmer, B. (1976). Social judgment theory and the analysis of interpersonal conflict, *Psychological Bulletin*, **83**, 985–1003.
3. Einhorn, H. J. (1972). Expert measurement and mechanical combination, *Organizational Behavior and Human Performance*, **7**, 86–106.
4. Kunreuther, H. (1969). Extensions of Bowman's theory of managerial decision making, *Management Science*, **15**, B-415–439.
5. Showers, J. L., and Shakrin, L. M. (1981). Reducing uncollectible revenue from residential telephone customers, *Interfaces*, **11**, 21–34.

### (ii) Conservatism

1. DuCharme, W. M. (1970). A response bias explanation of conservative human inference, *Journal of Experimental Psychology*, **85**, 66–74.
2. Edwards, W. (1968). Conservatism in human information processing. In B. Kleinmuntz (ed.), *Formal Representation of Human Judgment*, New York: Wiley.
3. Phillips, L. D., and Edwards, W. (1966). Conservatism in a simple probability inference task, *Journal of Experimental Psychology*, **72**, 346–357.
4. Phillips, L. D., Hays, W. L., and Edwards, W. (1966). Conservatism in complex probabilistic inference, *IEEE Transactions on Human Factors in Electronics*, Vol. HFE-7, 7–18.

### (iii) Non-linear extrapolation

1. Bar-Hillel, M. (1973). On the subjective probability of compound events, *Organizational Behavior and Human Performance*, **9**, 396–406.
2. Cohen, J., Chesnick, E. I., and Haran, D. A. (1972). A confirmation of

the inertial Ψ-effect in sequential choice and decision, *British Journal of Psychology*, **63**, 41–46.
3. Wagenaar, W. A., and Sagaria, S. D. (1975). Misperception of exponential growth, *Perception and Psychophysics*, **18**, 416–422.
4. Wagenaar, W. A., and Timmers, H. (1978). Intuitive prediction of growth. In D. F. Burkhardt and W. H. Ittelson (eds), *Environmental Asssessment of Socioeconomic Systems*, New York: Plenum.
5. Wagenaar, W. A., and Timmers, H. (1979). The pond-and-duckweed problem: Three experiments on the misperception of exponential growth, *Acta Psychologica*, **43**, 239–251.

*(iv) 'Heuristics' used to reduce mental effort*

1. Gettys, C. F., Kelly, C. W. III, and Peterson, C. R. (1973). The best guess hypothesis in multistage inference, *Organizational Behavior and Human Performance*, **10**, 364–373.
2. Kahneman, D., and Tversky, A. (1972). Subjective probability: A judgment of representativeness, *Cognitive Psychology*, **3**, 430–454.
3. Kahneman, D., and Tversky, A. (1973). On the psychology of prediction, *Psychological Review*, **80**, 237–251.
4. Knafl, K., and Burkett, G. (1975). Professional socialization in a surgical speciality: Acquiring medical judgment, *Social Science of Medicine*, **9**, 397–404.
5. Slovic, P. (1975). Choice between equally-valued alternatives, *Journal of Experimental Psychology: Human Perception and Performance*, **1**, 280–287.
6. Tversky, A., and Kahneman, D. (1971). The belief in the 'law of small numbers', *Psychological Bulletin*, **76**, 105–110.
7. Tversky, A., and Kahneman, D. (1974). Judgment under uncertainty: Heuristics and biases, *Science*, **185**, 1124–1131.

*(v) The decision environment*

1. Asch, S. E. (1951). Effects of group pressure on the modification and distortion of judgments. In H. Guetzkow (ed.), *Groups, Leadership and Men*, Pittsburgh: Carnegie Institute of Technology Press.
2. Einhorn, H. J. (1971). Use of nonlinear, noncompensatory models as a function of task and amount of information, *Organizational Behavior and Human Performance*, **6**, 2–17.
3. Janis, I. L. (1972). *Victims of Groupthink*, Boston: Houghton Mifflin.
4. Pollay, R. W. (1970). The structure of executive decisions and decision times, *Administrative Science Quarterly*, **15**, 459–471.
5. Wright, P. (1974). The harassed decision maker: Time pressures, distractions and the use of evidence, *Journal of Applied Psychology*, **59**, 555–561.

*(vi) Information sources*

1. Oskamp, S. (1965). Overconfidence in case-study judgments, *Journal of Consulting Psychology*, **29**, 261–265.
2. Slovic, P. (1982). Toward understanding and improving decisions. In W. C. Howell and E. A. Fleishman (eds), *Human Performance and Productivity*: Vol. 2, *Information Processing and Decision Making*, Hillsdale, NJ: Lawrence Erlbaum.

## C. Output

*(i) Response mode*

1. Grether, D. M., and Plott, C. R. (1979). Economic theory of choice and the preference reversal phenomenon, *American Economic Review*, **69**, 623–638.
2. Hogarth, R. M. (1975). Cognitive processes and the assessment of subjective probability distributions, *Journal of the American Statistical Association*, **70**, 271–289.
3. Lichtenstein, S., and Slovic, P. (1971). Reversals of preference between bids and choices in gambling decisions, *Journal of Experimental Psychology*, **89**, 46–55.
4. Lichtenstein, S., and Slovic, P. (1973). Response-induced reversals of preference in gambling: An extended replication in Las Vegas, *Journal of Experimental Psychology*, **101**, 16–20.

*(ii) Wishful thinking*

1. Cyert, R. M., Dill, W. T., and March J. G. (1958). The role of expectations in business decision making, *Administrative Science Quarterly*, **3**, 307–340.
2. Morlock, H. (1967). The effect of outcome desirability on information required for decisions, *Behavioral Science*, **12**, 296–300.
3. Slovic, P. (1966). Value as a determiner of subjective probability, *IEEE Transactions on Human Factors in Electronics*, Vol HFE-7, pp. 22–28.
4. Einhorn, H. J., and Hogarth, R. M. (1986). Decision making under ambiguity, *Journal of Business,* **59**(4), Part 2, S225–S250.

*(iii) Illusion of control*

1. Langer, E. J. (1975). The illusion of control, *Journal of Personality and Social Psychology*, **32**, 311–328.
2. Langer, E. J., and Roth, J. (1975). The effect of sequence of outcomes in a chance task on the illusion of control, *Journal of Personality and Social Psychology*, **32**, 951–955.

3. Perlmutter, L. C., and Monty, R. A. (1977). The importance of perceived control: Fact or fantasy? *American Scientist*, **65**, 759–765.


## D. Feedback

### (i) Outcome irrelevant learning structures

1. Brehmer, B. (1980). In one word: Not from experience, *Acta Psychologica*, **45**, 223–241.
2. Einhorn, H. J. (1980). Learning from experience and suboptimal rules in decision making. In T. Wallsten (ed.), *Cognitive Processes in Choice and Decision Behavior*, Hillsdale, NJ: Lawrence Erlbaum.
3. Einhorn, H. J., and Hogarth, R. M. (1978). Confidence in judgment: Persistence of the illusion of validity, *Psychological Review*, **85**, 395–476.
4. Fischhoff, B., Slovic, P., and Lichtenstein, S. (1977). Knowing with certainty: The appropriateness of extreme confidence, *Journal of Experimental Psychology: Human Perception and Performance*, **3**, 552–564.
5. Bushyhead, J., and Christensen-Szalanski, J. (1981). Feedback and the illusion of validity in a medical clinic, *Medical Decision Making*, **1**, 115–123.


### (ii) Misperception of chance

1. Cohen, J. (1972). *Psychological Probability: Or the Art of Doubt*, London, England: George Allen & Unwin.
2. Jarvik, M. E. (1951). Probability learning and a negative recency effect in the serial anticipation of alternative symbols, *Journal of Experimental Psychology*, **41**, 291–297.
3. Langer, E. J. (1977). The psychology of chance, *Journal of the Theory of Social Behaviour*, **7**, 185–207.
4. Wagenaar, W. A. (1970). Appreciation of conditional probabilities in binary sequences, *Acta Psychologica*, **34**, 348–356.


### (iii) Success/failure attributions

1. Miller, D. T. (1976). Ego involvement and attributions for success and failure, *Journal of Personality and Social Psychology*, **34**, 901–906.
2. Ross, L. (1977). The intuitive psychologist and his shortcomings: Distortions in the attribution process. In L. Berkowitz (ed.), *Advances in Experimental Social Psychology*, Vol. 10, New York: Academic Press.


### (iv) Logical fallacies in recall

1. Buckhout, R. (1974). Eyewitness testimony, *Scientific American*, **231**, 23–31.

2. Loftus, E. F. (1975). Leading questions and the eyewitness report, *Cognitive Psychology*, **7**, 560–572.
3. Loftus, E. F. (1979). *Eyewitness Testimony*, Cambridge, MA: Harvard University Press.
4. Snyder, M., and Uranowitz, S. W. (1978). Reconstructing the past: Some cognitive consequences of person perception, *Journal of Personality and Social Psychology*, **36**, 941–950.
5. Wells, G. L., and Loftus, E. F. (eds) (1984). *Eyewitness Testimony: Psychological Perspectives*, New York: Cambridge University Press.

*(v) Hindsight bias*

1. Buchman, T. A. (1985). An effect of hindsight on predicting bankruptcy with accounting information, *Accounting, Organizations and Society*, **10**, 267–286.
2. Fischhoff, B. (1975). Hindsight ≠ foresight: The effect of outcome knowledge on judgment under uncertainty, *Journal of Experimental Psychology: Human Perception and Performance*, **1**, 288–299.
3. Fischhoff, B. (1977). Perceived informativeness of facts, *Journal of Experimental Psychology: Human Perception and Performance*, **3**, 349–358.
4. Fischhoff, B. and Beyth, R. (1975). 'I knew it would happen'—Remembered probabilities of once-future things, *Organizational Behavior and Human Performance,* **13**, 1–16.

## V. MODELS OF DECISION BEHAVIOUR

There has been much interest in modelling how people make judgments and choices in given circumstances. These can be conceptualized under three headings: (a) linear models of judgement; (b) the lens model (see Chapter 1, Figure 1.1); and (c) heuristic combining models.

### A. Linear models of judgment

1. Meehl, P. E. (1954). *Clinical versus Statistical Prediction*, Minneapolis: University of Minnesota Press.
2. Hoffman, P. J. (1960). The paramorphic representation of clinical judgment, *Psychological Bulletin*, **57**, 116–131.
3. Yntema, D. B., and Torgerson, W. S. (1961). Man–computer cooperation in decisions requiring common sense, *IRE Transactions on Human Factors in Electronics*, Vol. HFE-2, 20–26.
4. Shepard, R. N. (1964). On subjectively optimum selection among multi-attribute alternatives. In M. W. Shelly and G. L. Bryan (eds), *Human Judgments and Optimality*, New York: John Wiley, 1964.
5. Sawyer, J. (1966). Measurement *and* prediction, clinical *and* statistical, *Psychological Bulletin*, **66**, 178–200.

6. Goldberg, L. R. (1968). Simple methods or simple processes? Some research on clinical judgments, *American Psychologist*, **23**, 483–496.
7. Hoffman, P. J., Slovic, P., and Rorer, L. G. (1968). An analysis-of-variance model for assessment of configural cue utilization in clinical judgment, *Psychological Bulletin*, **69**, 338–349.
8. Slovic, P. (1969). Analyzing the expert judge: A descriptive study of a stockbroker's decision processes, *Journal of Applied Psychology*, **53**, 255–263.
9. Goldberg, L. R. (1970). Man versus model of man: A rationale, plus some evidence, for a method of improving on clinical inferences, *Psychological Bulletin*, **73**, 422–432.
10. Dawes, R. M. (1971). A case study of graduate admissions: Application of three principles of human decision making, *American Psychologist*, **26**, 180–188.
11. Dawes, R. M. and Corrigan, B. (1974). Linear models in decision making, *Psychological Bulletin*, **81**, 95–106.
12. Libby, R. (1976). Man versus model of man: Some conflicting evidence, *Organizational Behavior and Human Performance*, **16**, 1–12.
13. Dawes, R. M. (1979). The robust beauty of improper linear models, *American Psychologist*, **34**, 571–582.
14. Einhorn, H. J., Kleinmuntz, D. N., and Kleinmuntz, B. (1979). Linear regression and process-tracing models of judgment, *Psychological Review*, **86**, 465–485.
15. Anderson, N. H. (1981). *Foundations of Information Integration Theory*, New York: Academic Press.

## B. The lens model

1. Hammond, K. R. (1955). Probabilistic functioning and the clinical method, *Psychological Review*, **62**, 255–262.
2. Hursch, C., Hammond, K. R., and Hursch, J. L. (1964). Some methodological considerations in multiple cue probability studies, *Psychological Review*, **71**, 42–60.
3. Hammond, K. R., Hursch, C. J., and Todd, F. J. (1964). Analyzing the components of clinical inference, *Psychological Review*, **71**, 438–456.
4. Tucker, L. R. (1964). A suggested alternative formulation in the development of Hursch, Hammond, and Hursch, and by Hammond, Hursch, and Todd, *Psychological Review*, **71**, 528–530.
5. Hammond, K. R. (1965). New directions in research in conflict resolution, *Journal of Social Issues*, **21**, 44–66.
6. Dudycha, L. W., and Naylor, J. C. (1966). Characteristics of the human inference process in complex choice behavior situations, *Organizational Behavior and Human Performance*, **1**, 110–128.
7. Hammond, K. R., and Summers, D. A. (1972). Cognitive control, *Psychological Review*, **79**, 58–67.

8. Hammond, K. R., and Adelman, L. (1976). Science, values, and human judgment, *Science*, **194**, 389–396.

9. Hammond, K. R., Mumpower, J. L., and Smith, T. H. (1977). Linking environmental models with models of human judgment: A symmetrical decision aid, *IEEE Transactions on Systems, Man, and Cybernetics*, Vol. SMC-7(5), pp. 358-367.

10. Hammond, K. R., Rohrbaugh, J., Mumpower, J., and Adelman, L. (1977). Social judgment theory: Applications in policy formation. In M. F. Kaplan and S. Schwartz (eds), *Human Judgment and Decision Processes in Applied Settings*, New York: Academic Press.

11. Camerer, C. (1981). General conditions for the success of bootstrapping models, *Organizational Behavior and Human Performance*, **27**, 411–422.

## C. Heuristic combining models

1. Dawes, R. M. (1964). Social selection based on multidimensional criteria, *Journal of Abnormal and Social Psychology*, **68**, 104–109.

2. Kleinmuntz, B. (1968). The processing of clinical information by man and machine. In B. Kleinmuntz (ed.), *Formal Representation of Human Judgment*, New York: Wiley.

3. Tversky, A. (1969). Intransitivity of preferences, *Psychological Review*, **76**, 31–48.

4. Einhorn, H. J. (1970). The use of nonlinear, noncompensatory models in decision making, *Psychological Bulletin*, **73**, 221–230.

5. Tversky, A. (1972). Elimination by aspects: A theory of choice, *Psychological Review*, **79**, 281–299.

6. Hogarth, R. M. (1974). Process tracing in clinical judgment, *Behavioral Science*, **19**, 298–313.

7. Russo, J. E., and Rosen, L. D. (1975). An eye fixation analysis of multi-alternative choice, *Memory and Cognition*, **3**, 267–276.

8. Payne, J. W. (1976). Task complexity and contingent processing in decision making: An information search and protocol analysis, *Organizational Behavior and Human Performance*, **16**, 366–387.

9. Simon, H. A., and Hayes, J. R. (1976). The understanding process: Problem isomorphs, *Cognitive Psychology*, **8**, 165–190.

10. Tversky, A. (1977). Features of similarity, *Psychological Review*, **84**, 327–352.

11. Nisbett, R. E., and Wilson, T. D. (1977). Telling more than we can know: Verbal reports on mental processes, *Psychological Review*, **84**, 231–259.

12. Smith, E. R., and Miller, F. D. (1978). Limits on perception of cognitive processes: A reply to Nisbett and Wilson, *Psychological Review*, **85**, 355–362.

13. Payne, J. W., Braunstein, M. L., and Carroll, J. S. (1978). Exploring predecisional behavior: An alternative approach to decision research,

*Organizational Behavior and Human Performance*, **22**, 17–44.

14. Tversky, A., and Sattath, S. (1979). Preference trees, *Psychological Review*, **86**, 542–573.

15. Corbin, R. M. (1980). Decisions that might not get made. In T. S. Wallsten (ed.), *Cognitive Processes in Choice and Decision Behavior*, Hillsdale, NJ: Erlbaum.

16. Abelson, R. P. (1981). Psychological status of the script concept, *American Psychologist*, **36**, 715–729.

17. Schustack, M. W., and Sternberg, R. J. (1981). Evaluation of evidence in causal inference, *Journal of General Psychology: General*, **10**, 101–120.

18. Russo, J. E., and Dosher, B. A. (1983). Strategies for multiattribute binary choice, *Journal of Experimental Psychology: Learning, Memory, and Cognition*, **9**, 676–696.

19. Fischhoff, B., and Beyth-Marom, R. (1983). Hypothesis evaluation from a Bayesian perspective, *Psychological Review*, **90**, 239–260.

20. Mackinnon, A. J., and Wearing, A. J. (1985). Systems analysis and dynamic decision making, *Acta Psychologica*, **58**, 159–172.

21. Johnson, E. J., and Payne, J. W. (1985). Effort and accuracy in choice, *Management Science*, 31, 395–414.

22. Kleinmuntz, D. N. (1985). Cognitive heuristics and feedback in a dynamic decision environment, *Management Science*, **31**, 680–702.

23. Keren, G., and Wagenaar, W. A. (1985). On the psychology of playing blackjack: Normative and descriptive considerations with implications for decision theory, *Journal of Experimental Psychology: General*, **114**, 133–158.

24. Brehmer, B., and Allard, R. (1986). *Dynamic Decision Making: A General Paradigm and Some Experimental Results*, Manuscript, Department of Psychology, Uppsala University, Sweden.

25. Klayman, J., and Ha, Y.-W. (in press). Confirmation, disconfirmation, and information in hypothesis testing. *Psychological Review*.

## VI. RISK

How do people make choices in the face of risk? This topic has attracted great attention in recent years. The following readings give some indication of this interest and have been organized under the following headings: (a) Expected utility theory and experimental challenges; (b) Measuring utility functions under risk; (c) Variants, and alternatives to expected utility; (d) Ambiguity and conflict; and (e) Risk in society.

### A. Expected utility and experimental challenges

1. Friedman, M., and Savage, L. J. (1948). The utility analysis of choices involving risk, *Journal of Political Economy*, **56**, 279–304.

2. Allais, M. (1953). Le comportement de l'homme rationnel devant le

risque: Critiques des postulats et axiomes de l'école américaine, *Econometrica*, **21**, 503–546.

3. Slovic, P., and Tversky, A. (1974). Who accepts Savage's axiom? *Behavioral Science*, **19**, 368–373.

4. MacCrimmon, K. R., and Larsson, S. (1979). Utility theory: Axioms versus 'paradoxes'. In M. Allais and O. Hagen (eds), *Expected Utility Theory and the Allais Paradox*, Dordrecht, Holland: Reidel.

5. Schoemaker, P. J. H. (1980). *Experiments on Decision under Risk: The Expected Utility Hypothesis*, Hingham, MA: Nijhoff.

6. Lopes, L. L. (1981). Decision making in the short run, *Journal of Experimental Psychology: Human Learning and Memory*, **7**, 377–385.

7. Schoemaker, P. J. H. (1982). The expected utility model: Its variants, purposes, evidence and limitations, *Journal of Economic Literature*, **20**, 529–563.

8. Slovic, P., Fischhoff, B., and Lichtenstein, S. (1982). Response mode, framing, and information-processing effects in risk assessment. In R. M. Hogarth (ed.), *Question Framing and Response Consistency*. San Francisco: Jossey-Bass.

9. Tversky, A., and Bar-Hillel, M. (1983). Risk: The long and the short, *Journal of Experimental Psychology: Learning, Memory, and Cognition*, **9**, 713–717.

10. Slovic, P. and Lichtenstein, S. (1983). Preference reversals: A broader perspective, *American Economic Review*, **73**, 596–605.

11. Goldstein, W. M., and Einhorn, H.J. (in press). Expression theory and the preference reversal phenomena, *Psychological Review*.

## B. Measuring utility functions

1. Becker, G. M., DeGroot, M. H., and Marschak, J. (1964). Measuring utility by a single response sequential method, *Behavioral Science*, **9**, 226–233.

2. Tversky, A. (1967). Additivity, utility, and subjective probability, *Journal of Mathematical Psychology*, **4**, 175–202.

3. Spetzler, C. S. (1968). The development of a corporate risk policy for capital investmant decisions, *IEEE Transactions on Systems Science and Cybernetics*, Vol. SSC-4, pp. 279–300.

4. Hershey, J. C., Kunreuther, H. C., and Schoemaker, P. J. H. (1982). Sources of bias in assessment procedures for utility functions, *Management Science*, **28**, 936–954.

5. Farquhar, P. H. (1984). Utility assessment methods, *Management Science*, **30**, 1283–1300.

6. McCord, M., and de Neufville, R. (1986). 'Lottery equivalents': Reduction of the certainty effect in utility assessment, *Management Science*, **32**, 56–60.

## C. Variants and alternatives to expected utility

1. Slovic, P., and Lichtenstein, S. (1968). The relative importance of probability and payoffs in risk taking, *Journal of Experimental Psychology Monograph Supplement*, **78**(3), Part 2.
2. Payne, J. W. (1973). Alternative approaches to decision making under risk: Moments versus risk dimensions, *Psychological Bulletin*, **80**, 439–453.
3. Coombs, C. H. (1975). Portfolio theory and the measurement of risk. In M. F. Kaplan and S. Schwartz (eds), *Human Judgment and Decision Processes*, New York: Academic Press.
4. Karmarkar, U. (1978). Subjectively weighted utility: A descriptive extension of the expected utility model, *Organizational Behavior and Human Performance*, **21**, 61–72.
5. Aschenbrenner, K. M. (1978). Single-peaked risk preferences and their dependability on the gambles' presentation mode, *Journal of Experimental Psychology: Human Perception and Performance*, **4**, 513–520.
6. Kahneman, D., and Tversky, A. (1979). Prospect theory: An analysis of decisions under risk, *Econometrica*, **47**, 263–291.
7. Chew, S. H., and MacCrimmon, K. R. (1979). *Alpha-Nu Choice theory: A Generalization of Expected Utility Theory*, Unpublished manuscript, University of British Columbia.
8. Payne, J. W., Laughhunn, D. J., and Crum, R. (1980). Translation of gambles and aspiration level effects in risky choice behavior, *Management Science*, **26**, 1039–1060.
9. Tversky, A., and Kahneman, D. (1981). The framing of decisions and the psychology of choice, *Science*, **211**, 453–458.
10. Bell, D. E. (1982). Regret in decision making under uncertainty, *Operations Research*, **30**, 961–981.
11. Loomes, G., and Sugden, R. (1982). Regret theory: An alternative theory of rational choice under uncertainty, *Economic Journal*, **92**, 805–824.
12. Machina, M. J. (1982). 'Expected utility' analysis without the independence axiom, *Econometrica*, **50**, 277–323.
13. Quiggin, J. (1982). A theory of anticipated utility. *Journal of Economic Behavior and Organization*, **3**, 323–343.
14. Lopes, L. L. (1984). Risk and distributional inequality, *Journal of Experimental Psychology: Human Perception and Performance*, **10**, 465–485.
15. Fishburn, P. C. (1984). SSB utility theory and decision making under uncertainty, *Mathematical Social Sciences*, **8**, 253–285.
16. Bell, D. E. (1985). Disappointment in decision making under uncertainty, *Operations Research*, **33**, 1–27.
17. Luce, R. D., and Narens, L. (1985). Classsification of concatenation measurement structures according to scale type, *Journal of Mathematical Psychology*, **29**, 1–72.

### D. Ambiguity and conflict

1. Ellsberg, D. (1961). Risk, ambiguity, and the Savage axioms, *Quarterly Journal of Economics*, **75**, 643–669.
2. Coombs, C. H., and Avrunin, G. S. (1977). Single–peaked functions and the theory of preference, *Psychological Review*, **84**, 216–230.
3. Gärdenfors, P., and Sahlin, N.-E. (1982). Unreliable probabilities, risk taking, and decision making, *Synthese*, **53**, 361–386.
4. Einhorn, H. J., and Hogarth, R. M. (1985). Ambiguity and uncertainty in probabilistic inference, *Psychological Review*, **92**, 433–461.

### E. Risk in society

1. Starr, C. (1969). Social benefits versus technological risk, *Science*, **165**, 1232–1238.
2. Howard, R. A., Matheson, J. E., and North, D. W. (1972). The decision to seed hurricanes, *Science*, **176**, 1191–1202.
3. Kunreuther, H. (1976). Limited knowledge and insurance protection, *Public Policy*, **24**, 227–261.
4. Slovic, P., Fischhoff, B., Lichtenstein, S., Corrigan, B., and Combs, B. (1977). Preference for insuring against probable small losses: Insurance implications, *Journal of Risk and Insurance*, **44**, 237–258.
5. Schwing, R., and Albers, W. A., Jr. (eds) (1980). *Societal Risk Assessment: How Safe is Safe Enough?* New York: Plenum.
6. Fischhoff, B., Lichtenstein, S., Slovic, P., Derby, S., and Keeney, R. (1981). *Acceptable Risk*, New York: Cambridge University Press.
7. Douglas, M., and Wildavsky, A. (1982). *Risk and Culture: An Essay on the Selection of Technological and Environmental Dangers*, Berkeley: University of California Press.
8. Arrow, K.J. (1982). Risk perception in psychology and economics, *Economic Enquiry*, **20**, 1–9.
9. Slovic, P., Fischhoff, B., and Lichtenstein, S. (1984). Behavioral decision theory perspectives on risk and safety, *Acta Psychologica*, **56**, 183–203.
10. Hammond, K. R., Anderson, B. F., Sutherland, J., and Marvin, B. (1984). Improving scientists' judgments of risk, *Risk Analysis*, **4**, 69–78.

### VII. CREATIVITY AND PROBLEM SOLVING

Much research has been done on creativity; unfortunately, the topic is difficult and results are somewhat discouraging. This short list should, however, prove useful.

1. Ghiselin, B. (ed.) (1952). *The Creative Process*, Berkeley, CA: University of California Press. (Reprinted by Mentor Books, New York.)
2. Osborn, A. F. (1953). *Applied Imagination*, New York: Scribner.
3. Wertheimer, M. (1959). *Productive Thinking* (enlarged edn), New York: Harper.

4. von Fange, E. K. (1959). *Professional Creativity*, Englewood Cliffs, NJ: Prentice-Hall.
5. Campbell, D. T. (1960). Blind variation and selective retention in creative thought as in other knowledge processes, *Psychological Review*, **67**, 380–400.
6. Gordon, W. J. J. (1961). *Synectics*, New York: Harper & Row.
7. Bruner, J. S. (1962). *On Knowing: Essays for the Left Hand*, Cambridge, MA: The Belknap Press of Harvard University Press.
8. Ogilvy, D. (1963). *Confessions of an Advertising Man*, New York: Atheneum.
9. Barron, F. (1965). The psychology of creativity. In T. M. Newcomb (ed.), *New Directions in Psychology*, Vol. 2. New York: Holt, Rinehart & Winston, Inc., pp. 1–134.
10. Guilford, J. P. (1967). *The Nature of Human Intelligence*, New York: McGraw-Hill, Chapter 14.
11. Maier, N. R. F. (1970). *Problem Solving and Creativity in Individuals and Groups*, Belmont, CA: Wadsworth.
12. de Bono, E. (1973). *Lateral Thinking*, New York: Harper.
13. Koestler, A. (1973). *The Act of Creation*, New York: Dell.
14. Adams, J. L. (1976). *Conceptual Blockbusting: A Pleasurable Guide to Better Problem Solving*, San Francisco, CA: San Francisco Book Co.
15. Stein, M. I. (1974–75). *Stimulating Creativity*, Vols. I and II, New York: Academic Press.
16. Whitfield, P. R. (1975). *Creativity in Industry*, Harmondsworth, Middlesex, England: Penguin.
17. Souder, W. E., and Ziegler, R. W. (1977). A review of creativity and problem solving techniques, *Research Management*, July, 34–42.
18. Ackoff, R. L. (1978). *The Art of Problem Solving: Accompanied by Ackoff's Fables*, New York: John Wiley.
19. Rothenberg, A. (1979). *The Emerging Goddess*, Chicago: University of Chicago Press.
20. Getzels, J. W. (1982). The problem of the problem. In R. M. Hogarth (ed.), *Question Framing and Response Consistency*, San Francisco: Jossey-Bass.

## VIII. DECISION AIDS

### A. Texts/overviews of decision analysis

1. Raiffa, H. (1968). *Decision Analysis*, Reading, MA: Addison-Wesley.
2. Schlaifer, R. (1969). *Analysis of Decisions under Uncertainty*, New York: McGraw-Hill.
3. Lindley, D. V. (1971). *Making Decisions* (2nd edn 1985), Chichester, England: John Wiley.
4. Brown, R. V., Kahr, A. S., and Peterson, C. R. (1974). *Decision Analysis for the Manager*, New York: Holt, Rinehart & Winston.

5. Keeney, R. L., and Raiffa, H. (1976). *Decisions with Multiple Objectives: Preferences and Value Tradeoffs*, New York: John Wiley.
6. Moore, P. G., and Thomas, H. (1976). *The Anatomy of Decisions*, Harmondsworth, England: Penguin.
7. Behn, R. D., and Vaupel, J. W. (1982). *Quick Analysis for Busy Decision Makers*, New York: Basic Books.
8. Kanfer, F. H., and Busemeyer, J. R. (1982). The use of problem solving and decision making in behavior therapy, *Clinical Psychology*, **2**, 239–266.
9. Keeney, R. L. (1982). Decision analysis: An overview, *Operations Research*, **30**, 803–838.
10. von Winterfeldt, D., and Edwards, W. (1986). *Decision Analysis and Behavioral Research*, New York: Cambridge University Press.

## B. Examples of decision analysis

1. Howard, R. A., Matheson, J. E., and Miller, K. E. (1976). *Readings in Decision Analysis*, Menlo Park, CA: Stanford Research Institute.
2. Bell, D. E., Keeney, R. L., and Raiffa, H. (eds) (1977). *Conflicting Objectives in Decisions*, Chichester, England: John Wiley.
3. Kaufman, G. M. and Thomas H. (Eds.) (1977). *Modern Decision Analysis: Selected Readings*, Harmondsworth, Middlesex, England: Penguin.
4. Hogarth, R. M. (1980). Judgement, drug monitoring and decision aids. In W. H. W. Inman (ed.), *Monitoring for Drug Safety* (2nd edn 1986), Lancaster, England: MTP Press.
5. von Winterfeldt, D. (1980). Structuring decision problems for decision analysis, *Acta Psychologica*, **45**, 71–93.
6. Keeney, R. L. (1980). *Siting Energy Facilities*, New York: Academic Press.
7. Ulvila, J. W., and Brown, R. (1982). Decision analysis comes of age, *Harvard Business Review*, Sept.–Oct., 130–141.

## C. Views on multi-attribute methods

1. MacCrimmon, K. R. (1973). An overview of multiple objective decision making. In J. L. Cochrane and M. Zeleny (eds), *Multiple Criteria Decision Making*, Columbia, SC: University of South Carolina Press.
2. von Winterfeldt, D., and Fischer, G. W. (1975). Multi-attribute theory: Models and scaling procedures. In D. Wendt and C. A. J. Vlek (eds), *Utility, Probability and Human Decision Making*, Dordrecht, The Netherlands: Reidel.
3. Gardiner, P. C., and Edwards, W. (1975). Public values: Multiattribute-utility measurement for social decision making. In M. F. Kaplan and S. Schwartz (eds), *Human Judgment and Decision Processes*, New York: Academic Press.

4. Fischhoff, B. (1977). Cost benefit analysis and the art of motorcycle maintenance, *Policy Sciences*, **8**, 177–202.
5. Einhorn, H. J., and McCoach, W. (1977). A simple multi-attribute procedure for evaluation, *Behavioral Science*, **22**, 270–282.
6. Johnson, E. M., and Huber, G. P. (1977). The technology of utility assessment, *IEEE Transactions on Systems, Man and Cybernetics*, Vol. SMC-7(5), pp. 311–325.
7. Humphreys, P. (1977). Application of multi-attribute utility theory. In H. Jungermann and G. de Zeeuw (eds), *Decision Making and Change in Human Affairs*, Dordrecht-Holland: Reidel.
8. Fischhoff, B. (1980). Clinical decision analysis, *Operations Research*, **28**, 28–43.

## D. Other aids

1. Einhorn, H. J., and Hogarth, R. M. (1975). Unit weighting schemes for decision making, *Organizational Behavior and Human Performance*, **13**, 171–192.
2. Linstone, H. A., and Turoff, M. (1975). *The Delphi Method: Techniques and Applications*, Reading, MA: Addison-Wesley.
3. Beach, B. H. (1975). Expert judgment about uncertainty: Bayesian decision making in realistic settings, *Organizational Behavior and Human Performance*, **14**, 10–59.
4. Spetzler, C. S., and Staël von Holstein, C.-A. S. (1975). Probability encoding in decision analysis, *Management Science*, **22**, 340–358.
5. Axelrod, R. (ed.) (1976). *Structure of Decision: The Cognitive Maps of Political Elites*, Princeton, NJ: Princeton University Press.
6. Kahneman, D., and Tversky, A. (1979). Intuitive prediction: Biases and corrective procedures. In *TIMS Studies in Management Science*, Vol. 12, 313–327.
7. Raiffa, H. (1982). *The Art and Science of Negotiation*, Cambridge, MA: Belknap Press of Harvard University Press.
8. Social judgement theory aids are exemplified in References 8, 9, and 10 under the 'lens model' sub-section (B) of Section V.

# Index